THE
BRANDENBURGER
COMMANDOS

D1153899

0 11557 03250 5

THE
BRANDENBURGER
COMMANDOS

Germany's Elite Warrior Spies in World War II

Franz Kurowski

STACKPOLE
BOOKS

Copyright © 1997 by J. J. Fedorowicz Publishing, Inc.

Published in 2005 by
STACKPOLE BOOKS
5067 Ritter Road
Mechanicsburg, PA 17055
www.stackpolebooks.com

www.jjfpub.mb.ca

Printed in the United States of America

10 9 8 7 6 5 4 3 2 1

FIRST EDITION

Library of Congress Cataloging-in-Publication Data

Kurowski, Franz.
  [Deutsche Kommandotrupps 1939–1945. English]
  The Brandenburger commandos : Germany's elite warrior spies in World War II / Franz Kurowski ; translated by David Johnston.— 1st ed.
    p. cm. — (Stackpole Military history series)
  Originally published in English: The Brandenburgers global mission. Winnipeg, Man. : J.J. Fedorowicz Pub., c1997.
  Includes bibliographical references and index.
  ISBN-13: 978-0-8117-3250-5
  ISBN-10: 0-8117-3250-9
  1. Germany. Oberkommando der Wehrmacht. Amt Ausl/Abw.—History.
2. World War, 1939–1945—Secret service—Germany. 3. World War, 1939–1945—Commando operations—Germany. 4. World War, 1939–1945—Military intelligence—Germany. 5. World War, 1939–1945—Regimental histories—Germany. 6. Germany. Heer. Panzergrenadierdivision "Brandenburg"—History. I. Title. II. Series.

  D810.S7K8613 2005
  940.54'8743—dc22

                        2005017821

Table of Contents

Note of Thanks

The author wishes to express his thanks to all former Brandenburgers and-members of the wartime Foreign Intelligence Service who helped him bring this project to a successful conclusion by providing advice and a number of illustrations.

They have helped establish the good name of the Brandenburgers and prove that the accusations made against them were groundless.

In the service of their country the Brandenburgers were unsurpassed by any other unit and it is hoped that this book will make this obvious even to the non-insider.

Franz Kurowski
Dortmund
30 March 1995

The OKW-AMT
Ausland/Abwehr

On 1 January 1935 Kapitan zur See Wilhelm Canaris became head of the German Abwehr. The Abwehr had evolved from the Reichswehr's Intelligence and Identification Service and joined the Navy's secret service in 1928. The combined secret service was later renamed Abwehr and in 1932 came under the command of Fregattenkapitan Conrad Patzig. In 1935 the Abwehr was subordinated to the Reich War Ministry and in 1938 to the Wehrmacht High Command (OKW). In 1939 its official designation was changed to the OKW Amt Ausland/Abwehr (OKW Office for Foreign and Counter-Intelligence).

Immediately after assuming his new post Wilhelm Canaris contacted his counterparts in foreign intelligence services, with whom he had already established ties through middlemen in the appropriate offices. In September 1935 in Munich he met with Colonel Mario Roatta, head of the Servicio Informazioni Militari—SIM, the Italian Secret Service. The Italians had tried to establish contact with Canaris' predecessor, Kapitan zur See Patzig, but in vain.

Patzig was brought down as a result of the Rohm affair, when after the series of murders on 30 June 1934 he demanded the removal of Heydrich because he had far exceeded the authority of Hitler and Goring and had caused officers of the Reichswehr to be killed who were innocent of any part in the "Rohm putsch." Patzig convinced the Minister of Defense, Generalfeldmarschall von Blomberg, to press for the removal of Heydrich.

Reich Minister of Defense Blomberg, who had secured the support of several cabinet ministers for this effort, made his move and was rebuffed by Himmler. Blomberg knuckled under. This slap in the face from Himmler seriously damaged his image, a thing for which he never forgave Patzig.

When Blomberg proposed that the Abwehr establish ties with the Italian Secret Service, Patzig rejected the idea, arguing that it was not trustworthy. Later, when Patzig gave orders for a special reconnaissance squadron—later to become Special Group Rowehl—to carry out flights

1

over Poland and France, flights which had been initiated by Hitler, Blomberg insisted that Hitler had forbidden the flights. In October 1934 the Minister of Defense learned that the Commander in Chief of the Luftwaffe's high-altitude reconnaissance squadron had photographed the entire Maginot Line. Blomberg summoned Patzig to him and declared curtly: "I can't use an intelligence chief who carries out escapades of this kind!"

Patzig had to propose someone to succeed him to Admiral Raeder. When he gave Canaris' name, Raeder rejected the idea brusquely. The Commander in Chief of the Reichsmarine didn't like Canaris and had already sent him into oblivion by placing him in command of the fortress at Swinemlinde. He wanted to retire Canaris in 1935. Patzig then raised a point that Raeder hadn't considered. He declared that in that case the Army would take over the Abwehr. Raeder relented and approved the naming of Kapitan zur See Canaris as head of the German counter-intelligence service. The white-haired naval officer moved into house number 72-76 on the Tirpitzufer on the Berlin Landwehr Canal.

On 1 May 1935 Canaris was promoted to Konteradmiral. He made all the former officers who had served as civilian employees with the Abwehr E-officers. One such was Major Hans Oster. Canaris also summoned old comrades from the Freikorps, men like Friedrich Wilhelm Heinz, a former cavalry officer, and Heinz Schmalschager. Former naval officer LeiBner came all the way from Nicaragua, and many others followed. One of Canaris' early collaborators was Major Hans Piekenbrock. Under Canaris' leadership the Abwehr grew into an extensive organization with three main departments; eventually, in the course of the expansion of the Wehrmacht, it became the Ausland/Abwehr, an agency that was to serve all three elements of the armed forces.

The central department was headed by Oberstleutnant (later Oberst) Oster. Head of Abwehr Department I was Major (later Oberstleutnant and General Staff Oberst) Hans Piekenbrock. Department I was responsible for secret communications and carried out active intelligence gathering.

The Abwehr's Department II was commanded by Oberst (later Generalmajor) von Lahousen- Vivremont. Department II handled all sabotage actions and special missions carried out by the Abwehr. Department III under Oberstleutnant (later Generalmajor) von Bentivegni, was the counter-espionage and counter-intelligence branch. In spite of this division of authority overlapping missions were not uncommon. The areas of responsibility assigned to these three groups were in turn organized into three sub-departments, with one responsible for each branch of the armed forces—army, air force and navy. Sub-groupings and the various special-ized intelligence objectives required further sub-divisions which shall be outlined briefly.

Each Wehrkreiskommando (Military Area Headquarters) had an Abwehr office that was under the command of the unit Ie and the Abwehr AO. The unit Ie was a general staff officer tasked with handling intelli-gence concerning the enemy. The AO was an Abwehr officer. Like the Abwehr itself, all Abwehr offices were organized into Groups I, II and III, which were responsible for intelligence gathering, sabotage and special missions, and counter-intelligence respectively.

The Abwehr Departments
I, II and III

The working plan of Abwehr Department Ausland I was as follows: For the command group: uniform direction of the secret message service. Summarization of all relevant intelligence sources. Cooperation with Departments II and III of the Office for Germans Living Abroad (Auslandsamt), the Foreign Office, the Gestapo and the Research Office (Forschungsamt). Execution of intelligence-gathering missions assigned by the Commander in Chief of the Armed Forces and of the three services: transmission of non-evaluated intelligence to the Ausland Department and the foreign offices of the three branches of the armed forces.

This department consisted of the following sections: Office Officer (West), Passes, Registry, Group I, and Army. Abwehr I Hd was responsible for directing the secret military message service in the west and south. Abwehr I H (West/North) Section was responsible for overseeing the communication of secret messages, utilization of value judgments by Department 3 of the Army General Staff concerning intelligence material delivered to it, as well as personal data and the evaluation of agents. Abwehr I H (West/South) handled the compensation of agents following their retirement as well as the impartial auditing of the rendering of accounts by the Abwehr offices. Section I H (West/North) was responsible for the countries of Belgium, Holland, England, Denmark and Luxembourg. Section I H (West/South) was responsible for France, Portugal, Spain, Switzerland, Italy and the overseas states, excluding Japan.

There were also subgroups for the secret message communications service in the east and southeast: Section, I H (East/North) was responsible for Poland, the border states, Finland, the USSR, Scandinavia, Japan and China, and Section I H (East/South) for Czechoslovakia, Hungary, Southeast Europe, Turkey, Iran and Afghanistan. Gathering intelligence on foreign weapons and military technology was the job of Section I Ht. Its mission was to obtain examples of weapons and military hardware abroad and explore the manufacture of chemical weapons by other nations.

4

Together with the command group, Abwehr Department II was responsible for the following areas: operation of the department as per instructions from the supreme command. Representing the interests of the department externally, uniform direction of the groups under its command and administration of funds.

Branch la was responsible for the mobilization calendar and the commander's secret material as well as administering the secret command matter files. As well it handled the internal service and took care of economic matters, dealt with the external service when expressly instructed to do so. Branch Ia was also given the job of maintaining the Ausland/Abwehr war diary.

Branch Ib controlled the laboratory responsible for technical research and maintained links with the armed forces office, the technical schools and institutes. It issued contracts for the procurement and stockpiling of materials and trained V men for special missions. Branch Ib was also responsible for issuing special directives, evaluating war experiences and using these for new special Abwehr missions.

The tasks assigned the branches of Group I with their responsible group leader included gathering intelligence on minorities and ferreting out organizations hostile to the state. An especially important role was that of spreading subversive propaganda within the enemy's armed forces. They were also to explore potential lines of communication with the political groups of potential enemies in peace and war, maintain the exchange of intelligence information with friendly powers, and produce memoranda concerning the goals and organizations of minorities and subversive groups.

This main branch had at its disposal various sub-branches. Sub-branch I ON was responsible for handling minorities and subversive groups in the Soviet Union, the Far East, Poland, Lithuania, Latvia, Estonia and Finland. Sub-branch 1 OS fulfilled the same role for Czechoslovakia, Rumania, Bulgaria, Yugoslavia, Greece and Italy, while Sub-branch I W was responsible for France, Belgium, Luxembourg, Switzerland, England, Ireland, Denmark, Sweden and Norway. Sub-branch I Db (Overseas) handled North, Central and South America and Spanish Morocco and Sub-branch 1 I Africa (less Spanish Morocco), Asia and South America. Sub-branch1 J was in charge of insurgency measures (promoting insurgent groups) world wide, as well as evaluating the press and books.

Group 2 and its group leader controlled the operations of the special service and were responsible for the organization of the service, establishing S-areas and producing memoranda on the economic and military situation of hostile states. Group 2 was also responsible for exploring offensive opportunities for the S organization, transport of materials and their storage with corps headquarters and at the nation's borders. It was also to ensure lines of communication and message transmission. In order to carry out these tasks the branch was divided into the following sub-groups:

Branch 2 (WS-1): France, Luxembourg, Belgium, Italy and
   Switzerland.
Branch 2 (WS-2): Spain, Portugal, Latin America.
Branch 2 (WN): England, Holland, Scandinavia, Denmark.
Branch 2 (OS): Czechoslovakia, Hungary, Rumania, Yugoslavia, the
   Balkan countries.
Branch 2 (ON): Russia, Poland, border states.
Branch 2 (Db): North America, special organizations.
Branch 2 (Mar): waters around Europe, Africa and Asia.
Branch 2 (Luft): conduct of the special service and liaison with the
   Reich Ministry of Aviation.
Branch 2 (Lab): Technical experiments, material administration.

Also part of Department II of the Ausland/Abwehr was what was later to become the 800th Special Purpose Instruction Regiment Brandenburg. When the Second World War began the unit was still in the formative stage; later, however, it was to play a decisive role in the actions of Department II.

The idea for the formation of this German commando force came from Hauptmann Dr. von Hippel, who in his early considerations outlined the role of such a unit: "to seize vital objects such as bridges, tunnels, crossroads and armaments plants and hold them until the arrival of the leading units of the German Armed Forces."

On 15 September 1939 Hauptmann Putz oversaw formation of the 1st SpecialPurpose Construction Instruction Company at the Bruck Troop Training Grounds. Hauptmann Verbeek was named company commander. His instructors included Leutnant Dr. Kniesche and Leutnant Grabert, as well as several NCOs and enlisted men.

The company itself consisted of volunteers from the Sudeten German Freikorps, ex-soldiers of the Czech Army, and other young men. From this one company was to evolve the Brandenburg Regiment, whose actions will feature prominently in subsequent chapters.

Abwehr Department III, whose command group was responsible for the overall control of German counter-espionage activities and also for the maintaining of finances, personal affairs and the war diary, was divided into the following groups and branches.

The administration officer, who was responsible for the running of the office and who had to catalogue all incoming mail. He administered the secret documents and handled personnel applications. Finance administration administered all funds, scrutinized incoming accounts and manned the pass control desk.

The registry handled business transactions, maintained the mail register and dealtwith accumulated mail. It administered the secret and non-secret files and digests, procured office supplies, saw to space requirements and administered the case files.

The role of Command Group III W (Armed Forces Counter-Intelligence) was the uniform conduct of counter-espionage activities within the armed forces. The command group leader was responsible for this. One of the group's chief responsibilities was the safeguarding of military secrets. It provided expert testimony in front of courts, especially the Reich court. The command group leader also fulfilled the role of the responsible deputy of the department chief.

Group III H was responsible for conducting counter-espionage in the army and evaluating the results. It gathered material for briefings and lectures, and maintained statistics on cases of treason in the army as well as on cases of desertion in the German armed forces. It also worked with Group III S in counter-sabotage operations. Branch III Kgf. directed and guided counter-espionage in the prisoner of war camps in cooperation with the Inspector of Prisoner of War camps through V-officers of the Abwehr III itself. This branch investigated German POWs abroad and escape attempts by POWs. It also carried out neutral missions and was responsible for prisoner exchanges. Like all other branches, III Kgf. was under orders to cooperate with Group III S in matters involving counter-sabotage.

Branch III M oversaw counter-espionage activities in the navy and monitored all attempts at subversion in the German armed forces as well as questions of precautionary maintenance of secrecy. It ran all counter-espionage activities in the Kriegsmarine and in the coastal fortification zones. The branch was also responsible for the maintenance of statistics on cases of treason and desertions in the navy, providing expert testimony before the courts, and the exchanging of prisoners. It was also under orders to cooperate with Group III S in matters of counter-sabotage.

Group III Luft: Responsible for counter-espionage in the Luftwaffe. It was required to investigate all Luftwaffe losses and handle the individual cases. Crimes of treason and cases of desertion within the Luftwaffe also fell within its jurisdiction, as did providing expert testimony before the courts.

The leader of Group III Wi (counter-intelligence in industry) was responsible for the uniform direction of defensive measures against espionage and sabotage in industry and to evaluate the group's experiences in this field.

Branch III Wi I's sphere of activity encompassed Military Areas I, II and X and the Abwehr offices in Kiel and Wilhelmshaven. Its purpose was to handle armaments questions concerning the navy and general Abwehr matters and to review the construction plans of the army and navy. As well the group was responsible for investigating press and police reports with regard to these themes, the release of navy military equipment for export, and assembling and evaluating the results of industrial espionage in the Nordic States, Russia and the British Dominions.

Branch III Wi 2 was responsible for handling the release of army military equipment for export, cooperating with the security service (SD), keeping track of foreign nationals, and conducting industrial espionage in Southeastern Europe and Asia(excluding Russia, China and Japan).

Branch III Wi 3 worked with the economic offices and the industry and trade councils. The monitoring of the labor exchanges and labor courts lay within its area of jurisdiction. It was also responsible for screening those businesses vital to the military and civilian economies. Its area of responsibility in the field of industrial espionage was Western and Southwestern Europe excluding England and Africa.

Branch III Wi 4 was responsible for checking all questions relating to Luftwaffe armaments, monitoring factory air defenses, aviation-related construction plans and the four-year plan, and directing important fuel-producing firms. It was also in charge of releasing air force military equipment for export and industrial espionage in Japan, China and the USA.

Group III C, which was divided into five sub-groups, carried out its missions inside Germany. Its sub-groups coordinated suspected cases of espionage, conducted counter-propaganda and monitored signals communications and passenger traffic.

The primary responsibilities of Group III F, counter-intelligence abroad, concerned counter-intelligence in the western and eastern states as well as the operation of passport offices in neutral countries. Five branches carried out these tasks.

Group III D, whose mission was "deception," consisted of two branches and was responsible for misleading potential enemies by means of counter-espionage and for monitoring the release of falsified material by Abwehr offices in conjunction with the general staffs of the army, navy and air force.

Group III S, anti-sabotage, required four branches in order to deal with its volume of work. It was responsible for combating all types of sabotage and activities detrimental to the defense of Germany at home and abroad; it also led anti-sabotage activities in the army, navy and air force as well as in the prisoner of war camps.

Group III G consisted of two branches and provided expert opinions dealing with cases of treason in the western and eastern states.

The last group was Group III Z Arch. (Central Archive of the Armed Forces High Command). Its job was to screen all female and male personnel hired by the OKW, OKM and RLM and to handle all cases of treason or loss of life that occurred in those areas. One of its most important duties was the precautionary maintenance of secrecy and the security of the headquarters of the OKW and of the Bendler, Tiergarten and Ltitzow Blocks in cooperation with the on-site commanders. All persons calling on the head of the OKW or on the Abwehr of Foreign Office had to be screened by this group. It handled the procurement of visas for official travel abroad and was responsible for security in the offices of Ausland/Abwehr III.

Also part of the OKW Office Ausland/Abwehr were the Foreign Mail Screening Office Berlin and the Foreign Telegram Screening Office Berlin. Both were authorized to examine correspondence of all types to or from persons classed as threats. They were also responsible for chemical investigations, and for scrutinizing the contents of private, business and military mail and in particular letters sent by prisoners of war. In its card index files were all those persons who came under suspicion in the course of monitoring communications as well as those already deemed worthy of scrutiny.

This completes the outline of the entire Ausland/Abwehr. The office had cast its huge spider web over the entire world and an awareness of this scope is necessary if one is to understand the extent of the actions of every type that were planned and carried out in and outside Germany before and during the war.

The "tension agents" (S-Agents) and "war agents" (A-Agents) began their work as soon as Canaris took charge of the office. The agency set up nets of agents whose sizes and diversity simply could not be plumbed by the enemy. The creation of this peacetime and wartime organization was Canaris' first priority.

Actions before the War

PREPARATIONS AND EXPANSION

In 1936 Canaris visited Estonia, where he had private discussions with the Chief of Staff of the Estonian Army and the director of Department 2 (the Estonian Secret Service). As a result of these talks an agreement was reached to exchange all results of espionage against the USSR.

Baron Andrei von Uexklill was named chief liaison officer between the two secret services. The Abwehr set up Group 6513 in Estonia. Technical specialists were dispatched to Estonia to step up radio espionage against the USSR.

Canaris had met with Colonel Mario Roatta, head of the Servicio Informazioni Militari, in Munich in September 1935 to discuss the possibility of cooperation in counter-intelligence. This was followed by a meeting between the two secret service chiefs in Rome in June 1936; the topic was joint action by Germany and Italy to intervene in the Spanish Civil war on the side of Nationalist Spain under General Franco.

In September of that year, the German military attache in Ankara, Oberstleutnant Rohde, reported that he had received reports from allied sources concerning shipments of military supplies for the Red Brigades in Spain from the USSR through the Turkish straits at the Bosporus.

In 1937 Canaris and his deputy, Oberst Piekenbrock, once again visited Estonia to step up the intelligence-gathering effort against the USSR and a short time later Canaris enlisted the exile organization of Ukrainian nationalists into the service of the Abwehr.

A German message center was set up in Shanghai in autumn 1937 to monitor the import and export of military supplies and their transshipment from this important port to all of East Asia.

Engineer Hermann Lang, an Abwehr agent working in the USA, reported on a highly-effective new bombsight that had come to his attention in the course of his duties as an assembly inspector with a major air armaments concern. A short time later he gained access to all the files on the new bombsight which resulted in further interest in the device. The files subsequently reached Germany.

Then in October 1937 Nikolaus Ritter, an Ausland/Abwehr expert from the Hamburg office, traveled to the USA. His orders were "to explore the possibility of establishing a extensive espionage net and the conduct of industrial espionage missions."

In 1937 an agent of the Ausland/Abwehr I Luft group was exposed by the US Secret Service; however with the help of friends he managed to escape to Canada by car and from there returned to Germany.

The Federal Bureau of Investigation now became active in this area and placed the "League of Friends of the New Germany," of which the exposed agent had been a member, under surveillance. When a Sudeten German named Rumrich then ferreted out a courier of the German Abwehr and proposed a major coup, the latter agreed. The idea was to kidnap an American officer after having tricked him into bringing the mobilization plans of the units under his command.

Rumrich sent a request to the Colonel in question to bring the mobilization papers to a specified place where he was to hand them over to a representative of the War Department. The letter was on War Department paper in an official envelope bearing a forged seal. The American Colonel became suspicious, however, and brought with him several FBI men, who arrested Rumrich. During interrogation the latter revealed the names of all the Abwehr agents known to him and their helpers.

Johanna Hoffmann, a hairdresser working on the Europa, was taking the place of the German V-man, who was on leave in Germany at the time. She was arrested when the Europa returned to New York. Hoffmann, too, told all she knew, resulting in a series of arrests. A total of eighteen persons were charged with treason. Also charged were several German officers serving with the military mission: Oberst Busch, Fregattenkapitan Menzel, Korvettenkapitan von Bonin and Korvettenkapitan Pfeiffer.

The Abwehr effort in Estonia was stepped up in 1938. It was clear to Canaris that gathering intelligence on the USSR could best be done from the Russian border states. His contact and that of the Abwehr officials so far had been Colonel Maasing. Maasing went to Berlin in 1936 to sign the agreement for joint intelligence gathering in the USSR which he and Canaris had worked out verbally. When Maasing was released to the reserve in 1938, he once again went to Germany to write down everything he knew about Department 2 of the Estonian General Staff. His successor, Colonel Willem Saarsen, had already been won over by the Abwehr while serving as department head. He developed the Estonian Secret Service entirely into a "branch office of the German Abwehr."

In the years up to 1938 Military Attaché Rohde carried out several trips from Ankara in the service of the Abwehr to Syria and Palestine, to

Iran and Iraq, and to Afghanistan. His mission was to discover everything that might be of use to the Abwehr and establish first contact with rebels and nationalists in those countries.

The Long-Range Reconnaissance Squadron of the Commander in Chief of the Luftwaffe, over which Canaris' predecessor had been brought down, had been flying intensive high-altitude reconnaissance since 1937 and made its first flights over the Soviet Union. Stationed at Berlin-Staaken, it received more and more high-altitude aircraft and was ultimately expanded into a group. The unit was commanded by Major Theodor Rowehl.

Beginning in 1940, with the help of Department 2 of the Estonian General Staff the Abwehr began infiltrating several German espionage and sabotage groups into the USSR. One figure who would later become well known was the agent leader Gavrilov. Ukrainian exiles, as well as a number of Estonian, Latvian and Lithuanian nationalists, were enlisted by the Abwehr. They were trained for missions in Poland and the Soviet Union at a special camp on the Chiemsee, near the Abwehr laboratory in Berlin Tegel and in Quenzgut in Brandenburg.

THE FEELERS ARE EXTENDED

The visit by Canaris and Oberst Groscurth to Baghdad marked the first attempt to extend feelers to the Middle East. The Germans held talks with Arabian forces who had spoken out against England and gone underground.

When the efforts of German agents became noticeable in the USSR, the Soviets abruptly closed the German consulates in Kharkov, Kiev, Leningrad, Novosibirsk, Odessa, Tbilisi and Vladivostock.

In May 1938 Hermann Lang, who was active in the American aviation industry as an engineer and an agent, returned to Germany to brief German technicians on production of the USAAF's modern bombsight. As a result of his efforts a copy of the bombsight was built in Germany within a short time. Lang soon returned to the USA and set up a network of agents there to spy on businesses producing war-related materials.

The year 1938 brought the Abwehr turbulent developments all over the world. In spite of the unmasking of eighteen agents—whose number included E. Graser, J. Hoffmann, Glinter-Gustav Rurnrich and Werner Voss—in America in spring 1938, the Abwehr was able to expand its efforts in the USA. Fourteen of the suspected spies were warned in time, and most fled to Mexico, from where they later returned to the USA to resume their work.

In June 1938 in Berlin a deal was worked out between the Abwehr and the Japanese military attache Major-General Hiroshi Oshima specifying the conditions for an official exchange of intelligence concerning the USSR and the Red Army. Oshima, head of the Japanese secret service's European control station, was the son of Japan's Minister of War. Both father and son were keen on obtaining as much information as possible on the Soviet Union. Their goal was to ensure that their country was fully prepared for a possible war against the USSR in which Japan would carve out a large piece of that nation's huge Asiatic land mass to provide living space for her people. This piece was to be large enough to ensure forever the dominance in the East-Asian sphere that Japan was secretly striving for. So "Junior" Oshima went to Germany to see to it that Russia was threatened from the west as well as east.

In Admiral Canaris, Oshima had found a counterpart who fully supported the Japanese plans concerning Russia. The two men were thus able to reach an agreement whereby the Japanese and German intelligence services would exchange information concerning the USSR. A preliminary verbal agreement had been reached in October 1935; however it was not considered worthy of a formal agreement as the Japanese government was not yet ready to cast in its lot with Germany by forming an alliance. After much negotiation, in which Foreign Minister von Ribbentrop was also involved, on 25 November 1936 Japan and Germany concluded the Anti-Comintern Pact.

When General Oshima returned to Germany in 1937 he brought a draft agreement for cooperation between the armed forces of both nations, including their air forces. Hitler declined, because the Japanese had invaded Northern China in July and he had no desire to allow himself to be drawn into a war in the Far East. General Keitel only went as far as to tell the Japanese that cooperation could be guaranteed even without a written obligation binding the German side.

In September 1937 Oberst Rohde once again journeyed to the nations of the Near and Middle East, including Afghanistan, in order to gather authentic material for the Abwehr. On his return he outlined for the first time the possibility of including the rebels and other enemies of Great Britain in actions that could be planned and conducted by the Abwehr. In an effort to further stimulate this promising state of affairs, Senior Government Advisor Dr. Woehrl, a specialist who had been carefully selected by the Abwehr, was sent to Teheran on Canaris' orders to assess the chances of reinstating the ex-king of Afghanistan, Aman Ullah, who was living in exile in Rome, and at the same time strengthen the position of the king's supporters.

Dr. Woehrl had worked in Kabul as an Abwehr agent for some time and he knew the land and the mentality of the leading members of the opposition groups. During discussions with Canaris he gave him the impression that it was possible to restore the ex-king to power by means of a putsch, thus creating a government friendly to Germany for the struggle against England.

In talks with the Abwehr, the Afghan specialist Woehrl was able to convince the Admiral that the plan was feasible. The latter sent Woehrl to Rome to see the ex-king and—once he had secured his agreement to take part—to Afghanistan.

Emir Aman Ullah had succeeded his father Emil Habib Ullah in 1919 and became king in 1929; however as a result of hastily-implemented reforms he was overthrown the same year by an Islamic revolt. The leader of the revolt was "Batscha-ji Saqqa—the son of a water bearer"—a tadjik.

With his support Aman Ullah's cousin Nadir became king in October 1929. The latter, now Nadir Shah, was murdered in 1933. He was succeeded by his son Saher, who was now to be replaced by Aman Ullah.

Following the return of Senior Government Advisor Dr. Woehrl and his report that the "wild" mountain tribes on the Afghan-Indian border were ready to risk a revolt, Admiral Canaris saw to it that these plans were presented to Hitler. He instructed his colleague Oberst Edler von Lahousen-Vivremont to draft a report for the Fiihrer in which the Abwehr's planned action in the west, the position of the Ukrainians, Operation Tibet and Operation Afghanistan were mentioned.

Hitler agreed that the "Afghanistan story" should be pursued.

The Wartime Organization of the Abwehr

The Ausland/Abwehr Office of the High Command of the Armed Forces began forming war organizations (KO) in most of the states of neutral Europe in 1936, a process that intensified during the course of the Second World War. They were housed by the German diplomatic missions in the nations concerned and their members were camouflaged as mission personnel. Depending on the Abwehr officers included in their staffs, these war organizations carried out missions for the three Abwehr Departments—I, II and III. Department III did not begin sending representatives to the war organizations until the outbreak of war, however.

In the war zones it was the Abwehr squads that selected agents from the population in areas where partisan warfare was being waged. Town and field commanders were also used to work for the Abwehr where and when this was promising. Even before the war broke out, therefore, Germany had laid an extensive counter-intelligence net over those states of interest to her, a net that abruptly increased in density in the course of the war.

The strands of the net came together in the Ausland/Abwehr office of the OKW. Cooperation between the Abwehr and Office VI of the Reichssicherheitshauptamt (Reich Central Security Office), as well as the Auslands Organization of the National Socialist Party under its chief, Gauleiter Bohle, began soon after the war started and this relationship was consolidated as time went on. As well, the Ausland/Abwehr Office worked with the Volksdeutschen Mittelstelle.

Cooperation with the three attaché departments of the elements of the armed forces, especially that of the army, referred to the evaluation of the foreign military attachés and their aides in relation to their possible recruitment for espionage activity for the Abwehr.

The Long-Range Reconnaissance Squadron of the Commander in Chief of the Luftwaffe under its commander Major Theodor Rowehl was responsible for long-range reconnaissance missions on behalf of the Abwehr. Tasked with delivering agents by parachute was the Reconnais-

sance Group of the Commander in Chief of the Luftwaffe, commanded by
Hauptmann Karl-Edmund Gartenfeld. Both officers were decorated with
the Knight's Cross for their actions deep inside enemy territory.

Communication between agents abroad and the Reich was achieved in
a number of ways. One was by mail to a cover address, which might be a
real or false private address. Mail to one of the latter was directed through
official channels to the appropriate post office. When letters addressed to
these fictitious addresses arrived, they had to be sorted by the post office
and forwarded without delay to the offices of the Abwehr. As well, such
shipments went to post office boxes. The letters were mostly open business
letters. The secret text was written between the lines with chemical inks
that were capable of passing any postal inspection.

Abwehr I's V-man in Lisbon, Major Kraemer-Auenrode, sent messages
to and received the same from England in the form of books or postcards
whose text had been determined in advance. However the best, fastest and
most secure method of communication was radio, even though in some
cases this could be ferreted out and located by means of radio location.
Not until after the outbreak of war did this radio traffic develop into a
worldwide net for the transmission of secret intelligence.

The Abwehr required outstanding radio stations for its worldwide
communications. The central radio station near Berlin conducted radio
traffic with all war organizations and the offices subordinate to them. The
major Abwehr offices, which also had to cover very large areas, likewise
had at their disposal first class radio stations.

The Abwehr office in Hamburg also set up a radio station in the suburbs of the Hanseatic port for radio traffic with agents; it had both large
receiver and transmitter installations, situated several kilometers apart. Set
up in the receiver site's Europe half, which picked up all European radio
transmissions, was a reception site with 20 receivers.

In the overseas hall, which picked up all radio transmissions from
overseas, were 23 receivers, which were manned around the clock. The
transmitters of every German agent in the world were linked with this
reception installation and every frequency was monitored by four radio
operators and a "stand-in" working six-hour shifts. Equally extensive was
the Abwehr office in Vienna, which controlled radio traffic in the entire
southeastern area. Transmission times for all frequencies were precisely
prescribed and were changed according to a specific pattern.

Finally, micro-photography was also used. Every war organization had
a device that was capable of reducing entire typed pages of text to a
microdot. In this way agents returning from abroad could easily carry all

intelligence on their persons, in such a way that it could never, even on the closest inspection, be discovered.

Shortly before the outbreak of war, in August 1939, the OKW Office Ausland/Abwehr issued an order for the quickest and most extensive possible securing of important information from the enemy's files. The primary objective was to use these sources to quickly create an accurate picture of the measures being taken by enemy leaders in regard to all military but also political questions, so as to be able to take appropriate steps. Furthermore through an intensive study of these sources it was hoped to be able to identify those persons and groups of persons who had been known or were now found to be potential enemies of Germany. Obviously this list included agents operating in Germany on "behalf of these nations who were active as underground agents.

It fell to Abwehr II to play a leading role in this effort, for it received orders to employ selected, specially-trained teams which, following close on the heels of, and in some cases preceding, the German assault units, were to enter the previously pinpointed archives of the countries being attacked and secure the desired files at all costs.

For this purpose the teams were provided with weapons, equipment, vehicles, and uniforms from the enemy states. One of the first assignments of this type read: "An Abwehr front-line reconnaissance detachment is to find, seize and secure all material from Polish intelligence offices and archives, especially from the archive of Department 2 of the Polish General Staff in Warsaw."

The Abwehr office in Breslau subsequently formed and equipped the necessary commando team; commanded by MaJor Heinz SchmalschHiger, it was sent by the Vienna Abwehr office in the direction of Warsaw.

After the fall of Warsaw the team was to secure all intelligence material from the 2nd Office (of the Polish General Staff, which dealt with reconnaissance and with espionage and secret service activities). Another source for the work of the Ausland/Abwehr was the German Geopolitical Institute, which even before the war investigated, listed and catalogued all material coming in from Russia and the Near and Mid East.

The institute had more than 1,000 employees who, after thorough analysis of the mass of incoming material, produced various summaries, especially reference books, in cooperation with the Economic and Armament Office of the Armed Forces High Command and military intelligence. This resulted in studies of Russia's armaments industry and its rail system, the capacities of the oil-producing countries of the Near and Middle East, and more.

The material used to produce these studies came to Germany via every possible avenue, from foreign trade, economic and foreign political institutions and units, but also via Abwehr agents in the German missions and embassies. Given Hitler's known aversion to the "Bolsheviks" it is no surprise that even before the war much attention was paid to the Russian armament industry and efforts were made to determine its locations and capacities and identify eventual bottlenecks in raw materials or energy problems. The temporary alliance with the Soviet Union did nothing to change this.

Of course another focal point of interest was the oil producing and refining industries of those states with oil industries, especially those that were important to German industry and to its war machine. Also of interest were some sources of other raw materials and their development, which were vital to German industry. One such was platinum from Columbia, which was vital to the aircraft and equipment industries. A special "Russia staff" was created to coordinate all sites in Russia to be examined.

THE COMMAND ELEMENTS OF THE ABWEHR
The Chain of Command

Hitler, who viewed the Abwehr as an important instrument of his leadership in the political as well as military fields, gave what was then still the Abwehr Department, called the Abwehr Working Group, his full support and had Canaris promoted from the ranks. Nevertheless this department at first led a shadow existence. It was not until the first German field marshal of the Third Reich, Generalfeldmarschall Werner von Blomberg, who had become the Commander-in-Chief of the German Armed Forces and Reich Minister of War, was dismissed and the Reich Ministry of War disbanded, that the Abwehr's hour arrived.

From then on Canaris and his intelligence apparatus were under the direct command of the Armed Forces High Command and thus General Keitel. Later Canaris received his instructions only from Hitler. As the senior department head, he even became Keitel's deputy in the OKW.

Thus the "midget", as he was called in the inner circle on account of his diminu tive stature, only about 1.6 meters tall, came to wield a level of power that was matched by few of the other leading figures of the Third Reich.

In 1939, when the Abwehr Working Group was enlarged to about 400 persons, this huge apparatus was renamed the Ausland/Abwehr Office. It was divided into several departments, and each of these groups was a complex in itself. they were:

Department I

Department I was responsible for foreign espionage and the secret reporting service. It was led by Oberst Hans Piekenbrock and later Oberst Hansen.

This department was divided into the four groups Heer IH (army), Luft IL (air force), Marine 1M (navy) and Technik IT (technology). As well there the secondary groups Wirtschaft IW (economics), Geheimwesen IG (secrecy) and Funk /J (radio).

The intelligence of all types acquired by this department was passed on to the three components of the armed forces.

As well the Wehrmacht Operations Staff under Generaloberst Jodi also received intelligence by way of Department III and Department II (Foreign).

Department II

As sabotage central, it had under its command all agencies which carried out such actions in Germany and abroad, in peacetime and during war. Its primary task was to find qualified men for these varied missions, attract them and train them.

All of these missions required professional soldiers and extremely well trained fighters; as a result a house unit was called into being. During the Christmas holiday of 1939 the unit was given the name "Brandenburger".

This was the origin of the 800th Special Purpose Construction Training Company Brandenburg. The unit's first commanding officer was MaJor Grosskurth. He was succeeded by Oberst Lahousen and in the summer of 1943 Oberst von Freytag Loringhoven.

Department III

The main function of this department was counter-intelligence. It, too, was organized into groups—Heer III H, Luftwaffe III L, Marine III M, and Wirtschaft III Wi. This department was led by General Staff Oberst Bamler and later by General Staff Oberst Bentivegni.

Department III F

This sub-department was led by Kapitan Protze. The department was assigned the job of directing the dispatching of agents to foreign countries by ship or submarine. These men were to infiltrate the intelligence services of various nations while others were to carry out acts of sabotage.

That counterintelligence had to work closely with the Reichssicherheitshauptamt was due to the fact that the Abwehr had no executive authority, so that all punishable acts had to be pursued by the police. Thus the German Armed Forces were never given the authority to take those measures that were required to prevent sabotage and espionage against the armed forces themselves. This regulation, that the police and not the armed forces themselves might decide on and punish these cases, dated back to the year 1869. It had never been taken off the books. This allowed the Secret State Police (the Gestapo) to claim responsibility in all cases of this nature. Unfortunately the Abwehr never protested against this anachronism.

The secret reporting service alone remained the sole province of the Abwehr. The Abwehr's foreign department, which was later elevated to a working group, was the central authority for military attachés in foreign countries. All military diplomats had to direct their reports to this department. Commander of this department was Konteradmiral Biirkner, who was also Admiral Canaris' deputy.

Central Department Z was a part of Abwehr Department III C and directed the Abwehr group in the administration. At the same time it was also administration central and was thus charged with the administration of the entire huge apparatus of the Abwehr. It also included the agent files, the legal department, the accounting office and the passport office. Head of this department was then Major Oster (promoted to Generalmajor on 1/12/1942).

Oster, later one of the leaders of the conspiracy against Hitler, had a close contact with the National Socialist Party in Graf Helldorf. His contact with the Reichssicherheitshauptamt was by way of Criminal Director Nebe. The latter was in charge of Office V of the Reich Criminal Police. All incoming reports passed through Oster's office. In his central office they were sorted and passed on to the various departments. It was an ideal place for sabotage, falsification of reports, and treason. At the beginning of the war the Abwehr office included 400 officers and approximately 30,000 agents.

One of the Ausland/Abwehr's special units was a reconnaissance squadron which conducted strategic reconnaissance with specially modified aircraft. After the war Generalleutnant Piekenbrock described the unit's operations:

Very early on aircraft were sent over Czechoslovakia, Poland, France, England, and Russia on high-altitude reconnaissance missions. Since such activities in peacetime were a breach of neutrality, the aircraft flew at altitudes of about 13,000 meters. They were neither seen nor heard. However, on account of the great heights involved, they could only be used in clear weather. Their mission was to photograph fortifications, airfields, their layout and usage, troop camps, railway traffic, and other prominent points such as barracks. The resulting photographs were used to create target maps for the Luftwaffe. The results were very good. It spared many agents and also provided source material for their use.

As per the terms of our agreement with the Luftwaffe General Staff, the Rowehl squadron had to be returned to the Luftwaffe when war broke out. But the Rowehl squadron also produced the Gartenfeld Squadron, which during the war delivered agents into Russia.

As commander of the unit, which for security reasons was designated "Reconnaissance Group of the Commander-in-Chief of the Luftwaffe," on 27 September 1940 Oberstleutnant Theodor Rowehl was awarded the Knight's Cross.

At that time, in terms of aviation and photographic technology, this aerial reconnaissance of enemy installations was unique in the world. It made an important contribution to the rapid successes of the later blitzkrieg. When, during the Nuremberg Trial against the "leading war criminals", Generalmajor Lahousen was asked about the activities of this special squadron by American Colonel Amen, he answered:

> Rowehl was a Luftwaffe colonel. He had a squadron for high altitude flight, which worked with the Ausland/Abwehr office in reconnoitering certain regions and states. Rowehl reported the results of his flights to Admiral Canaris and gave him the resulting photographs, which underwent some sort of evaluation by Department I's Air Group. These flights were made over Poland, then England and the southeast of Europe. I know that the squadron was based at Budapest for a time to monitor the southeast area. I myself once flew back from Budapest to Berlin in such an aircraft.
>
> When the war broke out these flights were stepped up and were carried out under strict secrecy.

It was only natural that the number of flights increased when war broke out in 1939. There now follows a brief history of the squadron.

The Rowehl Squadron and its Operations

The Luftwaffe Special Detachment Rowehl was formed in 1937 and that same year began carrying out photo-reconnaissance flights over the Soviet Union. It flew He 111 aircraft disguised as commercial transports.

In 1934 the German airline Deutsche Lufthansa had issued a contract to Heinkel to design a high-speed commercial transport for use on its network of high-speed routes; in addition to its crew, the new aircraft had to be able to carry at least 10 passengers. For aerodynamic reasons Heinkel decided on a twin-engine machine and gave it the type designation He 111. Its design was based on the principles used in the design of the He 70.

After it had completed its first flights as a passenger aircraft, the Reich Aviation Ministry ordered a bomber version of the He 111 that was to become the Luftwaffe's standard bomber. The first example of the horizontal bomber variant left the production line on 4 May 1937. Examples of the He 111 converted for high-altitude flight were delivered to the Rowehl Squadron. Some were fitted with pressurized cabins and flew as far as the Crimea and the Caucasus.

As previously mentioned, in spring 1939 the squadron operated its high-altitude reconnaissance aircraft from Budapest on flights over the areas of Kiev, Dnepropetrovsk, Zhitomir, Zaporozhye, Krivoy Rog and Odessa.

In July 1939 Oberstleutnant Rowehl presented Admiral Canaris with the results of his reconnaissance flights and was given a new assignment: the dropping of agents over Great Britain and Ireland as soon as England and Germany were at war. On 3 September 1939 Britain declared war on Germany. The dropping of agents began. As well, Rowehl's squadron was the first unit to conduct marine reconnaissance for the Luftwaffe and, to a very limited extent, for the submarine arm.

In January 1940 the Rowehl squadron began flying its reconnaissance missions mainly against the Soviet Union—from Seerappen in East Prussia, from occupied Czechoslovakia and from hastily-prepared airfields in occupied Poland, as well as from bases in Finland, Hungary, Rumania, and Bulgaria. Oberstleutnant Rowehl succeeded in locating and obtaining high quality photographs of Soviet military bases, airfields, industrial complexes, railway junctions, and especially bridges. Coastal and inland ports were reconnoitered and a precise target map was created which included airfields, frontier fortifications, depots and army bases. The anti-aircraft zones of Soviet cities were located and during operation "Oldenburg" Soviet sources and stockpiles of raw materials were targeted. The Moscow and Leningrad industrial districts were important targets of the reconnaissance flights, as was the oil-producing region from Maykop to Grozny and Baku as well as the western territory of the USSR.

Within the unit one part of the squadron became known as the "island squadron." This was on account of its secondary role of dropping agents over Ireland.

On 13 February 1940, in the OKW, Admiral Canaris was able to give General Jodi a comprehensive report, lavishly illustrated with air photos, and brief him on the special squadron's experiences during its missions over Russia.

On 28th April the squadron began flying from the Bardufoss airfield in northern Norway, which had fallen to German alpine troops under General Dietl. The first flights from Bardufoss went to Murmansk and the railway line leading to the port as well as Arkhangelsk.

Like the sorties flown over the Ukraine and western Russia, these missions could prove useful in the planning of operations by the Brandenburgers, so that in this connection the flights by the special squadron were also often of decisive importance to this unit.

At the beginning of 1941 the squadron flew sorties over Kronstadt, Kronstadt Bay and the units of the Soviet Fleet based there from several Finnish airfields. Activities were also stepped up over Leningrad, Murmansk and Arkhangelsk. With the help of target maps and the scouting of Soviet defense systems, when the campaign in the east began, Army Group North was supposed to be able to take Leningrad quickly. The primary purpose, however, was to facilitate a blockade of the USSR's northern sea routes and the Kola Peninsula.

Still in January 1941, the squadron flew missions from Rome and Sardinia over unoccupied France and Corsica, in order to obtain material from these critical areas in the event that a march into or through unoccupied France or the occupation of Corsica became necessary. 27 March 1941 saw the special squadron fly its first direct mission over Yugoslavia, when three aircraft took off from Wiener-Neustadt. A crisis situation in Yugoslavia could not be ruled out.

In summing up the squadron's operations, it can be said that the pilots of this unit distinguished themselves, often spent many hours over enemy territory, never lost track even in difficult situations, and always came home with excellent material.

Admiral Canaris' House Unit

FROM THE 800TH SPECIAL PURPOSE CONSTRUCTION TRAINING COMPANY TO THE 800TH SPECIAL PURPOSE TRAINING BATTALION "BRANDENBURG"

On 27 September 1939 Dr. von Hippel, Hauptmann in the Abwehr II/Ausland, obtained from his chief the order for the formation of a company of picked soldiers for use in the coming campaign in the west.

Admiral Canaris summoned Hptm. von Hippel on 15th October and gave him the job of raising this unit, which was to form the core of his house combat unit. At first it had to be capable of carrying out all kinds of operations. In addition to special missions for the western campaign, the program also included sabotage missions and surprise strikes.

The first volunteers for the new unit came from the ranks of the Abwehr. The site of the formation of the company, which was coming together gradually, was the city of Brandenburg on the Havel. The training site was a small estate on the Quenzsee. There was already a training base there for Abwehr people, who were trained to be radio operators and V-men there, but also explosives experts.

Residing there as the "maid of all work" was Major Maguerre, who had been given the job of providing all agents, V-men and sabotage teams with uniforms, weapons and equipment appropriate to the areas where they were going to see action, as well as radio equipment and explosives.

The first officers of the "Brandenburgers," as the company soon came to be known, received their final polish at this small estate on the Quenzsee. Wehrkreis III, Berlin was responsible for assigning all soldiers from every state in Germany who volunteered for the new unit.

Since the "Construction training Company" was to be involved mainly in the field of sabotage and demolitions, its training concentrated on the techniques and equipment used by combat engineers. Training was under the direction of Technical Inspector Kutschke, a great expert in the field.

In November 1939 Leutnant Siegfried Grabert and 11 soldiers of the German Special Purpose Company arrived from Sliac in Slovakia. They and other members of that company who soon followed were used to form

24

the 2nd Construction Training Company. Hptm. Fabian, who came from the artillery, took command of the 2nd Construction Training Company, which had been created from the German Special Purpose Company in ten days.

While the now two companies were being established, Hptm. Rudloff was transferred from the combat engineer staff of X Army Corps to Abwehr II. He was ordered to take 10 to 12 soldiers to Münstereifel and wait there at the disposal of Headquarters, 4th Army. When Rudloff arrived there, he was briefed on the missions that awaited him by General Staff Major Schwatlo-Gesterding. However, the planned attack in the west was postponed. Nevertheless, in Miinstereifel Hptm. Rudloff began training and preparing for other special assignments which were assigned him by the Abwehr.

At first with 12 soldiers, who were recruited from the Construction Training Company and who were later joined by a steady stream of new arrivals, Rudloff practiced commando-style operations. After receiving a new shipment of 70 soldiers and 3 officers on 23 November 1939, the Rudloff unit received the designation 3rd Construction Training Company Brandenburg. The constantly growing flow of volunteers to the unit made it necessary to form a battalion, which took place on 15th December.

The battalion's commanders and bases were as follows:

800th Construction Training Battalion based at Brandenburg-Havel	Hptm.Hippel
Headquarters Company based at Brandenburg-Havel	Oblt. Kutschke
1st Construction Training Company based at Innermanzing, Wienerwald	Oblt. Dr. Kniesche
2nd Construction Training Company based at Brandenburg-Havel	Hptm. Fabian (Obit. Dr. Hartmann)
3rd Construction Training Company based at Munstereifel	Hptm. Rudloff
4th Construction Training Company based at Brandenburg-Havel	Oblt. Walther

The following units were raised within the battalion and were later integrated into the unit:

a paratrooper platoon under Lt. Dlab
a motorcycle platoon under Oblt. Erwin Graf Thun
a North Platoon (or recovery platoon) under Lt. Zulch

a West Platoon under Fw. Kurschner, and

a Southeast Company.

As the plans for "Case Yellow", the code word for the assault on France, became known, the men around Hptm. Rudloff were formed into a company. They received instructions to guard sites in the area of the frontier when the western campaign began. This meant that they had to safeguard all important river and canal crossings in the western area before they could be blown by the enemy.

The 100th Special Purpose Battalion under Hptm. Fleck was deployed by the 6th Army in Bere with a similar mission. Proceeding ahead of the main body, it was to take possession of all the bridges over the Maas in the army's area, cut the ignition wires, and hold the bridges until the arrival of regular units.

At the end of January Feldwebel and officer candidate Hermann Kurschner was ordered by Hptm. Hippel to form a well-armed patrol for a mission in the west. Kurchner quickly agreed and gathered a group of volunteers which included members of the "Young Prussian League" as well as men from the mountain country around Kerkrade-Herzogenrath on the Dutch border who knew the area.

Kurschner presented his team to the headquarters company. Within a few weeks he had welded it into a potent small assault force. On 15 February 1940 Kurschner reported to Abwehr II where he was received by Oberstleutnant Lahousen and Major Stolze. There he learned the extent of his mission and received minutely detailed instructions.

At the end of March the Kurschner patrol, which by now had been given the cover title "Special Purpose Construction Training Platoon," was transferred to Erkelenz, and from it to be assigned to the 7th Infantry Division. Kurschner was briefed on his mission once again by the headquarters of the division. The order read:

> Proceeding ahead of our advance detachments, three to four hours before the start of the attack, the Kurschner platoon will advance to the four road bridges over the Juliana Canal due east of the Maas and seize them. The bridges are to be held intact until the arrival of the 7th Infantry Division. Planned crossing points: the bridge near Olbricht, the bridge near the village of Berg, and the bridges of Urmond and Stein.

Fw. Kurschner kept his people in shape with daily demolition and nocturnal patrol exercises. There were combat maneuvers with live ammunition, and practice with Czech hand grenades equipped with impact fuses. Special attention was paid to night orientation marches, because success in the coming actions very much depended on them.

"Dutch" uniforms were fabricated. They were to be worn over the German uniforms while approaching the bridges. When the fighting began they were to be removed. Only a few weeks before these commando-style operations Kurschner was promoted to Leutnant.

In addition to this assault unit, around 15 February 1940 the 1st Platoon of the 4th Company, Construction Training Battalion under the command of Lt. Witzel and Fw. Hermann Stohr with a total combat strength of 60 men was transferred into the Reichswald. It went into position in a concealed forest camp between Goch and the village of Asperden and prepared for its mission. The company's 2nd Platoon, led by Lt. Grabert, moved to Arsbeck, a village west of Rheydt. It consisted of 40 men.

While Lt. Witzel's platoon was subordinated to XXVI Army Corps, the Grabert Platoon was under the command of XI Army Corps. Both platoons had the same general assignment: "Seize the bridges over the Maas and the Maas-Waal canal before the arrival of the infantry spearheads, prevent their destruction, and hold them until the arrival of the infantry." The troops involved in this action were also to be dressed in enemy uniforms.

Thus the two commando units, each of roughly platoon strength, were to seize a total of eight bridges. Four of them lay in the area of the Grabert Platoon and four in the Witzel Platoon's. Approximately 7 to 11 soldiers would be assigned to each objective, as well as Dutch V -men. The teams were to move out to the attack at least three hours before the infantry.

At the beginning of May 1940 Admiral Canaris visited the forest camp at Asperden to observe several exercises for Operation "Rosy Dawn." He was visibly impressed by what he saw.

The bridges that were not to be seized by the Abwehr's house unit, the Brandenburg Special Purpose Battalion, were the Nymwegen and Arnheim bridges. They were to be seized and held by the 100th Special Purpose Battalion under Hptm. Fleck of the Oppeln Abwehr station. Fleck had formed this battalion from the 550 Abwehr men of the Oppeln station and other volunteers. It was allocated to the 6th Army commanded by Generaloberst Reichenau.

Sufficient Dutch-speaking leaders were provided by Oberst Erwin Edler von Lahousen Vivremont, the chief of Abwehr Department II. He invited the leader of the Dutch National Socialists, Julius Herdtmann, to take part. Herdtmann was only too willing to help. He immediately placed 200 members of his organization at the disposal of the Abwehr. Taken to an Abwehr II camp, they received military training and were prepared for their missions. Dressed in uniforms of the Dutch military police, they were to slip across the border and seize enemy installations. Even before the attack began, Lahousen had at his disposal a cadre of more than 1,000 men who were ready to attack.

Major Kewisch (later commanding officer of the Brandenburg Special Purpose Construction Training Regiment) also visited Munstereifel and was impressed by the high level of preparedness of the Abwehr unit.

One of the combat teams sent against the Grand Duchy of Luxembourg was commanded by Oblt. Eckart Schoeler, an estate overseer. His unit consisted of Germans who had previously lived in Luxembourg and who had been drawn from various units. Another was the platoon commanded by Fw. Eggers of the 2nd Company of the 800th Special Purpose Construction Training Battalion, which was moved to St. Thomas. From there, at the end of April it took up position in the Westwall's bunker line near Ammeldingen. These men were also under the command of the Abwehr and when the attack began they were to advance ahead of the infantry toward approximately 100 sites that they were to seize and hold.

Finally at the end of March a Brandenburger command center was set up in Berlin since these missions were too much for a battalion headquarters to deal with. It was equivalent to the operations staff of a regiment. In command of the operations staff was Major Kewisch. Major Kewisch came from the 8th Reconnaissance Battalion. He brought with him the aggressive cavalry spirit and became one of the leading commanders of the soon to be formed regiment.

INITIAL OVERVIEW

In the early morning hours of 10 May 1940, in several cases before midnight, the advance of the Brandenburgers began in Luxembourg, Belgium, the Netherlands and France. In France it was commando teams which saw action at Abbeville, in the Dunkirk-Calais-Boulogne-Arras-Lille area and near Verdun and Metz.

More important than these long-range missions, however, were those that were carried out near the frontiers to promote the advance by the infantry and armored units. The 3rd Company, 800th Construction Training Battalion stood ready for Operation Maastricht. The Abwehr special unit was ready to go as were the 200 Dutch guides under Julius Herdtmann.

The Schelde tunnel near Antwerp was occupied by an Abwehr special detachment. In The Hague, several Abwehr men familiar with the area led assault teams to the quarters of the Queen, the minister of parliament, to the headquarters of the High Command and to various other headquarters.

In Luxembourg the telephone system was destroyed at the outset and important installations, for example the Grand Duchy's main power plant, were occupied and the way was opened for a rapid advance by German forces through the Ardennes to the Meuse.

In Belgium the communications center at Stavelot was destroyed. But what happened at the bridges and special strong-points, to which the Brandenburgers set out at least three hours before the start of the attack on the early morning of 10 May 1940? Here is the story of their fantastic action from the beginning.

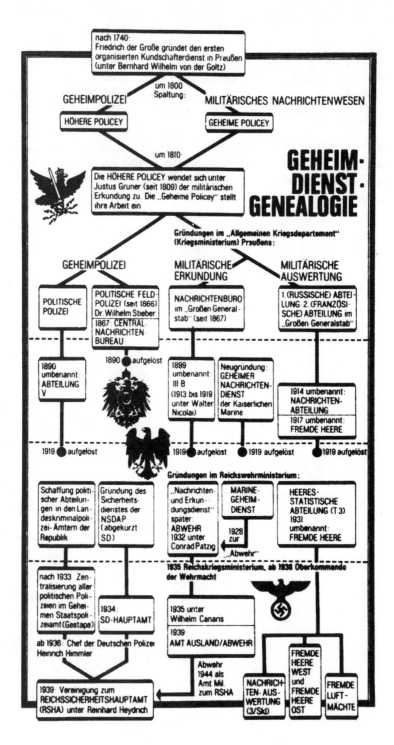

Genealogy of the Prussian-German secret service.

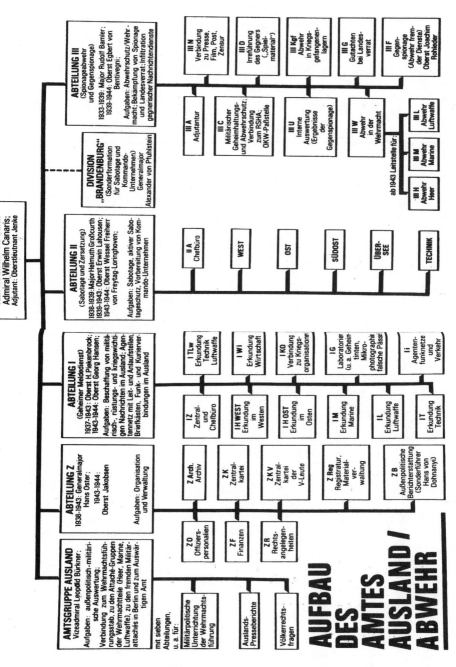

Expansion scheme of the Ausland, Abwehr.

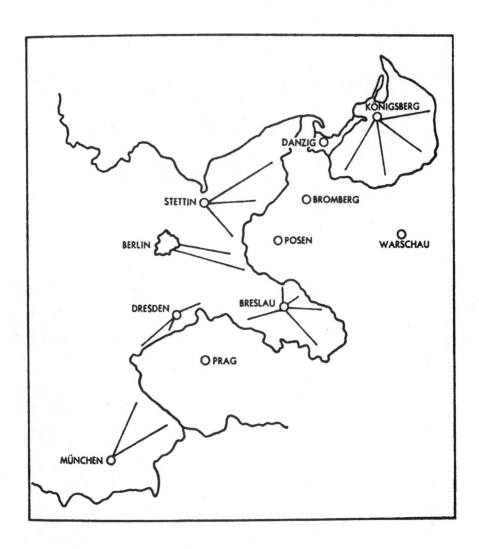

The German Abwehr offices in the east from 1923 to 1936.

Admiral
Wilhelm Canaris,
head of the Abwehr.

Admiral
Canaris and SS
Gruppenfuhrer
Reinhard Heydrich
head of the Security
Police and the SD
before the war.

Admiral Canaris
visiting the troops
at Brandenburg.

Allen W. Dulles,
head of US secret service in Bern.

General Pierre Louis River,
head of the French secret service.

Gen Lt. Von Benivegni,
head of Abwehr Department III.

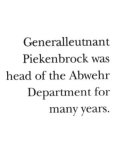

Generalleutnant Piekenbrock was head of the Abwehr Department for many years.

Gen Maj. Von Lahousen, head of the Abwehr's Department II, in conversation with Indian volunteers.

Dr. von Hippel, commander of the Brandenburg unit.

Erwin von Lahousen,
director of the Abwehr II department
(sabotage).

Oberstleutnant Oskar Reile,
Reconnaissance III/West.

Oberst Reinhard Gehlen,
head of the Foreign Armies
East Department.

Oberstleutnant Eisentrager, head of the Abwehr office "KO Far East" (KO = war organization).

SD chief Schellenberg with the head of the Gestapo, Müller, and Heydrich (at front, from left).

Oberstleutnant Gerhard Wessel, Oberst Gehlen's deputy.

Female auxiliaries
of Foreign Armies
East.

Martin Bormann,
too late identified
as an agent of the
Soviets.

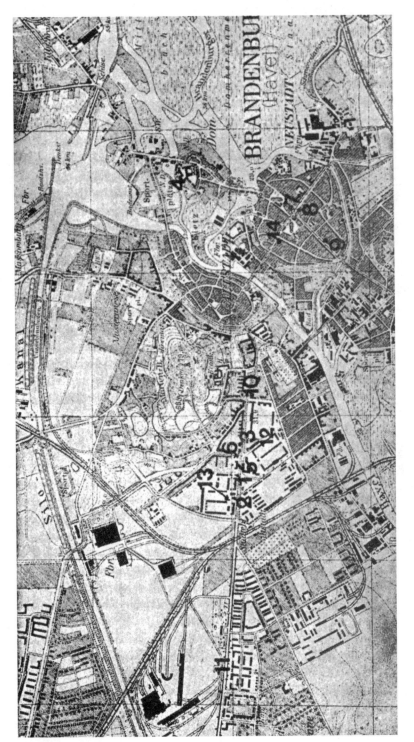

Brandenburg-Havel and the Brandenburgers' barracks.

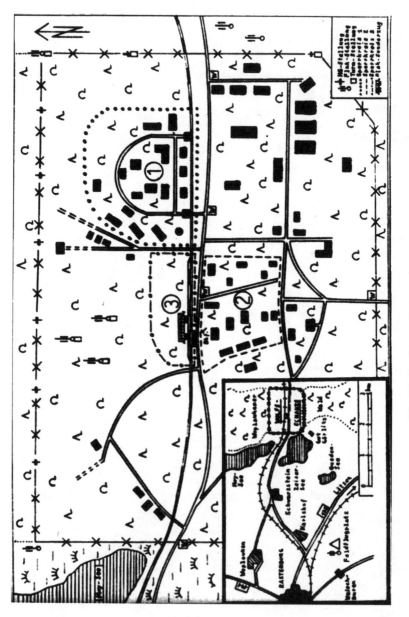

The Wolfsschanze Führer Headquarters.

The Abwehr at War

THE BRANDENBURGERS' FIRST COMBAT MISSION
BEFORE THE OUTBREAK OF WAR

It had been decided that the campaign against Poland would begin at 4:25 A.M. on 26 August 1939. However, as a result of Mussolini's intervention and Goring's negotiations with the Swedish mediator Dahlerus the date was postponed until 1st September. But the plans of the Armed Forces High Command also included two operations by the "German Company" and "Battle Group Ebbinghaus." As a precautionary measure the Jablunka Pass was to be occupied before the start of hostilities and held until the arrival of German armored forces. This action was to begin on 25 August 1939.

As well "Battle Group Ebbinghaus," consisting of the German Company and members of the former Sudeten German Freikorps, was deployed by the Breslau Abwehr station. Its members were to parachute into Poland and seize important sites, also before the official start of the war, and hold them until German forces arrived.

The Polish buildup was to be hindered wherever possible to the maximum possible extent. Additionally Ukrainian nationalists and ethnic Germans in Poland were to be equipped with arms and material to enable them to carry out acts of harassment and sabotage.

The special detachment commanded by Oberleutnant Dr. Albrecht Herzner was given the job of occupying the Jablunka Pass before hostilities began, disabling all demolition systems, and opening the way for the German combat division waiting in Sillein in the High Tatra. Dr. Herzner's thrown-together "fighting unit" was under the control of Abwehr II.

Other missions given the Abwehr: capture of the city of Kattowitz by a 400-manstrong Abwehr unit, seizure and holding of the vital Vistula bridge near Dirschau, and elimination of the Polish power station at Chorzow Jahm.

Dr. Herzner's special unit set out from Sillein on the evening of 25 August 1939. It rode as far as Dadca in vehicles belonging to the division for which it formed the advance group. While the army vehicles returned from there to Sillein, Dr. Herzner and his unit marched toward the

41

Jablunka Pass, five kilometers away. Toward midnight they reached the border and Dr. Herzner summoned all the squad leaders for final instructions.

From reconnaissance reports Dr. Herzner knew that a small Polish unit was stationed on the other side of the pass; it would have to be eliminated. He readied one platoon of his company-strength special unit that had been assigned to capture the enemy unit. None of the Polish soldiers must escape to sound a warning prematurely. For this reason the Polish quartering areas also had to be sealed off.

The leader of the pioneer platoon was instructed to search all likely looking places for explosives and remove the ignition wires of any that were found. Dr. Herzner stressed to his men that they should use their firearms only in an emergency, for any premature firing might threaten the viability of their mission.

Led by ethnic Germans who had volunteered for the job and were familiar with the area, the special unit set out divided into three battle groups. The first task was to take out the Polish forward sentries, which had been spotted by the Germans on the near side of the pass.

The first platoon walked up a path through the woods covering the steep slope toward the pass. When the men could look down and see the rail line, they spotted two sentries standing under a signal mast in front of the tunnel. They were obviously there to guard the tunnel entrance. While the soldiers stayed behind, the platoon leader and the guide crept down through a ravine to the railway embankment. Suddenly, in front of the Germans, a figure stood up from the ditch on the right of the embankment.

"Halt, who goes there," whispered a voice in Polish.

The guide threw himself on the man and knocked him to the ground. The second man of this previously unseen pair of sentries jumped up from the ditch and ran off in the direction of the tunnel. The platoon leader dropped his pack and ran after the second Pole. He caught him just before the signal mast, where the two sentries had been spotted. The two tunnel guards jumped up and grabbed the platoon leader, but the guide, who had overcome his first opponent, came to his aid and the second pair of sentries was overwhelmed without a shot being fired.

The platoon leader fetched the waiting soldiers, who had already followed him down the slope without waiting to be told to do so. Moving in a group, the men worked their way in the darkness along the tunnel walls, bent low. About halfway through the tunnel the platoon leader saw a glowing cigarette butt fall to the ground only a few feet in front of him and then a shoe extinguished the butt. It was the sentry stationed in the middle of the tunnel who served as a contact man between the two groups at the tunnel entrances. One of the men crept forward and silently overcame the unsuspecting Pole.

They moved on. Hushed voices could be heard from the far end of the tunnel, then it became lighter, and when they had approached to within a few dozen meters of the opening they could see that there were also four Poles at that end. The sentries were engaged in a conversation. Once the four soldiers stepped back a few paces, but then they returned to the tunnel entrance.

Four members of the special unit crept forward, waited for their chance and slipped out of the tunnel when the sentries walked away. When the Poles came back the waiting Germans jumped them and took them out without making a sound.

"You stay here until I report," ordered the platoon leader. Then he gave the sign for the guide to come to him. Together the pair crawled through the valley and after only three minutes they saw the small railway station of Mosty. More Polish troops could be seen there. Men were moving about at the storage shed. Farther to the rear they could see the three barracks of the Polish camp.

"Bring the men," ordered the platoon leader. When they arrived three minutes later he briefed them. First they had to overpower the guards at the station and the storage shed. Then they would seize the station and the shed simultaneously.

Oberleutnant Herzner had meanwhile arrived with the main body after receiving his platoon leader's report. After the guards had been eliminated, the Brandenhurgers worked their way toward the three buildings. They knew that one was the quarters for the NCOs, the second for the enlisted men, and the third served as an office.

The first to be overpowered was the commander of the Polish unit, a lieutenant. Then it was the turn of the remaining officers. The groups that entered the enlisted men's quarters worked just as quickly. However, there was an incident there when a Pole armed a hand grenade. One of the men grabbed it from him and threw it through the window. It exploded in the air. Warning shots into the ceiling drove the Poles back. That was the signal for several soldiers in the enlisted men's quarters to barricade themselves in. Dr. Herzener was able to persuade the Polish lieutenant to talk to his men in order to avoid unnecessary bloodshed. Dr. Herzner had convinced him that Germany had been at war with Poland since 4:25 A.M.

Relieved of their weapons, the Polish soldiers were taken to the storage shed and locked up. Meanwhile the demolition charges at both ends of the tunnel had been disarmed. The German divisions must show up at any moment. When they did they would find the way open.

But the German divisions did not come. The war had been called off and postponed until a later date. Battle Group Herzner had no working radio with which to receive this news. Seventy soldiers had taken possession of the Jablunka Pass. They had captured and disarmed about 800 Polish soldiers and now they were alone in enemy territory.

Suddenly there were noises. A steam whistle was heard and—by now it was light—then a huge goods train was spotted steaming from Polish territory up the hill toward the pass. One of the Polish Germans who knew the railroad signals set the station's signal to "stop." The train stopped before the signal for a few minutes but then rolled into the station anyway. It was a troop train carrying 1,200 soldiers. Several Polish officers got out of the forward car and walked into the station. They were met by waiting German soldiers with submachine-guns at the ready.

The colonel in charge of the train was taken to the lieutenant who had been captured earlier. The two men spoke. Finally they said that they were prepared to surrender the 1,200 soldiers on the train. The Poles locked up in the storage shed began pounding on the door. A burst of machine-gun fire over the shed silenced them at once.

Not until noon of 26th August was it possible to establish radio contact with the division in Sillein. The division commander told Dr. Herzner that the attack date had been postponed shortly after the special unit departed; the battle group was already an hour on its way and could not be recalled. Dr. Herzner was forced to tell his men that there was no war.

That evening the entire battle group headed back through the tunnel. It succeeded in slipping away from the Poles and set out for home. It had carried out its mission. If the war had begun at the planned hour, it would have delivered 2,000 Polish prisoners of war.

WARSAW FRONT-LINE RECONNAISSANCE DETACHMENT

When the German forces in Poland arrived at the gates of Warsaw, with them was the Warsaw Front-Line Reconnaissance Detachment under Major Schmalschliiger. Oberst von Lahousen had given him the job of securing all the files of the Polish secret service.

On 8th September it appeared that the Wehrmacht would soon be in Warsaw and the Abwehr detachment under Major Schmalschläger was ready. The detachment had just moved out, so as to reach the 2nd Department of the Polish Intelligence Service in Pilsudski Square and secure its files as quickly as possible, when it was called back by a dispatch rider. The unit, which had already entered Warsaw, was forced to withdraw. It was to be three-weeks, following air attacks on Warsaw and vain requests for its surrender, before the Polish capital finally fell.

But Major Schmalschläger was once again on the spot. He drove to Pil-sudski Square in a fast Opel Blitz truck and found the place empty. He did find about 100 steel cabinets in the office of the secret service—all were locked. The detachment leader had his specialists open them. They were almost empty. Only a few of the cabinets still held files, which had apparently been forgotten in the haste. Schmalschläger and his men did find a large quantity of files in several cabinets that contained material belonging to the 2nd Department's "German Section." Included was a complete collection of Wehrmacht publications, including weapons and service manuals. Some of the publications bore neat labels on which was written the name of the agent who had procured the material in Germany.

The military-geographical survey of Germany was very precisely made; the Germans were astonished to read in one of the studies that the Polish General Staff had believed that the Polish Army was capable of launching a surprise attack, reaching Berlin in eight days and bringing down Hitler's Germany. Of particular importance were German telephone books and an index card file of emigrants all over the world who had been recruited for special work or were still "sleeping" somewhere abroad.

But what they had hoped to find was not in the abandoned piles of paper: information on agents who had worked for Poland in Germany and were still working.

Major Schmalschläger had the men in the surrounding houses, those who had not fled, questioned. An hour later he had what he wanted to know. The Poles had carted the material away in numerous large army trucks eight to ten days earlier, when the city was already encircled.

The detachment commander gathered his men around him: "Gentlemen, the files of the Polish department are still somewhere in the city. It is impossible that such a number of trucks could have left the city. Therefore they must still be here somewhere."

"We have to check all the truck parks, Herr Major," observed one of the men, who spoke fluent Polish. Schmalschläger nodded. He split his force into two groups, then set out with his group to follow up on a lead he had received early on the second morning. He had learned that a truck convoy had driven in the direction of the fort during the night.

"They drove to old Fort Legionow," declared an army captain. "I saw six army trucks there."

Schmalschläger headed there at once, passed the roadblock, and followed the tire tracks down a dirt road until they arrived beneath the huge casemates of the old fort. There were trucks parked there, six of them. In them were fully packed boxes with all the files of the 2nd Department of the Polish General Staff. An initial inspection revealed that the highly valuable material had been found; it had obviously been brought there to be burned, for several boxes had already been piled up in a heap off to one side. It was somewhere where no one was likely to have gone, for the fort dated from the time of the Czars and was no longer in use.

After making this find Major Schmalschläger and two men armed with submachine-guns went inside the fort. They stopped before a locked door. It was opened, and in one of the ancient dungeons, where water dripped from the walls and it smelled of mold and decay, they found several boxes on rough-hewn shelves. They were opened; inside was found the Polish secret service's treasure: reports by the Polish military attaches in Tokyo, Rome, Paris, and Berlin and several cartons of material from the Bromberg branch office and others near the frontier. Apparently the Poles had wanted to save this material.

While still in Warsaw the files produced the names of 279 spies active in Germany; they were all arrested and brought before the federal court.

What the Warsaw Special Detachment did not know was that the material contained numerous clues about an espionage organization and a case of espionage that could be traced back to 1927. It was the case of Rittmeister Stosshowski, who had come to Berlin that year and established his net. Then in 1935, just after Admiral Canaris assumed command, he gained entry into the organization.

In addition to information, the captured files on Polish secret agents enabled the Abwehr to turn a number of them. Those with anti-Soviet sentiments were fully integrated into the German intelligence effort against the Soviet Union. The Warsaw mission had thus turned out to be a complete success.

THE FRONT-LINE RECONNAISSANCE DETACHMENTS AND THE WARTIME ORGANIZATION OF THE ABWEHR

Having already described an operation by one of the front-line reconnaissance detachments, it is appropriate that the formation and expansion of this special formation should be described here, especially since they played a significant role in subsequent events.

It began with the agent radio net, which had been established not just on the borders of, but also inside "potentially hostile" nations. One such radio net also existed in Poland. It was set up by Hptm. Horaczek. The agents' controllers were based in the Stettin, Berlin and Breslau Abwehr stations.

In addition to this network of agents, small Abwehr squads were formed and subordinated to large army units as "advance point units." Formation of such units was first suggested by Major Schmalschläger, an experienced counterintelligence officer. After these small units had achieved good success, particularly in searching for secret documents, in January 1941 the army general staff issued an order for military intelligence to create further units of this type.

Since these small units had been called Abwehr detachments and squads in the past, the newly created Abwehr Departments I and II were to receive a new designation. The so-called "Halder order" which provided for their formation designated them "front-line reconnaissance detachments." A specified number of front-line reconnaissance squads were placed under the command of these detachments. Later, on account of the large number of these detachments, control centers for front-line reconnaissance had to be established in the east as well as the west.

On average the front-line reconnaissance detachments consisted of up to 40 soldiers, while the squads were outfitted with about 12 to 25 soldiers. These included the interpreters, radio operators and officers. They were called front-line reconnaissance detachments because in wartime they were supposed to advance ahead of the spearheads of the attacking armies and through rapid intervention prevent the enemy from destroying important secret files prematurely. Their purpose was therefore roughly akin to that of the Brandenburgers and—what was decisive—they, like the Brandenburgers, were part of the Abwehr's fighting force.

As well as securing enemy documents, it was also necessary that the detachments evaluate them quickly and acquire new information through the use of informants, supplemented by practical statements from prisoners of war on the strength, organization and base of operations of opposing forces.

Furthermore, they had to take all necessary measures to safeguard friendly forces in the rear, areas with little or no protection, from acts of sabotage or partisans and act in the best interests of the unit under which they were serving. The units of Front-Line Reconnaissance I were directed by Abwehr I under Oherst Piekenbrock. Its primary task was to observe enemy forces and detect and report attack preparations. The role of Front-Line Reconnaissance III was to combat spies and saboteurs and eliminate terrorist groups in the area of the front. This meant that the front-line reconnaissance units were military units that, operating from the area of the front, had to carry out all tasks of a secret service and military nature.

These front-line reconnaissance units were commanded by the offices of the Ausland/Abwehr, but for purposes of discipline and administration they were subordinate to the armies or army groups in whose area they were operating. And thus it was that these detachments, which had been formed to supplement the Brandenburgers, were for the most part responsible for secret service missions, while the Brandenburgers took on the military special missions. It must be said that the first time the front-time reconnaissance units fully carried out these assigned tasks was in the Balkans Campaign, specifically in Yugoslavia and Greece. The following is a brief outline of those activities.

FRONT-LINE DETACHMENT X IN ACTION IN YUGOSLAVIA

In February 1941 the Abwehr office in Vienna received orders from the Ausland/Abwehr Department to immediately form and bring to readiness a front-line reconnaissance detachment to consist of several squads. An officer from the Abwehr's Group III assumed responsibility for the formation and command. He selected capable officers, the best Yugoslavian interpreters, radio operators, drivers and soldiers. The detachment ultimately consisted of 39 men. The squads under its command each averaged 12 men.

The detachment was sent to 12th Army under Generalfeldmarschall List in Sofia. When the invasion of the Balkans began on 6th April it accompanied the leading panzer units so as to reach its assigned objectives as quickly as possible. On the very first day of the invasion of Yugoslavia the squads captured a number of documents of the Yugoslavian army command that were of great value to the fighting forces. These included plans of Yugoslavian fortifications, special road maps showing blocking positions, and information concerning the load-bearing ability of various bridges. By the time the campaign against Yugoslavia was over, several boatloads of files had been sent up the Danube to Vienna.

Evaluation of the documents revealed that the Yugoslavian secret service had conducted only a limited program of espionage against Germany in the years before the war. It was learned, however, that the Yugoslavians had managed to infiltrate one of their agents into an Abwehr office, where he obtained some important information. A number of traitors from the German ranks and two intelligence swindlers who had sold bogus material were arrested or exposed.

An important side-benefit of these Yugoslavian acquisitions was the identification of several nations whose secret services were active in the Balkans—England, France and the Soviet Union.

FRONT-LINE RECONNAISSANCE AGAINST GREECE

When Denmark and Norway fell in spring 1940, the Abwehr office assigned to Headquarters, X Army Corps in Hamburg lost its area of operations and had to look about for new roles. Its commander, Kapitan zur See Wichmann, submitted his new proposal to the High Command of the

Navy. It read: "We must go to the Mediterranean, for it will soon become of great importance."

Wichmann's proposal was rejected, and he was told that the Mediterranean was the responsibility of the Italian secret service. Nevertheless he turned his attention to the Mediterranean, even though only at its fringes at first, by forming a front-line reconnaissance detachment for Greece. He first sent two Abwehr officers, disguised as businessmen, to Athens. They took with them a radio and transmitted their findings daily to Germany.

When the Italian adventure against Albania failed in the spring of 1941, Hitler was forced to make the decision to come to the aid of his ally to save it from defeat; at the same time he planned to destroy the British forces on Crete and the Greek mainland, because the British presence there threatened the vital oil fields in Rumania. Kapitiin zur See Wichmann was instructed to go ahead with the planned Abwehr detachment. It consisted mainly of members of the German navy. The detachment departed Hamburg in mid-March and in a few days reached the German marshaling area for the Greek offensive on the Bulgarian-Greek border. When the offensive began the detachment stormed ahead with the armored spearheads and on the morning of 27 April 1941 became the first German unit to reach Athens. The detachment immediately took possession of the ministry of the navy and seized all its secret files. The Greek admiral in command handed over the entire ministry to the young soldier commanding the assault team.

OPERATIONS IN THE WESTERN CAMPAIGN: PREPARATIONS

In October 1939, after the Polish Campaign ended, Admiral Canaris tasked Abwehr Major Horaczek with the formation inside occupied Poland of another espionage ring against the USSR, thus expanding the espionage effort against Russia. For this purpose Horaczek expanded the hastily organized temporary Abwehr stations in Radom, Chechanow, Lublin, Terespol, Krakow, and especially Suwalki into fully operational Abwehr offices. Furthermore, Terespol's airfield was enlarged for use by long-range reconnaissance aircraft of the Commander-in-Chief of the Luftwaffe's Long-Range Reconnaissance Group commanded by Major Rowehl.

On 10th October Admiral Canaris visited the Abwehr office that had been established in Warsaw and the same day, after consulting with the leader of Rumania's military secret service, ordered Abwehr II to place undercover operatives in the oil-producing region of Rumania around Ploesti with its oil wells, refineries, trains hauling oil tank cars, and shipping traffic on the Danube.

On the morning of 27/9/1939 Hitler assembled the Commanders-in-Chief of the army, air force and navy and the head of the Abwehr in the Reich chancellery and declared to them that he intended to take the offensive in the west in October. He outlined the necessary steps and declared that his first operational objective was Holland, Belgium and northern France, which was to act as a buffer zone between the enemy and the vital Ruhr valley. From this developed a number of plans for the seizure of various targets far in the enemy's rear; preparations were also made to launch surprise attacks on positions which might hinder the rapid advance to the west: bridges, canals, railway junctions. After this conference Canaris summoned Hauptmann Dr. von Hippel and instructed him to form a sabotage and assault company, which must include a number of men fluent in Dutch and Belgian (Flemish or Wallonian), to carry out surprise raids.

The first men with the necessary qualifications very soon began to assemble at Brandenburg-Havel. The Ausland/Abwehr had already had a training center for Abwehr agents set up near the barracks in the buildings of an estate on Lake Quantz. Its commander was Hptm. Seeliger. Here the agents of all three Abwehr departments underwent training necessary for their duties as radio operators, agents, photographers and spies. Materials needed for undercover operations, such as foreign uniforms, explosives, weapons etc., were obtained through Major Maguerre's office.

The company formed at Brandenburg received the designation "800th Special-Purpose Construction Training Company." Training, which emphasized combat engineer skills, was in the hands of Technical Inspector Kutschke.

In November 1939 Leutnant Strabert and two members of his "German Company" arrived at Brandenburg. After hearing rumors of what was going on there, he and his Sudeten Germans had come from Sliac in Slovakia to Brandenburg to volunteer. By 11th November the 800th Special-Purpose Construction Training Company, which became operational on 25th October, had been joined by the 1st and 2nd Special-Purpose Construction Training Companies.

On 10 November 1939 Hptm. Rudloff was ordered by Abwehr II to take a well-armed group of 12 Brandenburgers, as the members of the special companies were known on account of their base of operations, to Milnstereifel. With the beginning of the offensive in the west, which was to come in a matter of days, they were supposed to advance out of the 4th Army's marshaling area and occupy and secure any site that was considered important. The attack did not come, however; the process was repeated several times, but on each occasion the date of the attack was pushed back.

By the end of the year 1939 the Brandenburgers were already largely dispersed. With the exception of the training and headquarters company, the 800th Special-Purpose Construction Training Battalion, which had been created on 15 December 1939 with a strength of four companies under the command of Hptm. Dr. Hippel, had already moved to its operational areas. 1st Company had moved to its new base in the Wienerwald. At the request of Abwehr III Romanian-speaking personnel were sent to that country as a precautionary measure to safeguard its oil sources. The 2nd Company under Hptm. Fabian, with platoon commanders Lt. Grabert and Lt. Witzel, was still in the Ordnance General's Barracks at Brandenburg, while the 3rd Company under Hptm. Rudloff was in Münstereifel at the disposal of the 4th Army.

Ethnic Germans from all over the globe had come to Germany to serve in the German armed forces, especially in the 800th Brandenburg Battalion. The unit was first called" Brandenburg" during Christmas celebrations on Christmas Eve 1939 and the name stuck. The name was to remain a symbol of the unit throughout its life.

At the beginning of February 1940 the Brandenburgers learned of their new mission: "Seize a series of important bridges before the start of the offensive and hold them until the arrival of our ground forces." The troops trained in close combat and weapons handling and carried out demolition exercises to prepare for their mission. Special emphasis was placed on a stealthy approach. The platoon commanded by Feldwebel and officer candidate Hermann Kilrschner, which had been chosen for an offensive patrol at the end of January 1940, was now readied for the action in the west. In February Fw. Kilrschner reported to Abwehr II in Berlin; there he learned from the department's director, Oberst von Lahousen, and from Major Stolze, which missions he would have to carry out.

The Kilrschner Platoon was designated the "Construction Training Platoon" to conceal its true purpose, and at the end of March 1940 it was transferred to Erkelenz. From there it was to move out several hours before the attack in the west in advance of the 7th Infantry Division, take possession of the four bridges over the Juliana Canal, and hold them open for the division to cross the canal. Two platoons from the 4th Brandenburg Company had also moved west in mid-February. The 1st Platoon under Lt. Witzel and Fw. Stohr moved into the Reichswald near Goch-Asperden with 60 men, and the 2nd Platoon under Lt. Grabert to Arsbecl west of Rheydt. These two platoons had also been given missions in advance of the main force; they were to seize the bridges over the Maas and the Maas-Waal Canal and prevent the Dutch from destroying them.

OPERATION "WESERÜBUNG"

German intelligence stations had been established in Scandinavia before war broke out; operating from ports on the west coast, such as Bergen, Stavanger, Christiansand, Oslo and Skagen, German agents monitored merchant traffic and sent reports to Berlin. By the beginning of 1940 the system had been expanded to the point that it was possible to monitor all incoming and outgoing shipping. The reports were passed on so quickly that X Air Corps, whose headquarters was in Hamburg, could attack these ships at once. As a result, during the course of the winter of 1939-40, X Air Corps under Generalleutnant Hans Geisler alone was able to sink 150,000 tons of British shipping. Generalleutnant Geisler was awarded the Knight's Cross on 4 May 1940 for this success.

At the end of January 1940 the Abwehr office in Hamburg received a report that French alpine troops had left their former base at Matz and had been transported to the Channel Coast for shipment to England. It was clear to the Abwehr that there was going to be trouble in the north. The Abwehr was instructed to step up its intelligence-gathering activities in Denmark and Norway. This mission was passed on to the Hamburg office of the Abwehr. Operatives crossed the border into Denmark and returned with the locations of all Danish units. The Abwehr prepared armed squads. Their missions included the destruction of Danish communications between Gedser and Nykoebing as well as Operation "Sanssouci," the occupation of the railway station at Tingelv. They were also to occupy the main roads and prevent the railway bridge near Padborg from being blown, thus ensuring that the army could pass through Denmark as quickly as possible. The most important operation was the use of disguised troops to seize the major bridge over the Belt.

The Brandenburgers went into action in the north early on the morning of 9th April. Operation "Sanssouci" was carried out under the command of Fw. Sorgenfrey. The detachment succeeded in completing all its assigned tasks without complications. None of the locals paid any attention to the men in civilian clothes as they approached the bridge. The platoon under Lt. H. Lotzel was flown to the Großen Belt in gliders. They landed right beside the bridge and took possession of it without incident.

On the morning of 9th April the minelayer Hansestadt Danzig under Korvetenkapitän Wilhelm Schröder sailed into Copenhagen harbor carrying 1,000 men of the 308th Infantry Regiment under Major Glein, with motorcycles, bicycles and weapons on board. The ship was flying the Reich service flag. On the bridge with Korvettenkapitän Schroder was Kapitänleutnant Skipowski, who was to be the German naval intelligence officer in Copenhagen. The Hansestadt Danzig docked at the "long line" in Copenhagen and the assault company hurried ashore. The armored coastal vessel Niels Juel was seized and an hour later Schroder was able to report to Gruppe Ost: "Tub has arrived. Battalion landed." Copenhagen had been taken without a shot being fired.

When the landings in Norway began, the German steamer Vidar was in Oslo harbor. Since Oblt. Kempf of the Ausland/Abwehr was on board, he immediately used the ship's AFU set to establish contact with the radio station in Hamburg. In the morning he reported the arrival of the first aircraft and by afternoon had sent 240 transmissions to Hamburg which were immediately passed by telephone to the Abwehr and from there to Führer Headquarters.

Operations Staff Kewisch of the Ausland/Abwehr was set up in Oslo and it requested that the North Platoon waiting in Brandenburg be committed. Under the personal command of Major Kewisch, with Lt. Knauß and 41 soldiers, the North Platoon's mission in Norway began on I May 1940. Together with German alpine troops, it succeeded in carrying out a number of special missions before it returned to its base at Brandenburg-Havel after the Norwegian surrender on 12 lune 1940.

BRANDENBURGERS IN THE WESTERN CAMPAIGN—THE BRIDGES
The individual Brandenburger detachments for the operation in the west were assigned during the course of April 1940. A total of eight bridges were to be seized, four each in the areas assigned to the platoons commanded by Leutnant Grabert and Leutnant Witzel. Aerial photos were used to accurately simulate each objective in war games. The squads, each numbering between seven and nine men plus a Dutch interpreter, were to set off three hours before the leading army units. This lead-time was necessary, because the army troops assigned to the bridges were positioned approximately ten kilometers from their objectives and would surely be noticed as soon as they moved off. All members of the squads were issued Dutch army coats that they put on over their own uniforms. Each carried a submachine-gun concealed beneath the coat. "Pineapple" and stick type hand grenades were carried in the coat pockets. Pistols were stuck in pants pockets. In early May Admiral Canaris visited the Witzel Platoon's forest camp near Asperden and observed a final, thoroughly successful training exercise.

Also scheduled to take part in the operation, in addition to the two platoons, was the 100th Special-Purpose Battalion commanded by Hauptmann Fleck (from the Breslau Abwehr station). This unit was to seize the bridges at Nijmegen and Westerpoort, east of Arnheim. The Kilrschner Platoon was assigned the four road bridges over the Juliana Canal at Stein, Urmond, Berg and Obbicht in South Limburg. Late on the afternoon of

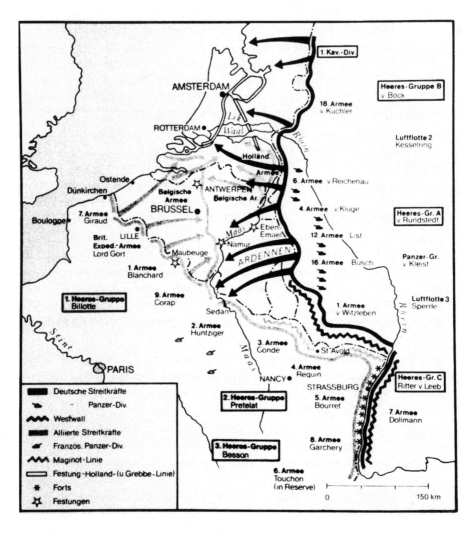

The plan of attack for the campaign in the West.

9th May the Brandenburg detachments and those of the 100th Special Purpose Battalion moved up into attack positions. They prepared for action and the men who were to seize the bridges over the Maas and the Maas-Waal Canal put on their Dutch uniforms.

At 12:30 A.M. the squad assigned to the bridge at Berg drove to Millen; from there it proceeded on foot to the border. At 1:30 A.M. the Dutch border was crossed. The soldiers crossed a foot-bridge over the two-meter-wide Geleen Brook. Led by Lt. Kilrschner, the squad bicycled to Berg. Lt. Kilrschner described what happened:

"With weapons slung we passed through the gap between two concrete pipes which had been filled with concrete and tipped on end as obstacles at the entrance to the bridge. We walked straight toward the Dutch soldiers standing on the bridge. Suddenly they ran away and I called after them in Dutch, 'Stop—where is the commander of the guard?' The Dutch stopped and when we were within range I said to them, 'Boys put down your weapons!' Then I disarmed the soldiers nearest me.

Suddenly one of the Dutchmen ran toward the demolition site on the bridge railing. Unteroffizier Bergner shot him in the leg, he cried out and fell to the ground. The rest of the Dutchmen were disarmed and led off the bridge. Amid their dismayed shouts of 'Don't shoot! Don't shoot!' I cut the ignition wires, which had been laid as a double line. We had done it."

A burst of machine-gun fire whipped across from the east bank. The machine-gun nest at the other end of the bridge was taken out. Lt. Kilrschner's engineers then removed the explosive charges. During this action he was shot in both thighs and the right foot. Gefreiter Frey dragged him on his back out of the enemy fire and was wounded in the process. The enemy was also prevented from blowing the bridge at Obbicht. There the commandos faced stiff resistance from a machine-gun on the western approach to the bridge. German machine-gun fire kept the Dutch from reaching the demolition site.

The advance detachment of the 7th Infantry Division arrived at about 7:00 A.M., and an anti-tank gun soon took out the enemy bunker from which the machine-gun was firing. This ended the fighting at the Obbicht Bridge. The same thing happened at the Stein and Urmond bridges. All four bridges were secured and the explosive charges removed from their recesses. The Born Bridge, which was especially strongly defended by the Dutch, could not be blown for fear of damaging the nearby lock. For this reason the Dutch positioned extra troops at the bridge.

Stationed there was a heavy infantry platoon under the command of Lieutenant Bekkering, with two 47-mm anti-tank guns, three heavy machine-guns and three light machine-guns. The three light guns were positioned on the east bank, where they had a clear field of fire. The German assault force neared the bridge at about 4:00 A.M.; but the Dutch defenders had already been alerted and opened fire. Later, when German troops arrived at the bridge, the leading trucks were shot up by the anti-tank guns. A heavy firefight broke out. In the midst of the battle Sergeant Engelaar and Corporal van de Bogaard crawled over from the Dutch side to the track-blocking system, which consisted of an iron grating, which Engelaar locked by cutting the wire. When one of the Dutch light machine-guns was put out of action, the other two withdrew to the west bank.

The German attackers were taking heavy fire from the casemate on the west bank. Finally the first German guns were moved up; they scored several direct hits on the casemate and also hit the two other bunkers left and right of the bridge on the west bank. The last Dutch defenders surrendered. The advance could continue. The entire 7th Infantry Division was able to cross the captured bridges and advance 30 kilometers into Dutch territory in the initial rush. After completing its mission, the detachment under Lt. Kilrschner was driven back to Erkelenz.

The Germans knew that the operation against the Maas bridges near Maaseyck would be especially difficult, because in order to reach it the bridge over the Juliana Canal at Oud Roosteren had to be crossed first. Additionally the Abwehr had identified a strong force of infantry in the area of South Limburg equipped with artillery, anti-tank guns and anti-tank rifles. The Hocke Special Unit, consisting of the 100th and 800th Special-Purpose Battalions, was to attack that area.

On the morning of 10th May 40 men of this battle group arrived at the town of Oud Roosteren east of the Juliana Canal and overran a Dutch infantry squad positioned there. They reached the bridge over the canal at Roosteren, where the bridge guard asked them for the password, which they did not know. But as they knew the previous day's password, the lieutenant of the guard on the east bank let them pass. The group was stopped again at the west end of the bridge. The corporal on guard there noticed something unusual about the steel helmets (which were made of papier-mâché) and called out the sergeant of the guard, who appeared moments later with the company commander, Lieutenant Braun.

The German squad leader, who called himself Captain Willemse, called for both men to surrender. When Captain Braun refused and reached for his weapon, he was shot by "Willemse." Seconds later "Willemse" was also shot at. The ensuing firefight resulted in dead and wounded on both sides. The Brandenburgers succeeded in taking the bridge. Corporal Velde was shot while attempting to set off the explosive charge and was taken prisoner. The bridge over the Juliana Canal was in German hands. The group immediately proceeded to the Maas Bridge near Maaseyk. It was spotted and placed under heavy fire. This prevented it from reaching the bridge in time and soon after the firing began it was blown up.

MORE BRIDGE ACTIONS BY THE BRANDENBURGERS

Under the command of Lt. Grabert, a 15-man V-squad with one man disguised as a Dutch lieutenant marched to Roermond at 2:00 A.M. It was one of the total of 15 combat teams sent against the bridges. The soldiers wore Dutch coats over their German uniforms and wore Dutch steel helmets. Marching through the middle of the city, Grabert and the V-squad finally reached a rail crossing. Since the barrier was closed, they turned to the left to go around it. A civilian followed them and all of a sudden they found themselves facing a patrol of six men.

"Halt!" ordered the patrol leader. "Show me your papers," he said to Lt. Grabert. The German officer showed him a falsified pass but the patrol was already suspicious. Lt. Grabert acted quickly. "Hands up!" he shouted at the Dutchmen. Three men raised their hands, one reached for his weapon and was shot down. Men came running from a side street—more soldiers. A brief firefight broke out, which delayed Grabert and his men from reaching the bridge. Then, with a thunderous roar, it was blown up before their eyes.

The bridge north of Roermond near Buggenum was supposed to be seized by a six-man team commanded by Uffz. Hilmer. Hilmer and his men were disguised as railroad workers and carried picks and shovels. Assigned to watch over the bridge were two Dutch NCOs and 20 men. Standing guard on the east bank at this time were Sergeants Touw, Jongkind and Kooyman. A steel mesh fence was stretched over the railroad track. The guardhouse on the east bank was connected by telephone to a bunker on the west side. That night Sergeant van der Wetering had taken up position there as commander of the guard. At precisely 3:00 A.M. Wetering was telephoned from the east side and a message was relayed by the Roermond police that a group of unidentified persons was moving along the rail line toward his bridge. There had been firing in Roermond. He was to immediately do everything required to secure his bridge as per orders.

Sergeant Wetering immediately had the steel mesh fence, which had been open, closed. About ten minutes later a suspicious group appeared at the eastern approach to the bridge in front of the mesh fence. The bridge guard stopped the group. One of the three, who was also a railroad worker, recognized one of the men and since the leader, Uffz.Hilmer, spoke with a German accent, extra caution seemed advisable.

Sergeant de Vries, the commander of the guard on the east bank, called the west bank to ask how he should handle the situation while his three guards kept a close eye on the group, which was obviously unarmed. Suddenly the "railroad workers" dropped their tools, pulled out their weapons and opened fire. Sergeant Touw was killed. Though wounded, Sgt. de Vries was able to warn the west bank. Kooyman and Iongkind had taken flight and ran, pursued by the Germans, toward the west bank. Before the pursuing Germans could open fire on the fleeing Dutch, they were themselves fired on from the west bunker. The first two Germans fell to the ground badly wounded. When the Germans reached the middle of the bridge the explosives were set off. Four huge explosions shook the structure and the Germans on the bridge were hurled into the depths along with the rubble.

Immediately after the Dutch guards on the east bank had been overrun, Uffz. Hilmer had fired signal flares to summon a German armored train waiting under steam just beyond the border. By the time it arrived at the bridge, twenty minutes later, it had been blown and the train could go no farther. The Dutch anti-tank gun opened fire. The first rounds struck the locomotive. The crew of the armored train was forced to abandon it due to the danger of explosion. The attempted seizure of the bridge had failed.

The raid on the railway bridge at Gennep went differently. It was supposed to be seized by an assault team of the 4th Company of the 800th Special-Purpose Construction Training Battalion under Oblt. Walther the company commander. Three Dutchmen, members of the Dutch national socialist party, took part in the surprise attack. They were dressed and armed as gendarmes. They wished to create the impression that they had intercepted and caught the nine men of the assault team somewhere in the area of the border and were now bringing them in.

When the group halted 800 meters from the bridge for Oblt. Walther to go over the attack one more time, one member of the assault team was missing. The ninth man had been left behind with one of the Dutchmen who had reconsidered and now refused to fire on his countrymen. Oblt. Walther accepted this but was cautious enough to leave one man behind with the Dutchman to prevent him from doing something stupid. When they appeared at the bridge they were met by four soldiers of the guard. Oblt. Walther and Fw. Stohr drew their pistols and positioned themselves so their movements and the weapons could not be seen from the west bank. In any case the bridge was 150 meters long and it was still dark. So the Oberleutnant held the four guards in check while Fw. Stohr went over to the guardhouse and with his jackknife cut every wire he could find. Meanwhile, however, the soldiers in the guardhouse on the east bank were able to ring the alarm bell. The warning was heard in both river casemates.

Oblt. Walther, an interpreter, a member of the assault team, and Fw. Stohr now went across the bridge. In the center of the span was another sentry who was supposed to monitor the water flow; he allowed them to pass. When they reached the other side Walther and his companions found themselves staring down a number of gun barrels. The Dutch marched them off after a half-hearted search, but they failed to find the concealed weapons. Suddenly Oblt. Walther shouted: "Aircraft, take cover!" He and his men burst free and pulled out their weapons. The Dutch, taken completely by surprise, were disarmed.

As soon as the east approach was secured Walther fired a signal flare. In the meantime the armored train had arrived. It came under fire from one of the casemates, but the Dutch gun jammed after firing a second round. The bunker crew surrendered.

The bridge at Gennep had fallen into German hands intact. A few minutes after the planned attack time the spearheads of the 256th Infantry Division rolled across to the west. On 24 June 1940 Oberleutnant Wilhelm Walther became the first Brandenburger to be awarded the Knight's Cross. After the war Walther was arrested by the Dutch military authorities.

THE BRIDGES OVER THE MAAS-WAAL CANAL

The bridges over the Maas-Waal Canal were more strongly guarded than those discussed so far. The bridge at Heumen, for example, which was located in the defense zone of the Dutch 26th Infantry Regiment, was under the command of Captain Dr. Postma. It was protected by several casemates. The defenders there had at their disposal five heavy machine-guns, an anti-tank gun, an 80-mm gun, and a mortar platoon.

A warrant officer and four sergeants of the police were standing guard on the bridge. At dawn on the morning of 10th May there appeared at the bridge four "Dutch policemen" with 30 German "deserters" led by Lt. Witzel. The sergeant of the guard allowed them to pass after checking their papers. When the total of 34 German soldiers reached the bridge they attacked casemates G8, G9 and Sl0 on the lock island on the far side of the river and took possession of them. The crew of casemate G7 saw them, however, and showered the attackers with a hail of fire.

Captain Dr. Postma, who was just inspecting the casemates, heard the firing and soon afterward was warned by one of the soldiers, who told him of the German ambush. Dr. Postma hurriedly drove back to the threatened position and there was hit by a stray machine-gun bullet. One of the Dutchmen who had led the way for the Germans, a man named Lucassen, was killed by the defenders.

The surprise attack had worked and the defenders were prevented from blowing the bridge, nevertheless the 4th Reconnaissance Battalion, which was supposed to follow the assault team, was unable to cross the bridge as it had been raised. Not until the Dutch lockmaster was forced to lower the bridge by hand (the electrical circuit had been knocked out by gunfire) did the first soldiers come across. A member of the assault team positioned a machine-gun in the center of the bridge and was shot from

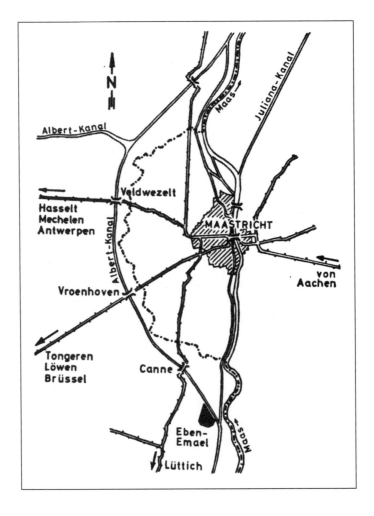

one of the casemates still in Dutch hands. Casemates G7 and G11, which were on the lock island, were still firing. The commander of the 4th Reconnaissance Battalion, Untersturmfiihrer Letz, was killed during the firing. There was a lengthy exchange of fire in which both sides suffered casualties. A Dutch counterattack, with the aim of retaking the bridge, failed under fire from the first German guns to be moved forward. Not until late afternoon was the 4th Reconnaissance Battalion able to cross the bridge.

The Malden Bridge was also guarded by a company of the Dutch 26th Infantry Regiment under Captain Peeters. Once again the defenders had medium and heavy weapons with which to fight off an attack. On the night of the attack one NCO and ten enlisted men were on guard. The bridge was barricaded with concrete rings and barbed wire obstacles. When the officer in charge inspected the guard at about 4:00 A.M., it was reported to him that four civilians had tried to cross the bridge. They had been turned back. The captain drove to his battalion commander, reported, and received orders to blow the bridge. In the meantime, however, a small force of Germans had seized the bridge. They had overwhelmed the guards, occupied the guard-houses and cut the wires to the explosive charges. With the same surprise and speed, the Germans took the bridge at Hatert. The Dutch did manage to set off one charge but it proved too weak to achieve the desired effect.

On the other hand, the night ambush against the roadblock near Didam failed. Incorrect uniform details gave the raiders away and they were fired on. The attackers were forced to withdraw.

In spite of several failed attempts, the missions against the bridges, together with the parachute operations, opened the door into Fortress Holland for the German Army and enabled it to wage a swift campaign.

OTHER ABWEHR OPERATIONS IN FRANCE

In addition to its efforts against the bridges, the Abwehr had planned a series of other operations with the objective of saving the secret files of the French general staff, and especially its 2nd Department, from destruction and taking possession of them. Another mission targeted the Dutch navy shipyard in Rotterdam. The objective was to acquire the Gaussing device, which could be used to counter German magnetic mines, and if possible its design documents as well.

Placed in charge of this operation was Korvettenkapitän Kilwen of the Abwehr. On 13th May he and his navy assault team succeeded in entering the shipyard, which was still in enemy hands. Kilwen and his men made their way to the design office, where two Dutchmen were about to burn the sought after papers. They managed to stop them and captured not just the important piece of equipment but the documents as well. They subsequently held out until Rotterdam was bombed and surrendered.

On 25th May another Brandenburger platoon stormed the sea locks and road bridges near Newport, Belgium and held them in the face of fierce resistance until the arrival of the armored spearheads. Once again both sides took heavy casualties.

When the attack on Reims began, a French staff car flying the corps standard drove into the city and, followed by a French truck, reached the citadel where the secret files of the French western army were kept. In his best French Abwehr Major Vossen, disguised as a French lieutenant-colonel, demanded that the files be turned over to him at once so that he might take them to safety in Paris. The French soldiers helped the two staff officers load the files into their truck. The Lieutenant-Colonel thanked the men and then drove away. Outside the city the two vehicles turned toward the German lines, ignoring the attempts of two wildly gesticulating sentries to prevent them from driving into "disaster".

On 30th May, with the fall of Paris imminent, a special group of Brandenburgers consisting of an assault team with two Abwehr officers, drove along the main road to Paris, worked their way into the melee of refugees and headed for the French capital. They reached the city on 9th June. Disguised as Dutch, French and Belgian refugees, they spoke to one another in those three languages. They were not found out. The assault team drove to the government quarter and stopped in front of the annex of the bureaus deuxiéme, the seat of the French secret service. The mood there was one of disintegration. Trucks sat in the courtyard. Soldiers were busy loading the secret files in heavy crates.

The Brandenburgers abandoned their disguises and seized the staff of the office. The soldiers were captured and the files secured. The French government left the city on 10th June. All the secret files captured in Paris by the Germans were shipped to Berlin aboard several trains. They included the central card index and the files of the sûreté nationale, the national security agency, which was subordinate to the Ministry of the Interior.

German troops entered Paris on 14th June. The waiting men of the Abwehr followed right behind them and established the Paris office of the German intelligence service.

On the afternoon of 18th June it was learned that French combat engineers were preparing to blow up the Pechelbronn oil wells in Alsace. A platoon of the 1st Brandenburg Company was sent there immediately. They raced toward Merkweiler-Pechelbrunn in two trucks and a fast car and drove straight to the oil wells. They jumped from their vehicles, ran into the engineers' quarters and arrested them. One of the men, an Alsatian German, showed them the wires leading to the explosives. They were cut at once and the danger was eliminated.

At the end of June Admiral Canaris ordered the establishment of the Abwehr and Abwehr branches in The Hague, Brussels, St. Germain, Dijon, Angers, Brest and Bordeaux. The Abwehr office in Brest set to work immediately, expanding the German espionage net in unoccupied France, in North Africa, on the Pyrencan Peninsula and in England.

Captured agents in Luxembourg and France were released on ISth lune. The front-line detachments also captured important files and documents in Abbeville, Guise, Saint Quentin, Cambrai, Arras, Doulens, Lille, Boulogne, Calais, Dunkirk and Verdun, which the French secret service had stored in its branches there. It was enough to keep the evaluators of the Ausland/Abwehr busy for years.

THE 800TH SPECIAL PURPOSE TRAINING REGIMENT
BRANDENBURG GUIDELINES AND FORMATION

The guidelines by which the 800th Special Purpose Construction Training Battalion was reorganized into a regiment came from the Chief of the Army High Command, Army Armaments Staff, and the commander of the Replacement Training Army AHA la (I). The order, Secret Command Matter No. 1450/40, was issued on 15 May 1940, for it had become apparent during the campaign in France that the command structure of a battalion was inadequate to allow the Brandenburger unit to meet the demands placed upon it.

The Brandenburger operations staff placed Major Kewisch, who returned from Norway in mid-June, at the head of the new regiment. Kewisch appointed Oblt. Zülch, whose abilities hc knew from the fighting in Norway, as adjutant in his staff. Both men were convinced that the Brandenhurgers were going to become a regular unit and as such should be raised and trained according to strict military rules.

In order to achieve this, Major Kewisch had young officers transferred to Berlin, where they joined the companies and battalions. In the process many older, experienced officers were passed over. The ensuing quarrels led to Major Kewisch being relieved at the beginning of October; he was replaced by Major von Aulock. But for him, too, the post was to be a brief one, for on 2nd November Oberstleutnant von Haehling assumed command. He would remain there for some years.

The uncertainty created by the frequent changes in command was now put to rest. The following is the list of the regiment's officer corps.

Note that a number of veteran officers, such as Hptm. von Hippel, were no longer present.

800th Special Purpose Construction Training Battalion

Regimental Commander:	Major Kewisch (until end Sept.)
	Major von Aulock (until end Oct.)
	Oberstleutnant von Haehling
Regimental Adjutant:	Oberleutnant Zülch
Ia: Oberleutnant Pinkert	
I Battalion:	Oberleutnant Walther (mWGb)
1st Company:	Oberleutnant Grabert
2nd Company:	Hauptmann Fabian
3rd Company:	Hauptmann Rudloff
4th Company:	Oberleutnant Walther
II Battalion:	Oberleutnant Walter
5th Company:	Oberleutnant Kutschke
	Oberleutnant Pinkert
	Oberleutnant Dr. Kniesche
6th Company:	Oberleutnant Meissner
7th Company:	Oberleutnant Kutschke
8th Company:	Oberleutnant Grabert
III Battalion:	Oberleutnant Baron von Acken
	Hauptmann Jacobi
9th Company:	Oberleutnant Kutschke
	Oberleutnant Wulberg
10th Company:	Leutnant Kutschera
	Oberleutnant Aretz
11th Company:	Oberleutnant Schoeler
12th Company:	Oberleutnant Schader

In order to reach their planned areas of operation within the OKH as quickly as possible, the regiment's three battalions were moved to the peripheries of these areas, as follows:

Berlin: for special missions on behalf of the Ausland/Abwehr: the regiment operations staff. Also quartered there was the signals company.

Brandenburg-Havel: for all missions of an interregional nature and for forming a point of main effort.

Baden near Vienna: for missions in eastern and especially southeastern Europe.

Aachen, later Dilren: for other missions in Western Europe and the planned Operation "Sea Lion."

OPERATION "EYRIE"—THE SEIZURE OF GIBRALTAR

On 23 July 1940 a certain Senor Guillermo arrived back in Madrid. After a sightseeing drive through northern Spain with his driver and a passenger; he immediately telephoned the German embassy in the Calle Castellana from a private apartment. The direct number connected him with the Military Organization Spain (KO Spanien). Oberstabsintendant Franzenbach, the financial head of the department, answered. He had been waiting for this call. He was relieved to hear that "Uncle" had arrived, for now he was certain that Admiral Canaris had arrived in Madrid without being recognized.

Franzenbach immediately passed the news on to the head of the Military Organization Spain, Fregattenkapitiin Wilhelm LeiBner. The latter operated in Madrid as "Honorary Attache" Gustav Lenz.

When "Uncle Guillermo" arrived at the embassy, the man with him turned out to be Oberstleutnant Hans Piekenbrock, head of Abwehr I's secret reporting service.

Admiral Canaris informed the amazed head of the Ausland/Abwehr department that a German staff consisting of various army and air force experts would soon be coming to Spain to determine if there was a possibility of conquering the British fortress of Gibraltar and thus block the Royal Navy's access to the Mediterranean and to Malta and Alexandria— and at the same time halt the supply of oil to these two bases. Canaris and Piekenbrock subsequently drove to the headquarters of the Spanish General Staff. Major-General Juan Vigón, head of the latter and a friend of Canaris, received the high-ranking German visitors, and when Canaris explained the German plan he called in Colonel Martinez Campos.

The head of the Spanish general staff immediately arranged a special audience with the Spanish leader General Franco. The caudillo liked the plan, but he realized that the British fleet would be a very powerful opponent. Nevertheless, it seemed clear to Admiral Canaris that Franco, and with him Spain, were willing to take part.

Meanwhile the members of the special Gibraltar staff had arrived in Madrid. Assigned to them was Lieutenant-Colonel Ramon Pardo of the Spanish secret service, who was to brief the members of the staff and provide the necessary technical information. The leaders of the German group were:

Oherstleutnant Hans Mikosch, who as commander of the 51st Pioneer Battalion had won the Knight's Cross on 21 May 1940 for actions in the western campaign; Major Wolfgang Langkau from the staff of the Jüterbog artillery school; two leading paratrooper officers: Rudolf Witzig, who won the Knight's Cross for leading assault group "Granite" which took Eben Emael and Hauptmann Osterecht.

This Gibraltar team assembled on 24th July and began gathering information. Lieutenant-Colonel Pardo provided the group with a vantage point at La Linea from which it could look directly into Gibraltar. From the lighthouse on the Punta Camero there was an excellent view of all the western defense works. Dressed as a Spanish city commandant, Oherstleutnant Mikosch flew from Sevilla to Cueta in a civilian airliner, passing close by Gibraltar's restricted zone. Hptm. Witzig and Hptm. Osterecht surveyed the entire area for possible landing sites for parachute and glider troops, while Admiral Canaris and Piekenbrock drove through the area by car. In Algeciras, where the Abwehr had three houses on the west bank, Canaris watched traffic in the harbor through high-powered binoculars.

Canaris especially enjoyed eavesdropping on several British officers in the Hotel Reina Maria Cristina in Algeciras. Spanish army sentries told him what they knew about the "fortress over there." What Canaris could envision was the fall of Gibraltar and the barring of the English from the Mediterranean, followed by the end of the war against England.

On 10 May 1940, after France was defeated in a six-week campaign, General Franco, who in 1939 had given a definite "no" to German plans to capture Gibraltar, declared: "Spain is no longer neutral, it is only not yet waging war." As confirmation of this, on 12th June he sent Spanish troops into Tangier and the Spanish crowds enthusiastically shouted: "Gibraltar para Espana!"

Gibraltar's position at the entrance to the Mediterranean made it one of, if not the most, important English fortress outside the motherland. Whoever possessed Gibraltar effectively controlled the Mediterranean.

Several days later the Spanish ambassador Margues de Magaz told the German state secretary in the foreign office, Freiherr von Weizsiicker, that Spain wanted not just Gibraltar, but all of Morocco, the area of Oran and other parts of the Sahara as well. In return his country would enter the war on Germany's side. As part of its entry Spain would also assist the German troops in seizing Gibraltar. All this encouraged Canaris, who immediately began preparations for the operation, as just described.

The spectacular successes achieved by the Brandenhurgers in the western campaign had greatly enhanced Canaris' image. Now the Admiral and chief of the Abwehr wanted to commit his house unit again; he would send them through Spain to seize the British island fortress. He had III Battalion in mind, which had been so successful in the west.

Canaris sent Hptm. Rudfloff to southern Spain. But now the matter became critical, and on 6Iuly 1940 Canaris hurried to see the Army Chief of

Staff, General der Artillerie Franz Halder, to ask his support for the operation. When Hptm. Rudloff returned from Spain he brought bad news. Any attempt to slip a large group of Brandenburgers through Spain without attracting the attention of British intelligence was out of the question. Cueta lacked the cranes necessary to transfer heavy guns from ship to shore.

Just as Admiral Canaris was about to let the Gibraltar file drop in the trash can, it was revived by Hitler and his advisors. As Hitler's planning chief, General Major Jodl, head of the Wehrmacht Operations Office, had written a memo titled "Further Conduct of the Struggle against England." In it the seizure of Gibraltar was given a great deal of space. Hitler waited several days for a peace offer from England, which after the fall of France he thought might be in the cards. Then, on 15th July, Hitler issued "Führer Directive No. 16," whose key sentence read: "Since England shows no sign of a willingness to reach an understanding in spite of her hopeless military situation, I have decided to prepare a landing operation against England and—if necessary—carry it out."

Operation "Sea Lion" was born and Gibraltar was shelved. But not entirely, for Hitler had concerns about carrying out "Sea Lion" and was therefore inclined to favor the less-dangerous Gibraltar operation.

When Canaris returned from Spain, as mentioned at the beginning of the chapter, he and his staff agreed that a surprise attack against Gibraltar was not feasible. Nevertheless a detailed plan of attack was worked out, according to which Gibraltar would be in German hands within three days. On 2nd August Admiral Canaris presented this attack plan to the newly-promoted Generalfeldmarschall Wilhelm Keitel, chief of the OKW, and General Major Warlimont, Jodl's deputy. Five days later Warlimont had worked out the "conquest of Gibraltar" and laid it before Hitler. The operation was code-named "Felix."

On 16th August Admiral Canaris again left for France. After visiting all the Abwehr stations there, he left his companion, Erwin Ritter von Lahousen und Vivremont, at that time still an Oberstleutnant in Abwehr II, behind in southern France and went on alone to Madrid. There he visited the Spanish general staff. After discussing all preparations for the Gibraltar landing, Canaris traveled on to Algeciras to speak to Major Fritz Kautschke, the senior Abwehr officer there. Subsequently he paid a brief visit to Lisbon.

Meanwhile, on 24th August Hitler authorized Operation "Felix." The strike against the English fortress was to be made by the 6th Army under Generalfeldmarschall von Reichenau. But "Felix" was destined never to reach fruition; instead the landing operation against England took center stage, and the plans called for the Brandenburgers to take part.

OPERATION "SEA LION" AND THE BRANDENBURGERS

Führer Directive No. 17 dated I August 1940, which dealt with a landing operation in the east and south of England, called for the troops of Army Groups A and B to assault the island from the Calais-Le Havre areas in three groups. From left to right they would be: the 26th Army, the 9th Army and the 6th Army. These troops were supposed to land on the east coast of England between Norwich and Brighton.

On 2 July 1940, I Battalion of the Brandenburgers commanded by Major von Hippel and the Rudloff battalion were placed on alert. Consequently the Brandenburg Regiment, which was still in the formation stage, was able to report both battalions ready for action in their assigned assembly areas on the Channel Coast. The von Hippel battalion moved into the area of the 16th Army. The battalion command post was set up in Nieuwport, east of Dunkirk. III Battalion under Hptm. Rudloff assembled in the 6th Army's sector. Its command post was located in Caen at the mouth of the Seine.

I Battalion was first supposed to destroy the locks at Folkestone in an airborne operation. A second part of the battalion was to make a sea landing on the Dungeness Peninsula and knock out the locks and power plants, but especially a battery of railway guns that had been spotted there.

III Battalion was to occupy the city and port of Weymouth; it would attack some time before the main body in order to divert attention from the latter's objectives—Plymouth and Portsmouth.

The 100-man-strong detachment of Brandenburgers, which had been formed from English-speaking foreign Germans, was to land in the first wave and strike out on light motorcycles deep into the enemy rear to carry out special missions and spread confusion. All seemed ready when on 12 October 1940 the navy received an OKW directive which stated that "the landing in England is to be kept up solely as a means of exerting pressure." This marked the death of Operation "Sea Lion." The ultimate cancellation of the landing in England followed on 10 January 1941.

Although the landing in England failed to take place as planned, the Brandenburgers assigned to it had enjoyed, as one of them put it, "a lovely swimming holiday by the sea."

But back to Operation "Felix." The following order of the day was issued on 2 October 1940:

Ib V: 35051/40 Secret   Berlin, 2/10/1940
Participation of Abwehr II in an attack on Gibraltar.
    A. Special Operations:
        Sabotage attacks on following facilities:

I. Fuel supply storage facilities.

(a) coal, (b) liquid fuel.

   2. Airfield, seaplane base.

      (a) repair workshop, (b) aircraft

   3. Power station.

   4. Sea water distillation facilities.

   5. Gas works.

B. Employment of the 800th Special Purpose Construction Training Battalion: Carry out the following missions before the start of the attack:

   I. Cut through or blow the iron fence that separates the English area from the neutral zone.

   2. Prevent the cut from east to west at the north foot of the rock (Devil's Tower) from being blown.

   3. Prevent the road west of the tidal basin on the northwest side of the rock from being blown.

Missions 2 and 3 will have to be carried out in part using motor torpedo boats and—if necessary—in English uniforms or civilian clothes. Further missions to more distant objectives at the start of the attack do not appear promising as they are heavily guarded and will depend on the progress of the fighting. Three officers and 100 men are required for the said missions.

An appendix listing the special missions, registration number 1694/152, was issued the same day. Its contents:

Appendix 1   1694/152

   Special Missions:

      1. Conling island fuel dump

      2. Sandy bay oil tanks

      3. Admiralty Mole coal dump

      4. Racetrack airfield

      5. Seaplane base

      6. Power station

      7. Sea water distillery system

Missions for the 800th Special Purpose Construction Training Battalion Brandenburg:

   I. Blowing up of iron fence,

   2. Prevent blocking of roads,

   3. Prevent demolitions at the north foot of the rock.

The detachments for these missions consisted of elements of the 5th Company the raider platoon commanded by Lt. Hettinger—and a 100-man battle group under Oblt. Graf Thun.

Hitler had a final conversation with the Spanish caudillo on 23rd October, during which he tried to overcome Franco's reservations and convince him to immediately join the operation, but in vain. After the meeting in Hendaye Hitler realized that he could not expect any help from Spain and General Franco, unless he, Hitler, approved Franco's territorial ambitions in North Africa. Hitler could not bring himself to do so.

The Italian invasion of Greece from Albania on 28 October 1940 had resulted in an immediate, massive intervention on the part of the British. Hitler had to act immediately concerning Gibraltar. On 4th December he sent Admiral Canaris to Madrid to negotiate with the Spanish government and General Franco and convince them to participate in the attack on Gibraltar and bring Spain into the war on the side of Germany.

While negotiations were going on in Madrid, Oberst Piekenbrock sent ten of the best-trained English-speaking agents into the British fortress; their mission was to seek out additional "weak spots" in the rock's defenses and relay the information by radio at once.

On 6 December 1940, while Directive No. 21 "Barbarossa" was being worked on, the Wehrmacht High Command gave Canaris instructions to at least obtain from General Franco Spanish permission for the Wehrmacht to cross over and over-fly the French-Spanish border and approval for it to march through to the south coast. As well he was to obtain Franco's approval for the stationing of German heavy artillery on the Canary islands and on Tenerife. The Brandenburgers were to be kept ready for action.

The next day the scouting staff from the Abwehr's Department I in Spain operating against Gibraltar and the Azores was bolstered by several officers from the army general staff. On that day, 7th December, Canaris asked Franco for permission for special units of the Brandenburgers to pass through Spain to take part in the conquest of Gibraltar.

On 8th December the "little Greek"—as Canaris was known, even though he came from Dortmund-Aplerbeck—was obliged to inform Hitler that Franco had evaded answering the question of Spain declaring war. Hitler instructed him to continue all espionage activities against Gibraltar, but at the same time said that the attack on Gibraltar, which was planned by 10th January, would not go ahead for the time being.

In an attempt to remove the roadblock standing in the way of the seizure of Gibraltar, on 10 December 1940 Admiral Canaris sent an official peace offer to Greece by way of the Hungarian ambassador in Madrid as well as an offer of mediation in the Greek-Italian conflict. Greece was promised that once it returned to neutrality it would be allowed to retain all the territory it had taken in Albania. What had happened to bring about this sudden change of mind on the part of Hitler?

On 28 October 1940 Italian forces from Albania had crossed the Greek frontier and thus opened a new theater of war in Europe. This gave Great Britain the grounds for immediate intervention and the German Armed Forces found themselves with another front to deal with.

On 10th December Hitler decided that "Operation 'Felix' will not be carried out. The necessary political conditions no longer exist."

One of the most important objectives in that phase of the war had been abandoned. At the same time, a new front had been created in the Mediterranean and ultimately North Africa that would involve significant German forces and deny them to the Eastern Front.

Hitler signed Directive No. 21 "Barbarossa" on 18th December. It stated that all preparations to attack must be completed by 15th May. As part of the preparations the Ausland/Abwehr was supposed to recruit and train Armenian emigrants of the Daschnakzutiun Party under Emin Resulzade, as well as members of the Georgian anticommunist Sai Schamyl, for use in the southeast part of the Soviet Union and the lands bordering on it.

For example, in Afghanistan contacts were established with the organization around the last Emir of Buchara and the sons and nephews of the last Emir of Chiwa. At the same time the military reconnaissance of the border areas of Libya and French Central Africa was begun. Conducted under the code name "Dora" the objective was to improve the accuracy of the existing maps and explore possibilities for out flanking attacks through the southern desert east to the Nile by the Africa Corps, which had meanwhile arrived in North Africa.

In rapid succession further activities against British positions in the border region of India were put in motion in Afghanistan with the help of native tribes. In India itself an espionage and sabotage organization was established with the help of the Indian politician Subhas Chandra Bose, who in 1921 had established a "disobedience movement" against the British and who in 1938 had become a deputy of the Congress Party. Bose was forced to flee to Germany in 1941. He directed operations by his group in India from there. From Germany and in 1943 from Japan he tried to form an Indian national army to fight England. Acts of sabotage and raids on British garrisons, depots and other installations were also planned.

At about the same time Argentina was made the main base for the secret service in all of South America.

On 16 February 1941 the German envoy in the Foreign Office, Grobba, negotiated with the Ausland/Abwehr over secret arms shipments to Iraq.

The Jablunka Pass detachment with its commander, Lt. Herzner.

In the campaign in Poland it was often the Brandenburgers who lit the spark. Hitler visits the troops in Poland.

The Branden-
burgers were the
first in action near
Mock. Here a
machine-gun covers
the crossing.

The bridge over the
Juliana Canal, initial
objective of the
Brandenburgers.

At the canal:
(from left) Kessel-
ring, Bodenschatz
and Göring.

The Maas bridge at Moerdijk was stubbornly defended.

One of the shot-up bunkers near the bridge.

The railway bridge over the Maas near Gennep.

River crossing in Holland.

He IIIs take off to strike Rotterdam.

Holland has surrendered. The Dutch commander in chief, General Winkelman, arrives in The Hague to surrender the army.

Hitler with his troops after the blitz campaign in France.

Der Oberbefehlshaber der Gruppe XXI., General der Infanterie von Falkenhorst, würdigt die Leistungen der Truppe mit einem Abschiedsschreiben:

Gruppe XXI   Drontheim, den 12. Juni 1940
Abt. Ia (Lg.)

[stamp:]
Lehr-Regt. „Brandenburg"
3. b. D. 800
Eing. 5- AUG 1940 ab
Az .... Br.B.Nr. ..... Az. .....
gef. Nbr. .... Nbr. .....

An das

    Baulehr - Regiment 800 z.b.V.
        (Carolus)
    z.Hd. des Herrn Regimentsführers
      Major K e w i s c h

Anlässlich des Ausscheidens der in Norwegen einge-
setzten Teile des Baulehr - Regiments 800 z.b.V.,
("Unternehmen Carolus") aus dem Bereich der Gruppe
spreche ich allen Offizieren, Unteroffizieren und
Mannschaften für ihr Einsatzfreudigkeit, ihren Schneid
und ihre guten Leistungen meine besondere Anerkennung
aus.

In elf Sonderunternehmen haben die mit der Durchführung
betrauten Offiziere, Unteroffiziere und Mannschaften
wertvolle Hilfe bei der Besetzung und Befriedung Nor-
wegens geleistet. Damit haben sie gleichzeitig die
Zweckmässigkeit eines solchen Einsatzes auch im Be-
wegungskrieg bewiesen.

[signature:] Falkenhorst

The Brandenburg Training Regiment receives a commendation from
GenOberst Nikolaus von Falkenhorst, later commander of the Wehrmacht.

Trouble Spot Afghanistan: The Afghan Company

The preparations were in full swing for the first transport of weapons and men to Afghanistan. The firm of Rheinmetall-Borsig AG had agreed to employ the affected agents as cover for their activities. On 29 April 1940—the Polish campaign was over and the invasion of France was about to begin—Hauptmann Morlock of the Abwehr arrived in Termez, Afghanistan to conclude some business. In addition to his small party he carried with him 30 "pieces of diplomatic baggage" which had a total weight of two tons. In fact they were small arms and a 20-mm anti-aircraft gun with ammunition and carriage. All were destined to arm the agent groups that had already been formed. Most of the agents had come to Afghanistan via the Todt Organization and were now armed, so as to be able to begin their assigned tasks.

Where they were to be used had been determined at the beginning of 1940 by Abwehr and Italian intelligence agents working closely together; they had visited the mountain tribes in the area of the India-Afghanistan border in 1938 and 1939 and sounded them out. Their main objective had been to mobilize and motivate the counter-revolutionary emigrant organizations of the last Emir of Buchara and the descendants of the Emir of Chiwa.

On 20 April 1940, the Fuhrer's birthday, the Abwehr sent a telex to the German embassy in Kabul authorizing and instructing it to initiate sabotage operations in the Afghan-Indian border region. These actions, which were coordinated by von Lahousen- Vivremont in close cooperation with the German embassy in Kabul, began on 24th April. In July 1940 the Abwehr Oberleutnant Dr. Oberdorffer and Abwehr leader Brandt were sent to Afghanistan to provide the isolated groups with a unified command. Operating under cover as a research group studying leprosy, for 32 days they traveled through Afghanistan with the Afghan Company and carried out the first anti-British actions.

The members of the Afghan Company had been trained by Rittmeister Habicht. The latter had also taken all precautionary measures and made the best possible preparations for the operation. But before the operation began, the Rittmeister was recalled by the Abwehr and tasked with the formation of the "Asad Hind" Indian Legion. (More of this in the chapter on India.)

The small Abwehr group moved through Afghanistan as far as the northwest border of India. There Dr. Oberdorffer established contact with the Fakir of Ipi, the acknowledged leader of the Afghan mountain tribes on the border, some of which extended into India. The Fakir of Ipi promised the Germans -his support for several missions against British installations. He provided the Abwehr men with three guides, who led the groups to the first sabotage targets. They made camp in the huts of an abandoned mountain village and the next day undertook the first scouting forays in this difficult terrain. Twice the two groups ran into British patrols, but thanks to the skill of their guides they were able to evade them.

They found the first bridge over a narrow gorge. Beneath it a roaring stream ran down the mountainside; they considered it a suitable target. They returned and reported to Dr. Oberdorffer. The latter decided to go ahead with the mission. The demolition group under the command of engineer Feldwebel Gerd Kessler set off on the following evening. Once again guide Amah Singh led the way. Shortly before reaching the bridge Singh went on alone. He returned a quarter of an hour later and stated that they could proceed with the action. They worked there way forward, reached the bridge and placed the first explosive charge under the support on the far side. Then they re-crossed the bridge, unrolled the fuse wire, and attached it to the second charge positioned on the near end of the bridge.

From the safety of a rock barrier at a turn in the path they set off the charges. With a mighty roar both of the wooden bridge's abutments flew into the air. The bridge itself crashed into the gorge. The attackers convinced themselves that they had done a thorough job and prepared to head back to camp. But then they came under fire from a higher position on the far side of the river.

'Take cover!" shouted Feldwebel Kessler.

For Heinz Schultze the warning came too late. He was hit in the throat by a bullet and fell to the ground. Kessler crawled over and pulled him into cover behind the rocks. Schultze tried to say something, but the blood pouring from the wound on the left side of his neck drowned every word. Schultze was dead before a pressure bandage could be applied. Kessler carried his comrade back to camp on his back. They had achieved their first success but it had cost them their first casualty.

In the weeks that followed they succeeded in destroying a forward radio station belonging to the British border guard. The Germans ambushed the site, after which the British there withdrew. Once all the documents present had been secured the radio station was blown up.

Four days later one of the native spies reported that a British patrol was on the move. That afternoon a British reconnaissance aircraft flew low over their village, which was camouflaged to look like a tribal mountain village. Everyone immediately took cover. The aircraft flew a wide circle and the spy and the guide waved.

"They didn't see anything," declared Sonderfuhrer Brandt. But Dr. Oberdorffer just shook his head.

"They have seen that this is no regular village. There are no women and children here. They will come back and bomb us out."

An hour later the spies were on their way to find a new campsite. They found another mountain village in which there were several unoccupied huts. The teams moved in. The same afternoon the lookouts reported aircraft. They hurried to the eagle's nest, as they called the lofty lookout site, and saw three aircraft dive low over the village and drop their bombs into the huts. Explosions followed, and smoke, dust and flames blotted out the former camp. The three aircraft then turned for home. That evening they celebrated their birthday. Dr Oberdorffer had saved them.

Soon afterward they risked venturing 30 kilometers inside India to attack a British telegraph station, but they were plagued by bad luck. They walked into a border patrol and became involved in a protracted firefight, during which they withdrew in steps toward the Afghan border. They were not even halfway back when it became light. An hour later six aircraft flew overhead and then they saw numerous parachutes billowing behind them, between their point and the border toward which they were striving. The English had dropped paratroopers in their rear in an effort to cut them off. An hour later they met the first of the paratroopers; now they were caught between two fires.

Dr. Oberdorffer covered the retreat with his pistol. He was able to see to it that the bulk of his men got through. During the final dash through the paratroopers' lines with Feldwebel Kessler they were involved in a firefight, during the course of which Dr. Oberdorffer was fatally hit in the chest. Kessler was taken prisoner.

This action, which also saw two of the native lookouts killed, ended the company's activities in this area. The Afghan Company dissolved. The men were scattered to the four winds. Under the command of Sonderfiihrer Brandt, the Germans in the group made their way to Kabul. There they took refuge in the German embassy until they were sent home.

From "Marita" to Rumania

RUMANIA'S OIL

Fuhrer Directive No. 20, the order for Operation "Marita," the assault on Greece, was issued on 13 December 1940. Long before this, however, plans had been made to secure installations in the southeast of Europe. The unit chosen for this task was the 800th Special Purpose Construction Training Battalion Brandenburg. The existing unit had to be enlarged and reorganized to be able to meet all the demands being placed upon it. The Brandenburg Regiment was born as a result.

The regimental headquarters in Berlin was also expanded so as to be able to keep pace with the growing demands on the regiment. The demands from the Abwehr's Department II had to be met, for after all that was the purpose of the Brandenburgers.

II Battalion, with its headquarters in Baden near Vienna, was allocated to the missions in southeastern and eastern Europe.

The headquarters of III Battalion, which was to take part in Operation "Sea Lion," moved into the Gallwitz barracks in Aachen, while Headquarters, I Battalion remained in the barracks on Magdeburger Straße in Brandenburg, Havel. After it became clear on 12 October 1940 that "Sea Lion" would not take place, the Abwehr withdrew III Battalion.

The Abwehr already knew in 1939 that something was brewing in the Balkans in the southeast of Europe. Material from the British and French intelligence services captured in 1939–1940 made it clear that both were going to carry out various types of sabotage missions against the Rumanian oil industry. Germany was dependent on this crude oil and its refined products, however. If the Allies could cut Germany off from its sources or destroy them, as in the First World War, then the war would be lost for Germany.

Already in mid-September 1939 two Frenchmen—engineer Leon Wenger and Captain of the 2nd Office Pierre Angot—arrived in Bucharest; their mission was to come up with a plan to destroy the drilling sites, the refineries and transport facilities, as well as the stocks in storage. On 18th September the French ambassador in Bucharest, Thiery, introduced

Wenger to the British envoy Sir Reginald Hoare. All went smoothly for engineer Wenger was no stranger to the experts. In 1916 he had worked with the English on plans for the complete destruction of the Rumanian oil sources and now he was to do it again.

Wenger examined everything, compared his plans with those of his English colleague and subsequently sent his report to the French government on I October 1939. He proposed destroying all parts of the Rumanian oil industry as well as production sites, transport facilities, stocks and refineries. The French ambassador, who had earlier conferred with Wenger on the morning of 28th September, immediately telegraphed the French foreign ministry. He urged that the Danube be blocked at key points immediately, thus closing this vital internal waterway between Germany and Rumania, over which much of the crude oil was shipped. The French secret police had already got wind of the fact that German Rhine vessels were being sent to the Danube to transport crude oil. The information available to the French suggested that this mode of transport was carrying 80% of all German oil coming from Rumania.

On 27 October 1939 the French foreign minister wrote to Corbin, the French ambassador in London: "Our special branches agree with those of the British that shipping traffic on the Danube should be blocked through suitable demolitions." The French authorities had already given their approval, while on the British side they were still waiting for the approval of the Foreign Office.

The Commander-in-Chief of the French Army, General Gamelin, had declared himself in favor of the destruction of the Rumania oil sources in a letter to the war ministry. He wrote:

"Implementation would be handed over to Mr. Wenger. I consider it appropriate that Herr Wagner be awarded the pro forma rank of colonel."

Captured documents revealed that the western allies also planned the destruction of the oil sources at Baku, for in 1940 Germany was still receiving oil from Russia, from the wells of Baku. The importance that Germany placed on its Balkan oil source was evident from a talk between Admiral Canaris and Generaloberst Keitel in August 1939. Two Balkan experts from his Department II had advised Canaris that all it would take would be for two cement-laden barges to be sunk in the iron-gate or some other suitable site to halt all shipping on the Danube for some time.

Keitel subsequently asked the admiral to personally establish contact with the Rumanian government and warn it against the French and British, who would not hesitate to destroy this vital source of income to Rumania if it fit their plans. A joint effort to protect the oil had to be proposed to the Rumanians.

Admiral Canaris immediately contacted Moruzov, the head of the Rumanian secret service, and met with him for a discussion. Both secret service chiefs agreed that they should immediately begin undercover operations to guard the oil. The operatives would be employees of several oil firms and sales offices held by German investors. The Siguranza (the Rumanian secret service) would take care of protecting these men.

When King Carol learned of this cooperation, he at first did not seem inclined to tolerate the game. Only after it was made clear to him that the Anglo-French plans of sweeping acts of sabotage were directed primarily at him personally and against the Rumanian people, did he approve the agreement. He was forced to see that his western friends England and France would have no scruples about ruining him and his country if it enabled them to strike a blow against their enemy Germany.

THE OIL PROTECTION ORGANIZATION

The oil protection organization began installing itself in Rumania. The Abwehr II sent 60 soldiers of the German Company from Sliac to Vienna under Fw. SuB. There he briefed the men, some of whom spoke Yugoslavian and Rumanian, on their mission to protect shipping on the Danube. Kapitan Schwarz of the Abwehr was placed in command of this oil protection unit and it was he who assigned duties. Not only were guards in civilian clothes put aboard every Danube oil tanker, but rail transports were also watched over by members of the Brandenburgers disguised as civilians. All the employees of the famous Danube Steamship Company at all the docking sites on the Danube were also Brandenburgers.

The secret services of Bulgaria and Hungary were informed of the oil protection operation since both nations were affected; they gave their approval for any measures that might become necessary to eliminate acts of sabotage.

In December 1939 three Abwehr non-commissioned officers—Süß, Stöhr and Kriegisch—traveled to Rumania to make preparations for the deployment of German security personnel. The now fully trained Brandenburgers followed in small groups, beginning in early 1940.

It soon turned out, however, that the protection they offered was inadequate. So at the end of August 1940 soldiers with the needed language skills were selected from the 5th Brandenburg Company under Oberleutnant Pinkert and were prepared for their mission in Rumania and on the Danube by Obit. Dr. Kniesche. Beginning on 10 September they were added to the protection unit.

Some of these Brandenburgers were sent to Ploesti, the center of Rumanian oil production, as a team of fitters. There they worked for

Rumanian companies as well as in the Standard oil refinery, which had been purchased by the German government. When even this bolstered force proved inadequate to deal with all eventualities, another entire company of Brandenburgers was sent to Rumania in mufti. They worked in the German-controlled plants and came up with the Viking Sports Club as a good cover for their meetings.

The Rumanian oil-producing region, which during this phase of the Second World War was the focal point of operations by the Abwehr, lies north of the capital of Bucharest. In its southern part lies the city of Ploesti, which for some time had been Rumania's most important industrial city. On the outskirts of Ploesti stood the twelve refineries that processed the oil from the drilling fields. In 1940 there were several very large and a few smaller refineries there. However each one included a large tank farm, pumping stations, loading facilities and pipelines.

Another very large refinery, together with several tank farms and oil-related facilities, was located at Campina, approximately 30 kilometers north of Ploesti.

The actual drilling area with its drilling towers occupied an area about 60 kilometers long and 20 wide to the northwest of Ploesti. The main city of this oil center was Moreni. From this oil-producing center a rail line and pipeline ran to Baicoi. In Gurgiu on the Danube there were further, smaller refineries and a large oil loading station, which was especially vulnerable. Other valuable facilities were located in Costanta and Bucharest.

THE BRANDENBURGERS AND THEIR HELPERS

The attempt by Anglo-American oil companies to reduce the annual output of Rumanian crude oil from 9 to 6 million tons, to drive up the price of Rumanian crude and thus starve out the Germans, appeared to work. King Carol II and his beloved Madame Lupescu, who both were involved in the oil business and had influential friends in England, at first agreed with this drastic rise in price. But thanks to the negotiating skill of Dr. Neubacher, the mayor of Vienna, an expert in Balkan affairs, the oil company was convinced to reduce the price by 50%.

Although the entire Ploesti oil region was off limits, citizens of France, Britain, Holland and Belgium repeatedly obtained special permission to visit the cities in the restricted area. In most cases they were secret service agents in mufti.

The German secret service established itself; it subsequently was able to intervene whenever matters became serious. Selected to lead the Abwehr team was Leutnant Dr. Drogler, a well-known chemist who went by the name of Dr. Luptar in Ploesti. Drogler knew well the Rumanian mentality.

Colonel Moruzov of the Siguranza assigned to him junior criminal police officials who spoke a little German. The Rumanians and the Brandenburgers worked in pairs, checking the various installations. This group was called in to investigate all acts of sabotage. They dealt with cases of arson, loosened pipeline connections, and sabotage of equipment and machines.

Brandenburgers rode the trains carrying oil to Austria disguised as railway workers. The head of the oil protection operation in Bucharest screened all incoming reports and sent copies to the Abwehr station in Vienna. There the Tarbuk brothers—five of them—separated the cases of sabotage. The missions were carried out under the leadership of Fw. Suß. When he reported that Russian troops were massing on the borders of Bessarabia and Bukovina, it was dismissed by the Abwehr in Berlin as a "latrine rumor." But on 26 June 1940 the Rumanian government received an ultimatum from the USSR; Rumania was to leave the two provinces by the 29th of the month and was warned not to oppose the Russian entry.

Dr. Luptar was now ordered to identify the man who had sent the report to Berlin, even though Süß was working under cover. Dr. Luptar radioed that Leutnant Suß had sent the report and that he knew nothing about his middlemen. Lt. Süß was subsequently ordered to Berlin. Immediately after his arrival in the Reich capital he reported to the Ausland/Abwehr, where he was "officially" questioned by Oberst Stolze. Süß told the head of Department II that he would not name his informants. He said that if he were ordered to reveal them he would do so and then ask for an immediate transfer to a combat unit. Oberst Stolze did not insist and Lt. Süß returned to Bucharest to report to Dr. Luptar.

By the end of 1940, not only did the Abwehr limit sabotage in Rumania to a minimum, but it also put together a personal file system containing several thousand names of reliable agents, enemy agents, possible saboteurs, and unreliable elements.

Stalin's demand for the surrender of Bukovina and the Bessarabia area placed the Abwehr team in Rumania on the highest state of alert. There were fears that the Russians would not stop at the Seret but would simply drive on and seize Ploesti, cutting the German lifeline to the Rumanian oil.

The German government declared that it had decided to guarantee the Rumanian border and would defend it by force if necessary. On 28th June Russian tanks rolled into the Bukovina and Bessarabia, but they halted at the Seret.

From that time on attacks by Allied sabotage teams increased in frequency. Finally in spring and summer 1940 it was found that huge quantities of sand and gravel and finally even steel balls had been transported into the center of the oil region. It was clear: the Allies had amassed all the materials necessary to render the oil wells useless. Their Rumanian allies had received orders to block up the oil lines. The Brandenburgers who were sent on a lightning raid found that the steel balls fit the drill holes precisely. If enough were dropped into the tubes, followed by concrete, then they would be useless for oil production for all time.

A fake assassination attempt on Dr. Luptar by two Brandenburgers got the ball rolling They were dressed so that they would be mistaken for two Englishmen who were the heads of the secret organization for the destruction of the oil fields. The Brandenburgers had stolen shoes from the two target Englishmen so that perfect footprints could be planted at prepared places.

The Rumanian criminal police were called on the night of the staged ambush. The "attempt on Dr. Luptar's life" barely failed. There were two bullet holes right over his bed. A resident said that he had seen a man in the moonlight. It was one of the two Englishmen. The shoe prints were taken. The matching shoes, only partly cleaned, were found in the possession of the Englishmen. The two suspects were expelled from the country. The Allied organization had been rendered leaderless but not powerless. Other Englishmen were rounded up in Ploesti, at Lake Snagov and in Bucharest. Searches of English cargo vessels turned up weapons and explosives. Altogether in those weeks and months the Rumanian security authorities expelled 1,300 English and French from the country.

Even though Shelmegeanu, the Rumanian Minister of the Interior, and Vantu, his under-secretary, were friends of England, they could not ignore the discovery of weapons on various English ships. The Brandenburgers had won the underground battle for the oil fields of Ploesti. This victory was crowned by Marshall Ion Antonescu, who on 4 September 1940 was named chief of state by King Carol II. Two days later he forced the king to step down and thus opened the door to Germany.

At the end of October 1940 the Marshall allowed the presence of German troops in Rumania. The German military mission immediately began the training of Rumanian troops. German air forces began providing protection for Rumania, especially the Ploesti area and the Rumanian Black Sea coast. England and France had lost the battle for the oil fields of Ploesti. The Brandenburgers who had taken part were able to put their uniforms back on.

Hitler sent additional instructors to Rumania in the course of this economic and political expansion toward the southeast, not least of all because of the offensive preparations against the USSR that were already under way. Immediately after this great development, Admiral Canaris set the course in discussions with the Wehrmacht operations staff and the military attaches in Berlin. All the military attaches whose host nations bordered on the USSR were given new tasks. Abwehr Oberst Brinckmann was dispatched by Canaris to Bucharest to organize the military mission and raise its efficiency to the maximum.

Admiral Canaris also traveled to Bucharest immediately after Marshall Antonescu took office and assured the Marshall of aid from Germany. When he returned to Berlin on 10th September, Canaris stressed to the OKW: "The Marshall is 100 percent in order, I can vouch for him."

On 11 September 1940 the Abwehr informed the Wehrmacht operations staff that it had, with the help of the German military attaché in Bucharest, Oberst Gerstenberg, succeeded in orientating the Rumanian head of state in a totally antiSoviet direction.

On 23 November 1940 Rumania joined the Tripartite Pact. At the end of 1940 another company of Brandenburgers was committed to secure the oil region and the Danube waterway. In spring 194 I the entire II Battalion of the 800th Special Purpose Construction Training Battalion Brandenburg was transferred to Ploesti from Baden-Unterwaltersdorf near Vienna.

During a private conversation in October 1940, Admiral Canaris informed Oberst Franz von Bentivegny, the head of Department III of the Ausland/Abwehr, that preparations had already begun for an attack on the Soviet Union. That same month Canaris told his subordinate that Generalfeldmarschall von Brauchitsch and General Halder had worked out the overall plan for the attack on Hitler's order. All preparations for the operation had been designated "Barbarossa."

In connection with this, in November 1940 Oberst von Bentivegny received a directive from Canaris calling on him to initiate activity by the Abwehr at sites where German troops were massing on the German-Russian border. In response to the directive, von Bentivegny issued appropriate orders to the Abwehr stations in Danzig, Konigsberg, Breslau, Krakow and Posen.

At Nuremberg the head of the Abwehr III stated, "Officially I was not informed about 'Barbarossa' until the end of January or the beginning of February after one of the meetings that were held every day. Admiral Canaris held all the department heads back and informed us that according to a message from GFM Keitel, Hitler had ordered all elements of the Wehrmacht to prepare for war against the Soviet Union. These preparations were to be complete by the end of May 1941."

"You, gentlemen," continued the Admiral, "are to carry out the necessary preparatory measures by the Abwehr for the attack on the Soviet Union. This matter is to be kept top secret."

The officers present were: the head of the Ausland Department, Admiral Burkner; the head of Department I, Oberst Piekenbrock, the head of Abwehr Department II, Oberst von Lahousen; and the head of the central department and Canaris' chief of staff, Oberst Oster.

THE WAR IN THE BALKANS AND THE BRANDENBURGERS

On 18 March 1941 Yugoslavia called into session the Royal Council in order to decide on the question of Yugoslavia's entry into the Tripartite Pact, which Hitler had been constantly urging her to join. The majority favored entry provided Germany agreed to rule out Yugoslavia as a staging area for further military actions.

After Germany agreed to this and a number of other conditions, on 25th March the Tripartite Pact was signed in Vienna. When this was announced, Colonel William Joseph Donovan, head of the US secret service in southeast Europe, and later chief of the Office of Strategic Services, contacted air force General Dusan Simovic and his Serbian nationalist group and convinced them to topple the government.

During the night of 27 March 1941 General Simovic seized power in a coup d'état, whereupon he mobilized against Germany. American promises of aid on a dizzying scale gave him hope that his coup would succeed. Hitler acted immediately and issued his Fuhrer Directive No. 25.

At noon on 27th March the chief of the Wehrmacht Operations Staff advised that, "the Fuhrer has decided to crush Yugoslavia." The Commanders-in-Chief of the Army and the Air Force were with him. A major speech was scheduled at 4:00 P.M. in the Reich Chancellery. That evening Hitler signed Fuhrer Directive No. 25—concerning the campaign against Yugoslavia. In a closed session orders were given for the air attack on Belgrade on 1st April and the start of Operation "Marita" the next day. No declaration of war was needed, since Yugoslavia already considered itself in a state of war with Germany, had enacted general mobilization and had broken the treaty.

On 28th March a letter from Mussolini with his support arrived in Fuhrer Headquarters. In these days before the start of the Balkan campaign all the Brandenburger units assigned to the southeast arrived at their departure points in rapid succession. The first teams already crossed the Yugoslavian and Greek borders in full or partial disguise to monitor important installations so that they could strike at the appropriate moment.

The detachments of II Battalion, Brandenburg Regiment were ready to move on the night of 6th April: the two half companies of the 5th Company under Obit. Kutschke with the 2nd Army in Carinthia and Steiermark, the 7th Company for a special mission at the Iron Gate, the 8th in the 12th Army's area at the boundary of the three nations. Behind them as the reserve unit was the 12th Company under Obit. Schader. It had been transferred from Duren to Baden near Vienna to maintain contact with the front-line detachments and bridge the empty area that would arise from II Battalion's advance. The Brandenburg Regiment ordered the formation of the 14th and 17th Companies to be accelerated and the units moved forward into the area south of Vienna. One of the first missions that the Brandenburgers' 5th Company had to carry out was to secure the Iron Gate, which absolutely had to be kept open.

As well as keeping a sharp eye on shipping, the Brandenburgers manning observation posts in this area also noted the positions of the field fortifications and bunkers which the Yugoslavians had erected on their side of the river and entered them on the target maps for the artillery. They discovered that a number of fully laden river barges had been tied up in hidden bays and reed beds upstream of the Danube gate. Nocturnal patrols had determined that the barges were packed full of sand, gravel and cement. If they were set free, they could, floating with the current, be wedged into the narrows in minutes and sunk there. It would then be months before the transport of crude oil by ship could resume.

In Berlin Oberst Bazing received orders from Admiral Canaris to take a selected group of 50 soldiers to the Rumanian airfield of Mehadica, which was situated directly opposite this danger point. There combat engineers were also to be put at Bazing's disposal. Then during the night of 6th April, prior to the morning attack, the entire force would be taken in trucks to Swijima on the Danube. Assault boats would be waiting there to take them to the Yugoslavian side of the river. Their mission there was to attack and eliminate the threat to shipping on the Danube.The mission went as planned. When the assault teams reached the bank of the Danube they immediately boarded the assault boats. They carried hand grenade bundles, hollow charges like the ones used against Eben Emael, and automatic weapons.

The assault boats immediately accelerated, raced across the Danube and beached at the selected landing sites. The engineers and the Brandenburgers jumped ashore. The Yugoslavian sentries were cut down in the initial hail of gunfire. Then the engineers ran to the bunkers and positioned their hollow charges. Explosions rumbled through the night. The Yugoslavian guards in the field works opened fire but against this well-drilled fighting team they had no chance. The firefight lasted all of seven minutes and then all was still. The attackers occupied the bunkers and the barges tied up in the bays. The situation there had been brought under control. The last sentence of the Wehrmacht communique of 17 April 1941 said:

At dawn on 6th April a combat group under Oberst Bazing made up of pioneers, elements of the Luftwaffe and special units crossed the Danube at the Iron Gate near Orsova under very difficult conditions. In a daring action the Yugoslavian bank was taken, stubborn resistance was broken, and all attempts by the enemy to block the river were frustrated. The determined efforts of a few German soldiers secured a vital shipping route and prevented it from being seized by the enemy.

THE BRANDENBURGER COMBAT TEAMS

Large numbers of Luftwaffe aircraft took off to attack Belgrade on the morning of 6th April. Their primary targets were army barracks, military installations, and government buildings. Belgrade's main railway station, a pontoon bridge over the Danube east of the city, and several freight trains were hard hit. That morning Air Fleet 4 under General der Flieger Lohr dispatched 400 Stukas and level bombers, 210 fighters, and 170 reconnaissance aircraft. The Yugoslavian air force was wiped out in one blow.

Sepp Janko, the leader of the German minority in Yugoslavia, part of which was armed, subordinated his people to the team that entered Yugoslavia from Hungary. Together they carried out Operation "Jupiter," in which two important bridges over the Drau were taken and secured. The Yugoslavian military airfield of Semlin was also seized.

In the point group of the 12th Army, the 2nd Panzer Division, combat teams of Brandenburgers advanced with the panzers. Their objective was to take possession of the Yugoslavs' secret archive before it could be destroyed. The detachment captured several Danube barges that were loaded with files. Among them were the plans to Yugoslavian fortresses and positions as well as special maps depicting the mining of roads, anti-tank barricades, and the load-bearing capacities of bridges, and extensive information on the Yugoslavian secret service. Battle Group Hettinger was transported to Jesenice to scout the 7,976-meter-long tunnel through the Karawanken in Rosenbach. It had orders to hold the facility and to eventually disarm the explosives installed inside.

On 7th April the battle group entered the tunnel and advanced as far as the border, which ran through the middle of the structure. As there was no draft, it was apparent to Hettinger that the Yugoslavians must have blocked the tunnel. The battle group then attempted to cross the mountain peak to the other side. During the night of 9th April the border was crossed on the mountaintop. The peak, which was 1800 meters high, was still covered by deep snow. Nevertheless, by the morning of 9th April the leading squads reached the tunnel entrance on the Yugoslav side. The guard was taken by surprise and overwhelmed. A party was sent in to scout the tunnel and after advancing about 40 meters it found it to be blocked. Explosives had been used to bring down the tunnel roof. The battle group set out for home and regained its starting point at Rosenach.

A further combat team of Brandenburgers under the command of Oblt. Grabert was to seize the bridge over the Wardar near Axioupolis; possession of this bridge from Bulgaria to Greece would enable the army to advance into central Greece. The structure was 400 meters long and made of wood. Once it was in German hands the 2nd Panzer Division could drive on Saloniki.

Together with his V-man and an interpreter, Oberleutnant Grabert went ahead to a vantage point from which he could observe the bridge. The V-man advised him that there were two British tanks on the other side. Peering through his binoculars, Grabert saw a dense stream of refugees moving toward the bridge. He had his 8th Company put on Yugoslavian helmets and greatcoats that the enemy had thrown away. Thus partly disguised, a platoon from Grabert's company drove toward the bridge in two trucks. On the way they were flagged down by a number of Yugoslavian soldiers, who were picked up. In this way the two trucks arrived at the bridge.

Suddenly the stream of refugees stopped in the middle of the bridge. Through his binoculars Grabert saw a British demolition team apparently preparing to blow the bridge.

"Berke squad come with me." The eight men jumped from the truck and ran toward the end of the bridge. Once there, a few bursts from their submachine-guns was enough to compel the British demolition team to surrender. The refugees loudly applauded the "Yugoslavian soldiers" who had kept their avenue of escape open.

All the Brandenburgers who had crossed got down from their trucks and secured the bridge. They allowed the refugees to pass freely. If enemy troops had appeared now the refugees would have taken the side of the Germans, who had doffed their disguises and were now directing and regulating traffic. Ninety minutes later the leading army units arrived and secured the bridge for good. This decisive act contributed to the rapid advance on Saloniki. For his role Oberleutnant Siegfried Grabert was awarded the Knight's Cross on 10 June 1941.

After entering Belgrade with the leading elements of the 11th Panzer Division on 12th April, the men of the Belgrade Special Detachment stormed the second office of the Yugoslavian General Staff, which had been heavily damaged by bombing. All documents were secured; several days later they were sent to Evaluation Station Southeast that had been set up in Vienna and examined there. Once again numerous valuable documents fell into the hands of the Abwehr.

Admiral Canaris spent 18th April in Belgrade to brief the Abwehr branch that had been set up there immediately after the entry of German troops on which documents to look for.

From the 21 st to 27th of April elements of the Brandenburgers' II Battalion occupied the Greek island of Evvia in the Gulf of Volos. This placed the unit in the English rear, forcing them to retreat. Elements of the battalion also occupied the Isthmus of Corinth and were first to enter Athens with the leading motorized German units. Greek-speaking specialists from the Hamburg Abwehr Station arrived in the Greek capital on 27th April. There they were met by agents from the German embassy who showed them the way to the Greek secret archives that were in the Ministry of the Navy. The Brandenburgers burst in and secured all the important documents, including some which were key to the subsequent conduct of the war and others which proved cooperation between Greece and the Anglo-French.

After visiting Bulgaria, Admiral Canaris traveled to Bucharest to sign an agreement with the new chief of the Rumanian secret service on an expanded security presence in that country by the Abwehr. From there the head of German intelligence flew on to Athens, where he inspected both Abwehr offices and wished the operations staff the best of luck in quickly realizing their own plans.

In Bulgaria the Abwehr chief had established secret service branch offices in Warna, Burgas, Plovdiv, Svilengrad and Cavalla. After returning from his trip to southeast Europe, on 13th May Admiral Canaris met with Hitler and gave him a detailed report on the situation in the Balkans.

An operation by elements of II Battalion against Maleme airfield during the attack on Crete on the morning of 20 May 1941 failed. The men were dropped into the middle of an enemy encampment and were wiped out in the subsequent fight. Their mission had been to advance from Maleme direct to Suda Bay, where they were supposed to sabotage English vessels to prevent the enemy from fleeing to Egypt.

The Abwehr in
the Eastern Campaign

THE PREPARATORY PHASE

During the course of preparations for the German invasion of the USSR, in early 1941 the Ausland/Abwehr organized an armed force consisting of Armenian emigrants belonging to the Daschnakzutiun Party, the remnants of the Azerbaizhani Mussawet Party, as well as supporters of the Georgian anticommunist Sai Schamyl, for use in the event of war with the Soviet Union.

Five months before the start of the campaign against Russia, in January 1941, Admiral Canaris formed three staffs designated "Walli I" to "Walli III." Hidden behind these cover designations were the front-line reconnaissance control centers that were to operate during the fighting in the east. The latter soon received instructions for sabotage, espionage and combat missions against Russia, and the orders came direct from the OKW Department Ausland/Abwehr or from "Foreign Armies East," which was directly subordinate to the Army High Command. All front-line reconnaissance detachments and teams were subordinate to these "Walli" staffs.

"Walli I" was stationed in the Polish town of Sulijewek and was later transferred to Vinnitsa in the Ukraine. "Walli II" was based in Suwalki. "Walli III," initially stationed in Breslau, was led by Oberstleutnant Schmalschläger and his first deputy, Hptm. Krickendt, who also led the evaluation team. The operations staff consisted of departments responsible for situation reports, evaluation, and Abwehr operational matters.

Under the direction of Oberst Eberhard Kinzel, who worked in the Foreign Armies East section in Berlin, a study was presented on I January 1941 titled Military Armed Forces of the Union of Soviet Socialist Republics. It should be mentioned that the predictions in the report concerning the Soviet Army and its equipment were completely inaccurate. As soon as the war in the east ended and the demarcation line between the German and Soviet occupied Poland was established, the Ausland/Abwehr began cultivating contacts with Ukrainian, Belorussian, Lithuanian, Estonian and Latvian nationalists in the Soviet zone and setting up an established net of agents. According to the Soviet secret service, its counterintelligence forces uncovered and flushed out 95 German spy rings operating in close proximity to the borders of the USSR.

The leader of the Organization of Ukrainian Nationalists (OUN) was arrested by the Russians in the Lvov area. Other arrests began in spring 1941. 1,596 German agents were claimed to have been arrested and subsequently shot. Since the German side published nothing about its use of agents and their capture and execution by the Soviets, this number cannot be confirmed.

The Strelitz Battalion, 2,000 strong and based in Krakow, the Ukrainian Legion in Warsaw, and the battalion of Ukrainian fighters raised and trained in Luckenwalde, were the key groups for the planned operations in the USSR. Ukrainian nationalists were transported across the border into the USSR. Beginning on 2 February 1941 the teams of the 1st Company of the Brandenburgers moved into bases in the Allenstein area of East Prussia and began their special training for operations in Russia.

On 15 February 1941 Admiral Canaris received a secret command matter that was signed by Generalfeldmarschall Keitel. In it the Abwehr chief was named "coordinator of all secret service and military actions to conceal the German buildup against Russia."

On 19th February Admiral Canaris sent the head of Abwehr II, von Lahousen-Vivremont, to "Camp Zeppelin" near Zossen, where the army general staff was based. All joint actions involving the Abwehr and the army were to be coordinated with it. Canaris himself traveled to Krakow on 28th February to discuss with the head of the Abwehr station there how the enemy in the east could be surprised. When he returned to Berlin, Canaris gave the head of Abwehr III, Oberst Bentivegny, the following instructions:

Prepare all arms of Abwehr III for active espionage work against the Soviet Union, for example:
(a) Paralysis of the activities of the Soviet intelligence centers.
(b) Misleading of foreign intelligence services by our agents, specifically by leading them to believe in an improvement in relations with the Soviet Union and the preparation of a strike against England.
(c) Abwehr measures to maintain the secrecy of preparations for war against the Soviet Union and the security of the secret transporting of German troops to the east.

Oberst von Bentivegny placed Group III D on alert. In cooperation with Department L of the OKW and the general staffs of the three branches of the armed forces, it composed the false reports that were to be leaked to the enemy by agents of the counter-espionage service under Oberst Rohleder (Group III F).

On 11th March Canaris received instructions to mislead the Russian military attaché in Berlin, Major-General V. I. Tupikov, by means of false information. This was done through Soviet agent Orestes Berling, a member of the Soviet security service attached to the Soviet embassy in Berlin. Berling had been unmasked and turned, and he was ideally situated to pass on the latest "discoveries" that had been cooked up as a deception. These erroneous reports reached the desk of the Russian general by way of Berling.

The Russians were so completely deceived that on 20 March 1941 the then head of the Red Army's secret service, General Fedor Igor Golikov, told Stalin that the rumors of German troops massing in the east and of an imminent invasion of the USSR by Germany had been cooked up solely by Russia's enemy, the British, who wanted to provoke a war between Russia and Germany in order to get themselves out of the trouble they were in.

In his situation report to the British high command on 13 March 1941, director of military intelligence Major-General Francis Davidson wrote: "We have no reason to assume that a German attack on Russia is imminent."

The Abwehr's Department III had pulled off a major coup. This situation, together with the fact that the Red Army had moved its troops in the western frontier districts up to the demarcation line and that the Red Army's strength there had grown to 171 infantry divisions and 40 motorized brigades by 4th April, led the Abwehr to dispatch as many special units to the east as possible. This situation led to a revival of the idea of using Ukrainian nationalists, which had been forbidden by Hitler in autumn 1940.

The head of Abwehr Department III, von Lahousen, had repeatedly tried to use the Ukrainian nationalists as agents and couriers for his service. Hitler, however, had issued orders for these men to be released and sent away. In November 1940 SS-Oberfuhrer Muller, head of the Gestapo, tried to have these men arrested and executed. Admiral Canaris was able to prevent this by ordering his departments not to use the Ukrainians any longer. Lahousen was left with no choice but to separate himself from the nationalist leader Jary and his compatriots on 13th December—the day he met with the nationalist leader. He did intimate to Jary, however, that they would probably be able to use him again very soon.

With the departure of these agents from Abwehr III's intelligence service, the Abwehr was blinded as far as the Soviet Union was concerned, for all the important information on the USSR reaching Berlin came from these sources. But now that there was a requirement to establish a functioning espionage service as quickly as possible and install a dense net of spies to provide Brandenburger commando teams with information they could use on their missions, von Lahousen turned once again to the Ukrainians and the nationalist fringe groups in the Baltic States, who had proved to be knowledgeable about the Russian rear areas. He used his existing contacts to give the signal "green" for these men to return to service as German agents.

Following a confidential talk with Admiral Canaris, the latter officially ordered that contact was to be reestablished with Colonel Melnyk, the head of the OUN, and his deputy Jary, as well as with the Ukrainian Bandera.

Oberstleutnant Erwin Stolze, Lahousen's deputy as head of Abwehr Department III, recalled this recall action before the Nuremberg tribunal.

WORKING FOR THE ABWEHR

At the end of March 1941 the then Oberstleutnant Stolze received an order from his superior, the head of Abwehr II, Oberst von Lahousen-Vivremont, to come to his office. There he told Stolze that the German attack on the Soviet Union was about to begin. In connection with that he gave Stolze the following order: "Evaluate all the information we have on the Soviet Union. From that determine all the necessary missions and the measures to be taken. You are to consider the information I have just given you top secret."

Stolze asked von Lahousen- Vivremont which directives had been issued to carry out the resulting missions. Lahousen- Vivremont stated that under his, Stolze's, direction, a special group was to be formed to be called simply "Group A" whose sole purpose was to carry out preparations for sabotage and subversive activities inside the Soviet Union. He then also gave Stolze an order from the Wehrmacht Operations Staff containing the "guidelines for subversive activities in the territory of the Soviet Union after the German invasion of Russia."

When Stolze had left the meeting room and returned to his office he took a closer look at the order. On the last page he saw the signature of Generalmajor Warlimont, who had signed on behalf of Generalfeldmarschall Keitel. There were just two words on the cover page: OPERATION BARBAROSSA.

The order contained the following directive for the Abwehr II: After the initial strike by the Luftwaffe and the army's advance, it was to establish a network of agents which was to cover all of the USSR as soon as it was conquered. Stolze also discovered the agency's first mission:

"Establish contact with Ukrainian nationalists in the service of the Abwehr and other groups well disposed towards us."

Later that same day Stolze invited the leader of the Ukrainian nationalists, Colonel Melnyk, or "Konsul I" as he was known, and the left wing revolutionary leader Stefan Bandera to come to see him. He instructed them to make their way to the Ukraine as soon as German forces invaded the USSR and incite the national forces there to rise up against the hated Soviet regime. The objective of this action was to decisively weaken the power of the Red Army in its own rear areas.

On 2 May 1941 representatives of all three branches of the armed forces met at Krampnitz near Potsdam for a conference chaired by the deputy chief of the Wehrmacht Operations Staff, Generalmajor Warlimont. One of the topics of discussion was employment of the Brandenburgers and other special units.

Besides Warlimont and the three armed forces chiefs of staff, present at the meeting were the head of the Wehrmacht propaganda department, Oberst von Wedel, Oberst Rudolf, Oberst von Lahousen-Vivremont, and Oberstleutnant Stolze as the representative of Abwehr II. All of the proposed special missions were discussed during the course of the conference; these proposals were subsequently presented to Generalfeldmarschall Keitel and General Jodl.

INITIAL PREPARATIONS FOR "BARBAROSSA"

On 1 June 1941 Abwehr II ordered the formation of the three named front-line reconnaissance detachments for the Army Groups North, Center and South.

One hundred trained Estonian resistance fighters in Russian uniforms were deployed from Finland; acting as spies and radio agents, they were to carry out Operation "Erna" in the area of the former Baltic States. Two groups of these agents were transported by sea from Pellinge Island to Kumna Bay. One was discovered by Soviet torpedo boats in the Bay of Finland and was forced to turn back. These men later parachuted into Estonia, where they worked for Army Group North in the Aegviidu, Narva, Tallinn and Wesenburg areas.

Ukrainian nationalist volunteers were infiltrated over the Soviet border even before the campaign began, with the mission of making lists of the names of Russians who were either particularly loyal to the Soviet regime or fanatical opponents of the same. Both were equally important.

At the Tirpitzufer in Berlin they were already celebrating the plans for a German-Ukrainian friendship and a partnership of the German armed forces and the Ukrainian volunteer units.

Abwehr II also formed teams planned for use in the north of the Eastern Front in the area of the Baltic Republics of the Soviet Union—Latvia, Lithuania and Estonia.

Together with his chief von Lahousen-Vivremont, Oberstleutnant Stolzc began forming the Abwehr detachments that were to be sent to the German army groups in the staging area in East Prussia. Parallel to this, directives were sent to the Abwehr stations in Konigsberg, Krakow and Warsaw, as well as to the war organization in Finland, by the head of the Abwehr, Admiral Canaris, telling them to step up espionage activities against the Soviet Union to the maximum. Furthermore, the 800th Special Purpose Construction Training Battalion "Brandenburg" was placed under the direct command of the head of Abwehr II, von Lahousen. The latter was to arrange the initial missions as well as all those to follow.

On 10 June 1941 Admiral Canaris and the leading officers of the Ausland/Abwehr attended a major conference; on this occasion the Abwehr commander discussed the job of occupying Russia with SS and police officers of the Reichssicherheitshauptamt. Canaris made an agreement with Heydrich for his agents to cooperate with those of the SD and the Security Police.

One day later six agents from the Krakow Abwehr station were sent across the border; their mission was to blow the rail line from Stolpunova to Kiev during the night of 22 June 1941. The mission was a failure, however.

Beginning on 15th June, a large number of combat and sabotage teams crossed the Russian border by night. They infiltrated deep into the enemy rear, where they waited to strike as soon as the German attack began. Their mission was to cut telephone lines, blow up radio and telephone masts, destroy bridges and railroad tracks, and occupy positions vital to the advance and hold them until the arrival of German troops. In the final weeks before the invasion the Abwehr dispatched its front-line reconnaissance teams to join the three army groups. Technically and operationally they were subordinated to the army headquarters. The units familiarized themselves with the terrain before they joined the point units with which they would advance, so that they could better recover the first secret documents from overrun positions and destroyed fortresses and send them to the Walli staffs.

The number of front-line reconnaissance detachments in service corresponded to the number of German armies in the field. One such unit was subordinated to each army, which sent it into the most forward assembly area where the panzer units or fast advance battalions waited for the starting shot. Their first objective was not just to secure intelligence-related material, but also to search for tactical material in the overrun division, corps and army headquarters of the Red Army and recover orders of all kinds from which conclusions could be drawn as to Russian intentions.

During the course of 21 June 1941 the armies sent the front-line reconnaissance detachments ahead to the panzer divisions and reconnaissance units. At 1:00 A.M. on the morning of 22 June 1941 the Abwehr command was advised by radio that its front-line combat units were ready and had moved into their jump-off positions.

At 3:00 A.M. and 3:15 A.M. these Abwehr detachments advanced with the panzers; the three Walli staffs waited for the first material to come in so that they could set to work. There were 150 Abwehr teams, three to ten men strong, taking part in the initial advance. They comprised Abwehr Detachment 104. It was made up exclusively of volunteers who were ready to carry out any orders given to them. All material they might find was to be sent to Abwehr station Walli III in Breslau. Since the distances soon became too great, Walli III moved, first to Lemberg (Lvov) and then to Vinnitsa.

The OKW's Foreign Armies East section also wanted all information concerning the enemy as quickly as possible. It was primarily interested in obtaining Red Army orders of battle, combat manuals and the like so as to fill existing intelligence gaps as quickly as possible. By implementing appropriate procedures, Foreign Armies East's liaison officer to the Ausland/Abwehr, Oberstleutnant Cartellieri, ensured that such documents were quickly forwarded to Walli III.

The Abwehr combat teams assigned to the northern sector, which were first deployed in Latvia and Lithuania, Baltic Republics of the Soviet Union, received a number of important missions. One of the first was to seize the railway tunnel and bridge near Vilna. In Latvia combat teams were to take possession of the bridges over the Western Dvina, hold them until the arrival of German forces, and prevent them from being blown at all costs.

Together with his superior, the head of the Abwehr's Department II, von Lahousen-Vivremont, Oberstleutnant Stolze began forming and drilling these detachments. When they were ready for action they were moved into Army Group North's concentration area in East Prussia.

The 800th Special Purpose Construction Training Battalion" Brandenburg", which was directly subordinate to the head of Abwehr II, was prepared for action. Its units' bases and commanders were:

I Battalion:	Brandenburg, Havel:	CO: Major Heinz
II Battalion:	Baden near Vienna:	CO: Rittmeister Jacobi, later Major Heinz
III Battalion:	Duren:	CO: Hptm. Jacobi

Some of the regimental units, the 4th through 17th Companies, were still in training or—like the 13th Company—were being reequipped as the Tropical Company Africa.

In the east the units of the regiment saw action from the very first day: the 4th Company less the Lutke Parachute Platoon and the 7th and 8th Companies went to Northeast Prussia. the 10th Company was transferred from the Duren area to East Prussia for commando operations. The 9th and 12th Companies were earmarked for operations in the east and would be sent there later. The following is an exact chronological survey.

On 3rd June III Battalion, Special Purpose Construction Training Battalion Brandenburg under Hptm. Jacobi was ready for action in Duren. On orders from Oberst von Haehling the II th Company was removed from the battalion formation for other duties. A half company consisting of one officer and 124 men, with a 14-man train and 11 Palestinians with 5 three-ton trucks, three cars, three motorcycle-sidecar combinations and a solo motorcycle were to carry out four missions. The company headquarters squad, which accompanied this half company, consisted of two officers and seven men as well as an eight-man squad. This battle group thus had a total of 164 men at its disposal.

This Special Unit "Fendt" under the commanding officer of 11th Company, Oblt. Fendt with Lt. Einem-Josten and Lt. Leuffen, was to become the 1st Company of the 288th Special Unit; the unit, some of whose soldiers spoke Arabic, was supposed to be deployed to the Near East and was thus unavailable for Barbarossa.

The following bases were chosen for the regiment prior to the start of operations in the east:

I Battalion: based at Brandenburg with
    1st Company, including HQ Company, combined as V-company, stayed in Brandenburg.
    2nd Company, preparations for Operation Barbarossa
    3rd Company, ditto
    4th Company, ditto
II Battalion: based at Baden near Vienna with
    5th Company (elements already in action guarding the Danube waterways). Rest in Baden near Vienna.

6th Company in Rumania guarding the Ploesti oil fields. Preparations for action with the 22nd Infantry Division in the southeast.

7th Company main body transferred to Northeast Prussia.

8th Company ditto

III Battalion: based at Duren with

9th Company in formation. First available for operations in the east on 1/9/1941.

10th Company in East Prussia preparing for commando operations.

11th Company mustered out, planned as core of Special Unit Felmy (2SSth).

12th Company transferred back from Baden near Vienna to Duren. Scheduled for operations in eastern campaign.

Regimental Units

13th Company being reorganized as Tropical Company "Africa"

14th (Replacement Training) Company earmarked as training company for II Battalion

15th (Light) Company being reorganized as "Finland Company"

16th Company under formation in Duren. Earmarked for combined air-sea action against the island of Osel.

17th Company under formation. Subsequently renamed 1st Company, 800th Special Purpose Construction Training Battalion Brandenburg.

Since the Wehrmacht High Command reckoned that the war in Russia would be another "blitz" campaign and that Army Group North would be able to reach its objective of Leningrad within a few weeks, the Brandenburger combat teams were moved into areas close to the border in order to cross over ahead of the main force and carry out their missions in the enemy rear. The Brandenburgers in this area were under the command of Hptm. Walther.

Under the command of Obit. Grabert, the 5th Company was shipped by fast train from Neuhaus in the Vienna Forest to Tilsit. From there it moved up to Tauroggen near the border. After Oblt. Grabert was put out of action by an accident, Oblt. Knaal was placed in command of the 8th Company. The coming missions had already been "handed out." Each company or half company wanted to be first in line and more than once Oberst Haehling had to step in to decide which unit received which mission.

The 7th Company was split into two. One half company under Lt. Pfannenstiel moved into the area of I Army Corps, 18th Army. Following its rapid transfer from Duren the 10th Company under Oblt. Aretz took up quarters in Schonwalde near Allenstein. On 18th June it received its mission order:

"Advance from the tip of Suwalki near Sudauen, through Augustowo along the road to Grodno, secure intact all road and rail bridges and hold them until the arrival of the infantry."

In order to complete its mission the company was also divided into two half companies. The first was led by Lt. Kriegsheim, the second by Lt. Kohlmeyer. The 12th Company, commanded by Oblt. Schader, was sent from Vöslau to East Prussia on 8th June. Its final preparations were made near Modlin near the German-Soviet demarcation line. Its mission:

"Move by night against the major road and rail bridge over the Bug. Secure it, prevent it from being blown, and hold it until the infantry arrives."

The parachute platoon under Lt. Lutke was pulled out of training and placed on alert. It was issued jump equipment, weapons and weapons containers and was sent by fast train to Suwalki, where it was to establish contact with the waiting infantry divisions that would assign it a special mission. The object of the first parachute action by the Brandenburgers was to drop behind enemy lines, seize an important bridge, and hold it until the arrival of German forces.

I Battalion under Major Heinz was assigned to the area of Army Group South.

Unit liaison officer in army group headquarters in Krakow was Lt. Dlab. While the 1st Company stayed in Brandenburg, on 28th May the remaining companies transferred to Zakopane in the High Tatra. There the battalion was joined by the two companies of the "Nightingale" Legionnaire Battalion under Oblt. Herzner and Oblt. Oberlander, that had been subordinated to it. There Major Heinz received the following mission order:

"Advance as far as Przemysl with the 2nd and 4th Companies and the subordinate 'Nightingale Battalion. Using the cover designation 'Assault Company Schulze,' the 3rd Company led by Oblt. John will make its way into the assembly area of III Panzer Corps, General der Kavallerie Eberhard von Mackensen, and stand by at the Bug for action."

On 20th June the 10th Company under Oblt. Aretz moved into the forest north of Plaska about 2,500 meters from the demarcation line, which was formed by the "Augustovsky," a narrow but marshy stream. It was vital that all the bridges on the advance road be captured intact so as to facilitate the infantry's advance.

Everything was ready. The war against Russia was about to begin and no one knew that it would last four years and claim millions of victims. The soldiers hoped that they would be home by winter and celebrate Christmas with their families.

The Abwehr in the Campaign against Russia

THE RAILROAD BRIDGES AT AUGUSTOVO, SIOLKO AND HOLYNKA AND THE BRIDGE AT LIPSK

At about 1:30 A.M. on 22nd June Lt. Konig, the leader of a 12-man combat team, raised his fist and began to move. The men followed in close single file, trying to make as little noise as possible. All were under cover, which meant they were wearing Russian uniforms. At the border they moved through the German wire, in which the engineers had cut a narrow gap. The team's target was the railroad bridge at Augustovo. When the team reached the stream that formed the boundary they found the patrol reports confirmed. The enemy had removed the planking from the wooden bridge over the stream. All that was left was the pilings on both sides.

The planking the team had brought with it was placed on the wooden posts and one man was sent across the stream to scout ahead. Suddenly a gasping voice rang out from the darkness on the other side. The Ivans had caught the scout—that much was clear. Lt. Konig decided to wait for the artillery barrage before he crossed the stream. The barrage began at 3:05 A.M. and the team crossed over. They found the corporal, who had been strangled by a Russian sentry.

The team reached the road and slipped into the mass of retreating Russians. In this way they arrived at the Augustovo Bridge without being unmasked. The bridge was unguarded but it had been prepared for demolition. The wires were cut and as the team was throwing the explosives, which had been removed from their chambers, into the river, the enemy opened fire from the east bank.

Leutnant Konig was shot in the chest; he died immediately. The men took cover and fired at the shadowy forms moving toward the bridge on the far side. The enemy withdrew and the assault team was able to hold the bridge with its automatic weapons until the leading German infantry arrived. The advance battalion rolled across and put the enemy to flight.

South of Siolko just three Brandenburgers in Russian uniforms crossed the bridge and rendered the demolition charges harmless by cutting the lead wire. There was an exchange of gunfire with the Russians and two of the men were killed. Uffz. Zollner, the team leader, held the bridge alone until the arrival of the first infantry.

Feldwebel Rennkamp, who with 10 soldiers was supposed to seize and hold the bridge at Holynka, got through to the bridge and took possession of it. However, they could not find the lead wire and the bridge was blown by remote control just as they were about to empty the explosives tubes.

Leutnant Kriegsheim, accompanied by just two ethnic Germans and an agent who spoke excellent Russian, made his way to the Bobr bridge south-west of Lipsk. This mission was more difficult than the others, for in order to reach its target this small team had to cross the Augustovo-Grodno road before it could reach the 100-meter long wooden bridge. The team was also accompanied by a war correspondent, but he had to be left behind when they crossed the road. When the small team was stopped by two Russian sentries and asked for the password, Kriegsheim and his men gave "Astrakhan." This was incorrect and the Russians therefore decided to take them to their command post. What that meant was clear, for they were in Russian uniforms.

They neared the building and were surely about to be exposed. Lt. Kriegsheim drew his pistol from his pocket, opened his coat to show his German uniform underneath, turned around and fired at the first Russian. The second Russian pulled the trigger of his weapon, which he was carrying at the hip, but Kriegsheim shot him down. Immediately after this exchange of fire, illumination flares were fired from all sides, bathing everything in harsh light. There was no way now that they could get through to Lipsk. Lt. Kriegsheim ordered his men to take cover in a ditch.

Approximately forty minutes later—the German barrage had begun at 3:05 A.M. the leading German units appeared. The Brandenburgers tried to identify themselves, but they were still wearing Russian coats and they were fired at by their own people. Two of the team were wounded.

The remaining two men, Lt. Kriegsheim and an Obergefreiter, now set off in the direction of Lipsk. They slipped into a column of retreating Russians and continued with it toward their objective unnoticed. The Gefreiter who spoke Russian even asked a sentry for the fastest way to the bridge. Following his directions, the pair arrived at the bridge over the Bobr and saw that it was the scene of hectic activity. Densely packed columns of vehicles and foot soldiers crossed the bridge in an endless stream.

Several small units were trying to cross, obviously in a hurry; had they heard that the bridge was about to be blown? Lt. Kriegsheim and the corporal began searching for the lead wires and even checked the bridge pilings; none of the Russians thought to ask them what they were doing there. But they were unable to find the wires or explosives. Then a detachment of about 40 Russians appeared on the other side of the bridge; they began unrolling several drums of wire and unloaded explosives from a truck. When they approached the bridge, the two Germans threw off their Russian coats and opened fire from a range of 70 meters.

The Russians took cover and returned fire. The corporal was fatally wounded in the neck. Kriegsheim, who had taken cover, was certain that he was about to meet the same fate when the Russians suddenly redirected their fire. A German advance battalion had arrived on the scene.

Lt. Kriegsheim raced over to the corporal to dress his wounds. As he bent over giving the man something to drink, three Russians, who like him had been hiding in the bushes on the riverbank, came up behind him. One of them stabbed him in the back with a bayonet. The Leutnant lost consciousness. He was evacuated to the rear as quickly as possible. Meanwhile, the infantry rolled across the bridge. One more step had been taken in the German advance.

OPERATION "BOGDANOV":
IN THE FORTRESS OF BREST-LITOVSK

The Lütke parachute platoon, which had expected to see action on 22nd June, was not transferred to Varene airfield, 70 kilometers northeast of Suwalki, until the next day. The platoon's objective had already fallen to a rapid armored advance. Now Lt. Lütke and his men were to carry out Operation "Bogdanov," the seizure of a bridge over the double rail line from Lida to Molodechno. The mission was to begin at 5:00 A.M. on 24th June.

The platoon took off in three Ju 52 transport aircraft and flew low over the hedges and the heads of the German infantry toward a small landing site that had been located about 1,200 meters beyond the bridge. From the landing site a narrow wood stretched down to the bridge. Using it as cover, they would have an easy time of it or so they were told. Flying at only 40 meters above the ground, the three Ju 52s came to the plateau and began their landing approach. Suddenly they were met by a hail of machine-gun and rifle fire. The pilot of the lead aircraft was wounded in the mouth; two other men in the aircraft were also injured.

Directly ahead could be seen the bridge bunkers. The aircraft made a steep left turn back to the drop site. From a height of 55 meters the platoon commander gave the order to jump. When Lütke saw that the aircraft's wounded radio operator had not released the weapons container he asked the pilot to make another pass. The wounded pilot did it. As jump director Lütke was not supposed to jump. But after he had released the weapons container he nevertheless leapt out the door into space. He landed safely.

The platoon was assembled. It turned out that they had landed very close to the target. That probably saved their lives, for no less than 16 enemy tanks were parked on the road at the edge of the plateau. Had they come down elsewhere the tanks could have decimated the platoon with their machine-guns. While the platoon worked its way toward the bridge the crews of the Russian tanks tried to hit and set off the demolition charges. Mortars also opened fire. The paratroopers reached and secured the bridge. An hour later three German armored cars that had left the forces pursuing the fleeing Russians arrived and gave Lütke and his platoon fire support. They were followed by the point elements of a motorcycle battalion approaching from the south. Then, on orders from the battalion commander, they turned north and headed straight toward the bridge.

Soon afterward the three armored cars linked up with the Lütke platoon and gave it direct support. Two Russian counterattacks, whose objective was the destruction of the bridge, were beaten back. The major Russian attack expected early on 26th June did not materialize.

Both bridges had fallen into German hands intact. Over them the advance continued to roll east at a rapid tempo. When relief arrived on 27th June the Lütke parachute platoon, which had lost four dead and 16 wounded, was commandeered by the army troops on the spot and in spite of all protests was incorporated into a battalion. Ultimately only seven men returned to their battalion on 4 July 1941. Leutnant Lütke was not one of them, for he had died in a forest battle while fighting as an infantryman.

The missions by the Brandenburgers in the first days and weeks of the Russian campaign were so manifold in number and nature that it is impossible to do more than name a few to illustrate the extent of the unit's commitments.

Abwehr front-line reconnaissance teams advanced with the leading elements of Army Group Center assaulting the fortress of Brest-Litovsk. Their mission was to secure files, orders and important documents before they could be destroyed by the Soviets. While the battle for the fortress still raged, a Russian staff car roared up from the southeast and, pursued by German mortar fire, drove into the fortress. At the wheel was a commissar, in the back seat a Red Army colonel. They were in fact members of a special Abwehr team that was supposed to secure the important documents in this the largest Russian land fortress. The colonel showed the guard an original order from the STAVKA that even bore Stalin's signature.

The order stated that Colonel Goluyev was to secure the important secret documents from the fortress and take them to Smolensk. With the colonel were eight soldiers, who were to transport the files. The loading of four trucks proceeded quickly, interrupted only when the men were forced to take cover by German artillery fire.

By the time they were finished German troops had already taken parts of the fortress. Only the Red Army's commissar school, the headquarters of the citadel and several secondary forts were still holding out.

Colonel Goluyev was urged to leave as quickly as possible. Two of the four trucks had been loaded. Unimportant files were supposed to be burned. The men of the driving team climbed aboard the two trucks and shortly after midnight of 27th June the small convoy, led by the staff car, left the fortress and headed southeast with headlights shielded. After about four kilometers it was detoured by Brandenburger guides and an hour later reached its destination behind the German lines with its terrific haul. There Colonel Goluyev once again became Leutnant Bauffke. The Brandenburgers had pulled off one of their greatest coups without a drop of blood being spilled. It later turned out that the Leutnant had been lucky, for the next day the Russian headquarters and the commissar school in which he had spent the night and drank vodka with Russian officers was attacked by German bombers with 1000 kg bombs.

All the captured documents were sent to the experts of Walli III. Additional evaluators came from Berlin to study the documents, which gave the German armed forces important clues as to Russian troop strengths and intentions.

OTHER COMMANDO OPERATIONS

Obit. Knaak and his battle group accompanied the advance group of the 8th Panzer Division with the objective of seizing the bridges over the Dvina. Commanded by General Erich Brandenberger, this panzer division, the spearhead of LVI Panzer Corps, advanced along the Wilkomierz-Utena road toward Dvinsk.

At dawn on 26th June Battle Group Knaak separated from the point unit. Riding in two captured Russian trucks, Knaak and his men drove alone toward the east at high speed. One of the two trucks reached the Dvina bridge and drove across unchallenged. Not until it reached the eastern approach was it fired on. The truck drove down an embankment. The men seized their weapons and jumped out. The second truck was only one third of the way across the bridge when it was fired on by a Russian heavy machine-gun. The men in the truck jumped down and, firing from the hip, ran toward the far end of the bridge. This group suffered heavy casualties, but the survivors linked up with the first group. It had dug in at the other end and had stopped several attempts by the enemy to recapture and blow up the bridge. The detachment leader, Oblt. Hans-Wolfram Knaak, was one of those killed. He was subsequently promoted to Rittmeister and on 31 November 1942 was awarded the Knight's Cross posthumously. Fw. Prohaska, who assumed command after the death of the chief, was later named in the Wehnnacht communique. Meanwhile Obit. Grabert, having recovered from the injuries suffered in his accident, hurried back to his company and took command.

During the night of 30th June Lvov was seized by elements of the Brandenburgers' I Battalion. This strategically and technically important site was taken and secured. On that 30th June the Brandenburg Regiment was bolstered by the now operational 13th and 17th Companies.

As well the Brandenburgers carried out a series of other risky, commando-style raids. On 17 July 1941 the Commander-in-Chief of Army Group North, Generalfeldmarschall von Leeb, wrote to the head of Abwehr ü, that "use of the special forces provided by Abwehr Department ü played an important and in places decisive part in the rapid and successful conduct of operations by Army Group North." The field marshal went on to say:

> Through their courageous actions the men of this regiment have paved the way to victory for the armored forces and other units and secured positions whose loss would have been irreplaceable for the conduct of operations. In a daring and selfless advance the numerically weak operations groups stormed and held seven important bridges and carried out successful patrol operations. Their heavy casualties are a sign of heroic willingness and German soldierly virtue. Before the fallen we lower our flags in respect and gratitude.
>
> I express my gratitude and full appreciation to all participants for their outstanding accomplishments. Signed von Leeb, Generalfeldmarschall.

Just as in the northern sector, the Brandenburgers also completed their assigned missions in the central and southern sectors. In Army Group Center's area the Schulze assault company was ordered to establish a bridgehead around the railroad bridges over the Styr near Rozyszce. First, however, the two enemy-held villages of Rudnia and Duza had to be taken. The defense included snipers and light tanks. This costly attack was called off by Oblt. John.

In spite of this setback a bridgehead was soon established across the Styr. The railroad bridge across the deep gorge was secured and its destruction by the enemy prevented, but the company lost 16 of its soldiers. Operation followed operation in the subsequent weeks and months. The Brandenburgers turned up wherever the action was. When vital installations had to be taken the Brandenburgers were thrown into the game, the trump card of the German command.

BATTLE GROUP HEINZ IN ACTION

When the 17th Army halted on 28 June 1941 it stood astride a line Grodek-Jagiellonski-Hszana-Kozize, about nine kilometers west of Lemberg (Lvov) and Rokitno, about ten kilometers to its north. The attack on this heavily fortified defense line was planned for 30th June. At the suggestion of Major Heinz the Brandenburgers were deployed in front of the German troops in the sector of XXXXI Mountain Corps in order to seize Lvov the night before the attack and thus divert the attention of the defenders from their western front.

The Brandenburgers' I Battalion was joined by the "Nightingale" legionnaire battalion. This unit, which had been formed in Neuhammer from Ukrainians of the Organization of Ukrainian Nationalists under Melnyk (at the urging of Abwehr ü), was initially rejected by Hitler. Not until the invasion of the USSR was imminent did he authorize its use. Many of its soldiers came from Lvov and were ideally suited to the nocturnal operation because of their familiarity with the local area. In addition to the German battalion commander, Oblt. Dr. Herzner, the Ukrainians were led by their own military commander, Sconprynka. Hptm. Dr. Oberlander functioned as political advisor in Ukrainian affairs and had nothing to do with the command of the battalion.

The battalion received its special name "Nightingale" because it had a choir which compared favorably even to the Don Cossacks. After darkness fell on 29th June Major Heinz moved his unit up close to the defense line of the Red Army troops defending Lvov. Only the mountain troops' outposts and forward observers were that far forward.

The order to attack was given at 11:00 P.M. The Ukrainian companies raced toward Lvov, meeting only sporadic resistance. The enemy positions turned out to be fakes. The NKVD and the regular Red Army troops had abandoned Lvov under cover of darkness. When the legionnaires reached the building occupied by the NKVD they found the bodies of massacred countrymen, murdered by the NKVD.

Major Heinz sent his own combat teams in an hour later. He and 30 of his men led the way in motorcycle-sidecars and raced for the Lvov city hall.

Heinz ordered his men to put out the fire that the NKVD had set in the cathedral. The beautiful Lvov church was saved and the relics inside were rescued, as was the bishop of the United Church of the Ukraine, Count Czepticki, who had been left tied up inside by the NKVD. At the city hall Uffz. Fielitz, who had accompanied Major Heinz, was ordered to occupy the NKVD central with his squad. He and his men drove there on their motorcycles and discovered several mass graves in the inner courtyard of the building. Some were still open, some partly covered. It looked as if several thousand must have been murdered there.

When the squad drove back to the city hall at about 8:00 A.M., it was escorted by the wildly jubilant people of the city, happy to at last be free of the fear of death at the hands of the NKVD. The Ukrainians took charge of the building that housed the radio station. At 11 :00 A.M. their leader issued a proclamation announcing the formation of a free, independent state of Western Ukraine. At about 2:00 P.M. the German mountain troops marched into the city in perfect order, unopposed.

Part of I Battalion—2nd Company under Hauptmann Dr. Hartmann, which had entered Lvov from the north—remained in the city with the "Nightingale" battalion for several days. For a week Major Heinz was the city commandant of Lvov.

In his combat report to the Ie of XXXXI Mountain Corps dated 30 June 1941, Major Heinz stated: "In all three prisons in the city of Lvov there were thousands of brutally murdered people."

The Ie's response: "The 1st and 4th Mountain Divisions are instructed to assign their press and photo reporters to these acts of cruelty. The corps' senior judge advocate, as well as the recently arrived liaison officer from the Foreign Office to Headquarters, 17th Army, have been sent to Lvov for a closer examination."

The 603rd Military Administration Headquarters moved into Lvov on 30th June. Field judge advocate Tomforde visited the Brigitti prison (previously used as an NKVD jail), taking with him medical officer Stabsarzt Dr. Georg Saeltzer.

Afterward they visited the Samarstinov prison, which had served as a military jail. There they questioned surviving witnesses and civilians. Field judge advocate Dr. Tomforde subsequently filed a report. Senior judge advocate Dr. Wilke, judge in the headquarters of XXXXIX Mountain Corps, was also involved. After conducting extensive research he wrote:

> The appearance of the bodies found in the GPU prison suggested
> that the murders were preceded by severe beatings and torture.
> Most of the murdered were Ukrainians, the rest Poles. According

to statements by witnesses, two wounded German airmen were also delivered to this prison. An airman's belt and a flying helmet were found in the rooms of the prison. It is to be assumed with certainty that these two airmen were among the murdered who could no longer be identified.

The experts assigned to view the bodies and determine how and with what weapons these people had been killed—Generalarzt Dr. Richard Eckl, veterinarian Dr. Joseph Brachetka, and Staff Sergeant (Reich Labor Service) Kurt Dittrich—were questioned until 6 July 1941.

The 17th Army's "flying army judge" questioned other witnesses, Polish and Ukrainian survivors from the three prisons and those who had escaped. The bodies were already in a state of decay when found. The bottom layers in the first four cellars examined could not be identified. "Among the 423 bodies which were laid out in the courtyard of the Brigitti prison for identification were boys aged 10, 12 and 14 years and young women of 18, 20 and 22 years, as well as elderly men and women."

Also found in the former GPU cellar were articles of clothing from the uniforms of the airmen. "The military jail was situated in the north of the city. There the cellar was piled to the ceiling with bodies. 460 bodies were recovered. It was only possible to enter the cellar wearing gas masks. The heat was such that everything had begun to decay."

Finally, three dead Luftwaffe soldiers were also found in the military jail. Four more members of the Luftwaffe were found in the NKVD jail. The 17th Army's pathologist, Dr. Herbert Siegmund, established that the wounded men had been shot in their beds. The other four soldiers, who had been captured uninjured, were found to have been shot in the back of the neck. The people murdered here had been in Russian custody for many months. The Polish manager in the surgical department of the hospital gave the following statement to judge advocate Dr. Moller:

"The shootings began two days before the outbreak of war. All those who were on a 'black list' were killed. They all died but 12. Eight men and four women escaped the massacre." (After the war the Polish witness to one of the massacres, who had given a truthful account of what happened, was banished to Siberia by the Soviets. He was released in 1975 and immigrated to the USA.)

The Ukrainian Red Cross participated in the investigations from the beginning. On 7th July eight Ukrainians told the commandant of the city that "more than 4,000 bodies had been found in many houses in Lvov alone, including some that had been hanged. One was a girl of about eight who had been hung naked from a ceiling lamp."

"As well," reported the Ukrainian Red Cross, "bodies were found in various cellars of people who had been tied up and walled in alive."

During the Nuremberg trials held by the victors, German troops were charged with these acts, including Brandenburgers, who were the first to enter Lvov. These events are related here because the facts and dates undoubtedly prove the guilt of the NKVD in the deaths of these people. These facts were confirmed by a US congressional committee that convened in 1954. The chairman was Senator Charles J. Kersten. Eighteen other members sat on the committee, including Senator Ray J. Madden, who had headed the Katyn Committee in 1952. Witnesses were questioned in Munich, New York and Chicago. The concluding report stated: "In the first days of the Second World War the NKVD shot all political prisoners in every city of the Western Ukraine, with the exception of a very few who miraculously survived."

In autumn 1959 Professor Dr. Theodor Oberlander, then Minister for Exiles in Chancellor Dr. Adenauer's cabinet, was accused of being responsible for these acts of murder committed in Lvov from March to September 1941. Then on 5 September 1959 an article appeared in the Radianska Ukraina which tried to confirm this accusation. The result was a witch-hunt against the soldiers of this unit, who had had no authority over the "Nightingale" battalion and who had nothing at all to do with the action. Yet the following appeared in the Soviet newspaper: "Eighteen years ago the fascists committed a terrible crime in Lvov during the night of 29-30 June 1941. Using a prepared list, the Hitlerite 'Nightingales' arrested and brutally murdered hundreds of communists, comsomolites and non-affiliates in the courtyard of the prison in Zarmarstynovska Street."

This miserable lie, which surpassed even the lies about Katyn, Vinnitsa and others, was very quickly revealed to be such by a German court. The intense denunciations of Dr. Oberlander by "good Germans" led to a judicial inquiry by the senior prosecutor of the regional superior court in Bonn.

The court reached the unanimous decision "that not a single shred of proof could be found for any of the claims and accusations and that no guilt could be placed on Oberlander for any massacre. On the contrary, based on reports from German, neutral and opposing (USA) sides, the following statement was released: "During the first days of the war the NKVD shot all political prisoners in every city in the Western Ukraine with the exception of a very few who miraculously survived."

An international committee that included four former resistance fighters attempted at the same time to find evidence of Dr. Oberlander's guilt. The committee members were Norwegian lawyer Dr. Hans Cappelen, former president of the Danish Reichstag Ole Bjorn Kraft, the Dutch socialist Karel van Staal, Belgian university professor Floor Peeters, and Swiss lawyer and deputy Dr. Kurt Schoch.

The committee sat five times. Four of the meetings were held in The Hague, where testimony from witnesses was heard. Several eye-witnesses from Lvov appeared. The committee disbanded at the fifth sitting without having completed its work, because nothing was left of the accusations against Dr. Oberlander. Questioning of the witnesses, who had been in Lvov at the time, revealed without a doubt that it had been the Russian NKVD that had committed the murders. So as not to have to publicly confirm this and in this way appear to be "national idiots," the committee members issued the following statement: "After four months of investigation and screening 232 witness statements from all participating circles, we have reached the conclusion that the charges which have been raised against the 'Nightingale unit and the former lieutenant and present federal minister Dr. Oberlander are totally unfounded."

However the committee could not bring itself to admit that it was the NKVD that had committed these crimes. Later in a letter to author Alfred M. de Zayas written on 31 March 1977, Dr. Hans Cappelen did honor the truth and stated: "After a thorough investigation the committee, including myself, reached the conclusion that Dr. Oberlander did not participate in the murders in Lvov in 1941.—It was the NKVD that committed these murders."

Now the world knew what had happened at Lvov and who had carried out this inhuman butchery. But the events at Vinnitsa, at Uman, at Lopatin, at Berdichev and at many, many other places in the Ukraine during the Second World War which were blamed on German soldiers, and what was said at Nuremberg to obtain the conviction of many German soldiers, including Generalfeldmarschall Erich von Manstein, introduced into the proceedings with great pathos by the Soviet prosecutors, were nothing but lies so atrocious that any reader who knows history can only react with disgust.

For much of what we know about these events we are indebted to the Ukrainian author Borys Lewytzkyi, who wrote the following in the Polish exile magazine Kultura in Paris:

The responsibility of the Soviet authorities for the murders in the Lvov prisons, as well as for the murders in other prisons in Galicia and the Ukraine, is so clear that it seems likely that there were provocateurs in the Soviet ranks who tried to shift the blame for these atrocities on to the German occupation forces or the Gestapo.

The shootings that took place in Kiev, blame for which was also shifted on to the Germans, were carried out by the NKVD. Not until after the war and many diplomatic and non-diplomatic inquiries did the Polish embassy in Moscow obtain the admission that "many former senior Polish officials were killed in the jails of Kiev."

The shootings in the jails of Lvov in those tragic days in June 1941 were common knowledge to the entire population of the land far and wide.

Thus it has been proved beyond a doubt that neither the Heinz unit of the Abwehr nor the "Nightingale" battalion that was subordinated to the Abwehr had the least thing to do with the murders in Lvov of which they were accused.

SPECIAL MISSIONS

At the end of July 1941, Brandenburgers under the direction of Korvettenkapitän Cellarius, leader of the secret Finland-Estonia war organization, carried out a glider operation against the fortifications on the island of Osel. The aim of the attack was to neutralize the enemy batteries on the south tip of the Baltic island and thus facilitate the attack by the infantry. However the operation went wrong and the Brandenburgers lost 11 killed and missing.

In order to handle the constantly growing number of missions and to be able to assess the flow of information and documents, in September 1941 the Ausland/Abwehr established new branches and sub-branches in Kaunas, Lithuania; Riga, Latvia; Tallin, Estonia; Vilna, East Poland; and Minsk, Belorussia. Counter-espionage and other missions continued to be carried out from there.

At the beginning of October 1941 the 9th Brandenburg Company was sent deep behind the Russian front on a special mission. Target of this operation, which out of necessity was conducted under full cover using Russian uniforms, was the Isdra dam in front of Moscow. This daring mission was a failure.

When it began to sink in at the end of 1941 that the new blitz campaign had failed, it was decided in an intense discussion between Admiral Canaris and the Abwehr department heads to carry the agent missions deep into Russia. Groups were to be put down in the Caucasus, the Volga region, the Urals, and Central Asia. The necessary experts were on hand. At the same time Admiral Canaris said that it was necessary to restore the strength of the front-line reconnaissance units on the German-Russian front and to increase their combat strengths to at least 1,000, otherwise they would be incapable of carrying out the missions assigned to them.

In a Finnish forest camp near Rovaniemi Brandenburgers from alpine lands were prepared for another important mission. They were to sabotage the strategically vital rail lines from Murmansk to Leningrad and from Murmansk to the interior of Russia, thus cutting the supply line to the Russian northern armies and the only avenue for the delivery of supplies and food to encircled Leningrad. Cutting the Murmansk rail line would also prevent Allied weapons and munitions arriving at Murmansk and Arkhangelsk from reaching the armed forces at the front. This would also give German bombers a chance to attack and destroy the supply dumps in Murmansk. The choice fell on the 15th Company.

The operation by German and Finnish forces was only a partial success, for the rail line was never disabled for more than a few days. The operation did, however, tie down considerable enemy forces.

Since the end of 1941 the Walli üI staff had infiltrated agents into the growing Soviet partisan movement. They used Russian deserters and officers from the camps whom had been identified as being reliable and anticommunist. At the end of January 1942 the joint German-Finnish effort to explore the Russian military post office numbering system was also concluded. Not only had it enabled conclusions to be drawn concerning the distribution of Soviet armed forces, but also allowed a number of other useful facts to be analyzed.

The most active unit in the north was the company commanded by Leutnant Adrian von Foelkersam. Consisting of independence-minded Balts, it carried out numerous missions into the Russian rear. In one daring action von Foelkersam ambushed the headquarters of a Russian division and brought back important documents.

The first Brandenburger snowshoe detachment went into action in the winter of 1941–42. In April the unit's soldiers set out for the rail line to Murmansk disguised as Russians, on the way they came upon Russian depots and strong-points at Alakwetti and on the Liza. They attacked and destroyed the installations but then were beaten back and pursued by Russian security forces.

IN THE COMMAND CENTER OF THE AUSLAND/ABWEHR: RUSSIAN PEACE FEELERS

On the second day of the Russian campaign Admiral Canaris had emphatically pointed out to the head of Abwehr ü, Oberst von Lahousen-Vivremont, that the department was to engage only military targets. Several times during the first six months of the campaign he stated that the organization was to "maintain extreme reserve in all political questions." It must make no political promises or hold out the likelihood of the same to any national group—such as the Ukrainians—no matter how large it might be. In any case this was recorded in von Lahousen-Vivremont's war diary.

Then on 16 July 1941 Obergruppenführer Heydrich made an agreement with Generalleutnant Reinecke, the chief of the General Office of the Wehrmacht, according to which the Gestapo and the SD would be allowed to sift out all the members of the Red Army in Wehrmacht prison camps and shoot all those who were thought to be Bolsheviks or exposed as commissars. Admiral Canaris immediately raised objections. Unfortunately he did not complain where it was necessary, but instead only within Abwehr circles. Instead he sent Oberst von Lahousen-Vivremont, the head of Abwehr ü, into this battle with the Gestapo because he, according to Lahousen, "did not wish to commit himself too much to a negative attitude toward the ideological tendencies of the order."

And so in the ensuing discussions with General Reinecke and Obergruppenführer Müller it was Oberst von Lahousen who had to be one to argue that this order "contravened the conventions under international law and that furthermore such shootings would have an adverse affect on the morale of the troops."

The Ausland/Abwehr official responsible for international law, Helmuth James Graf Moltke, was instructed by his department head, Admiral Bürkner, to draft a memorandum for a presentation he intended to make to Generalfeldmarschall Keitel. Finally the memorandum would also be signed by Admiral Canaris. The concerns raised in the memo concentrated on the fact that the order as issued contravened the norms of military law and set aside much that was not only militarily expedient but also necessary to maintain the discipline and effectiveness of their own forces. Furthermore they were worried about the military and political consequences.

The response from Generalfeldmarschall Keitel, which was directed not to Admiral Canaris but to Admiral Bürkner, the chief of the foreign department, emphasized that these concerns were entirely in keeping with the soldierly ideals of chivalrous war, but that what was at stake here was the destruction of a world view.

Canaris then got himself in serious trouble by daring to employ a man of Jewish origin as a V-man in Tangiers. Himmler heard about this "case" and in February 1942 he reported to Hitler that the Ausland/Abwehr was using a number of Jewish liaison and middle-men abroad.

Hitler gave orders for the admiral to be suspended from further service and for Admiral Bürkner to assume command of the agency. Through the Führer's adjutant, Oberst Engel, Canaris succeeded in gaining an audience with the Führer. The admiral was able to convince Hitler of his loyalty and was reinstated. He had learned, however, that his authority stood on feet of clay.

THE ABWEHR AND RUSSIA'S PEACE FEELERS

The Soviet Union was in desperate straits in September 1941. In the summer it had suffered heavy losses in men and materiel in six great battles of encirclement, and the Red air force had been practically swept from the skies. That month the command center of the Abwehr began picking up suggestions that there were people in Russia, diplomats as well as party leaders, who might be ready to "get together with the Germans again."

Agent Edgar Klaus of the Stockholm Abwehr station, another Jew from the Baltic states, had an excellent contact in Alexandra Mikhailovka Kollontai, his bridge partner and the Soviet envoy to Sweden. He reported that there were signs of disintegration in the USSR and that Mrs. Kollontai wanted to change sides and come to Germany. After pursuing this channel more intensively, the Abwehr found repeated Russian hints and concealed offers to reach a peace. But Admiral Canaris was not interested as long as the German run of success continued.

When the German summer offensive of 1942 bogged down, further signals were received from Moscow indicating a readiness on the part of the Soviets to negotiate. At the end of 1942 it was once again agent Klaus who informed Admiral Canaris that the Russians were ready for serious negotiations with Germany. The Russians wanted to "seek a settlement with Germany in order to end this war, which was so costly to both sides, as quickly as possible."

Even after their victory at Stalingrad the Soviets were ready to negotiate and they hoped that given the situation Hitler might be turned in this direction. Now it would have been up to Admiral Canaris to explore this opportunity and ultimately present it to Hitler. But the head of the Abwehr did not take this step. He did not want to negotiate with the communist leaders or their representatives.

This happened at precisely the time when the "Red Orchestra" spy ring was being uncovered and destroyed, revealing the full extent of Soviet espionage in Germany. The fact that an Abwehr officer was involved made things all the more difficult for Canaris. The officer responsible for air-landed and parachute troops in Abwehr II, Oberleutnant Herbert Goll-now, had been a member of the "Red Orchestra."

During his trial on charges of treason, Wilhelm Canaris stated that the activities of the "Red Orchestra" had cost the lives of 100,000 German soldiers. It was learned that ten sabotage teams of the Abwehr and the Brandenburgers had been caught behind the Russian lines and liquidated as a result of Gollnow's treachery. All this (as well as the fear of incurring Hitler's disfavor if he raised this touchy theme) kept Canaris from pursuing this hot lead.

Another now stepped into his place. Diplomat Peter Kleist, an employee of Foreign Minister von Ribbentrop, established contact with the Russians in Stockholm after talking to agent Klaus. The Russians had become even clearer in spring 1943. They wanted to make peace. In April 1943 the three members of the Soviet embassy in Stockholm Mikhail Nikitin, Alexei Tatadin and Boris Jarcev met with German diplomats on an estate near the Swedish capital. Some initial understandings were reached, pointing to a positive outlook for future negotiations.

The next meeting was held in June at the Swedish Baltic resort of Saltsjobaen. A few days later Klaus informed the German legation that a senior official of the Soviet foreign commissariat by the name of Alexandrov wished to speak to a gentleman he knew in the German foreign office. He was referring to Peter Kleist. Kleist came to Stockholm on 17 June 1943. The next day he was visited in his hotel by V-man Klaus, who informed him that Alexandrov wanted to meet him on 7th July.

When Hitler learned about this by way of the foreign office he at once forbade the meeting, which could have paved the way for a totally surprising turn in the course of the war. Soon afterward it turned out that the matter had not died in spite of Hitler's ban; agent RR 3117 from Lisbon, who was also employed in Stockholm, reported to the Hamburg Abwehr station that the Soviets were still interested in negotiating with the Germans. The Hamburg station advised Abwehr central that the Portuguese agent had overheard a report by the envoy in Stockholm to the foreign ministry in Lisbon. In it he spoke of rumors that a German-Russian peace was imminent.

At this point Baron Vladimir Kaulbars, a former cavalry captain in the Imperial Russian Army and a friend of the Canaris family who now and then served as an interpreter for the Abwehr and instructed the admiral in the Russian language, became involved in the affair. Baron Kaulbars had worked with the French and Soviet secret services before changing sides. He urged his friend Canaris to take up the matter, enter into secret negotiations with the Soviet envoy and help end the war.

However, since Roosevelt and Churchill had declared at Casablanca in January 1943 that they were demanding Germany's unconditional surrender, Admiral Canaris had been cultivating contacts in the west, not the east. Freiherr Kurt von Lernsner, for example, had met with the American naval attaché in Istanbul, Commander George E. Earle, a friend of Roosevelt's.

In this consultation Canaris offered a cease-fire in the west with a continuation of the war in the east "in the name of the powers standing behind him." Von Lernsner wanted to fly with Earle from Turkey to the USA. With him he would take promises of support from the pope, cardinal state secretary Maglione, the nuncio Roncalli and others. Roosevelt's answer to this proposal was curt and simple: "no." Earle was ordered to withdraw from the negotiations.

After extending a number of other similar feelers, in summer 1943 Canaris was able to invite the head of the US secret service, Donovan, and General Menzies from England to Santander. There the heads of the European secret services sat around a table and Canaris outlined his peace plan: cease-fire with the west, removal or handing over of Hitler, continuation of the war in the east. Abwehr officer Justus von Einem, who had accompanied Canaris to Santander, later stated that the three secret service chiefs were in agreement on the basis of Canaris' proposals.

However the leaders of the two allied nations did not want to hear anything about the story. Unconditional surrender to all the allies, including the Russians, was and remained an iron rule from which they could not deviate one iota. Admiral Canaris had chosen the wrong side for peace talks. Had he approached the Russian side he would have achieved his goal.

Wilhelm Canaris, who had often helped people in trouble, stepped in once again in late summer 1942. He was able to have 12 elderly Berlin Jews, whom he had earlier identified to the Gestapo as agents, transported out of the country, allegedly for service in the USA. When Canaris later became entangled in similar affairs, and when it became known that he had maintained secret contacts with the Vatican and others, the RSHA and the SO began spying on him and keeping him under surveillance, which ultimately led to his removal.

REFORMATION AND REORGANIZATION OF THE ABWEHR

In autumn 1941 the German offensive in the east, and especially in the central sector before Moscow, ground to a halt. All of the Brandenburg units deployed in the east suffered heavy casualties in several weeks of bitter defensive fighting. The bulk of the Brandenburg units had returned to their home bases to reorganize, rearm and take on replacement personnel.

By December 1941 the only units still at the front were the "Tropical Company" under Oblt. von Koehnen in Africa, the 9th Company under Oblt. Dr. Kniesche in the area northwest of Moscow, and the 6th Company under Oblt. Bansen in the Crimea. The commander of the Brandenburg Training Regiment, Oberst von Haehling, issued new guidelines for all the units that had come back to their home bases. These were first issued as individual orders, though it was planned to publish them in combined form after the reorganization and retraining was complete. Here is that document, so important to the subsequent employment of the Brandenburgers, which according to Oberst Haehling's reports to the Ausland/Abwehr was written by the latter:

Head of Abwehr II: Report No. 1509/42 Secret dated 26/6/1942
General Duties:

The mission of the 800th Special Purpose Construction Training Regiment Brandenburg is undercover military operations against targets of tactical, strategic or military-economic importance. These take place where other units of the fighting forces cannot as yet or no longer fight. In view of the significance of movement in modern war, the taking of transportation facilities, especially bridges, is of primary importance.

Units of the 800th Special Purpose Construction Training Regiment Brandenburg engaged in special operations shall use military stratagems of all kinds to deceive the enemy and seize from him objectives of military importance. Exploiting the success of these special operations tactically and strategically is the role of the command of the following forces.

Guidelines for operations:

(1) The units of the 800th Special Purpose Construction Training Regiment. Brandenburg are exclusively combat instruments of a war of movement. Their employment in the vanguards of motorized and armored units is therefore the rule. Their employment in rear guards can be appropriate and necessary in special cases.

(2) The units of the 800th Special Purpose Construction Training Regiment Brandenburg are to be withdrawn from the front with the advent of positional warfare. Lengthier periods of defensive fighting are to be used by units of the 800th Special Purpose Construction Training Regiment Brandenburg for accelerated testing of and conversion to new methods of fighting. Only in this way will the element of surprise be assured in the future against an 'alerted' enemy.

(3) Since its troops have been selected for special operations, specially trained, and are difficult to replace, the employment of the entire training regiment or its units in the infantry role is war-

ranted only in cases of extreme emergency and then only temporarily.

(4) The combat unit for special operations by the Brandenburg Training Regiment is the company. It is divided into two half-companies each capable of independent operation and one heavy platoon. The total strength of the company is 300 (!) men.

(5) The companies of the Brandenburg Training Regiment are put at the disposal of army groups or armies. Their use is determined by the focal point of combat and will change accordingly.

(6) Whenever possible a company of the training regiment is to be assigned to only one division. A division of the company between more than two divisions endangers its fighting strength and is to be categorically rejected.

(7) The strength and composition of the forces assigned to each combat mission depend on the situation and the objective.

(8) From the time companies of the Brandenburg Training Regiment enter the area of the armies, they are tactically and—insofar as the operation is concerned—disciplinarily subordinate to them. Otherwise responsibility for the welfare and care of personnel stays with the regiment even during the operation.

(9) Commitment of Brandenburger units happens exclusively and responsibly according to the directives of the fighting forces.

(10) As a rule, as part of each mission the Brandenburg Training Regiment will assign a liaison officer to the command responsible for that action. The liaison officer will inform the unit command responsible for the operation of the strength, organization and fighting style of the subordinated regiment units.

Since the Brandenburgers were required to operate together with army units, simultaneous with this order the regiment's weaponry and equipment as well as its weapons training, often involving new weapons, were brought in line with those of the army. In the course of this reorganization everything associated with missions for the Abwehr's Ausland II Department was eliminated. This included the Abwehr's training facility on the Quenz estate near Brandenburg, which fell under a new area of command.

The 1st Company based at Brandenburg, which to date had served as an assembly and operations base for V-men and special missions, was taken over by a V-Battalion, becoming A Company. Also in the V-Battalion was the company commanded by Oberleutnant Johannes, one of the original Brandenburgers.

The commander of I Battalion, Major Heinz, was tasked with the setting up of an Abwehr school and from December 1941 was placed in command of the V-Department. His successor as commander of I Battalion was Hauptmann Walther. Heinz left the battalion on 28th October after introducing the new CO.

Formation of the V-Battalion under Major Heinz was complete by 19th November. It moved into temporary quarters at the Meseritz troop training grounds, which was known as "Camp Earthworm." The Instruction and Training Company under Rittmeister Dr. Harbich based there was subordinated to the V-Battalion.

By the end of 1941 the reorganized 800th Special Purpose Construction Training Regiment Brandenburg was ready to return to action. Its order of battle was as follows:

Regiment Commander:	Oberst Haehling
I Battalion:	Hauptmann Walther
1st Company:	Oberleutnant Babuke
2nd Company:	Hauptmann Dr. Hartmann
	Oberleutnant Pinkert
3rd Company:	Oberleutnant (from 1942 Hptm.) John
4th (Light) Company:	Oberleutnant Kürschner
II Battalion:	Major Dr. Paul Jacobi
5th Company:	Oberleutnant Zülch
6th Company:	Oberleutnant Bansen (still in the Crimea)
7th Company:	Oberleutnant Kutschke (from 1942) Oberleutnant Oesterwitz
8th Company:	Oberleutnant Grabert
III Battalion:	Hauptmann Jacobi
9th Company:	Oberleutnant Kniesche (outside Moscow)
10th Company:	Leutnant Kriegsheim (wounded) Hauptmann Auch
11th Company:	Position still not filled
12th Company:	Oberleutnant Schader
15th (Light) Company:	Leutnant Trommsdorf

The latter was one of the last companies in action in the high north. The following is a brief outline of its activities.

THE TROMMSDORF COMPANY WITH HEADQUARTERS, LAPLAND ARMY

The idea of employing a special company originated from the then Leutnant Trommsdorf. With the agreement of Department II of the Ausland/Abwehr about ninety soldiers gathered at the Zossen troop training grounds; each was an expert in his field. Consequently this tiny unit included both expert combat engineers as well as, for example, dog handlers from the army dog school in Sperenberg, who had volunteered for a special mission in the far north. The soldiers were trained to use pistols, rifles, automatic weapons, and light artillery. Their number also included two fully trained radio teams and a first-aid section with a doctor and six medics. On account of the intended area of operations, the volunteers of course had to include first class skiers.

The "half company" was put together quickly then shipped into the northern area. Lt. Trommsdorf reported his unit ready for action to Generaloberst Dietl, who welcomed the group warmly, especially since there were several well-known skiers in its ranks.

In the course of a short briefing by the staff of the Lapland Army Trommsdorf learned that a new German offensive was planned for the spring. Dietl had assumed command of the newly formed Headquarters, Lapland Army on 14 January 1942 and was promoted to the rank of Generaloberst the same day. He and his chief-of-staff, Generalmajor Ferdinand Jodl (the younger brother of Alfred Jodl, head of the Wehrmacht Operations Staff) moved into their new headquarters in Rovaniemi, in the Hotel Pohjanhovi.

At the end of March 1942 the Russians had begun reconnaissance and offensive patrols there with the objective of preparing the planned advance by their southern forces north to the "Russian road." The Red Army's spring offensive was imminent.

This situation forced Trommsdorf's soldiers, who had been in the far north for some time, to curtail their training. The company had been bolstered through the addition of 30 Finnish volunteers. Dietl, who kept an eye on the company, saw that it acclimatized itself to the prevailing conditions quickly. At the end of March it was time. Operation "Lutto" could begin. Lutto was the name of a small river southwest of Murmansk near Alkawetti. The operation was led and seen through by Generalleutnant Ferdinand Schorner, commander of XIX Mountain Army Corps since 15 January 1942.

The role assigned the Brandenburgers in this attack, which was to begin on Easter Sunday, 6 April 1942, was to drive deep into the enemy rear and there to sever or at least disrupt the flow of supplies to the enemy through ambushes and harassment tactics. Its most important objective was to sever the route from the huge Russian depot near Ristikent southwest of Murmansk to the front.

The Trommsdorf Company went into action on 6th April. Although it had a Finnish guide, the heaviest snow for some time caused the company to miss the rendezvous point with the mountain battalion, which was supposed to take the Russian strongpoint in the village of Lutto. The mountain battalion also arrived late, however and it attacked the enemy without waiting for the night raids by the Trommsdorf company which were supposed to facilitate its advance. The attack, which took place in bright daylight, was a failure and casualties were heavy. The Trommsdorf company, which arrived soon afterward, did not go into action at first; it was alone in the terrain and with warmer temperatures melting the snow it had to fight its way back in stages. The men wandered all day through the deep snow of the forest and ate the last of their rations. Not until a patrol of mountain troops came upon them did they make their way back to their camp.

In mid-April Leutnant Trommsdorf was ordered back to Berlin. He was succeeded by Lt. Sölder.

At the beginning of May 1942 the Russians filtered through the German-Finnish lines in Carelia, northwest of Kiestinki; as a result the Brandenburgers of the Trommsdorf company were once again sent against special targets. They succeeded in sealing off several attempted breakouts by the Russians, halting the enemy with skillfully placed minefields and decimating them in night raids. One nocturnal raid led by Lt. Sölder recaptured a forward post being used by four Russian snipers. The action resulted in hand-to-hand fighting which ended in the Brandenburgers' favor, although casualties were heavy.

The company, now down to about 60 effectives, defended the newly won position against repeated Russian counterattacks and held it until June, when the Red Army suddenly ceased its attacks.

Pursuing the enemy to the north, German and Finnish troops reached the area far north of Kestenge. Soviet losses on the Murmansk Front alone, where it made 119 attacks in which 37 battalions of the Red Army took part, were 8,000 dead and 200 captured. As it later turned out, this was to be the Red Army's last major attack in the far north. Nevertheless the Lapland Army under Generaloberst Dietl had also suffered heavily. 680 German soldiers, including 16 officers, were killed. 2,630 men and 163 officers were wounded and 163 soldiers, including 3 officers, were reported missing.

The mission of the Brandenburgers in Finland and northwest Russia was over.

Ausland Abwehr II—Operations in Iraq

FIRST CONTACT

Germany extended the first feelers to Iraq in 1937. During that and the following year the German military attaché in Greece and Turkey, Oberstleutnant Rohde, undertook several extended journeys through Syria, Palestine, Iraq and Iran and even traveled on to Afghanistan. It was his objective to seek out all the facts that might be of interest to the Abwehr and gauge the mood of the nations he visited.

Following Rohde's report the head of the Ausland/Abwehr, Wilhelm Canaris, who had just been promoted to Vizeadmiral (on 1/4/193S), traveled to Baghdad accompanied by Major Groscurth to have talks with Arab leaders and sound out their readiness to fight against England.

From that point in time the Ausland/Abwehr set about forming an "Arab Brigade" which was created within the Brandenburg Regiment and which was prepared for its mission in the Near East—Lebanon, Syria and Iraq.

The initial objective was to support the independence movements in Afghanistan, Iran and Iraq and as well ensure deliveries of food and oil from those lands.

Beyond this, however, gaining a foothold in the above mentioned lands would bring Germany to the Russian border. Operating from bases there German aircraft could bomb the Soviet oil-producing sites of Batum and Baku. Later there would exist the possibility of launching a fast raid to seize the oil fields of the southern Caucasus and restore them to production for German use.

In the above-mentioned lands sympathy increasingly turned toward the German side. Should it come to open rebellion and war against England in these regions, it would endanger her long sought after land link between India and Egypt, now threatened by the arrival of the Africa Corps in North Africa, and would mean the potential isolation of the Arabian Peninsula and the equally threatening presence of German troops on the borders of Turkey, Vichy Syria and Iran. It was obvious to Great Britain that she would have to safeguard Iraq by invading. British hegemony in the "approach to India" had to be maintained.

The Ausland/Abwehr established further bases in the southeast in autumn 1940 and then in January 1941, including in Afghanistan. Oberstleutnant Rohde traveled to Afghanistan in September 1940 to gather relevant information for the Abwehr. Following his return he briefed Canaris on the initial proposals for drawing that country into the war against England.

But back to Iraq.

The Kingdom of Iraq was born after the First World War. The new kingdom, which belonged to the Ottoman Empire, resulted from the peace treaty of Sevres and was declared part of the British mandate. Abdallah, son of the Sherif of Mecca, Hussan Ibn Ali, was the British governor in Iraq, until finally at the Cairo Conference in March 1921 Faisal was proclaimed king of a new Iraqi monarchy. This was how the state was created that England tried to conquer in 1941. In spite of its admission to the League of Nations on 30 June 1930, this kingdom was nothing but a farce. Every minister and even the king received a British "advisor." England trained the Iraqi Army, maintained soldiers in Iraq and in the event of war Iraq had to serve Great Britain. When England demanded that Iraq follow her declaration of war on Germany, made on 3 September 1939, the Iraqi government refused to tow the British line.

In 1930 Yasin al Hashimi had founded a "patriotic brotherhood" against the England-sponsored ruling class governing Iraq. After his death in 1937 leadership of the organization passed to Rashid Ali al-Gailani, a lawyer. After King Faisal's death in April 1939 Abd al-Ilah took over the regency. Nuri Tes-Said had been prime minister since 1938.

After the first sounding-out visit by the Germans, in June and July 1940 the Arab Committee held talks with the Italian envoy Gabbrielli. The latter declared the objective of Italian policy to be: "Securing the independence of all lands of the Arabian east."

The Arab Committee dispatched Unman Hatted to Berlin. Following lengthy talks he received a "German declaration of sympathy for Arab nationalism."

In Iraq Ali-el-Gailani received an ultimate demand from the British "garrison" to "break off all contacts with the Axis powers." It did not go into why the British ambassador left Baghdad and why all of Iraq's assets in foreign banks were frozen. The thriving arms trade was put on ice and finally US President Roosevelt asked the government in Baghdad to step down.

Rashid Ali el-Gailani, prime minister since 1940, refused, and the regent could not force him to step down even if he wanted to. Regent Nuries-Said submitted his resignation on 21 January 1941. After several more gestures of ill will Iraq stood on the brink of civil war. Finally Gailani stepped down after all. His removal had a fateful effect on Iraq's international relations. Then Gailani was named to head a provisional government because the man holding the office, Taha, was no longer exercising his office and Nuri, the regent, had fled to the south.

So Gailani became Iraq's head of government again on 10 April 1941. On the night of 16th April the British government informed Iraq that it was going to occupy the country. England's war against Iraq officially began on 2nd May.

Meanwhile the German-Iraqi negotiations of 15 February 1941 had blossomed into a first action. The Abwehr had arranged weapons deliveries for the planned anti-British action by General Rashid Aliai-Gailani with envoy Grobba of the foreign office. The arms were to be delivered by transport aircraft flying a suitable route over Turkey with a stop on Rhodes, but also by submarine to Latakije in Syria. The military expert assigned to the operation was General der Flieger Felmy.

Starting on 11th May, half of the Brandenburgers' Arabian Brigade was dispatched to Iraq, where the Iraqis were offering resistance to the British forces. The Arabian Brigade began harassing raids and was able to destroy or capture two British gunboats and about 50 supply ships. At the same time preparations were made to block the Shatt el Arab waterway by sinking a German ship in the entrance, thus preventing British troops from being transported from India to Basra.

On 22nd May the Arabian Brigade was engaged in heavy fighting by the British

Arab Legion on the major caravan road from Damascus to Rutba.

On 25th May the Arabian Brigade achieved a major success when it completely wiped out a force of about 100 British, including 11 officers, in an ambush in the Tigris valley.

On 27th May Hauptmann Berger of the Abwehr, who led the Arabian Brigade, attempted to lure the British Arab Legion into a trap. The attempted ambush was unsuccessful.

On 30th May the leader of the Iraqi government, Rashid Ali al-Gailani, and the Grand Mufti of Jerusalem, who had been living in exile in Iraq for more than a year, were forced to flee Baghdad. They found asylum in Iran and from there they later made their way via Turkey to Germany. There, they and one of the Egyptian princes in their entourage were looked after by the Abwehr.

On the same day the Arabian Brigade was forced to withdraw into Iran before the British forces. Further missions were to wait for it there. On 31st May the cease-fire was signed with England in Baghdad.

But what measures were taken by Germany to assist Iraq?

LUFTWAFFE UNITS IN ACTION IN IRAQ

Already on 24 April 1941, in a discussion with Foreign Minister von Ribbentrop, Reichsmarschall Goring made a promise that five Ju 52s would deliver about 100 tons of material to Syria in 10 flights. Another 600 tons were to reach there by train via Turkey. Hitler gave his approval when, on 27th April, foreign minister von Ribbentrop showed him the first figures on Iraq's economic potential and the significance to England of the loss of that country. Germany now had to get the Vichy government to agree to release the French weapons stored in Syria and, most importantly, to obtain landing rights for German aircraft and aviation fuel for them in Syria. The former envoy in Baghdad, Fritz Grobba, was instructed to fly to Baghdad and establish close contacts with the Iraqi government. Subsequent events were determined by the outbreak of fighting in Iraq on 2 May 1941.

In a further deal France, in return for major German concessions, obligated herself to defend Syria "with all the forces at her disposal" in the event of a British attack on this French mandate.

Envoy Grobba, who had received orders to establish a political link to Iraq, was an expert in Near East affairs but he was in no position to assess the capabilities of the Iraqi armed forces. Nevertheless he enjoyed a high standing among the Arabs.

On 6th May the Grobba mission flew to via Foggia to Rhodes and from there on the 9th to Aleppo in two He IIIs of the "Führer Courier Squadron" piloted by Hptm. Leytheuser and Oblt. Grauthoff.

On 10th May the aircraft landed at Mossul. Grobba contacted the head of the Iraqi government and was told to come to Baghdad at once. Grobba and the other members of the mission—consular secretary Hornberger, interpreter Dr. Falkenstein, press attaché Steffen, radio operator Emde, the liaison officers Hptm. Darjes of the Luftwaffe operations staff and Hptm. Kohlhaas of the Abwehr II (Foreign), and two Palestinian-Germans, Feldwebel Wienand and Feldwebel Bulach of the Brandenburgers—reached the capital by car.   .

The second group from Germany, the foreign minister's delegation led by legation counselor Grenow and Obersturmführer Laux, von Ribbentrop's "house photographer," arrived in Baghdad aboard three Ju 52s. It also included two Brandenburgers, Uffz. Brass and Uffz. Krautzberger. These four Brandenburgers were under orders to destroy all oil facilities in the event of a German withdrawal. Several hundred kilos of high explosives had been placed on board the Ju 52s for that purpose.

Legation counselor Hans Ulrich Granow had American and British bank notes in his luggage. On 25th May 640 kilos of gold was also made available for the Iraqi national bank. Envoy Grobba was to deliver the gold to Iraq, which he did. When asked which Luftwaffe officer should lead the mission in Iraq, Göring's choice fell on Oberst Werner Junck, commander of the fighter element of Air Fleet 3 based at Deauville. Junck had experience in the tropics, having served as chief instructor of the German military mission in Bolivia under General Kundt in 1930.

On 6th May Junck met with Reichsmarschall Goring; he was briefed on the situation in Iraq and his mission by Generalleutnant Jeschonnek, Goring's chief-of-staff.

Named "Commander of Aviation Iraq", he was now in charge of the Junck special detachment. The transport element was commanded by Major Pinagel. At his disposal were three Ju 90s and ten Ju 52s. The detachment also included nine He III s and twelve Bf 110s The He IIIs, of 4/KG 4, were led by Hptm. Schwanhauser, while the Bf 110 Staffel, 4/ZG 76, was led by Oblt. Hobein.

A reconnaissance group was to precede the unit. This was led by Major Axel von Blomberg, son of Feldmarschall von Blomberg.

Oberst Junck flew to Munich on 11 May 1941. At the same time eight He III s took off from Silistea for Athens, where several Ju 52s and Ju 90s were standing by. Ten more Ju 52s under Hptm. Rother were in Kothen ready to depart.

The first six He IIIs arrived on Rhodes on 11th May. When Oberst Junck arrived in Athens on 12th May he found that the bomber squadron had already flown on. Two Ju 90s had meanwhile arrived at Damascus.

On 13th May the officers of the reconnaissance group under Oblt. Knemeycr with Leytheuser and Hptm. Schwanhauser assembled in Mossul. Oberst Junck arrived in Mossul via Rhodes and Palmyra. There he was met by the Iraqi air force liaison officer and the Mutasarrif of Mosul, as well as the commander of the 2nd Iraqi Division, a lieutenant-general, which indicates the importance the Iraqi leadership placed on the presence of the German air force.

OPERATIONS

After the fuel question was cleared up, on 15th May the German airmen flew their first mission in Iraq: a desert patrol over Syrian territory.

Oberst Junck was received by the Iraqi command in Baghdad, where he was welcomed by Rashid al-Gailani, head of the Iraqi armed forces General Salman, and the Iraqi chief-of-staff Zaki. There, Junck got his first first-hand look at the situation and quickly realized that the level of training of the Iraqi forces was very uneven.

On 16th May Oberst Junck ordered the first offensive missions. Three He IIIs attacked hangars and quarters of the British base at Habbaniya. In the process they shot down a Gloster Gladiator and bombed the entire facility; one He III was damaged and made a forced landing. The subsequent strafing attack by six Bf 11 Os was a significant success. As well as destroying additional hangars and a fuel dump another Gloster Gladiator was shot down in air combat.

Two heavy fighters carried out another attack on an airfield between Habbaniya and Falluja, where they destroyed a Hurricane on the ground and inflicted other damage. British aircraft attacked the Baghdad airfield in response. The Bf 110s that took off to intercept were involved in a turbulent dogfight and lost one of their number shot down. Another was forced to make an emergency landing. Already the lack of another squadron of He III s and especially a squadron of Bf 109s was making itself felt. But so soon before the invasion of Russia the Luftwaffe high command did not want to release any more aircraft to this secondary theater. This was a serious mistake, for at the end of May Iraqi resistance collapsed and with it all the other German plans.

At the same time the operation against Crete by paratroopers and air-landed troops had begun; no less than 151 Ju 52 transports were shot down there during the fighting which lasted from 20th to 30th May. Of these about 20 were supposed to have delivered weapons and supplies to Iraq. As a result of these unforeseen losses the Luftwaffe command had no aircraft available to fly supplies to Iraq.

Nevertheless the handful of He III crews continued to fly and fight. On 18th May four Bf 110s took off from Mossul to attack the British "Habforce" advancing through the Syrian Desert. The remaining four serviceable Bf 110s flew to Kirkuk, from where they would be in a better position to intercept British aircraft attacking the Baghdad area. On the evening of 18th May only one Bf 110 was serviceable. It flew reconnaissance and subsequently attacked advancing British forces.

Meanwhile three Italian Savoia Marchettis had arrived at Mossul. The Italian declaration that they would be followed by 60 (!) transport aircraft was not realized.

The 20th of May saw the climax of Luftwaffe operations in Iraq. One He III flew reconnaissance and three others, which were now serviceable again, attacked the Habbaniya airfield again, scoring hits on parked aircraft and hangars. Four Bf 110s strafed ground targets near Falluja; during the course of this mission they shot down a Blenheim and a Gladiator. Herbert Schlüter told the author: "If we had had an entire squadron of 18 to 20 machines, we would have been in a position to provide our ground forces with effective and perhaps decisive help and support."

The RAF responded by attacking the headquarters of the Iraqi air force at Hinaidi near Baghdad. During the raid a Bf 110 that had made an emergency landing there was destroyed.

On 20th and 21st May Oberst Junck dispatched two more Bf 110s to Kirkuk, leaving only two heavy fighters at Mossul.

On 21 May 1941 a decision was made in the Luftwaffe High Command and Führer Headquarters to create a military mission for the entire Middle East area and first send only training personnel but later a combat unit from the Abwehr's special Brandenburg unit in at least battalion strength to Syria. The soldiers were to be outfitted with tropical uniforms with Iraqi insignia and rank badges.

While legation counselor Rahn served as the Reich's political representative in Syria and Grobba in Iraq, General der Flieger Felmy was named chief of "Special Staff F". He was also a veteran of the Middle East, having served on the Sinai Front as an airman in World War One.

The Luftwaffe effort on 22nd May saw two He III s and five Bf 110s attack a large British truck convoy near Habbaniya, Subsequently two Bf 110s flew another attack against British motorized columns near Falluja, while two He IIIs with a Bf 110 escort attacked Habbaniya again, setting the power station on fire.

Two Bf 110s and a He 111 were lost on this day. The 23rd of May saw two Bf 110s fly two armed reconnaissance missions over the British base at Falluja. Two Gladiators rose to intercept and both were shot down. Two He Ills bombed Habbaniya again and a third flew reconnaissance. The last two He III s were made serviceable again. Meanwhile two Bf 110s again attacked Habbaniya, but both were lost. One made a forced landing while the second went missing. It later turned out that it had been shot down by Hurricanes.

4/ZG 76 had been completely wiped out. The surviving crews, who were at Kirkuk, had no aircraft. One of them was the young Lt. Wilhelm Herget, who would later win the Knight's Cross with Oak Leaves on 11 April 1944 as commander of the night fighter unit I/NJG 4.

On 26th May the British raided Baghdad and other targets while a single He III flew the last attack on Habbaniya. The Heinkel placed its bombs on target and returned safely. The British answered by sending five Vickers Wellingtons to Mossul, where they damaged one of the last He III bombers.

On 27th May Major Hansen of the OKH and Major Arnold of the Abwehr's Department II arrived. When Hansen told Oberst Junck that he could not expect army forces and replacements for his Luftwaffe units for three months, Junck suspected that these officers, whose number also included Hptm. Roser of the Abwehr Department I, already had plans to wind down the German effort. He nevertheless requested two heavy fighter groups and a squadron each of bombers, fighters and reconnaissance aircraft.

While the Abwehr officers discussed the planned destruction of all oil facilities in Iraq—pure fantasy for four members of the Brandenburgers against the strong British forces—on 28th May in Baghdad envoy Grobba declared that his group would be leaving Iraq in a few days.

The eleven Italian CR-42 fighters and one Savoia transport that landed at Mossul on 28th May were too late. Nevertheless they flew two missions from Kirkuk on 29th and 30th May before they left Iraq again on the 31st. Even while Oberst Junck was in Athens begging five more Bf 110s from Command Staff F, on 28th May envoy Grobba ordered everyone out of Baghdad. He did not even think it necessary to notify Oberst Junck or the German airmen still at Mossul.

At the same time as this hasty departure was taking place six more Ju 52s landed at Mossul with weapons, ammunition, and medical supplies. Major Hentschel had meanwhile had two He IIIs made flyable in order to send them out with the aircrew about noon. One of the two Ju 52s kept back followed at 2:00 P.M., while the flak crew, the staff and the signals platoon remained in Mossul until 4:00 P.M.

When Grobba arrived in Mossul on the morning of 30th May he found the base abandoned. This was the consequence of his omissions in regard to direct instructions for the personnel.

Even though Oberst Junck, who on 30th May was on Rhodes ready to depart for Iraq with three He IIIs and five Bf 110s in order to continue the fight, bore no responsibility for this disaster, he was relieved of his command and replaced by Major Schemel I. On 3rd June, however, this unfair measure was personally corrected by Reichsmarschall Goring. The German legation reached the Syrian border and safety during the night of 1st June.

THE SUMMING UP

The defeat of Iraq by Great Britain was also a heavy blow to the German command, not least because by August 1941 it resulted in the loss of Syria and Iran.

Nevertheless Special Staff F remained in existence and during the course of time received several well-equipped German intervention units that also included volunteer Arab troops. If stronger air forces had been sent to Syria and Iraq in spite of the imminent invasion of Russia, General Felmy and Oberst Junck would certainly have been able to master the situation.

At his own request Oberst Junck was called before the honor court of the Luftwaffe; there he stated that had he received another group of He III s, a further Bf 110 group and a well-equipped fighter squadron, he could have halted all movement by British forces in May. That this lay within the realm of possibility was shown by the effectiveness of the handful of He IIIs, which gave the British command in Iraq a very hard time.

Werner Junck was completely rehabilitated. The achievements of his handful of airmen were given their full due. However, this rehabilitation did nothing to change the fact that Junck did not receive the Knight's Cross until 9 June 1944, soon after he was named commanding general of II Fighter Corps.

While the German units escaped the country, Iraq's top military leaders, in particular all senior commanders and commanders in chief of the army and air forces, were court-martialed and for the most part sentenced to death on the gallows.

FURTHER OPERATIONS IN IRAQ

From 9 June to 3 July 1941 the Ausland/Abwehr II's "Arab Brigade" withdrew from Iraq to Syria to continue the fight against British troops there. However this was not the end of German activities in Iraq.

On behalf of Major Schulze-Holthus of Abwehr II, in Iran the German geologist Friedrich Kümmel went to the Paitag Pass on the Iraqi border in order to investigate the possibility of getting through on the road to Baghdad. As well he was instructed to make his way through the pass and Iraq to Ankara, Turkey, where he was to contact the Near East War organization based there. Friedrich Kümmel was caught by Kurds and was handed over to the British for a few pounds of tea and sugar. The unlucky German was sentenced to be shot for spying.

On 15 July 1941 Hitler met with Prime Minister Rashid al-Gailani who had escaped from Iraq. The latter declared his willingness to serve as an announcer in broadcasts to the Near East of anti-British propaganda.

In the autumn of 1941 a plan was worked out by the Abwehr II to seize the British oil fields in Iran and Iraq. A condition for this operation was the conquest of the Caucasus region and the passage of German troops through this mountainous land to Baku and Grozny.

During that same autumn all the heads responsible for the Near and Middle East gathered at Abwehr headquarters in Berlin. Present on the

German side were Admiral Canaris, General Felmy and Erwin Edler van Lahousen-Vivremont. The latter had come to the Ausland/Abwehr as an Oberstleutnant and Austrian intelligence specialist; he advanced very quickly and soon attained the rank of Generalmajor. Representing Italy were General Cesare Arne and the commander of the Italian Arab Legion, Colonel Ivrea. But the man at the center of attention was the Grand Mufti of Jerusalem, Amin al-Husseini. All those present agreed to establish a center in North Africa for all areas of anti-British subversion.

On 15th September Admiral Canaris and General Felmy met in Rome with Rashid al-Gailani and Amin al-Husseini to discuss the union of the German-Arab Instruction Battalion with the Arabian Freedom Corps. The anti-British coalition suffered a setback in October when one of the agents still operating there, Hamudi Janabi, was arrested.

It was the Grand Mufti of Jerusalem, Amin al-Husseini, who was to give the Ausland/Abwehr early warning of the imminent landing by Anglo-American forces in Northwest Africa at the beginning of November.

In November 1944 the Ausland/Abwehr decided to drop five men into Iraq. One of the men was an Iraqi general staff officer, who was to rejoin his troops in Iraq. They were acting on the orders of Amin al-Husseini, the declared enemy of England whom was under Hitler's special protection. In addition to a considerable arsenal of weapons, ammunition and explosives, the five agents carried with them money, jewelry and various gifts.

At 4:29 on the afternoon of 27 November 1944 a Ju 290 of I/KG 200, a unit that specialized in unconventional missions, took off from the Wiener-Neustadt airfield to fly to Mossul. On board was the pilot—group commander Hptm. Braun—the crew and the five men who were to parachute into Iraq. Led by Lieutenant-Colonel Ali al-Rashid, they were made as comfortable as possible in the cargo hold of the huge machine. By 4:29 P.M. it was already pitch dark. Navigation was a difficult task as their destination lay about 3,000 kilometers to the east. Once his own radio beacons and transmitters lay behind him, the navigator had to depend on dead-reckoning navigation, which was complicated by the fact that they must not fly over the Black Sea or Turkey. Hauptmann Braun had strict instructions to fly over Hungary, Yugoslavia and Greece.

After reaching the optimum cruising height of 3,000 meters, Hptm. Braun trimmed the aircraft for level flight. The aircraft's speed increased and he retarded the throttles of the four engines to achieve the most economical cruising speed.

The huge aircraft flew toward its destination at 300 kilometers per hour. From here everything would depend on Braun's skill as a navigator.

They must reach Mossul and then fly a little farther until they arrived at one of the airfields still in German hands where they could land and refuel. One possibility was the island of Rhodes. Another Ju 290 would fly the necessary fuel there.

The moon rose as the aircraft was crossing the border between Bulgaria and Greece, providing another reference point. Mossul was still six hours away.

An hour and a half later Rhodes came into sight. An hour after that the Ju 290 began to descend and everyone breathed a sigh of relief when the Tigris was found. In spite of the darkness, from a height of 500 meters the crew spotted the railway line they were searching for.

"Three-hundred meters, Herr Hauptmann," called out copilot Leutnant Pohl. "Open the port hatches."

The five Iraqis stood ready, the jumpmaster with them. When he heard the command to get ready he put his hand on the shoulder of the Lieutenant-colonel. The next command was the one to jump, and he pressed hard on the Lieutenant-colonel's shoulder and gave him a slight nudge. The jumpers left the aircraft; after them went the cargo containers and their parachutes.

The jumpmaster reported everyone out and Hptm. Braun pulled the aircraft into a climbing left turn. The engines strained at climb power and after turning through 180 degrees the aircraft steadied on to a westerly heading.

The dashboard clock showed 5:10 A.M. when the aircraft arrived at Rhodes four hours later. It over flew the island at low level and Braun spotted green signal flares rising from the ground. That was the airfield. He turned, approached the airfield in a wide arc, sighted the runway and turned on to final. At 5:20 P.M. Braun set the machine down smoothly and taxied in. Thirteen hours had passed since takeoff from Wiener-Neustadt. It was a masterful accomplishment, but one which drew little attention, for such missions had become routine for KG 200.

The second Ju 290 was waiting. Braun's aircraft was refueled while the crew sat down to a hearty breakfast in the officers mess.

The next evening Hptm. Braun took off when the moon rose, but a mechanical problem forced him to land again after a few minutes. A second attempt was made but the problem reappeared. Meanwhile the supply aircraft, which had taken off behind Braun, had already disappeared to the northwest. Once home, its crew would report that Braun had taken off then disappeared. Contact with base was impossible.

After an intensive search for the problem Lt. Pohl, an engineer in civilian life, not only located the problem, but removed, cleaned and reinstalled all elements of the hydraulic system. The aircraft was now completely serviceable.

On the third night they took off again. A few minutes after takeoff one of the Brandenburgers smelled something burning. All the electrical systems failed except for the radio altimeter, but the aircraft was flyable and when Lt. Pohl succeeded in getting the compass working again it was decided to continue the flight. When they passed the first Alpine peaks in the moonlight Braun initiated descent. Lt. Pohl called out the readings: height, speed, etc. They broke through the clouds and Lt. Pohl saw a flat, snow-covered plain before them. They had made it.

They approached Wiener-Neustadt from the east. Their recognition signal was answered by the base flak. Braun hauled the machine around and then crept toward the airfield at treetop height. He over flew the airfield perimeter and then cautiously set the heavy machine down on the snow at the edge of the field. It rolled out and finally came to a stop without having hit anything or rolled into a ditch.

Something should be said of the nature of this group and all of KG 200, which was commanded by Oberstleutnant (later Oberst) Baumbach and which operated under the orders of Air Fleet 6 led by Generaloberst Ritter von Greim.

The Geschwader was formed on 20 February 1944. Nine days later the Geschwader and Gruppe headquarters and I/KG 200 reported ready to commence operations. The three squadrons of I/KG 200 had been formed from the Commander-in-Chief of the Luftwaffe's test unit, Transport Column XI "East", and the remnants of the 5th Long-Range Reconnaissance Group. The latter unit had been based on the Atlantic coast with its Ju 290 long-range reconnaissance aircraft.

I Gruppe was commanded by Major Karl-Edmund Gartenfeld, who had received the Knight's Cross while serving as a squadron leader in the Luftwaffe Commander-in-Chiefs Strategic Reconnaissance Group (No.5). Then from April 1944 until the end of the war it was led by Major Koch. The unit was equipped with aircraft of every type, from training aircraft to long-range bombers, from cargo gliders to tactical reconnaissance aircraft. Because the nature of the missions flown by the unit almost always required it to operate for long periods over enemy territory, it also used Italian, French, British and American types including the B-17 and B-24.

In mid-November 1944 III/KG 66 was incorporated into KG 200 as its II Group, while the former II Group was re-designated III Group. The Geschwader's IV Group was formed in November 1944; the new unit was responsible for general training and for providing new airmen joining the Geschwader with additional and specialized training. All the unit's aircraft were prepared for their special roles at the Finow airfield near Berlin. On account of its special status the Geschwader had at its disposal specialized technicians who installed new equipment and converted aircraft for their new roles. Also stationed there were the parachute and cargo-drop specialists.

In October the Geschwader's first commander, Oberst Heigl, was called away from the unit; his successor was Werner Baumbach, who was to hold this position until the end of the war even though he was summoned to Fiihrer Headquarters for a special mission just before the end of the war. Baumbach was placed in command of anti-bridge operations.

On 17 April 1945 I/KG 200 was placed at the disposal of the Reich Chief Security Office. II Group at Burg bei Magdeburg and III Group at Blankensee were subordinated to Air Fleet Reich, while Operational Detachment 200 at Parchim was assigned to a battle group commanded by Oberst Helbig. Because of the subordination of I Group to the RSHA, after the war there were rumors that the "Secret Geschwader 200" had flown leading Nazis out of Germany, mainly to Spain and South America, and that one or another machine had disappeared without a trace.

All this fell into the realm of fables and fairy tales. The Geschwader was disbanded shortly before the end of the war and its various parts were committed in widely scattered locales. The victor's hunt for Hitler's "espionage Geschwader" came to naught because there was no such unit. True, orders had been issued to make ready to fly senior political leaders to Barcelona, but this flight, too, was canceled by the Luftwaffe high command; as a result the pilot tasked with the flight, Hauptmann Braun, was able to fly 70 of his comrades back to Germany with him from Horsching near Linz in his Ju 290, coded PJ + PS.

Hauptmann Braun and his crew were arrested there by the Americans and had to spend several weeks delivering a variety of German and foreign aircraft that the Americans wanted to take to the USA from departure bases in southwest France.

At Orly near Paris this experienced and capable long-distance flyer trained an American crew to fly the Ju 290. He was thus the last active officer and pilot of the German wartime air force.

BATTLES IN IRAQ

To what has been said about the fight for freedom in Iraq there remains to be added that on 3 November 1939 Oberst Oskar Ritter van Niedermeyer passed a study entitled "Policy and Warfare in the Near East" to the

Wehrmacht High Command via the Abwehr. With it he put into motion a development that within a few months was to expand into the previously-described uprising in Iraq.

In his study Niedermeyer proposed employing agents in the Near and Mid East with the objective of exploiting the Arab freedom movements. However—as already related—it was to be the end of 1940 before the Abwehr II could begin forming an Arabian Brigade and using it in Lebanon, Syria and Iraq.

The Secret Near East War Organization was set up in Ankara. It concentrated on organizing espionage, sabotage and diversion in all the lands of East and North Africa. General der Flieger Felmy was chosen as military expert and leader of the organization. The question of what assistance was needed for Iraq was discussed in the Foreign Office with Oberst Brinkmann of Abwehr II. On 28th April came a declaration of sympathy for the Iraqi nationalists. But this was just the beginning.

On 11th May half of the Brandenburgers' Arab Brigade was slipped into Iraq, where it saw action with the goal of interfering with the British buildup.

On 23 May 1941 Fuhrer Headquarters issued Fuhrer Directive No. 30, which stated in part:

1. The Arab freedom movement is our natural ally against England in the Middle East. In this context the uprising in Iraq is of special significance. This strengthens the forces hostile to England in the Middle East beyond the Iraqi frontier, disrupts English communications, and ties up English troops and shipping at the expense of other theaters.

   I have therefore decided to hasten developments in the Middle East by supporting Iraq. Whether and how it may be possible, in conjunction with an offensive against the Suez Canal, finally to break the British position between the Mediterranean and the Persian Gulf is a question that will be decided only after 'Barbarossa.'

2. In connection with my decision I order the following for the support of Iraq: (a) Support by the air force. (b) Dispatch of a military mission. (c) Arms deliveries.

3. The military mission (cover name—'Special Staff F') will be under the command of General der Flieger Felmy. Its tasks are: (a) To advise and support the Iraqi armed forces. (b) Where possible, to establish military contacts with forces hostile to England outside Iraq. (c) To obtain experience and intelligence in this area for the German armed forces. The

composition of this organization will be regulated, in accordance with these duties, by the Chief of the High Command of the Armed Forces. Chain of command will be as follows: (a) All armed forces personnel sent to Iraq, including the liaison staff in Syria, will be under the command of the head of the military mission with the proviso that orders and guidelines for the aviation units will come exclusively from the High Command of the Air Force. (b) The head of the military mission will be subordinate to the Chief of the High Command of the Armed Forces, with the proviso that orders and guidelines for the aviation units will come exclusively from the High Command of the Air Force. (c) The members of the military mission are, for the time being, to be regarded as volunteers (in the manner of the Condor Legion). They will wear tropical uniforms with Iraqi badges. Also, Iraqi markings will be worn by German aircraft.

4. The Air Force: The employment of the air force in limited numbers is intended, apart from its direct effects, to increase the self-confidence and fighting spirit of the Iraqi armed forces and people.

5. Arms Deliveries: The Chief of the High Command of the Armed Forces will issue the necessary orders in this respect. (Deliveries to be made from Syria, in accordance with the agreement reached with the French in this matter, and from Germany.)

6. The direction of propaganda in the Middle East is the responsibility of the Foreign Office, which will cooperate with the High Command of the Armed Forces, Operations Staff—Propaganda Section. The basic idea of our propaganda is: 'The victory of the Axis will free the countries of the Middle East from the English yoke, and will give them the right to self-determination. All who love freedom will therefore join the fight against England. No propaganda is to be carried out against the French in Syria.

7. Should members of the Italian Armed Forces be employed on duties in Iraq, German personnel will cooperate with them on the lines laid down in this directive. Efforts will be made to ensure that they come under the command of the Head of the German Military Mission.

The Supreme Commander of the Armed Forces
signed: ADOLF HITLER

There was a special reason for Syria's removal from the machinery of propaganda. There were approximately 150,000 French troops under General Weygand based there, apparently loyal to the Vichy regime.

OPERATIONS IN MESOPOTAMIA

After the English-supported government of Hashemite Prince Abdul Illah, acting regent for King Faisal II, then just six years old, was brought down by General Gailani's secret organization "The Golden Rectangle", Germany immediately recognized the new government and established diplomatic relations with it. England thus faced the loss of the country and the port city of Basra on the Persian Gulf. Consequently English troops entered Iraq by way of Basra on 2 May 1941.

It seemed clear that the Iraqi Army, poorly equipped with out of date weapons, could offer no serious resistance to England's well-trained, expertly drilled troops. In view of the tremendous distances involved, rapid and effective German support was not possible. For 30 days the English forces advanced rapidly. The English forces were joined by Australian, South African and Free French volunteers and regular troops.

How this campaign was fought and what part the Brandenburgers played in it will be described in the following chapter.

In preparation for the deployment of the Brandenburgers to Iraq the chosen leader of the unit and Chief of the German Military Mission in Iraq, Major van Blomberg, departed by air with his operations staff for Baghdad.

As the aircraft approached Baghdad and flew low over the desert, armed Bedouins were sighted below riding in the direction of the Iraqi capital to join the fight against the hated English at the side of their General Rashid Ali el Gailani. On Blomberg's order the pilot throttled back and went lower. Below them thousands of Bedouins were riding toward Baghdad. Then suddenly some of them pointed their guns upward and opened fire, suspecting an English aircraft. The passengers waved to the Arabs and as the aircraft had not been hit assumed that this was some sort of welcoming salute.

Then the aircraft approached the Baghdad airfield and landed safely. Only then, when Major van Blomberg's party urged him to leave the aircraft, was it discovered that he was dead. He collapsed suddenly and fell back in his seat.

A reconstruction of the events surrounding his death revealed that one of the bullets fired at the aircraft by the Arabs had pierced the window against which the major had pressed his face for a better view. Because of the noise being made by the others and a running fan, the breaking of the window had not been heard. The fan also prevented the draught from being heard.

The German Military Commission had lost its leader. At the same time scouts reported that Indian troops under British command were on their way from Basra to Baghdad, though still 800 kilometers away.

The Grand Mufti of Jerusalem now unleashed a feverish activity. So far he had lured fickle sheiks and princes with money provided by the Abwehr and the Foreign Office. But now he bought weapons wherever he could find them. His trusted agents in Beirut sent whatever they could lay their hands on. This in turn attracted the attentions of the Secret Service, which had the arms dealers under surveillance.

The British Middle East High Command immediately ordered the part of the British commandos under Colonel Stirling, which was then on the Sudan border, to Iraq. While Stirling flew to Cairo to get his orders from the High Command, his Long Range Desert Group was already on its way to Lebanon. This formation was the British equivalent of the 800th Special Purpose Construction Training Regiment Brandenburg.

Before the commando got to Baghdad the Iraqi government confiscated all aircraft there, whether military or commercial airliners. Among them were several belonging to Pan American Airlines. These machines were used to transport weapons purchased in Beirut to Baghdad and were flown by military pilots.

Within 24 hours there were sufficient weapons in Baghdad to arm 2,000 Arab volunteers, who were to be employed under German command. Altogether the German military mission that was hastily ordered to Iraq had 25,000 volunteers under its disposal for the fight against England. They had streamed in from every country in the Near and Middle East, from Iran and Jordan, from Egypt, Lebanon and Syria, from Saudi Arabia, Yemen and Hadramaut.

The German officers selected only those men trained in the use of weapons and armed them. Approximately 300 officers of the Iraqi, Egyptian, Jordanian and Syrian armed forces formed the core of the "Arab Brigade." They formed infantry companies as quickly as possible. Special groups were directly trained by the Brandenburgers. These men were of various nationalities, but they had a common faith, Islam, and a hate, that of England.

The formation of this Arab Legion, which was begun by Oberst von Lahousen-Vivremont and Major Meyer-Ricks, was completed immediately after the formation of Special Staff F. The Arab Legion was placed under the command of General Felmy. Half of the brigade, commanded by Brandenburg Lieutenants Brecht and Dreesen, remained in the Kut-Hilleh area. It was under orders to guard the rail line from Basra. Under Abwehr Hauptmann Berger, the second half marched and tried to sever the supply lines to the British troops approaching from Basra.

At the same time a special detachment of Brandenburgers was dispatched to Shat el Arab to sink German and Italian ships lying there and thus prevent British troop transports from India from reaching Basra via Shat el Arab. At that time the British troops were marching from the confluence of the Euphrates and the Tigris directly toward Baghdad. When they reached the Urku lake region they were able to sever the rail line running to Kut.

So as to be independent of roads and rail lines, British supplies were sent north by ship. Altogether 50 of these ships—which were limited to 100 tons, anything larger would have been unsuitable for river use on account of their deeper draught—were sent up the Tigris in convoy.

When this fleet reached a critical point and during the night of 11th May tied up on the river bank, the English command had half dock on the right side, the other half on the left. The ships lay in so-called packets, side by side. Running boards joined the first to the second and so on and several of these packets lay one behind the other. The two escort vessels, British gunboats, anchored in the middle of the river so that they could fire to both sides in the event of an alert. So as to be prepared for any eventuality, the British also had the core of their Arab Legion establish bridgeheads on both sides of the landing site.

After darkness fell, the Arab Brigade under the command of Hptm. Berger used the plentiful river reed beds to fashion floating islands beneath which they could drift toward the ships unseen. They approached the two gunboats anchored in midstream, went on board, overpowered the sentries and secured the passageways. Then, almost silently, they took prisoner the crews of both gunboats.

Afterwards the Iraqi volunteers, led by the Brandenburgers, swam over to the supply vessels to quietly take them as well; but then submachine-gun fire ripped the night from the bridgehead on the right side of the river. Hand grenades exploded.

A wakened by the shooting, the crews of the ships tried to get on deck, but the Brandenburgers had already secured the gangways and the rudely-awakened British found themselves staring into the muzzles of automatic weapons.

Meanwhile the battle sounds in the two bridgeheads had become a terrific din. More troops joined the fighting. After the ships' crews had been disarmed and locked up, Hauptmann Berger sent the men from the ships into the nearest bridgehead. The rattle of machine-guns and the crash of hand grenades rose to an ear-splitting din. The darkness was pierced by flashes of flame. The British and Indian troops gave up and Hauptmann Berger put volunteers in enemy uniforms on the ships. The convoy resumed its river journey as if nothing had happened.

Toward noon British aircraft appeared overhead. They announced their friendly intentions by waggling their wings. They were obviously unaware of the daring seizure of the ships by the Germans and their Arab allies. The Arabs disguised as English and Indian sailors waved their caps in the air.

That evening the second part of the Arab Brigade, which had taken over the ships and armed itself with the weapons of the English and Indian crews, reached a deep bay on the west side of the river only a few kilometers from the north shore of Lake Schiban. The war materiel that was on the ships was hurriedly removed and taken to the lake. Waiting there were Arabs, who transported it by camel and wagon to the rail line not far away. The British prisoners were taken away by the same route.

The first British reconnaissance aircraft appeared over the unloading site at dawn on 12th May. Hptm. Berger urged his men to hurry up and unload the last transport ship; later he and his staff and a small, armed force were the last to leave the bay.

They had not gone far when a squadron of British bombers appeared on the scene and bombed all the ships, including the two captured gunboats. There was no return fire. Whether or not there were still prisoners in the ships was apparently of little concern. The British river supply system had thus been broken for there were no more suitable vessels available.

Hauptmann Berger began a forced march to the west. Several hours later he linked up with the first elements of the brigade. From there he sent a radio message. It read: "XB 3 to XB 4: Am with entire brigade about 20 km west of Uruk by the rail line to Kut, north of Lake Schiban. We are expecting a massive British air attack in the coming hours. Captured war materiel from the English supply fleet is in our hands. Urgently request orders." The answer from Baghdad read: "The air force's first and second squadrons transferred to Kut. Technical personnel on the way from Kut to the designated brigade camp. Readiness in 30 minutes."

But there was no British air attack on the Arab Brigade. They were apparently satisfied with the destruction of their own war materiel and the ships. General Wilson, the senior commander in the Middle East, was later relieved of his command for not bombing the Arab Brigade.

This omission gave the Arab Brigade the chance to reorganize and reequip itself. All surplus weapons were sent back to Baghdad, for thousands of freedom fighters were waiting there for arms prior to joining the brigade. In the coming days the weapons did not have to be transported any closer to Baghdad, for when news of the great victory reached the Iraqi capital a huge column of volunteers headed for Lake Schiban and the camp of the Arab Brigade.

It was estimated that 30,000 men had gathered there by the early morning of 15th May. At about 10:00 A.M. there arrived from Kut a large automobile column bearing the Grand Mufti of Jerusalem, who had come to inspect the volunteers and bless them for the holy war. There was a mood of jubilation and confidence in victory.

Dressed in his familiar long black coat, a white turban on his head, the Grand Mufti congratulated the German liaison officer on this victory. Then he turned to the victors of Susa and the other volunteers and called upon them to wage "holy war" against Great Britain. Then he reviewed an assembled honor guard.

Early on 16th May this hastily formed and extremely undisciplined army marched through the Tigris Valley, initially unopposed. The absence of the British bombers was due to the Iraqi Army's attack on the British base at Habbaniya, about 100 km south of Baghdad. Another factor in their absence was the activities of the German fighter squadron, which shot down a number of British aircraft.

When the brigade's vanguard, a battalion commanded by Leutnant Dreesen, sighted a force of British troops approaching along a side valley of the Tigris, Dreesen immediately had his men spread out and position themselves at the mouth of the valley. He posted the two captured machine-guns in front of and behind the planned encirclement point. The enemy came into view. There were eight British officers and about 90 Gurkha soldiers.

They marched through the side valley directly toward the road, apparently with the intention of halting the Arab Brigade and holding it there until reinforcements arrived to take it in a pincer movement and wipe it out. When the Gurkha command group, led by a tall British captain, arrived at the exit point only 150 meters from the forward machine-gun, the weapon opened fire. The march stopped and the Gurkhas fell back under machine-gun and rifle fire.

Within half a minute the firing rose to a wild crescendo. One group of about 30 Gurkhas led by a lieutenant took advantage of a jam in the front machine-gun to get within thirty meters of it, but then they were met by hand grenades. They lobbed their own grenades and took out the machine-gun nest before the last of them ceased fire.

This ambush in the Tigris Valley ended in a duel between snipers. None of the approximately 100 British soldiers were left alive. For this action Leutnant Dreesen was awarded the Iron Cross, First Class. He had not only stopped, but had literally wiped out the enemy.

Under the command of Leutnant Brecht the rear guard succeeded in breaking through and splitting up the British march column, which was several kilometers long. The Leutnant isolated one part of the column and by attacking repeatedly prevented the British troops from continuing their advance. When dusk fell Brecht and his men moved out of the desert, broke into the enemy ranks, raked them with fire, and then withdrew into the desert again. Pursuing English patrols were intercepted and wiped out in fierce night combats in which neither side gave any quarter.

On 17th May the officers of the German military mission met with the officers of the Iraqi general staff. Both agreed that the enemy would now withdraw as quickly as possible.

This was to prove to be a fundamental error. True, a smaller group of forces had withdrawn at a high tempo toward the confluence of the Tigris and the Euphrates, but the main body had a completely different direction. The English not only moved into the lake region and through the Tigris Valley in the direction of Baghdad, but also sent the main body of their Arab Legion under its leader Glubb Pasha down the big caravan route toward Rutba and Damascus. By the evening of 15th May this legion force had reached the area 100 kilometers east of Rutba.

They, too, were harried by the Bedouins of this open country by night. The sniper war cost the British a number of casualties; as well the physical exertions bordered on the unbearable.

The Iraqi garrisons along the way should have been in a position to repeatedly stop this main English battle group and engage it in costly fighting. Instead, however, they allowed themselves to be overrun without a fight. Aided by the British, a number of the senior officers were already plotting against their own head of state.

But lurking behind the sand dunes along the caravan route were the Bedouins, who waged their own small-scale war of ambush against the British. They poisoned the wells from which the British had to get their water. In the end it was so short of water that transport aircraft had to fly in containers of water for the Arab Legion.

Behind the British force the Bedouins closed the caravan trail; Glubb Pasha's Arab Legion was thus on its own. Nevertheless, the British commander continued to march. The German-Iraqi-led brigade had departed its big camp on Lake Schiban on 15th May. Traveling by rail, it reached Ramadi. There was no resistance, even though the line passed close to the hotly contested British base at Habbaniya.

The rail line ended 10 kilometers from Ramadi. Trucks had been ordered there to enhance the brigade's mobility. First, however, it was driven to Ramadi, the brigade's forward directing center. There it picked up additional volunteers from Baghdad. From Ramadi the brigade set off down the major Rutba-Damascus caravan route, along which the Arab Legion was approaching.

On 21st May, after a 48-hour march through the desert in the burning heat, the Arab Brigade reached the Salah oasis. It was here that the decisive battle was to be fought. Motorized patrols reported that the enemy was still two day's march away.

THE DECISIVE BATTLE

In spite of a murderous sandstorm that claimed several lives, Lt. Brecht and Lt. Murat had marched straight through the desert and reached the Salah oasis. Only 8,000 of the 10,000 volunteers made it to the oasis, however. The rest were somewhere behind in the trackless, burning desert. Their comrades took no notice. They were engaged in a great holy war, proclaimed by no one less than the Grand Mufti of Jerusalem. If they fell they would go at once to paradise, where they would be entertained and celebrated by beautiful women.

The first skirmishes between leading elements took place on 22 May 1941. The Arab Brigade dispersed and began encircling the still advancing Arab Legion under Glubb Pasha. However this did little to impede the latter. He had his special forces crack the encircling ring and continued to march toward Baghdad. From then on his march tempo was significantly slower, however, as both flanks of his legion were harried by night ambushes.

Special elements of the German-led brigade infiltrated the rear guard of the British force. It was the start of a dirty little war that cost both sides heavy losses. As a result the British march tempo, which had been 65 kilometers per day, fell to just 30.

"Deserters" made their way to Glubb Pasha's force. The men who undertook this hazardous mission were in fact Brandenburgers who spoke perfect Arabic and who came from the Near or Middle East, as well as a number of Iraqi volunteers. They told Glubb Pasha that the Arab Brigade, backed up by Iraqi troops, had established a strong defense line with tanks and heavy guns west of the Salah oasis and that only heavy weapons and air support could break it.

Glubb Pasha called a rest stop and requested air reconnaissance from his superiors. This took an entire day, which was put to use by Hauptmann Berger and his 8,000 men at Salah. They built dummy positions and thus stopped Glubb Pasha's advance. It was two days before patrols revealed that the position did not really exist and that it consisted merely of mock-ups and a few soldiers.

Glubb Pasha ordered his force to attack. Led by armored cars and troop carriers, it smashed through the weakly manned position at once.

The large British force now marched about 50 kilometers parallel to the main road to Baghdad. Since Glubb Pasha did not report this unauthorized move for fear of being recalled, the transport aircraft dropped the legion's supplies over the old route, as a result of which they fell into the hands of the Arab Brigade. A battle group under Leutnant Murat camped at the former British campsite and collected the supply containers.

Meanwhile the main body of troops under Hptm. Berger hurried back approximately 50 kilometers and set up a strong blocking position south of Salah. If Glubb Pasha kept to his march-route, he must run into this position where 8,000 fighters were waiting for him. The remaining units, which were following Glubb Pasha's Arab Legion, received orders by radio to stay close on the enemy's heels and "to harass him until, without water, he collapses totally exhausted."

For hundreds of the British Arab Legion it became a death march.

Exhausted and thirsty, they lay at the side of the march-route and begged for water.

It was thanks to Leutnant Brecht that they did not simply die of thirst. The pursuing German-led group gave the abandoned men water and often had to protect them against Bedouins attacking from the desert in search of booty. This was not always successful, however, and the dead littered both sides of the advance route. Not until Glubb Pasha had lost fifty percent of his force on this forced march did he report his last position to the high command of Middle East forces and request immediate assistance.

The German plan to lure Glubb Pasha's troops into an ambush was negated, for the British command ordered him to halt in order to ensure that help reached him. The halt came just ten kilometers from the prepared German ambush position. Glubb Pasha had saved himself and his command.

The situation in the desert had turned into a standoff; but that did not bother the British, for on 20 May 1941 a group of their bombers took off from Basra to attack Iraqi cities. As well, the British troops advancing up the Tigris Valley arrived in Baghdad the same day. While they were stopped at the outskirts of the city and in the suburbs, the Iraqi command under Rashid Ali el Gailani and the Grand Mufti of Jerusalem collected everything of value and fled the city to the northeast with their intimates.

Surrounded by a fiercely loyal bodyguard, they drove toward the border with Iran. From there they made it to Turkey, which will be dealt with in more detail in the following chapter.

The reign of General Gailani and his German-supported government in Iraq had lasted less than a month.

Following the English into Baghdad was the Prince Regent Abdul Illah, who immediately formed a new government and promised his foe General Gailani a "fight to the finish." The politicians left behind in Baghdad signed a cease-fire with Great Britain on 31 May 1941. For all practical purposes the war in Iraq was over. But the German-led Arab Brigade was still under arms. The new Iraqi government under Nuri es-Said Pasha demanded that it lay down its arms to the Arab Legion, its former opponent. The men of the brigade were promised a full pardon if they complied. The German military mission also fled to Mossul by air on 30th May. From there it radioed instructions for the German command and troops of the brigade to withdraw immediately.

The German soldiers and the remaining Iraqi and other volunteers followed the order and withdrew to the Iraq-Syria border, which was crossed on 9th June. There they fought at the side of those Arabs who were waging a bitter struggle in Syria against the British, who had taken the cities of Sur in Lebanon and Dera in Syria.

The Brandenburgers and their friends fought on until 3rd July. Then, with the surrender of Syria, the fighting there also came to an end.

✠

At the beginning of August Admiral Canaris and his deputy Oberst Piekenbrock visited Ankara to personally see to the subsequent pursuit of the objectives of the Arab freedom movements. They had lengthy discussions with the secret Near East war organization in the embassy with the knowledge and tacit approval of the Turkish general staff. The Germans sought not only to promote anti-Soviet subversion and secure the straits against a breakthrough by the Russian fleet, but also future actions against British forces in the Middle and Near East with the continued objective of tying up as many enemy troops in this area as possible.

Also in Canaris' party was the former leader of the Secret War Organization Netherlands, Oberstleutnant Zermatt, whom Canaris had chosen as the new leader of the War Organization Near East. From there agent Jacques Graewer, who operated under the disguise of a sales agent for the Hamburg Import Company in Teheran, was instructed to set up a radio message center and establish "line" traffic with the embassy in Ankara in order to keep up with the latest developments.

The fighting in Iraq was over but not the activities of the Abwehr in Iran, which will be described in a following chapter. But first more details concerning the flight of the Iraqi general and the Grand Mufti of Jerusalem.

THE FLIGHT FROM IRAQ

For the Prime Minister and General Rashid Ali el Gailani and the Grand Mufti of Jerusalem it was high time to get out of the city if they wished to avoid capture and imprisonment by the English.

On 30th May they crossed the Iraqi-Persian border near Chanekin and asked Shah Resa, the father of the last Shah before Khomeni seized power, for political asylum. This was immediately granted to both high-ranking politicians.

After the Russians invaded Iran without warning on 25 August 1941 and later British and American troops moved in from the south, the German military commission, which had initially coordinated the resistance against the aggressors, had to abandon the fight. The Arab leaders were delivered safely to Ankara by an escort of six Brandenburgers. From there they made their way via the Balkans to Germany.

The journey had to be made under conditions of total secrecy, for Rashid Ali el Gailani and all his supporters had meanwhile been sentenced to death in absentia by the English-backed Prince Regent Abdul Illah. For this reason the Iraqi general was taken to Berlin first. The Grand Mufti of Jerusalem was to follow.

Meanwhile, however, the Grand Mufti's hiding place in the German embassy in Ankara had been found out. Both the British secret service and the Turkish police, whom had an extradition request from the Iraqi government, waited for the Grand Mufti to leave this safe place so they could arrest him and hand him over to the English. However the German ambassador and his staff skillfully mastered this critical situation. First they staged an accident involving a member of the embassy staff complete with blood from a hidden pig's bladder. Afterward the "accident victim"—dressed in an embassy uniform and wearing a thick head bandage—was taken to the airport, carried onto an aircraft and flown to Germany.

Until news arrived that the Grand Mufti had arrived in Germany, the embassy secretary, who was supposed to have been involved in the accident and who was about the same size as the Grand Mufti, had to stay out of sight. Only when the Grand Mufti of Jerusalem Amin al-Husseini appeared publicly in Germany was the game of hide and seek ended and the British secret service ended its surveillance of the German embassy. The Grand Mufti was provided with a stately residence, the Fuschl Castle, where Foreign Minister Joachim van Ribbentrop had resided for a time.

At the end of January Egypt expert Berner of the Brandenburgers joined Special Staff Felmy as its anti-British sabotage expert for Africa and the Near and Middle East.

On 15th July Hitler received former Iraqi head of state General el Gailani in the "Wolf's Lair." He assured him that everything would be done to win back his country. Ali Rashid el Gailani went on to work as a propaganda speaker in broadcasts that were beamed into the Near and Middle East.

At the beginning of September 1941 Admiral Canaris, General Felmy and Oberst van Lahousen-Vivremont, as well as General Ame, chief of the Italian secret service, met to discuss the future of the German and Italian Arab Legions. Also present were the commander of the Italian Arab Legion, Colonel Ivrea, and the Grand Mufti of Jerusalem. The objective was to establish a center for Arab units under fascist control in North Africa.

Admiral Canaris and General Felmy met again with the Grand Mufti of Jerusalem in the middle of the month. This time the topic of discussion was the creation of a German-Arab Instruction Unit and the Arab Free Corps then being formed. The meeting was concluded with no result.

On 21 September 1941 Special Staff F, stationed in the south of Greece, received a list of instructions directed specifically at it from the Wehrmacht Operations Staff. The directive authorized the Ausland/ Abwehr to assign espionage and sabotage missions to it and the special unit it had formed. The core of the special unit consisted of 2,200 officers and men who were divided into three companies. The bulk of the unit's personnel were former Palestinian Germans or Germans who were natives of Middle East countries and spoke the native language perfectly.

Operations in Iran

THE TÄBRIS ABWEHR STATION

At the beginning of 1940 the Ausland/Abwehr together with the SD established three anti-British agent offices in Iran. This was the foundation of a development that would end with a Persian civil war. The centers were located in Teheran and in the Kashgais and Bakhtiar areas.

On 22 February 1940 the Abwehr sent Hauptmann Paul Leverkuehn, disguised as a diplomat, to Täbris in Iran by way of Moscow to serve as consul. So far the Near and Middle East had had no significance at all to the German war strategy, for no one in their wildest dreams thought that German troops would be sent to such a distant region of the world.

The Abwehr, therefore, at first concerned itself with possibly motivating the Russians to attack Afghanistan and thus exert pressure on the northwest frontier of India. This would have forced England to deploy substantial numbers of forces there, which would then be unavailable for use in Europe or later in North Africa.

This notion had to be abandoned as did a second that culminated in the Russians advancing out of the Caucasus toward the Mossul oil fields or even driving through Persia to the Persian Gulf.

It was Oberst Warlimont, chief of the National Defense Department within the OKW, who proposed the covert scouting of Azerbaidzhan to Admiral Canaris. He also suggested that they investigate the strength and fighting power of General Weygand's army in the Near East. During a meeting on 22 February 1940 Canaris proposed one of his officers, Hptm. Leverkuehn, for this assignment. Hauptmann Leverkuehn traveled to Täbris at the beginning of March 1940. The new consul was soon able to form a picture of the situation in Iran. The road through the Kara Dagh was passable for alpine troops and in Leverkuehn's estimation two motorized divisions would be sufficient to drive through the mountains and then through the steppe to the Russian oil fields at Baku. From his base in northern Persia the consul had the militarily and geographically important Shibli Pass southeast of the city of Tabris scouted as well as the Kaflankuh Gorge.

After the German victory in the west eliminated the threat posed by Weygand's army, which sided with the Vichy government, the way was clear for German operations in the Near and Middle East. Secret files captured in France revealed that Daladier, the French Prime Minister, had instructed Chief of the General Staff Gamelin and Head of the Navy Admiral Darlan to look into the possibility of an attack on Baku. When Hauptmann Leverkuehn's identity was accidentally revealed, Admiral Canaris sent a Major of the Abwehr I department, Julius Schulze-Holthus, to Tiibris under the cover name Dr. Bruno Schulze. His secret mission was to scout the oil-producing region of Baku and report on anything else he learned while traveling through the Soviet Union.

When he returned to Berlin Schulze-Holthus made his report to Admiral Canaris. He was then sent to Tiibris by Canaris to serve as consulate secretary. Together with SD agent Thielicke he directed the activities of agents from Täbris.

THE BRANDENBURGERS IN OPERATION "AMINA"

Operation "Amina" began in June 1941. It was prepared by an Abwehr group under Leutnant Merzig. The objective of the attack was the destruction of the Abadan oil refinery. This was supposed to deny fuel to the British Near East Fleet and British land forces.

The second group involved in Operation "Amina" was under the command of Leutnant Dr. Heinrich Meinhard. It was brought from the island of Samos in the Dodecanese to the Turkish border and reached the Turkish city of Afkon Karahisar on 13 July 1941. This group, which was made up of men from Admiral Canaris's house unit, the Brandenburgers, crossed the Reza Mountains and reached the Persian city of Choi, where, as per their mission orders, it contacted the Kurdish Prince Murchen. The prince, who had no official functions, was nevertheless considered the uncrowned ruler of this area even though it was officially administered by the governor of the military district of Sawalan and the mayor of Choi. Nevertheless Prince Murchen's authority was absolute; if he gave the order there would be war and if he wished it there would be peace.

Although the Brandenburgers had orders to go to Teheran and set up a radio station there, they were detained by the prince in his residence. He wanted them to instruct his tribesmen in the use of firearms. The prince had a direct line into the garrisons in the south of the Soviet Union and had learned that a Soviet invasion was imminent. He wanted to meet it with his fighters. After receiving Teheran's permission, the small detachment stayed in Choi. It moved into the mountains and began training.

The second group under Leutnant Merzig was brought to the Libyan coast by submarine and put ashore in an inflatable boat.

At about the same time, bitter fighting had broken out south of Beirut between Arab and Vichy French forces and British troops who had landed there. This German group succeeded in getting through to Beirut, where it reached the address of a contact, one Abdul Rasman. He led the group to Damascus. Office VI of the Reichssicherheitshauptamt had stationed an agent there under the name of Dr. Smith. Smith now put his contacts to use. He succeeded in chartering an aircraft, received takeoff clearance and flew the second group to Baghdad. From there it made its way to the Persian Gulf.

Its mission: destroy the oil refineries at Abadan and terminate production of fuel for the Near East Fleet and the British Army. The men successfully reached Basra. There they were betrayed to the British secret service and forced underground. As a result the third group assigned to Operation "Amina" under Leutnant Helferich was deployed. Its mission began in Eleusis on 19 July 1941 and took it via Rhodes and Cyprus through Syria and Iraq toward Teheran.

The aircraft carrying the party crashed into a mountain between the cities of Hamadan and Teheran; however, all the soldiers parachuted to safety shortly before the crash. They managed to reach Teheran where they were taken in by Prince Baktshari—an intimate of the Shah.

This group soon transmitted all the intelligence from Teheran to Germany. Then they were ordered to kidnap Prince Shirwan, who was supported by England. According to the files of the Middle East War Organization the prince intended to support the invasion of Persia by the English with all the forces at his disposal. As well he was in close contact with the English and their secret service, which was very strongly represented in all of Persia.

Under Iranian law the prince's behavior was high treason, but the Shah was too weak to be able to punish him accordingly. Prince Shirwan had signed a decree for his friends, according to which all the Iranian arms depots in the south of the country were to be emptied and transported north. By doing so he wished to prevent the generals who were faithful to the emperor from resisting the English invasion in the south.

In the meantime the remnants of the Arab Brigade from Iraq had assembled in the army districts of northern Persia. Additional volunteers crossed the border from Iraq by night to join them. This led the small group of German military to hope that they might use these fighters and the weapons being sent to the north to achieve victory before the arrival of the English and pave the way for a government friendly toward Germany. The weapons transports rolled from the south into the north of the country. A large portion ended up in the hands of the freedom fighters, some voluntarily, some as a result of hijacking the transports.

On 25 August 1941, British and Soviet forces entered Persia from the south and north simultaneously. The country resisted fiercely but was overpowered and forced to surrender on 28th August. Shah Resa Palavi abdicated in favor of his son Mohammed Reza on 17th September and was sent into exile in South Africa by the British. He died in Johannesburg on 26 July 1944.

Under English pressure, the new government in Persia immediately implemented measures to "root out German nests of subversion." The German Military Mission and the secret detachments were pursued and largely ferreted out. Only Major Schulze-Holthus and his wife were able to escape.

The first "Amina" group under Leutnant Dr. Meinhard, which had trained Prince Murchen's tribesmen in northern Persia and then carried out raids on supply and communications installations in and around Soviet border cities, was able to carry on without English interference. This relieved the British of having to step in themselves against their ally on the northern border.

The underground war in Persia was not yet over, however. At the beginning of 1942 the Abwehr deployed about 100 of its Indian operatives in East Persia as saboteurs, with orders to reach India from there. They, too, caused the English many sleepless nights.

For the rest of the year there was radio silence in Iran in the truest sense of the word; then at the end of 1942 the work was resumed in a joint effort by Abwehr Departments I and II and Office VI of the SD. In charge of these renewed efforts was Korvettenkapitän Schiller together with SS-Hauptsturmfuhrer Kurt Schuback of the RSHA. These new groups, some of which were to act as radio teams and others as sabotage teams, achieved some quick and spectacular successes. They blew the Bushir and Shira roads, attacked fuel dumps, bridges and tunnels, and so incited the Luren that they began a revolt against the government. Military advisor to the Kashgais was Schulze-Holthus. Only the lack of a constant radio link to Germany and sufficient heavy weapons prevented victory by Nasr Khan, the declared leader of the Kashgais in southern Persia.

On I September 1943 agents and radio teams were deployed over all of Persia in larger numbers. The landings, by aircraft and parachute, were made in various parts of the country. After establishing contact with native leaders these teams set about their sabotage activities. These mounted to such a degree that the Persian government was left with but one response. On 9 September 1943 it declared war on Germany with the following words:

"German agents have been dropped into our country by parachute in considerable numbers and have inflicted serious damage. This is an attack on our country by the German Reich which we can only answer with this declaration of war."

The group under Major Schulze-Holthus, which officially called itself a military mission, was overpowered and handed over to the English in an operation worthy of a spy thriller. Here is the complete story of this group, which essentially consisted of Major Schulze-Holthus and several assistants.

ODYSSEY OF A MISSION

After Major Julius Schulze-Holthus met with his superior of the Abwehr I, Oberst Piekenbrock, and suggested that he personally take charge of the Baku matter, he was installed in the Tiibris consulate by the Foreign Office. At first, however, the major was met by skepticism. Oberst Piekenbrock had not forgotten that a short time before Hptm. Dr. Paul Leverkuehn, a member of the Abwehr, had traveled to Täbris in the guise of a German consul in order to establish a net of agents from there to the oil sources of Baku. The effort had failed, for a Jewish acquaintance of the new consul from Berlin, who had helped him escape Germany, inadvertently blew his cover.

Schulze-Holthus had prepared himself well for this conversation. He brought with him a map that he used to show that the area of Azerbaidzhan was cut in two by the Russian-Persian border. Oberst Piekenbrock pointed out that the Foreign Office had got cold feet after the disaster with Dr. Leverkuehn and that the German envoy in Teheran, Ettel, would also not be in agreement. The Major asked to go to Teheran personally in order to present his plans to envoy Ettel, even though he knew that his prospects were not good.

Schulze-Holthus received Piekenbrock's approval and now drove to see his superior, Senior Government Advisor Dr. Bruno Schulze, in the Ministry of the Interior. There he received a transit visa for Russia and instructions to monitor traffic on the entire run from Moscow to Baku and count the number of trains and their cars. He was to note all new construction at the stations and along the line and record the locations of watering facilities, oil tanks and coalbunkers.

During the journey through Russia the major repeatedly excused himself and disappeared into the toilet—claiming to be suffering from stomach pain and diarrhea much to the amusement of his traveling companion, an Armenian oil director. In fact he used his absences to record his observations. As soon as he arrived in Baku Schulze-Holthus was set upon by a woman of the Intourist travel bureau who took him to the hotel for foreigners and attended to him over eagerly. The major said that he wanted to travel on to Teheran to inspect the German technical school there.

The journey to Teheran was finally continued across the Caspian Sea. The landing in Bender-Pahlewidem harbor and the drive along the shore of the Caspian Sea brought Schulze-Holthus into the Persian capital city, where he immediately reported to the German legation, which was in the diplomatic quarter. Major Schulze-Holthus asked to see the trade attaché, one Herr Specht, who was an Abwehr officer and his contact man. He passed him the courier mail and the latter opened the conversation by complaining about envoy Ettel, who was a stolid bureaucrat and had no inkling of the Abwehr's activities.

When Schulze-Holthus asked him how they could convince the envoy to back him for the consulate post in Täbris, Specht replied, "It would be easier to get a hippopotamus to sing Christmas carols."

After the lunch break the major met with the envoy. Ettel, short and wiry with sharp facial features, fixed him with a stare and asked what he wanted in Teheran. When Schulze-Holthus told him that he would like to become consul in Täbris, Ettel put him off politely, however the major refused to take no for an answer. He made it clear that Baku, as a long-range German objective needed to secure its own oil supply, could only be monitored and observed effectively from Täbris. He promised to have a copy of every report to the Abwehr sent to Ettel so that he was always aware of everything that was going on. The German envoy agreed, but on the condition "that you act nothing like Leverkuehn." Schulze-Holthus was permitted to go to Täbris as consulate secretary, but at the insistence of Ettel he had to take his wife with him. This settled the matter, and Schulze-Holthus sent two coded telegrams to Germany. The first went to Oberst Piekenbrock, the chief of Abwehr I, the second to the Benesch Firm in Hamburg. the text read: "Please establish contact immediately between me and Achmed Asai in Teheran."

Less than 48 hours later he was face to face with Achmed Asadi in the house of Franke, the senior German salesman in Teheran. Asadi assured himself that the visitor was destined for Tiibris as Dr. Leverkuehn's successor and that he had also been assigned Baku as part of his working area. The Iranian assured Schulze-Holthus that he could count on his help and declared that the SD's representative was not working cleverly enough.

Ahmed Asadi explained to the major the particulars of the Azebaidzhani underground movement, from which a large group under its leader Mulli Mudafai was sympathetic to Germany, while the Musawad, the core of which was comprised of former oil magnates and land holders dispossessed by the Soviets, were also in favor of cooperation if special concessions were made to them.

"The Germans," explained Achmed Asadi, "have great possibilities here, because they are not among the oppressors of other colonial peoples."

The next day Major Schulze-Holthus received instructions from Berlin to come home and report. After landing at Baku he was met by the same employee of the Intourist Bureau. She promised to take him to a fire worshippers' temple in the middle of the Baku oil fields the next day. Traveling as senior government advisor Dr. Bruno Schultze, Schulze-Holthus spoke knowledgeably about the sect and charmed his guide while furtively recording to memory the oil pipelines, the waterworks and the two new airfields. There were new roads and barracks in Baku and even a new rail line.

They reached the temple of the fire worshippers. The building was small. A vital part of the temple was the natural gas line that led from a storage tank up to the roof. There the priests could regulate the height of the flame with a cleverly concealed hand wheel, so that the flame appeared to rise directly from the roof of the temple while the faithful kneeled in the open. The "senior executive officer" was also permitted to climb the narrow stairway to the roof, from where he was able to make out a number of new facilities.

When Schulze-Holthus arrived in Moscow two days later he dictated a twelve page report on Baku to the German military attaché; this was immediately encoded and sent to Abwehr I in Berlin. After Schulze-Holthus had reported back to Oberst Pie ken brock, the latter told him that his report on Baku had already been forwarded to Admiral Canaris. In the afternoon the major met with Canaris. The latter gave him the green light for his new mission and at the end of their talk said,

"You have to work quickly and eventually drop your cover. I must have your results here by the middle of June."

The Schulze-Holthus couple arrived in Täbris in mid-May. Consul Bohn, the major's immediate superior, was at first mistrustful. But his reservations soon disappeared. He was expecting to be recalled anyway, for he had maintained a friendly relationship with the English consul even after the outbreak of war. One of the major's first informants was a sergeant in an Iranian division based in Täbris. Schulze-Holthus very soon established contact with the Armenian underground movement Dashnak-Zakan, whose leader, Achmed Asadi, immediately offered him assistance. One of the organization's middlemen was prepared to supply the Germans with all-important information concerning Russian Azerbaidzhan. Ten days later Schulze-Holthus received the first reports from Baku.

On 15 May 1941 the major received an urgent order from Berlin to immediately reconnoiter the air bases in the Kirovabad area. Wasiri, the only Persian middleman who spoke with the major, dispatched three small groups. By 20th June they were not yet back. They had been spotted and fired on by Russian border troops. Six of the men died from their wounds. The next day Russian radio in Baku broadcast to the world that there was a German espionage center in Täbris. The same day Berlin stepped in again and ordered the final scouting of the Baku area as quickly as possible. Special attention was to be paid to the appearance of new Russian fighter units in the border area.

In the late afternoon—it was 22 June 1941—the legation in Täbris also learned that Germany had attacked the Soviet Union. In the following weeks it became difficult to obtain additional material. The borders were sealed tighter than usual. In spite of this further material was acquired.

At about 5:00 A.M. on the morning of 25 August 1941 the inhabitants of Täbris were rudely awakened by heavy anti-aircraft fire. Then the first explosions were heard. The Soviets had begun their attack across the Persian border. Consul Wussow, who had succeeded Bohn as envoy, informed his deputy that they would have to begin preparations to leave. The German colony was advised. The Germans arrived at the consulate with their bags and a short time later left by car for Teheran. The German engineers involved in railroad construction in the north of the country were advised by telegraph. The legation's files were burned in the courtyard, the last coded messages were sent, then the convoy set out for Teheran. When they arrived in Teheran Consul Ettel was not present. His deputy, Legation Councilor Dittmann, received his colleagues from Täbris.

The question now was whether Ambassador Ettel would succeed in obtaining permission for all Germans to depart Iran for Turkey. If he did not, the only remaining possibility was to get to Turkey on their own with their diplomatic passports or make their way east toward Afghanistan. When Major Schulze-Holthus informed the German ambassador that he wanted to head for Afghanistan the latter called his plan sheer madness. Ettel insisted that Schulze-Holthus and his wife were personnel of the diplomatic corps, for whom he had obtained free passage to Turkey. To reach Afghanistan meant crossing the Lut desert. All the other routes had already been blocked by the Russians.

Several days afterward Schulze-Holthus, his wife, and engineer Hirschauer, who had worked on railroad construction and wanted to join the couple, secretly left the embassy by car. At first they took the major road to the south. On the way the car's axle was damaged. Nevertheless they carried on as far as Isfahan at 40 kilometers per hour. After repairs to the car they resumed their journey the next morning. Next they had to drive via Ysad and Kerman to Barn; but they did not reach their destination, because they were stopped in Kerman and escorted back to the road to Teheran.

The three Germans decided to try and make a break for it. They drove through the city at 120 kilometers per hour, escaped the police, and were free. When Barn came into sight they stopped outside the city so as to avoid running the same danger. After Hirschauer had purchased boards and shovels, in the evening the group drove into the desert. They covered 80 kilometers in six hours, but then they became stuck for good in the loose sand.

Early the next morning a herd of camels led by several men came in sight. The group hired two drivers and eight of the animals, and while Hirschauer and the major each climbed onto one of the riding animals, Mrs. Schulze-Holthus steered the car while it was pulled by the other camels.

Forty-eight hours later they had passed through the Lut desert. The two drivers took them to the black tents of the Belutschen where they received a warm welcome. The Belutschen told them the way to an unguarded border crossing between Lake Helmand and the Good-i-Zirreh marsh.

The small group now drove along the main road that led along Persia's eastern border from Zaidan in the south to Mesched in the north. When they finally reached the border east of Schusp, they found themselves facing an impassable mountain chain. They drove back to Schusp, where they were advised to drive to Tabbas. There a caravan trail led across the border. After arriving in Tabbas the group learned that rock falls caused by an earthquake had blocked the pass road in several places. The only possibility left was Yasd.

In Birshand the Germans' car was again stopped by the police and the three were taken to jail. The provincial governor, to whom they turned for help, read aloud to them an order from the war ministry: "The German consulate official Schulze-Holthus from Täbris, who is on the run with two companions, is to be arrested immediately: if necessary armed force is to used and they are to be held in custody until further instructions are received."

Ten days later a police detachment arrived from Teheran to take the Germans back to the Persian capital. The journey back to Teheran was made in several stages and the prisoners were quartered in the old summer embassy in Schemiran near the capital. There they learned that ambassador Ettel and the entire legation staff had already left for Germany and that of the German civilians with no diplomatic status 350 had had to be handed over to the British and 104 to the Russians. It was to be expected that they, too, would be handed over to the English: provided that they were lucky enough not to be claimed by the Russians.

An escape plan was worked out. Several days later, after their surprise breakout succeeded, Schulze-Holthus and his wife drove into the mountains with Iranian friends. Engineer Hirschauer remained behind. There were tense moments when a Russian armored column passed them and a tank became stuck in a tight turn right in front of them. They had to wait, but this danger passed too.

After moving through two hiding places near Teheran, they finally found the security service agent in the city, Sturmbannfiihrer Mayr, who informed them that General Zahidi, commanding general of an army corps in Isfahan, had told him that "large parts of the Iranian Army are ready to strike at England on a signal from Germany. Several high officials are behind me." Mrs. Schulze-Holthus, who managed to reach Täbris and from there Schapur, took this intelligence with her so that she could pass it on at the earliest opportunity.

Schulze-Holthus himself established contact with Dr. Friedrich Kümmel. His cover in Persia as a geologist had failed; he would have been in a position to carry out the necessary intelligence gathering. After a game of hide and seek a friend found Schulze-Holthus with Major Esfendiari of the Teheran police; there he was visited by three Persian general staff officers. The colonel who led the group held forth the prospect of an early uprising and war of liberation against England. He made reference to the possibility of German troops marching into Teheran, which could be done at three places and access roads. One of these was from the north via Baku-Lenkoran-Astara, from where German troops could advance directly to Kaswin, the jump-off position for a drive to Teheran. The colonel declared: "The German headquarters must be set up in Isfahan, because the Persian general staff is based there."

In conclusion: sites were chosen for landings by German parachute troops as well as drop sites for weapons and munitions—including anti-tank guns, anti-aircraft guns and mortars. The "Milli Mudafai" and other guerrilla groups, as well as the tribes under the Kashgai prince Nasr Khan, would ensure that the Persian rail installations remained intact.

Schulze-Holthus made a complete report on this talk and passed it on to SD man Mayr, who was to take it to Berlin. Several days later Schulze-Holthus was contacted by Dr. Kümmel. The latter had carried out a scouting mission for the Abwehr at the Paitag Pass and had gathered valuable intelligence, which he now wanted to take to Berlin. Dr. Kümmel also took the report by Schulze-Holthus with him. The maps that Kümmel was given were drawn in invisible ink on a handkerchief, which "was deposited, somewhat soiled, in my pocket and which at first attracted not the least interest."

When the British security service uncovered Dr. Kümmel's secret apartment the next day, the "bird had already flown." Since his landlord had been arrested, it was to be expected—in the words of Major Esfendiari—that they would now also be looking for Schulze-Holthus with him. The fate of Dr. Kümmel remains uncertain. He did make it to the border, but there he was captured by the Kurds who lived in the area and handed over to the English. He was interrogated and a member of the British secret service discovered the drawing on the handkerchief. Dr. Kümmel was sentenced to death for spying.

Schulze-Holthus, who had found a new hiding place, received an invitation from the Kashgai leader, Nasr Khan. The latter had a "private army" of 20,000 men under arms in dangerous proximity to the British-controlled Persian oil fields. British troops were supposed to drive him out of there. Schulze-Holthus reached Nasr Khan with several Persians, including the division adjutant of the Teheran garrison and the Persian deputy Nobacht. In spite of being checked several times by British sentries they made it to the Khan. There they were first taken to the leader of the 20,000 Kashgai horsemen, Prince Ibrahim, in the tent city where Nasr Khan resided.

Then the Germans and their friends were invited to see Nasr Khan. Schulze-Holthus learned that the prince had 8,000 men with an equal number of First World War rifles as well as 12,000 old shotguns. His force also had 20 light machine-guns. He asked that his request for anti-tank weapons, heavy machine-guns, modern rifles and the necessary ammunition be passed on to Germany. Major Schulze-Holthus gave the list with the prince's wants to Nobacht, who in turn passed it to Standartenführer Mayr. When the Persian director of the Anglo-Iranian Oil Company came to Nasr Khan and requested on behalf of the English that he hand over the German major, the prince declined. Nasr Khan's request for weapons could not be transmitted to Berlin as Mayr no longer had communications with the Reich capital.

An airfield for use by German transport aircraft was built near Fiirshband. Soon afterward Schulze-Holthus learned that his wife had not reached Germany but was in jail in Baschkaleh. The secret notes she had sewn into an undershirt had been found. Immediately afterward Schulze-Holthus found out that Standartenführer Mayr had been betrayed to the

British consul general in Isfahan and that they had found in his possession a whole suitcase full of secret documents.

To make matters even worse, the head of the Persian resistance movement, General Zahidi, disappeared. He had been arrested by General Wilson and his bodyguard and taken away. British forces began hunting down all Persian officers under suspicion.

THE LAST ACTIONS IN PERSIA

The final operation conducted in Persia was a parachute mission by six members of the Brandenburgers, who were dropped in the area of Teheran. They landed at night in the salt desert of Darya-je-Niimiik. Uffz. Corell, the team leader, spoke fluent Persian. Dressed like a Persian, he walked from the landing site to Teheran, where he sought out the agent of the RSHA, Standartenfiihrer Mayr. He then went back to fetch the other members of the team. Corell and the others returned to Teheran. During his double march through the desert he contracted a typhus infection. The men of the Milli Mudafai resistance movement cared for him until his death.

Schulze-Holthus had to promise Nasr Khan that he would make direct contact with Mayr and through him request that a radio team be inserted into the south of the country, which would soon be the front line. Nasr Khan also brought up his request for arms again and the major promised to pass that along as well.

Then in March 1943 when deputy Nobacht arrived in the camp by horse, it was learned from him that the English had convinced the Teheran government to begin the offensive against the south in April and that General Shabahti would lead it. His participation was just window dressing, because in reality a British command staff had worked out the operation and would also direct it. The command staff received its orders direct from the Commander-in-Chief of British forces in Persia, General Frazer.

A concentric attack was planned on Giirmesir. It was to be carried out by five Persian brigades. The Kashgais under Nasr Khan were to be driven out of their settlement area into the desert, there to starve or die of thirst. The politician also brought news that one of the six members of the radio team that had parachuted near Teheran had died in the city. A delegation made up of a colonel and four staff officers from the headquarters of General Schabathi appeared in Nasr Khan's mountain valley to negotiate with the Kashgai leader. Khan found the government's terms unacceptable and rejected them; civil war was imminent. Near Ghaleh Piirian Kosro Khan, the younger brother of Nasr Khan, inflicted the first defeat on the enemy.

The Kashgais were victorious until a few days later a huge army appeared above their valley and moved heavy guns and mortars into position. The British attack began three days later with barrage fire from guns and mortars. Then the infantry units moved forward, firing at everything in their path. The Kashgais held fire until the enemy had approached to within about 100 meters; then they opened up, concentrating on the officers. The first attack collapsed. There was a succession of attacks and counterattacks and finally it settled into positional warfare at the Muk Pass.

The Kashgais were taken by surprise when the Kamseh joined the battle on the side of the government forces and sent 1,000 of their men against the Kashgai rear. They fell back to the upper reaches of the Kara-Agadsch River with the command staff below the fortress of Ghaleh Piirian. The attack on the fortress failed.

While the front there remained static, Nasr Khan's brother Kosro Khan had taken the fortress of Samirum and captured a large number of mortars. He reported that his warriors were ready to advance on Osfahan. Since Nasr Khan did not trust the SD officer Mayr, he asked Schulze-Holthus to ride to Teheran to negotiate with the government and also use Mayr's radio to contact Berlin.

The next morning the German major departed with an escort of 25 horsemen. On the way they ran into two messengers from Kosro Khan, who reported that another radio team, consisting of four men, had parachuted into Kosro Khan's forces between Samirum and Desch-i-Kurd. They had a large quantity of gold and dynamite and a message from Hitler to Nasr Khan. The party now rode for Kosro Khan's camp. When they arrived they found Kosro Khan there, but the German radio team had already ridden on. The latter consisted of an officer and two NCOs of the SS and a Persian named Farsed.

Korso Khan also showed Schulze-Holthus photos of Nasr Khan's other three brothers, who were in Berlin as negotiators and who were later to play a special role. According to Kosro Khan, the Germans were supposed to set up a radio station in the Biirm-i-Firuz Mountains.

The next day Schulze-Holthus set out for the mountains. He and his party arrived there after 36 hours and found the radio team's dark green tents and the two 10-meter antennas, between which an antenna was stretched. Schulze-Holthus met SSHauptsturmfiihrer Kurmis, a Balt. He passed on greetings from Mrs. Schulze-Holthus, who he had met with Major Berger in the offices of the Abwehr. She had made it to Germany after all. Kurmis also told him that he—Schulze-Holthus—was to be flown out in one of the next aircraft to leave there. They intended to make him responsible for the entire Orient. This was no less than his being gotten rid of by the SD.

Not until 15 October 1943 did the four radio operators succeed in establishing contact with Berlin. The delay was due to an error in setting the frequency of the radio, which had been set at 400 kilohertz. Then two of Nasr Khan's brothers were captured while returning from Berlin to Persia. They were taken to Cairo, tried by the British and sentenced to death. It was now surely all over for Major Schulze-Holthus and the radio team, for in return for pardoning Nasr Khan's brothers the British demanded that he hand over the entire German military mission.

At first the Germans were supposed to be shot, but then they were handed over to the English. With the British officers there was also a short civilian. He introduced himself to the German major as Major Jackson, English consul in Shiras, and told him that the English government had made an agreement with Nasr Khan to treat the Germans well.

They arrived in Teheran after a twenty-hour automobile trip. It was early morning and they were taken direct to the headquarters of the Secret Service. Schulze-Holthus was interrogated five days later. Afterward he was taken to a camp. In the camp at Emmaus the major met the SD agent Mayr and Dr. Kümmel as well. Schulze-Holthus was exchanged for a British intelligence officer in early 1945 and returned to Berlin by way of Switzerland. A terrific odyssey with equally terrific but unexploited opportunities was over.

Long-Range Missions
by the Abwehr

FRONT-LINE DETACHMENT 200 IN AFGHANISTAN

The activities by the Abwehr special detachments in the Near and Far East described in Chapter I were not the end of operations by the German intelligence service in Afghanistan. Oberleutnant Dietrich Witzel-Kim, head of the Abwehr's Front-Line Detachment 200, was ordered to Kabul with his Afghan and Indian agents and the men specially trained for this mission. From there he was to drive and walk to the Indian border, locate a suitable site, and establish a base equipped with a transmitter. As well Witzel-Kim was to organize the subsequent dispatch there of radio equipment and operators, seek out a landing strip in the operating area of the Fakir of Ipi, and secure the good will of the leaders of the mountain people, for without their assistance and support nothing could be achieved in northeast Afghanistan.

At the same time Major Shenk, who resided in Kabul, received an order from the head of Department II of the Abwehr to mobilize the White Guard emigrants living in Afghanistan and prepare them for anti-Soviet activities in the southern, Moslem states of the USSR.

Operation "Tiger" could begin. Three weeks later the Abwehr officers in Kabul, Major Schenk and Oberleutnant Witzel-Kim, whose warrior name there was "Pathan," reported that radios, explosives, weapons and ammunition were ready for transport into the rebel-held areas and soon afterward that the training of agents to handle the radios was complete.

On 16 September 1941 the Abwehr informed Oblt. Witzel-Kim of his mission and revealed to him the plan of operations against the USSR. On 25th September, following lengthy negotiations, Major Schenk met with the exile Uzbeks working against Russia, whose leader was Mahmud. Then he went on to see the Fakir of Alinbar and was able to convince him to join the anti-Soviet movement. Working on behalf of the Abwehr, Jacub Khan had his informants spread out. Their reports were passed on to the operations staff. The attacks could begin.

On a single night, 19 October 1941, three Russian border posts and a railroad terminus were attacked and blown up. Before the Russians could react, the next night a railroad repair facility and a small power plant that also supplied power to the Russian border garrisons were destroyed.

On 13 January 1942 Oblt. Witzel-Kim reported from Afghanistan that the Abwehr sponsored Bose Indian nationalist organization already had more than 5,500 deserters in the border area, among them 2,000 armed soldiers of the British colonial army. They now trained Indian and Afghan guerrillas in many border villages. According to Witzel-Kim's report, the Bose organization already had cells established in all of Northern India and in Madras from which acts of sabotage were carried out against British installations and supply routes. Frequent targets of the saboteurs were railway workshops and the jute factories in Calcutta.

On 15 March 1942, acting on orders from Abwehr II, Witzel-Kim and his native radio operator Doh went back to the mountains of the Afghanistan-India border. There he organized a number of acts of sabotage and surprise attacks against British patrols and outposts, supply routes and installations, and the communications services. At the end of May Oblt Witzel-Kim was ordered to ride the entire stretch of road from Kabul to Baraki and Barah and from there to Saiydabad and Ghasni and back to Kabul. While doing so he was to look for potential sites to sabotage this strategically important supply and communications road.

Witzel-Kim and Doh set off on 3rd June. Both were dressed as mountain dwellers. Witzel-Kim had rubbed himself all over with walnut juice until he was as brown as Doh. On this ride they experienced the strangest things. Once they tagged along with a small caravan that was escorted by a British patrol against the threat of robbers.

Oblt Witzel-Kim ended up talking to a British captain who tried to recruit him for the British armed forces. The German pretended he was interested and listened as the officer told him all about life in the service of the British forces. On the fourth day of their ride they were discovered by another patrol while sketching a crossing over a riverbed; the British observed them from the mountains with binoculars. Doh noticed the sun glinting off the optics and warned his chief. He immediately replaced the page that he had been using with one already prepared showing mountain herbs and began to draw on it.

When the patrol reached them the excellent drawing convinced the enemy, and the Oberleutnant explained to them the importance of these herbs using numerous botanical terms, assisted by Doh. They even obtained a note from the patrol leader to his chief to the effect that he should allow the botanist and his assistant to come and go freely. As a result Witzel-Kim was also able to ride through several side valleys and see important military and technical sites that were later sketched.

When they arrived back in Kabul on the evening of 10th June they brought with them a wealth of valuable intelligence. It proved very valuable in supplementing the survey undertaken by the Todt Organization in 1940. Should the army succeed in driving through the Caucasus, it would have all the information necessary for a quick occupation of the country and the securing of all the important roads.

Sahir Shah's Afghan government, which had maintained a neutral stance, had to bow to pressure from the British embassy, which was riddled with secret service personnel, when it delivered Jacub Khan into its hands. This top German agent was arrested on 15 August 1942. Six days later another Abwehr agent working independently in Kabul was arrested. This was the signal for everyone to cease their activities temporarily and find new hiding places; they would not become active again until the secret service agents had been eliminated.

On 8 September 1942 a relay station was set up in the Caucasus in order to make the radio link between Kabul and Berlin more secure and less prone to breakdown. The operation, code-named "Tiger's Castle," was carried out under extreme secrecy. Long after the Caucasus had been evacuated by German forces, four Abwehr radio operators and two Caucasian assistants remained and made possible the continued work by German agents and Front-Line Detachment 200 in Afghanistan and India.

Operations in India

SUBHAS CHANDRA BOSE AND THE FORWARD PARTY BLOCK

Once removed from Operation Afghanistan, Rittmeister Habicht set to work immediately and established the "Asad Hind—Free India" Legion, which was incorporated as a unit of the 4th Regiment, 800th Special Purpose Construction Training Division Brandenburg. The Indians who made up the legion were mostly soldiers who had served in the North African desert with the 5th Indian Division. They were quartered and trained in the so-called "camp earthworm" near Meseritz.

The men of the Indian Legion wore German uniforms; the legion's unit emblem, a shield bearing a leaping tiger, was worn on the sleeve and the turban. Their training concentrated on jungle and mountain operations. The Abwehr had already conducted its first operations in the Afghanistan-India border region. This positive experience led the German and Italian intelligence services to agree that they should carry the fight to India.

Germany at first turned its back on Subhas Chandra Bose, who had visited Germany in 1936 as mayor of Calcutta, and who had been received by Adolf Hitler. A secret anglophile, Hitler sympathized with England and hoped to be able to get this "Nordic brother race" on his side.

From Berlin Bose traveled to Rome; there he had talks with the Italian Duce, Mussolini, which were equally fruitless. On the way to Rome Bose met in Prague with Dr. Otto Strasser, the leader of the Black Front, who had emigrated from Vienna to Prague after his break with Hitler. Bose explained to Strasser his and India's position as a people forced to live without sovereignty. He said that in the event of a Soviet victory Nehru would become leader of India and that should National Socialism prevail he, Bose, would be elected leader of India. He said that Hitler's and his goals were the same, and that Nehru's objectives and his own in regard to India's freedom were the same though their methods were different. Both Bose and Ghandi had been jailed for their efforts to free India and separate it from the British Empire.

Following the outbreak of war in Europe, the Indians were at first ready to support England under certain conditions. England rejected any conditions, but when her position became serious after Dunkirk and she turned to the Indian Congress, the latter was again prepared to support England if it guaranteed India's freedom.

Winston Churchill then decided the matter when he said, "I became prime minister to defend England and not to sell off the British Empire." With this rejection a secret agreement worked out between Nehru and Bose in New Delhi took effect. After Nehru rejected an offer from the German government to visit Berlin in 1937 it was Bose's hour. He publicly agitated against Nehru and pointed the finger at his antifascist but pro-Soviet and pro-Chinese speeches. Bose was kicked out by Nehru and banned from holding public office for three years.

Subhas Chandra Bose now founded the "Forward Block", which opposed Viceroy of India Lord Linlithgow's declaration that India was in a state of war. In this situation Bose had three possible allies: Germany, Italy and Japan.

In January 1941 Bose, who was closely watched in Calcutta, was able to slip out of his house, which was watched by the secret service round the clock. With the aid of the Abwehr, which had extended its web to Calcutta, he crossed India disguised as a Moslem and reached Peshawar. From there supporters of the Aga Khan slipped him into Afghanistan. Waiting at the border was a group of "road building engineers" of the Todt organization—in reality an Abwehr detachment—who escorted him safely to the Russian border.

At the Russian border the NKVD took charge of this important visitor and took him to Moscow, where he was handed over to the German ambassador, Friedrich Wemer Count von der Schulenburg. Several days later Bose was flown from Moscow to Berlin in a special courier aircraft. Aboard the same aircraft were the "road building engineers" and several men of the Abwehr II.

Bose was met at Berlin's Tempelhof airfield by the deputy of the Foreign Office's head of protocol and was driven in a closed car to Wilhelmstrasse. This time Bose was accepted by Hitler as a necessary evil, especially since the Indian was especially concerned about the "Asad Hind" Indian legion and was calling for the Indian soldiers trained there to join the fight against England.

Bose was able to raise his standing with Hitler by broadcasting for the Axis powers over the "Asad Hind" transmitter, which had been set up near Nauen, and later from Lalaya. Hitler also agreed when it was proposed to him that an Indian government in exile be formed with Bose at its head. Thus the "Indian National Congress" was born. The negotiations then being carried out by Sir Stafford Cripps with India failed. Nehru and other Indian leaders were thrown in jail; consequently Bose found more and more supporters for the planned seizure of power. Bose worked closely with Rittmeister Habicht, and when the latter said that the time had come for the first missions and that they had to take place in India, Bose acted.

Japan also took an interest in this up and coming man, possible head of a major nation within their sphere of interest. Through General Oshima the Japanese leadership named Bose head of the Indian freedom movement and offered him a residence in Singapore, which they had conquered in February 1942. The authorities in Berlin agreed with this move, especially after Bose declared that the Indian Legion would remain under German control.

At the beginning of February 1943 Subhas Chandra Bose traveled with his adjutant Dr. Habib Hasan and two officers of the Indian Legion to Kiel, where the submarine U 180 was ready to sail under the command of Fregattenkapitän Musenberg. On 9 February 1942 the Indian group was taken by motorboat out to the submarine in Kiel Bay. The captain was told that they were engineers of the Todt Organization, but he was not fooled for he knew Bose from photos in the newspapers.

The voyage was uneventful, because the boat had orders to run submerged when in the vicinity of any other vessels. It reached the Indian Ocean unopposed and there rendezvoused with a Japanese submarine. In the night the four men transferred to the Japanese submarine, which took them to Singapore. There they moved into a prepared residence in Rhe, a residential area of Singapore. Following an initial inspection, Bose traveled on to Tokyo, where he held negotiations with the Japanese government.

When he returned to Singapore his assistants had already brought to Singapore the persons chosen for the government in exile. Bose formed the government and all that was left now was to bring the Indian Legion to India.

THE ROLE OF THE BRANDENBURGERS IN OPERATION "TIGER"
Bose had already been given the plan of action for the Indian Brigade worked out by the Abwehr at the end of August 1941. After the German armed forces had driven through the Caucasus and reached the Caspian Sea, the legion was to be flown to India to touch off the uprising against the British oppressors. There were also to be parachute landings in northwest India.

In the future the Abwehr' s main agent for India, also middleman and liaison officer between the Italian and German intelligence services and the Bose organization, Rahmat Khan, was to work for Germany only. He acted as courier between Kabul and Calcutta. In preparation for the main operation, in January 1942 the Abwehr dropped 100 fully-trained Indians of the Indian Legion into east Iran. Their mission was to reach India via Baluchistan and carry out acts of sabotage against the British and prepare everything for the great national uprising.

This Operation "Bajadere" was a complete success and Oberleutnant Witzel, who was active in Afghanistan, reported the effectiveness of the 100 men to Kabul, from where the reports were forwarded to Germany.

On 13 March 1942 Keppler, State Secretary in the Foreign Office, held extensive talks with Oberst von Lahousen-Vivremont and Major Marwede of Abwehr II concerning the subversion that was to be initiated. Also discussed was Germany's advance from Afghanistan to India. Once Bose's transfer to Singapore had been initiated, Abwehr specialists and the Brandenburger coastal raiders went to work transporting the command element of the Indian Legion to India.

This operation was to be one of the Brandenburgers' greatest feats. It was organized by Abwehr II in cooperation with the operations staff of the Brandenburg Regiment and a special detachment from the High Command of the Navy (OKM).

Of the 14 available blockade runners, four were to take the officers and best soldiers of the Indian Legion to Singapore. One of the ships was converted into a Swedish ore freighter and set out for Singapore as the Brand III. Brandenburgers with the necessary qualifications—they had to speak Swedish—were soon found. The interior of the ship was partitioned in such a way that a thin layer of ore could be placed in the upper part of the cargo hold, while the soldiers were accommodated in an open area beneath it. Some Indian soldiers, those with experience as seamen, were made part of the ship's crew.

After the upper part of the cargo hold had been filled with Swedish ore, the Brand III took on fuel in the port of Malmo. British agents in Malmo reported to London on all ships coming from the Baltic. The passage of the Brand III was also reported and it was allowed to sail through the Channel unchallenged.

The ship was stopped in Gibraltar and its manifest inspected. The ship's cargo of "ore" was destined for an iron foundry in South Africa. An agent from Capetown had sent the order to Sweden. Of course the verification check in South Africa confirmed the order and a check of the trade register confirmed the existence and status of the iron foundry. The Brand III continued through the Mediterranean and passed through the Suez Canal. Prior to this it had passed inspection by British officials after it was sent to the roadstead while British warships, which enjoyed priority, passed through the canal.

On another occasion the vessel was inspected by US ships in the Bay of Bengal. Shortly before reaching the Sunda Strait a Japanese cruiser picked up the Brand III and escorted her to Singapore. The first advance party of Indian troops had arrived safely and was placed at Bose's disposal.

While trying to sail around Africa, a second blockade runner, also with men of the Indian Legion on board, was challenged by English warships west of the Cape of Good Hope and ordered to stop. The blockade-runner made smoke and headed into the falling darkness at top speed. The resulting search operation forced the ship far to the south and it was listed missing.

The Bose government in exile now had soldiers with the training necessary to instruct others. Operations could now begin. Bose's "Freedom Radio" in Singapore urged all Indians to leave India and join his army of freedom fighters. English troops were sent to the frontier to halt the stream of Indians hurrying to join the Bose army. In a single day 4,000 Indians were stopped and sent back.

Soon afterward the Indian Legion was renamed the Indian Freedom Army. It fought the English along the Burma Road, waging a fierce guerrilla campaign against their supply convoys. The Indians used the jungle as cover from which to launch surprise raids on road junctions and intercept truck columns. These actions tied up a large part of the Indian Colonial Army. Two regiments alone had to be deployed full time to guard the Burma Road. Japan supplied the Indian Freedom Army with weapons, ammunition, vehicles and food, for the forces it engaged could not be used against Japan.

Not until the English began sending the families of known Bose supporters to internment camps did the number of operations fall significantly; nevertheless, the struggle in India led by Subhas Chandra Bose went on even after the end of the war in Europe and ended only when Japan was forced to give up Burma and Singapore.

Not until the day Japan surrendered did Bose disband his army. He himself disappeared without a trace. It was said that he had been killed in a plane crash near Taipei on 18 August 1945 and that the Japanese had even buried his ashes in Tokyo, but the rumors that Bose was still alive would not die. It was rumored that he had joined the Chinese communist leader Mao Tse Tung immediately after the war, took part in the great march and became China's political advisor for Indian affairs.

Nothing is known of the Brandenburgers and the men of Abwehr II who remained with the Indian Freedom Army. The majority of them were rumored to have joined the French Foreign Legion in Saigon.

Operations in Africa

PREPARATIONS—FIRST OPERATIONS

At the beginning of 1940 a special unit of the Abwehr/Ausland consisting of scientists, geographers, geodesists, geologists, mineralogists, meteorologists and road builders set about to begin gathering intelligence on north and central Africa from central Libya. The codeword for this broad-based operation was "Dora."

In August of that year the Abwehr station in Münster was tasked with evaluating all cartographic material relating to Morocco, Algeria, Tunisia, Libya and Egypt captured as a result of the successful campaigns to date.

This search operation was code-named 'Theodora." It involved German cartographers and geographers as well as former officers of the French colonial army who had volunteered for this duty. They were assembled at a remote castle in the Rhineland. There they began working on a veritable mountain of files, conducting numerous economic and military-historical studies, which were of significance to a possible German intervention in Africa. After the German armed forces began their participation in the Italian struggle in Africa against the British with Operation "Sunflower" on 12 February 1941, the time had come for various special units to go into action.

The information acquired in Operation "Dora" was now put into practice. The Brandenburgers began military reconnaissance work in the border region between Libya and French Central Africa in order to make accurate and complete existing maps. Patrols crossed areas of desert using tracks known only to the native Bedouins in order to find routes that the Africa Corps could use to outflank and encircle the enemy.

In January 1941 a Brandenburger patrol was sent into the Italian colony of Eritrea. When British troops entered the territory the Brandenburgers withdrew into Abyssinia, which had been annexed by Italy.

At first General Rommel was entirely opposed to the use of agent groups and special formations, possibly using enemy uniforms. Not until the enemy began using similar tactics was he convinced that the German side also needed a special force.

176

Special Unit 287, which was formed in the Runienberg barracks in Potsdam from the 11th Brandenburg Company and trained for action in the desert, included men with desert experience.

Special Unit 288 was of similar composition and underwent the same training. The area of operations for both units was to be the western desert and the Suez Canal, or an even more extensive operation which, following the conquest of the Caucasus, was to lead through Persia and Iraq to the Suez Canal.

When the English entered Addis Ababa on 4 April 1941, elements of these special units fought the British invaders and inflicted casualties on them. When the English neared Massaua on the Red Sea, another detachment sank a fully loaded Italian freighter, blocking the passage.

On 3 May 1941, on orders from Oberst Piekenbrock, an agent under cover as a scientist together with two escorts slipped into French West Africa via southern Libya. His job was to scout the region for following Brandenburger commandos.

Beginning in mid-1941, the 13th Company of the 800th Special Purpose Construction Training Regiment Brandenburg was readied in Brandenburg as a "catch basin" for the formation of a tropical company. On 28 October 1941 the first half-company under Oblt. Wilhelm von Koenen departed Brandenburg for Tripoli via Naples. It was to be employed as a supply company.

The first live action by the Brandenburgers in North Africa took place during Panzer Group Africa's eastward advance that began on 22 January 1942. When the spearhead units reached the Egyptian border on 24th January, Brandenburgers under Oblt Bisping were with them; however, nothing is known of their orders or actions in which they took part.

On 22nd January another commando under Oblt von Leipzig set out from the Libyan village of Tarabulus, where they had transformed themselves into Arabs, for the British garrison city of Murzuk. The first radio-equipped agents were installed behind the British troops and in January 1942 another detachment of Brandenburgers constructed a forward airfield at Gatron so that reconnaissance aircraft could fly from there over the Tibest and Tümmo Mountains.

Oblt von Leipzig's operation south from Tripoli was begun with the considerable force of 100 men equipped with captured British trucks, including 12 mounting 40-mm Bofors cannon. As well they had Jeeps armed with anti-aircraft machine-guns, a command car, and tanker trucks for water and gasoline. The group also included a repair unit commanded by an experienced technical sergeant and a captured Spitfire aircraft. The aircraft was flown by a Hauptmann of the Brandenburgers.

The march was first supposed to lead to Murzuk, the Italian's forward base in the desert. From there Oblt von Leipzig's force was to split into three to carry out reconnaissance missions:

Patrol A: Commanded by Oblt von Leipzig, was assigned the main operation. It was to advance south to the Tümmo Mountains and from there to the Tassili Plateau, along which it was believed ran the British supply road.

Patrol B: Commanded by Feldwebel Stegmann, was to scout toward the Tibesti Mountains.

Patrol C: Commanded by Leutnant Becker, was to advance west to Gath on the Algerian border.

The operation, which was to cover 4,000 kilometers, began after two weeks of preparation. Its primary objective was to halt the flow of supplies to the British army over the west-east route which began in the Gulf of Guinea in the west and led across Central Africa to Port Said.

At first the unit advanced quickly through the Gafara area south of Tripoli. It was to scout passable tracks, find water holes, and then carry out the reconnaissance missions. Many of the group's soldiers spoke fluent English, some Arabic. Their commanding officer, Oberleutnant von Leipzig, came from Southwest Africa.

After driving 1,000 kilometers through the desert the group came upon the track that led from Misurata to Hun and Socna. Finally, that afternoon, Murzuk was reached. Residing there was Major Matteo Rinaldi, a desert-experienced officer who had taken part in the campaign against the Senussi with Marshall Graziani. He and his garrison of four Italians and 150 native camel riders stood guard on the border of the Italian empire. When the subject of constructing an airfield was raised, Major Rinaldi suggested Gatrun. Gatrun lay about 100 kilometers southwest of Murzuk. As conditions there were favorable, the engineers immediately set to work.

The reconnaissance element of the operation began with the main group's planned advance to the Himmel Mountains. Fw. Stegmann and his smaller group drove to Tibesti and Lt. Becker headed west for Gath on the Algerian border. The group soon transferred its base from Murzuk to the forward airfield at Gatrun. The radio station was also set up there and it was joined by the repair unit and two self-propelled guns to guard the field.

On its way to Gath the Becker group had to deal with a road that scarcely warranted the name. It also had to cross the pass beyond Serdeles. Conditions improved on the other side. The road to Wadi Tenezruft was good. When the group reached the wadi on which Gath also lay, they were met by a white man in Arab dress. It became evident that he was German, a native of Hamburg, who had landed in Ghat after deserting from the French Foreign Legion.

It turned out that the man was able to describe the entire desert area south of Gath that the group was supposed to reconnoiter. The Becker group took his directions in carrying out its mission and created a map of the area south of Ghat. When the Becker patrol returned to Gatrun the men found a proper supply dump there complete with military post office.

Oberleutnant von Leipzig and his group advanced into the Himmel Mountains. On the very first hill they encountered a French patrol driving through the desert in an armored car. Disguised as British troops, the Brandenburgers were not recognized. The two groups exchanged greetings and best wishes and then went their separate ways. It was different at Ghezedia, where the patrol was stopped and identified. There was a brief firefight in which two vehicles were shot up by the enemy. The crews climbed into the surviving vehicles and the patrol withdrew. It turned out that they had driven into a well-camouflaged French camp.

Although the de Gaulle troops did not give chase, they did man all the passes and hilltops, from which they could monitor the entire area with their field glasses. The Tümmo Pass was especially heavily manned.

The remaining group under Fw. Stegmann drove through the desert village of Aui to the Wadi Arabi at the foot of the Tibesti Mountains, where it was able to establish first contact with the Tibbu living there. In the Tibbu camp they learned that the French had also set up a forward base there and kept a sharp eye on the area south of the Tibestis. The Brandenburgers also learned that a German aircraft had attacked Fort Lamy seven months earlier. The French had taken heavy casualties in the attack and since then they had bolstered their garrison in the fort and had advanced to the foot of the Tibesti Mountains. They had established observation posts on several of the mountaintops.

A radio message was dispatched requesting that the special unit's Spitfire aircraft be sent. By the time it arrived the group had cleared a narrow landing strip with the Tibbu's help. Hauptmann Gerlach carried out a number of reconnaissance flights from the desert strip similar to those he had earlier flown from Gatrun. He determined that the low hills south of the Tibestis were occupied by French troops. He located the French headquarters in Bardai and Vur.

His aircraft was never fired on, for it was painted in British colors and was assumed to be an aircraft of the RAF. Four days after his arrival Hptm. Gerlach took off on a flight to Lake Chad to reconnoiter its south and southeast shores. The result was the same: French troops were everywhere.

As a result of the three reconnaissance forays Oberleutnant von Leipzig was forced to report that, as planned, the advance from Gatrun into Central Africa would be possible only with a strong motorized force of at least three divisions. A single division would not get past the Tümmo Pass. As well the operation would require a bomber group and a fighter group for escort.

The plan died then and there, for Rommel could not spare a single armored division from his meager force in Africa. These facts confirm one thing, however: with a German division and the necessary air forces in Iraq and another in this last area, the entire operation, the conquest of Alexandria and Cairo and an advance from Iraq into the Russian oil region, could have been brought to a successful conclusion.

Following the failure of the German attack on the British positions at El Alamein, the tropical company under Oblt von Leipzig had to be ordered out of Murzuk and the area to the south near Gatrun if it was not to be cut off. It withdrew into Tunisia, which after the Allied landings on 8 November 1942 had also become a battleground.

OPERATION "SAALAAM"

At the same time as part of the Tropical Company was beginning its operation in the south, in the north the rest of the company initiated and carried out several other actions which were more or less of a reconnaissance nature. The most outstanding of these was Operation "Saalaam". The object of the operation was to make contact with Egyptian nationalists who had withdrawn to the Fayum oasis. These nationalists were sworn enemies of Great Britain. An attempt was to be made by the Brandenburgers to use them against English installations.

These men were also to form a sort of industry protection force so that when German forces entered Cairo they would find all the important facilities still operating. Preparations for the operation had begun in November 1941. It had to be postponed, however, after the Africa Corps was forced to retreat in November following the launching by the British of a major offensive. Not until German forces resumed the offensive on 21 January 1942, resulting in the capture of Tobruk on 20th June, did the operation move from the preparation phase to execution.

Leader of the battle group was Hauptmann Laszlo Count Almaszy, who knew Egypt very well. Before the war he had been active as a flight instructor in Cairo and had cultivated reliable contacts in the country. Almaszy was assisted by another German from Egypt. There was also a foreign correspondent who had spent a long time in London and also knew Egypt. Hptm. Almaszy had a letter of recommendation from the Grand

Mufti of Jerusalem, which in the Arab world was worth its weight in gold. The letter was given to a pair of agents before they were sent into Cairo to gather intelligence. All the information they gathered on troop movements and preparations by the enemy was radioed back to Rommel.

The two agents, who came from the interpreter school where they had taught, had ten years of experience in Egypt. The rest of the group was made up of Brandenburgers who had volunteered for the operation. The greatest difficulty associated with the mission was the 3,000 kilometer journey to the objective.

The operation began in Tripoli on 29 April 1942. The group, which was equipped with two captured Ford cars and two 1 1/2 ton Ford trucks, made good progress as far as the Gialo oasis. From there the "route" consisted of a compass course to follow. All the men wore German uniforms. The cars were marked with German crosses, however these had been smeared with mud and were identifiable only from close range. The following is a detailed account of the operation.

THE OBJECTIVE IS CAIRO AND THE NILE: POLITICAL ACTIONS IN EGYPT

The only detailed report on Operation "Saalaam" was submitted by Hauptmann John W. Eppler of Abwehr II. The thoroughness of the report was a reflection of the high priority and importance given the operation.

"Shortly before 11 A.M. the next morning, 12 April 1942, I arrived before the entrance of the Hotel Uaddon and prepared to go in to see Rommel. The Uaddon was on a small rise at the edge of Tripoli. It had been built for Air Marshall Italo Balbo as one of his residences in the country. From there one could see the sea as well as the countryside and all of Tripoli.

When I walked into the lobby past the saluting double sentry, I saw with relief that Almaszy had already arrived. One by one the others arrived: Oberstleutnant Maurer, liaison officer to the Centro Militare Offizia Informazione (the official designation for the Italian intelligence service), Oberst Melzer and Admiral Canaris.

We were all in uniform, although Canaris appeared in civilian clothes. While we were exchanging friendly greetings General Rommel arrived. This day he was wearing field gray. On his stiff officer's cap sat a pair of driving goggles, which were from captured British stocks. I noticed for the first time that he wore a scarf with his otherwise extremely correct uniform. This gave him a somewhat folksy appearance and softened his hardness.

The discussion was casual in form. We sat together cordially over beer and General Rommel once again outlined his next objectives."

At that time the German Africa Corps was in the great Syrte arc near the Arco dei Fileni. His intention was to advance to the Halfaya Pass and from there take Sidi Barani and Marsa Matruk. For Rommel it was decisively important to advance as quickly as possible and take full advantage of the enemy's weak period, for Rommel's motto was: 'Exploit, exploit!'

For Rommel it was a foregone conclusion that he would not only retake the area of Tripolitania he had given up the year before, but also liberate all of Libya and advance to Alexandria in a rapid, decisive drive and thus open the way for an uprising against Great Britain by the nationalist forces in Egypt which were waiting for such an advance."

Rommel wrote:

Führer Headquarters is aware of the importance of the efforts of the Africa Corps.

Before us stands the great and difficult task of driving through to the Suez Canal and taking Egypt. If we succeed it will mean the loss to England of the entire Near East. The huge oil region there will fall into our hands and can be used by our entire armed forces. Only thus will it be possible to equip the army and air force as well as the navy with greater numbers of motor vehicles and this will be a severe defeat for the Allies.

We would control the Persian Gulf with all its ports and thereby prevent the extensive deliveries of war materiel by the Americans to the Soviet Union.

This would not be all, for after such a victory Malta and Cyprus and ultimately Gibraltar would fall to us. This would secure the flow of supplies not only for the Africa Corps, but also for the troops that will then be stationed in Syria, in Iran and Iraq, and in southeast Russia near Baku and the Caspian Sea.

All this is still in the distant future. First we must create the necessary conditions for it.

John Eppler continued: "After this introduction General Rommel turned to our direct mission: 'We need intelligence on the enemy, above all reliable intelligence. Even the smallest report can be of significance. The information from Cairo sounds favorable. Since July, as Admiral Canaris has confirmed to me, the Abwehr has had the code used by the US military attaché in the US embassy in Cairo. Everything radioed to Washington from there by Colonel Feller is decoded by us, and being a conscientious officer Colonel Feller reports on all movements by the British 8th Army and reports every convoy and every reinforcement of British troops from Iraq or Palestine.

'But this cannot last forever. This leak will be discovered and plugged some day. They will use a new code. By then we have to have set up a perfect intelligence apparatus with a secret transmitter in Cairo which can keep us informed of the latest happenings in Egypt. It is therefore of decisive importance for you, Hauptmann Eppler, and for you and your men, Major Almaszy, to get to work in Cairo. You will provide us with the latest intelligence and trends in Egypt and above all in the Egyptian resistance.'

Rommel turned to Admiral Canaris. 'This is why I immediately agreed to your proposal, Canaris. For the coming time we need not only the most extensive intelligence gathering on the enemy, but also an assessment of the mood among the young officers of the resistance. This must be a well thought out and above all fully functioning operation."

"General, our soldiers, especially Major Almaszy, an expert in desert reconnaissance in the Sahara, and Hauptmann Eppler, son of an Egyptian pasha, both of whom can converse in Arabic, and Hauptmann Eppler's assistant, who will take part in the action as an American, are members of the Abwehr and are skilled in all aspects of undercover operations. Nevertheless, there cannot be one hundred percent certainty. But I have confidence that this operation will proceed without a hitch. It has been extremely well planned, will be carried out by desert experts, and has the best prospects for the Cairo mission. The remaining participants in this Operation Saalaam were personally selected by Hauptmann Eppler and myself. Since all have received a clean bill of health all the requirements have been optimally met.'

At the end of the meeting, after Rommel had exchanged a few words with Almaszy, he observed in his typical Swabian way, 'You know the crazy have the most luck. Why should you have none?'

Finally Rommel said goodbye to the men of the commando mission to the Nile personally. He shook hands with each of them and wished them good luck for the operation.

The final preparations were made. These included selecting the radio code and confirming the operational status, especially of the receivers, of the main radio station at the headquarters of Panzer Army Africa and the two backup stations in Smyrna and Alexandrette. All transmissions would come from the main station with the panzer army.

The code was as simple as it was unbreakable. The book Rebecca by Daphne Du Maurier was used to find the appropriate words. All the radio stations were issued completely identical editions of this work. When a transmission was to be sent the words to be used had to be taken from this book. The page numbers were then encoded by using a certain system, so that the enemy would have to assume that it was a numerical code.

The agreed-upon transmission times were 6 A.M., 1 P.M. and 7 P.M. The ten men of the entire team prepared for the start of the mission, which was scheduled for 29 April 1942. The two operators of the main radio station were taken as far as Memelin in the Cyrenaica, near Rommel's headquarters, where they were dropped off to set up their radio station. The vehicles to be used were five captured from the British, two Fords and three $1\,{}^1\!/\!{}_2$ ton trucks.

An MG 15 was mounted on each vehicle. The conversations centered around one question: 'Can we make the estimated 3,000 kilometers through the unexplored Sahara?' Little mention was made of the fact that we would have to cover another 3,000 kilometers to get back. What was involved beyond the already mentioned intelligence gathering missions was secret, but those in the know of course knew that they also had to free and bring to Germany General Asis el-Misri, who had been chief of the general staff of the Egyptian Army when war broke out and who, because of his pro-German stance, had been removed in 1940 under great pressure from the English. The Fama reported that the general was going to be arrested.

The attempts to free the general had begun in February 1941. At that time Major Ritter of the Abwehr's foreign department had won over the scientist and desert traveler Almaszy for this unusual action. Immediately before this, Nikolaus Ritter had outlined his adventurous plan to Admiral Canaris: with the support of X Air Corps a team of 10 Abwehr men led by Count Laszlo von Almaszy would set out for Egypt to free the general.

At first General Misri Pasha favored a plan that would see him picked up by a submarine from Lake Berollos in the Nile Delta. This could not be done by a German submarine, however. He then agreed to the proposal that he be brought out of the country by aircraft.

Not until 30 May 1941, after the successful conclusion of the Crete operation, was Major Ritter able to obtain two He III aircraft from General Geißler who commanded X Air Corps. The aircraft came from Kampfgeschwader 26. The site chosen for the landing was a strip at the Red Djebel on the big oasis road. General el Misri Pasha could reach it from Cairo in a few hours. the first attempt was called off after General Misri was in a car accident. Then, on Saturday, 7 June 1941, the two aircraft took off from Derna and headed east.

Hauptmann Haller, commander of a group in Kampfgeschwader 26, flew the first aircraft. His radio operator was Hptm. Blaich, who had experience in desert flights. Major Ritter flew in this, the escort aircraft. Almaszy was in the second aircraft. It was to land and pick up the general while the escort aircraft kept any opposition at a distance. When the aircraft arrived over the landing site at about 6 P.M. there was no sign of the passenger. Almaszy had the pickup aircraft fly along the road to Cairo at low level. When the spires of the city came into view it turned around. The general had not come.

The next day the radio operator in Cairo reported that the general had been arrested and that his transmitter had probably also been betrayed and that radio activity had to be terminated immediately. This was another argument for setting up a new radio station. General el Misri Pasha had taken off in an aircraft for the meeting place, but when a British aircraft appeared his aircraft, which had taken off from Heliopolis airfield, descended steeply as the pilot prepared for a forced landing. It struck the top of an olive tree and crashed.

A British sentry drove to the crash site and took the general into custody. A double was used to fool the British authorities and instead of the general a major, one of the conspirators, went into prison in place of the general, while he continued to stay in contact with the conspirators under Nasser.

What of the conspirators and nationalists in Egypt? Who led them and what were their relations with each other and the occupying power England?

THE EGYPTIAN CONSPIRATORS

In addition to the underground activity of the Arab nationalists under Shiikrti elKuwatli in Syria and Beshara al-Khury in Lebanon, there were also officers of the army and other nationalists at work in Egypt.

Cairo and Alexandria, which had become rear area centers for the British forces after war broke out, suffered under the occupation and the constant British malice. King Farouk I succeeded his father, Faud I, to the Egyptian throne after the latter's death on 28 April 1936, although he remained under a regency until 29 July 1937, when he was declared to be of age.

The young king admired Mussolini but especially Hitler and sought to emulate him, which was impossible under British occupation. He and the pashas of the ruling Wafd Party realized that a victory by the Africa Corps and an ultimate victory by Germany would mean complete freedom from Great Britain for Egypt. The founders of the Saghlul Pasha and—during the Second World War—Nahhas Pasha Parties were ardent supporters of Egyptian national independence. To them it seemed that through Germany it was a certainty. Hasan el-Banna, the military leader of the Moslem Brotherhood, was also anti-British. The overwhelming majority of Egyptian students and intellectuals were so encouraged by the possibility of the German Africa Corps reaching Cairo that in 1941 and 1942 they openly held demonstrations in the streets of Cairo. It was reported to Germany that demonstrators shouted; "We are Rommel's soldiers!" Another slogan was "Out with the English!"

In the army it was primarily the young officers who prepared their revolution while the Africa Corps battled the British. Furthermore the broad mass of the population supported all those who fought against England, which they considered to be their oppressor.

When the Africa Corps launched a lightning offensive at the end of January 1942 and recaptured all of Cyrenaica in seventeen days, London took action to forestall a prepared uprising. On 4 February 1942 the British ambassador in Cairo, Sir Miles Lampson, and a group of officers entered the Abding Palace with pistols drawn. At the same time tanks and personnel carriers surrounded the palace, which was the residence of the Egyptian king. Sir Miles Lampson stormed into the king's office and presented him with an ultimatum: he had 24 hours to name the leader of the Wafd Party, Nahas Pasha, prime minister, or be removed and deported.

Nahas Pasha was also an opponent of England, but as expected he remained neutral after King Farouk I charged him with reforming the government. The Wafd was thus transformed from a freedom party into one of the institutions that suppressed freedom. Now it was up to the officers with nationalist leanings, who were led by two young officers: Anwar el Sadat and Gamal Abd el-Nasser.

The young officers of the Egyptian Army were in contact with Rommel's Panzer Army Africa in 1941 and even more so in 1942. Several times they were ready to unleash the uprising, but each time something happened that seemed to make it inadvisable.

The leader of the officer conspiracy was the former chief of staff of the army General Asis el-Misri. He had worked out the plans according to which the army was to seize power and help Rommel's panzer army to march into Cairo via Alexandria. These conspirators contacted the headquarters of the Africa Corps by courier and Rommel declared himself ready to work with them. General el-Misri was asked to leave Egypt covertly and present his plans to Rommel in person and determine the strategy and tactics to be used.

This was the beginning of what the later Colonel Sadat called the "Egyptian patriots' streak of bad luck."

The officers subsequently worked out a plan which Sadat described as follows: "An armed coup d'état was supposed to bring down the government in Cairo and install a national cabinet. The Egyptian Army was supposed to wage a small-scale war against the British to weaken the enemy, tie down large numbers of troops and thus weaken the British units facing the German front. The fate of the British Empire would be decided as soon as we linked up with the troops of the Axis powers."

This time Admiral Canaris took a personal interest in the second attempt to free the general from Cairo and the participation of Rommel for the purpose of working out a joint plan for the defeat of the British in Egypt. Two Abwehr agents disguised as Egyptian dervishes had tried to reach Cairo at the same time as Eppler. Both made it to Fayum Oasis, a center for the Egyptian nationalists, and established contacts there. From there they were to be slipped into Cairo.

Canaris now went all out. In mid-June 1941 he called a meeting at his headquarters. To the assembled officers he said: "Rommel needs reliable information from the British concentration areas in Egypt. His strategy is based on tricks and surprising the enemy. Every bit of intelligence from the enemy camp that is of help to him is worth more than an armored battalion."

Major Ritter was unable to go to Derna because he had to complete all the preparations for a second air mission. This foresight proved to be useful, for when two German captains named Klein and Mühlenbruch arrived at his headquarters a short time later things came to a head. Both men were experts in Arabic and spoke the language perfectly. They had lived in Alexandria and Haifa for a long time and had indicated their willingness to spy for Germany in Cairo. Hauptmann Almaszy of the Abwehr, who was still in Derna, used his experience as a desert geologist to draw a map illustrating a caravan route from Farafrah oasis to Deirut on the Nile. On it Almaszy marked a hill 100 kilometers from the Nile that could be used as a "prominent feature in the field."

"Also," he told the assembled members of the special detachment, "there is a broad strip of firm desert ground called the Serir ground. An aircraft can land on it easily. The flying time there from Derna is about 4 1/2 hours. From there it is only another 100 kilometers to the Nile Valley." They agreed that a light motorcycle could deliver the two quickly over the 100 kilometers. A machine would therefore be provided and on 16 July 1941 the He III was to land at Derna, pick up the team and take it on its way.

The aircraft did not arrive. Major Ritter ordered the aircraft allocated as escort to be used to transport the agents, and the escort was dispensed with. The first aircraft later arrived after all, having had a tire problem, and it was assigned to the escort role. The aircraft took off one close behind the other from the Derna airfield. They flew east at a height of 500 meters; they then climbed to 4,000 meters near enemy territory when a sandstorm reduced visibility below.

After just five hours in the air the line of hills that was their target came into sight. While the escort aircraft stayed at 1,000 meters, the transport descended. The aircraft commander ordered the young pilot to land. The pilot did not do so, however. He had seen a British armored car heading in their direction. The pilot flew a wide circle, commenced his approach to land, then pulled up again when he saw that the site he had chosen was too rough. During the next approach the sun suddenly disappeared; it had simply gone down. Major Ritter was forced to order the pilot to return to Derna. When they approached their destination the radio operator received a message not to land as the airfield was under attack. The nearest alternate was Benghazi. Then an engine failed and the pilot turned back toward Derna, as Benghazi could not be reached on one engine.

To make matters even worse the Heinkel was fired on by a British bomber. The inexperienced pilot, whose aircraft was supposed to have been the escort, took evasive action and found himself over the Mediterranean. Soon afterward the fuel ran out and he made a' forced landing in the water. The machine impacted heavily and agent Miihlenbruch was killed. Major Ritter was rescued with a concussion. Pilot Hptm. Leicht was also badly hurt but was pulled into the life raft.

The survivors spent two days in the water, with four sitting in the raft and two clinging to it, before the waves cast them up on the beach. The survivors reached an Arab village; the inhabitants alerted the desert rescue squadron, which picked them up. Major Ritter was flown to hospital and his place was taken by Hauptmann von Almaszy of the Abwehr.

On arriving in Gialo Hauptmann von Almaszy learned that his team had set out on 29 April 1942. However, it encountered conditions different from those reported by the Italians—"smooth sand so hard that a motor vehicle can drive on it easily"—instead it discovered a belt of dunes between Gialo and Kufra oasis 450 km to the south which had to be skirted.

Now Hauptmann von Almaszy had to personally go up on a scouting mission. He obtained an aircraft at the Italian airfield at EI Agheila and flew the planned route. What he found confirmed the information from the locals. Furthermore the water in the Gialo oasis was not good and began to foul after three days. Drinking water was brought from Bir Butafall, which was about 20 km east of Gialo oasis and known only to the natives.

Nevertheless, after stocking up with water they departed Gialo on 4th may. In Hauptmann von Almaszy's vehicle was the leader of the two-man Abwehr team, Hans Eppler. He had previously served in the German embassy in Cairo on special duties with his friend Gerd Sandstede.

After Rommel's energetic intervention, in which he called for first-hand information on the enemy, Eppler, his friend Sandstede and Count Almaszy had been chosen by Admiral Canaris for this undertaking. Each of the following three cars also carried two Abwehr men. The first day the cars covered a considerable distance quickly. Not until the second day did the terrain become more difficult. Negotiating the high sand dunes required great skill on the part of the drivers. The group covered just 40 kilometers in the 48 hours of the second and third days.

The doctor was the first to suffer the so-called desert staggers. This practically ended the mission for the entire group, for such an illness, whose symptoms included clouding of consciousness and circulatory disturbances, made continuing impossible. Then the Brandenburger NCO who was serving as technical expert suffered a heart attack. They headed back the way they had come and reached Gialo oasis five days after they had left.

The team set out again on the morning of 11th May. The two men who had fallen ill were not replaced. Von Almaszy had selected a new route. It led south along the well-known Italian "iron bar route" which was called "Balifikata." This well-marked route led around the area of sand dunes. After six days under way the team came to a huge rocky area, a so-called garet, as the Bedouins called these boulder fields that included huge chunks of basalt.

Almaszy and Eppler led a patrol to scout a way around the field. They found a passable route but the going was slow. The detour lasted six hours before the terrain became more friendly. Now they could see the high plateau of the Kebir Mountains before them. Count Almaszy had driven through them while on research expeditions between 1930 and 1932 and in 1937. Now they had to find a pass to take them through the mountains.

At the foot of the Gilf el Kebir Almaszy even found a water depot he had left there in 1937. The water in the sealed canisters was still drinkable. From there—where one vehicle was left as depot for the return trip—Almaszy sent a radio message to Gialo that they had reached this first objective. Three hours later Almaszy found a way through the mountains. On reaching the plateau they carried out measurements for a landing strip. From there to the Nile and Cairo was exactly 700 km by air.

The southernmost point had been reached. On 22nd May the team headed east, and a short time later northeast, until it arrived at the Charga oasis about 270 kilometers northwest of Aswan. They spent the night at a safe distance from the oasis, which lay in a depression, before scouting it on foot the next morning. No English troops were found at the oasis.

It was Sunday, 23 May 1942, when they drove toward the oasis in two vehicles each carrying three men. The third vehicle had been left behind in a ravine outside the oasis as the second vehicle depot. They were stopped by an Egyptian sentry just short of the oasis. When the Egyptian asked what they were doing, Eppler, on the advice of Almaszy, told him that they were the advance party of a British division headquarters and the general would soon be following soon.

They were allowed to pass. In this way by afternoon they reached the area 10 km southwest of Assiut, a city on the Nile in which Eppler and his associates were supposed to be dropped off so as to continue to Cairo by train.

On arrival the two agents fetched their things from the storage compartment. They had brought everything needed to transform them into Cairo businessmen, including notebooks with Egyptian writing and a letter from an Egyptian auto club for an auto trip through the desert. In one of their bags were the two secret transmitters with which they were to communicate with Rommel's headquarters from Cairo. Hidden in a second bag was 20,000 Pounds, then worth about 400,000 Reichsmarks.

While Eppler and Sandstede went to Assiut, Almaszy turned his two vehicles around and began the return journey. Along the way he carried out precise mapping of the terrain. Beyond the Gilf el Kebir they joined up with a column of Sudanese for a time. Then they came upon an unguarded supply dump that belonged to their opposite number, namely the Long Range Desert Group. The Germans helped themselves to water, gasoline and food from the 12 trucks.

The radio operator tapped out the following message to the radio station in Cyrenaica: "Operation Saalaam completed, returning to base."

A few days later Hauptmann Almaszy reported his team's return to General Rommel. There he learned that his small radio station had been incorporated by Rommel's headquarters and had been captured by the English during the fighting in the Knightsbridge area. This was later to have fatal consequences for the two agents in Cairo. Rommel promoted Almaszy to Major and expressed hope that he would see him again soon in Cairo.

TO ASSIUT AND CAIRO

Along with his radio operator, who was now using the name Peter Monkaster and who called a genuine American passport his own, John

Eppler, now Hussein Gaafar—his father's name—drove out of Charga toward Assiut along the hard-packed road. It was 23 May 1942. Shortly before Assiut they parted ways with Almaszy and their friends and continued alone to Assiut. With them they had two suitcases, the radio equipment hidden in one and the money in the other.

They reached the edge of the city and found themselves facing a British army camp being used for a training exercise. Eppler and his radioman reported to the captain overseeing the exercise. They said that they had driven into the desert, that the engine of their car had failed, and that they had been walking for two hours. The captain had a jeep take them to Cairo and promised to look after their car in the coming days.

With much luck and the help of a servant named Achmed whom they hired in Helwan, the two agents managed to get their valuable bags through a British checkpoint at the Cairo railway station. They had successfully taken the first step in the operation.

As the son of the judge and pasha Gaafar, Eppler knew Cairo very well. He first moved into an Italian-run rooming house, from where his operator dispatched the first message to Mamelin. The receiving station answered at once. Operation "Condor", as it was now known, had begun successfully. Operator Hans-Gert Sandstede had every reason to be proud, for in the coming days the radio link functioned smoothly. It was he who came up with the line that caused everyone to laugh: "Allah knows everything, Adolf Hitler knows everything better!"

Meanwhile he had memorized the book *Rebecca*—of course his copy was in English—which enabled him to encode messages quickly.

Eppler went to the famous "Kit Kat" nightclub, which was located on the Nile island of Zamalek, and there he found an old friend, the dancer Hekmat. It happened that he took a seat at a table where a representative of the British intelligence service was sitting. Through Madame Amer, a native of Austria, he established contact with his family living in Cairo and on their large estate. He met with his brother and learned that his father had died several weeks before.

With the help of old friends Eppler was able to rent a houseboat on the bank of the Nile. His neighbor was Major Dunstan, know known to Eppler as head of Secret Investigations Middle East. Eppler presented himself as Hussein Gaafar, son of the later superior judge. First contacts were made. The ruling head of the Cairo Muslim Brotherhood, Prince Abbas Halim, assured him of his full support.

Meanwhile the receiving station in Africa had suddenly ceased to communicate. What had happened? When Count Almaszy reported to Rommel west of Bir Hacheim at the beginning of June, the latter said to him:

"You know, Almaszy, the whole thing is very embarrassing to me. When we got into trouble south of Gazala near Knightsbridge on 28th May and had to break through to the west, the Tommy snapped up part of my signals echelon. With it, unfortunately, was the radio truck with Aberle and Weber and all their papers."

Count Almaszy could imagine what this must mean for Eppler and Sandstede. He gave a report on his own operation and declared that he had found and mapped an area about 600 km southwest of Cairo where an airfield could be built for bombing the British. Rommel promoted Almaszy to major on the spot and ordered radio traffic with Cairo stopped in order not to endanger the radio operator there.

That was the reason for the silence of the African receiving station. Both of the other receiving stations were forbidden to transmit, nevertheless they received all the transmissions from Cairo.

The dancer Hekmat was able to inform Eppler that the British Near East Command had ordered the transfer of the 10th Army from Syria and Palestine. A little later she told him that a load of 100,000 mines had been delivered to the Alamein front to stop the Germans there. As well he learned that the 2nd New Zealand Division had been moved to the fortress of Marsa Matruk, in order to stop the Africa Corps there should it succeed in taking Tobruk.

The reputation of the parties on the houseboat grew. Once Anwar el Sadat was invited. He was not happy with what he saw and to him the boat was a veritable den of iniquity. Accordingly this made him distrustful of the two agents. He saw Eppler as the lazy son of a rich man.

The fall of Tobruk produced an atmosphere of gloom and doom in Alexandria and Cairo. Many secrecy officers burnt their files. Gasoline had to be poured over the tall stacks of files in the courtyard of the British headquarters in the Hotel Semiram in order to get them to burn. The population of Cairo gloated as they watched this development. They prepared for the arrival of German troops. Graffiti covered the houses, slogans such as: "Sieg Heil!", "Duce, Duce!" and even "Go home you bastards!" Less than proper English, but the point got across.

At the beginning of September Sandstede and Eppler were arrested by the intelligence service. They came—as was the case the world over—at dawn, a time that is the most favorable for arrests of all kinds. Handcuffs were placed over their wrists. Fortunately Sandstede had been able to burn the most incriminating of their papers. While the British were busy with Eppler, Sandstede had prepared the boat to be scuttled. The pair were interrogated by the British in the camp at Maadi; although they were threatened with revolvers they admitted nothing.

The next night Sandstede slit his wrists and Eppler thought that he had "died unnoticed by the guards." Not until months later did he learn that Sandstede was still alive; the British had found him in time to save his life. As they refused to confess, Eppler and Sandstede were subjected to increasingly brutal treatment. Eppler finally agreed to write a confession. He was taken to a special cell and given special food. It took him four weeks to write his "confession." It consisted of one word; all 200 pages contained the one word "station."

The end of this "song" was a severe beating by eight soldiers under the command of Major Kennedy, already known for his brutal methods. Nevertheless, the "station story" was received with some amusement in British headquarters.

After the pair had made several statements without "blowing the whistle" on a single German agent or Egyptian nationalist, they were brought before a military court. The verdict: "Sentenced to death by firing squad."

A week later their sentence was commuted, and at the request of British officers, however this was not revealed at first. Prior to this Winston Churchill, who was in Cairo to meet with Chiang Kai Shek and Ibn Saud, suddenly appeared at the cell where the two were sentenced to die were being held. When, in the course of their brief conversation, they asked the British Prime Minister if, in a similar situation, he would have given away his people behind the scenes and confessed, the latter said, "Not a word".

"Not a word" was said by Eppler and his friend.

Several days after the end of the war Rommel's two spies were released to return to Germany, not to freedom but rather to the former concentration camp at Neuengamme. There they were just "two figures among 8,000 Nazis," who were starved, beaten and killed. On 17 July 1946 they were shipped to Hamburg and there simply thrown out of the jeep at the market. They were free.

LEBANON AND SYRIA

Before describing the subsequent operations by the Brandenburgers in Africa, a brief survey of events in Syria and Lebanon in 1941.

Already in September 1940 Oberleutnant Roser of the Abwehr had been sent to Beirut, Lebanon as its "advance detachment." The first elements of the Brandenburgers' Arab Brigade were sent to the Near East beginning at the end of 1940 for operations in Lebanon, Syria and Iraq.

On 7 March 1941 the Ausland/Abwehr urged the Foreign Office to finally approve German operations in those lands. On 24th March Admiral Canaris, together with officers Bürkner, Piekenbrock and von Lahousen and Oberstleutnant Stolze, conferred in the Foreign Office with representatives from the Near East on the planned measures. What was requested was the widening of the spy net, especially in Turkey, Egypt, Syria and Iraq, and the provoking of anti-British actions that would culminate in revolts in Palestine, Trans-Jordan and Iraq. The revolutionaries in Palestine as well as those in Trans-Jordan and especially Iraq were to be strengthened by deliveries of arms of all types. The main attention of the Abwehr was initially focused on Iraq, which has been dealt with already. But Syria was also in the Abwehr's plans, which even included a request to bomb the Haifa oil refinery in Palestine.

On 9th June a detachment of the Arab Brigade crossed the border between Iraq and Syria and fought on against the British until 3rd July. Under the cover of a diplomat, Abwehr officer Rahn established himself in Syria to gather intelligence on troop strengths and camps there as well as their corps headquarters in Trans-Jordan and Palestine. On 25th June Oberleutnant Roser, the representative with the ceasefire commission in Damascus, withdrew with his small party into Turkey. By 30 June 1941 he and his men were joined by about 300 Iraqi, Syrian and Palestinian nationalists. They had been provided with German passports by the Abwehr so that they might slip into Turkey and from there travel to Germany. Few succeeded however.

Beginning in summer 1941 Arab agents were trained for operations in the Syrian desert at a camp near Cape Sunion on the south tip of the Greek mainland. However, they were unable to carry out the planned actions, because Syria had meanwhile been taken over by the Free French.

THE FREE FRENCH IN SYRIA

On 8 June 1941 leaflets rained down on the surprised inhabitants of many of the cities in the Near East. They bore the signature of General Georges Catroux. He was acknowledged as an expert on Africa, for he had served and fought there and in Indochina and was governor of Indochina from 1939 to 1940. He had joined the movement headed by General de Gaulle and in early summer 1941 was named by him to be Senior Commissioner in Syria. He initiated the leaflet operation over Beirut and Tripoli, Damascus, Homs and Aleppo, and all the other cities and towns of Syria and Lebanon on behalf of General de Gaulle. The essence of the leaflet propaganda was:

"We have come to put an end to the Mandate regime and to free Syria and Lebanon and make them independent states."

The British government lent its support to this propaganda declaration and undertook to guarantee that the promises made would be kept.

The same day British, Free French and Indian troops from Iraq, Trans-Jordan and Palestine marched into Lebanon and Syria. This was a flagrant breach of the treaty Germany had concluded with the Vichy government under General Pétain. Since the attempts to get the Vichy government to voluntarily abandon the agreement had failed, it was now done by force. General Pétain's representative in Syria and Lebanon, the High Commissioner, was General Dentz. He was obliged to see to it that the terms of the German-French cease-fire were carried out and to work loyally with Germany. By the time of the invasion the rebels in Iraq had received the bulk of their arms from Syria. In Syria the German aircraft—too few in number, unfortunately—had landed to refuel and departed. The German agents in Syria could deploy freely without fear of being arrested by the high commissioner.

Once again it was Winston Churchill, the British prime minister, who made the decision to wipe out this wasps' nest and take both Syria and Lebanon from the Vichy French and place them under the Free French.

The operation was prepared under the code name "Exporter." But Vichy was unwilling to let these two countries go, which carried with it the risk of being seen as unreliable by the Germans, who might then occupy the free zone of Vichy France. Marshall Pétain ordered the Vichy forces to resist. When the US ambassador Admiral Leahy reproached the elderly Marshall for representing the interests of Germany and not France, he replied: "We know that we will lose Syria, but were are determined to fight to the end." The fighting began on 9th June and lasted until 12 July 1941. On that day a ceasefire was signed. Two days later General Catroux and the British General Wilson entered Beirut.

Some weeks later General de Gaulle also visited a part of "his territory." The Lebanese and Syrian politicians were very soon to learn that the French and English were at loggerheads. England was in favor of giving both countries their promised independence. De Gaulle, however, was of the opinion that mandate rule could not possibly end before the war was over. Furthermore, he demanded for the Free French exactly the same rights over both lands that had previously been exercised by France, because these had been set down by the League of Nations.

De Gaulle was certain that the English did not really want to see an independent Lebanon and Syria, but instead were supporting the idea in order to eliminate France for good as a competitor in the Near East. The general, who had the same effect as a red flag in England and in the free part of France, telegraphed his views to Churchill even before the fighting was over.

On 23rd July de Gaulle, who had got his way, reached an agreement with the British Minister for the Near East, Sir M.O. Lyttleton, according to which he—de Gaulle—might exercise all the rights due to France in

Syria and Lebanon. He had to, however, accept an Englishman as military commander-in-chief. The English General Spears was placed in command of the forces of both countries. The latter dared to characterize France and the French in Syria and Lebanon as inept.

Standing between these two hostile "allies" were still the Arab leaders, with Schükrü el Kuwatli in Syria and Beschara al-Khury in Lebanon. They succeeded in holding elections in August 1943. Both leaders won and the new parliament in Lebanon declared all the remaining limitations on independence invalid and mandate rule "at an end."

General Catroux was now forced to act. He declared the Lebanese declaration invalid and had arrested the president-elect Beschara al-Khury, the prime minister and most members of the government in Beirut. At this point the English stepped in and demanded that the men who had been arrested be released. Cairo and Baghdad supported the demand as did the USA; the latter did so only in secret and under the cover of a secret telegram. The French had to release their prisoners and so lost face in Lebanon and Syria.

Following the de Gaulle line, French troops attempted to retain control of the country after the war and even went so far as to bombard Damascus on 29 May 1945-as they had done twenty years earlier with good results. Then British troops intervened and "restored order."

After a mutual agreement was reached in December 1945, the last French troops left Syrian territory on 14 April 1946 and that of Lebanon on 31 December 1946.

THE BRANDENBURGERS IN TUNISIA

During the night of 30 October 1942 a meeting was held in the command post of the 800th Special Purpose Instruction Regiment Brandenburg near Voroshilovsk which resulted in the regiment's 13th Company and a platoon from the Light Pioneer Company under ObLt. Kuhlmann being separated from the rest of the regiment.

The two units were to form the basis of a special unit that would be joined by platoons from various units. Chosen to command the unit was Hptm. Wilhelm Koenen, a veteran of the African Theater, and it needed no prophet to predict that the unit would be sent to Africa.

The 9th Company of the III Battalion, Special Purpose Instruction Regiment Brandenburg, which had been deployed in the Dorogobush area on anti-partisan duties, was likewise sent back to Germany. There the men were examined for tropical suitability and in November 1942 transferred to North Africa, where the enemy had launched Operation Torch, an attempt to strike at the rear of Panzer Army Africa.

In October in the Trapani area the Kuhlmann Platoon was enlarged to a company and incorporated into the von Koenen Tropical Battalion as its 5th Company. On 12 November the units under Hauptmann Friedrich Koenen were given the official designation Tropical Battalion von Koenen. This independent unit was at first deployed on coastal defense. Not until weeks later did it take part in a special mission.

On the evening of 26 December 1942 two operations were launched from Bizerte airfield only minutes apart. The first, which was led by Hptm. von Koenen, was aimed at the railway bridge at Sidi bou Bakr, while the target of the second under the command of Leutnant Hagenauer was the railway bridge north of Kasserine.

Helmuth Spaeter, who later served as a staff officer in the Brandenburg Division, described "Operation Clormann" in his book on the Brandenburgers.

The battle group, which consisted of 30 men, was supposed to be flown to the target in three gliders. The operation was under the command of Lt. Hagenauer, who joined the Brandenburgers just prior to the mission. However, only two gliders were available instead of the desired three. The covering squad under Fw. Clormann had to be left behind, for the pioneers were the main actors in this play. Only Clormann and one of his men took part, armed with an MG 42 machine-gun. The Hagenauer group's mission was to blow up the road and rail bridge north of Kasserine. If successful, they would sever the main supply route of the English forces.

Towed by two Ju 52 transports, the gliders arrived in the target area on the evening of 26 December 1942. Met by heavy anti-aircraft fire, they were forced off course and landed in a side-valley. The gliders came down so far apart that only one crew was able to reach the objective. The glider pilot broke both legs and had to be left behind in the aircraft. Lt. Hagenauer was also injured and had to be carried by the nine remaining men. The NCO in charge of the pioneers was also injured and Fw. Clormann assumed command of his squad. The group found itself 20 kilometers from its target. The men set out in the afternoon, carrying the demolition equipment.

As dusk was falling the Germans came upon a lone rider on a camel. They stopped the man and convinced him to load their supplies on his animal and guide them to the bridge. They arrived at a dry riverbed that was crossed by the bridge at some point. Since it was already daylight they sought cover where they could spend the day. Leutnant Hagenauer, who had recovered sufficiently to assume command, instructed Clormann to take his machine-gunner and head toward the bridge until they could keep it under observation. The pair set out for the bridge on foot. This saved their lives, for two hours later they heard hectic rifle and submachine-gun behind them from the direction of the camp. They ran back a way until they saw a large number of French troops swarming toward the group from three sides, keeping it under fire.

"We mustn't go on," observed Obergefreiter Wodjarek, Clormann's gunner. "That's at least a company, they'll cut us to pieces."

The pair set off in a northwesterly direction. Their objective was Kairouan, where there were German troops. However, Kairouan lay 180 kilometers away. Lt. Clormann described what happened:

"We had 67 cigarettes, 2 boxes of matches, a box of Schoka Kola and a box of Cola Damlan. We had a total of 14 rounds of ammunition in our two pistols. We walked for six nights. When the hunger became unbearable we went into a Bedouin farmhouse. We identified ourselves as Germans and were well received and cared for. There were two handfuls of couscous and chicken broth for each of us, as well as three hot cups of coffee. We changed clothes in the hut, replacing our uniforms with native clothing. We then wandered another two days with our friends.

Near Piochon we unexpectedly came upon a German sentry. Keeping his distance—for after eleven days on the run we surely didn't smell too good—he took us to his company commander. After some questions and showing our pay books they believed us and we were sent back via battalion and regiment to the Air Commander Tunis, where we made our reports."

The Brandenburgers learned that all those of their comrades who had survived the disaster had been taken prisoner and were sent via. the English interrogation camps to Canada.

On 10 January 1943 another group led by Leutnant Luchs took off for Wadi el Melah. The bridge there was their target. The men reached the bridge, placed their explosives and detonated them. The bridge was only partly destroyed. An Arab V-man subsequently blew up the two bridge supports left standing, putting the bridge out of action for good.

In mid-January 1943 a British submarine dropped a commando team off the coast. The commandos were spotted by elements of the 13th Company as they paddled ashore in rubber rafts. Pursuit of the team of eight, which was led by a captain, began. The British officer and his two radio operators were supposed to serve as a radio team to direct the insertion of further commando teams and brief the new men as they arrived. The remaining members of this advance party were to seek out the headquarters of the von Koenen Tropical Battalion so that it might be attacked and taken out later by an assault team.

The German reaction included patrols from the Arab Legion under the command of Oberst von Hippel. The operation was a success and the British captain and his seven men were captured in their hiding place.

Using the commando team's radio equipment, Major Rudloff of the Abwehr, an expert in radio deception, was able with the help of a "turned" radio operator to maintain a long-running contact with the English commando base in Malta. When the command post in Malta requested a new, safe landing site for another commando team, one was transmitted immediately. The Brandenburgers advised that the commando team should land wearing French uniforms.

When the submarine of the British 10th Flotilla based in Malta surfaced off the coast of Hammamet, a signal lamp flashed the agreed-upon signal. The lamp had been part of the equipment of the first commando team.

A Brandenburger who spoke perfect English guided the rubber rafts to shore and led the men to a ravine. Other Brandenburgers were waiting there to capture and disarm the commandos. The submarine received a short message in Morse—OK which meant: landed safely, all in order.

The radio game was maintained for another four weeks. The English even complied with a request for "tea for the Bedouins," which the Brandenburgers enjoyed immensely. But then there was a change in frequency and the British caught on. The source was lost forever.

The German Arab Instruction Battalion had been transferred to Tunis in December 1942. Its mission: incite the Arabs in Tunisia to lead all the Arabs in French North Africa to rise up and join the fight against the Anglo-Americans. Oberst von Hippel, one of the senior Brandenburgers, had formed the battalion. Its first station was Stalino, before it was shipped to Northwest Africa.

A conference of the Western Allies took place in Casablanca from the 4th to the 21st of January 1943. The results of the conference, including a demand for Germany's unconditional surrender, were passed on to the Abwehr within a few hours. Rumors that even the Sultan of Morocco was acting as a German agent turned out to be false.

THE RAID ON SIDI-BOU-ZID

Early on the morning of 14 February 1943 Hauptmann von Koenen led a large force in an attack on the village of Sidi-Bou-Zid, located a few kilometers west of Faid. There was no artillery preparation. Exactly one month later the village was to be the scene of a battle involving the 10th and 21st Panzer Divisions. The village was held by American troops. Three groups of vehicles—mostly captured enemy equipment—roared into Sidi-Bou-Zid like a storm wind. Reaching the village square, the men leapt from their vehicles, stormed through the gate past the American sentries to the US headquarters.

The cry went up from house to house: "Rommel's boys are attacking!" The Americans threw down their weapons and fled. One participant told the author; "all we could see was heels and dust."

The Americans headed for Sbeitla, where they expected to find help. On the way they divested themselves of anything that slowed them down. In addition to small arms and other items of equipment, the Brandenburgers captured 27 tanks and armored troop carriers, 23 guns, machineguns and ammunition and a large quantity of fuel.

The Brandenburgers scouted ahead as far as Feriane. They found the area completely empty. Not until Gafsa did they come under weak enemy fire, which indicated that the empty area ended there.

Driving by night, von Koenen's battle group headed back over roads made bottomless by steady rain. Progress was slow as the vehicles frequently got stuck in the mud. It was already too late to report this opportunity to Generalfeldmarschall Rommel. Rommel struck on 14 February 1943; Panzer Army Africa attacked shortly after the Brandenburgers set out for the breakthrough area. Rommel's forces drove to just short of Tebessa, but his plan to take Tebessa, as had happened at Gafsa, in the enemy's rear, was frustrated near Thala on the evening of 20 February.

Rommel was able to send his 10th Panzer Division toward Thala on the evening of that decisive day, but the Allies had bolstered their defenses there at the last minute. The main body of Panzer Army Africa, which on the 21st advanced through Tebessa and took Djebel el Hamra, seemed to have a clear path, for on the 21st the 10th Panzer Division took Thala.

But there the emergency measures taken by General Alexander, who had just taken over as Commander-in-Chief of Allied Forces, began to take effect. He sent the British 9th Armored Division forward and also ordered the 6th Armored Division to attack. After taking heavy losses the 10th Panzer Division was forced to give up Thala and withdraw. That was the situation when Hauptmann von Koenen reported to Rommel that another way was open.

The decision was made at a final staff conference on the evening of 22nd February: the retreat began. Panzer Army Africa's last big opportunity had passed. The heroic effort by the Brandenburgers, which was supposed to spark the assault, had been in vain.

Following a visit to the tropical battalion by the commanding officer of the Brandenburgers, Hptm. von Koenen was called away to assume new duties. His place in Africa was taken by Oberleutnant Hoffmann. (Friedrich von Koenen was killed in action at Vizegrad, Croatia on 20 August 1944 while serving as an Oberstleutnant and commander of the 4th Light Infantry Regiment Brandenburg.)

Under its new commander Oblt. Dr. Wagner, the tropical battalion's 5th Company was assigned to coastal defense in the Cap Bon area. For this task it was subordinated to the Naval Command Tunisia, Kapitän zur See Meixner.

Other elements of the battalion were deployed in the north of the Tunisian Front with the hastily formed von Manteuffel Division. It undertook the mining of roads and installations and carried out armed reconnaissance into enemy-held territory.

In late April, with the final phase of the battle in the Tunisian bridgehead in sight, the Brandenburgers' special equipment and key personnel were flown to the mainland. Privileged to secret information of the first order, they could not be allowed to fall into enemy hands. The 5th Company set up a number of depots in Arabian ports and hiding places. They hid away boats and stocks of fuel so that they might escape Africa when the end came in Tunisia. The wounded Brandenburgers were taken to the airfields and flown out by night in Ju 52s.

Early on the morning of 8 May 1943 the last Brandenburgers, under the command of ObLt. Dr. Wagner, left the port of Ferryville in two large assault boats and sailed to Cape Ras Zebib. The next day the two boats were commandeered by a navy headquarters and it took a radio message from the army to get them released. The last Brandenburgers to leave Africa boarded their assault boats on the evening of 9 May 1943. They cast off and set sail toward the Italian mainland.

For the Brandenburgers, some of whom, under the command of ObLt. Hoffmann, were forced to remain behind in Africa, the operation in North Africa was over.

The Brandenburgers fought in the North African deserts from the first day of Germany's involvement to the last. Erwin Rommel said of the Brandenburgers: "Koehnen and his men are worth an entire regiment to me."

British wartime Prime Minister Winston Churchill in Africa, right General Bernard Montgomery.

The CIC enjoys the same tinned rations as his men.

A Brandenburger on forward lookout duty behind a scissors-type periscope.

Hptm. Graf Almaszy at the Japsa Pass. He was a desert expert.

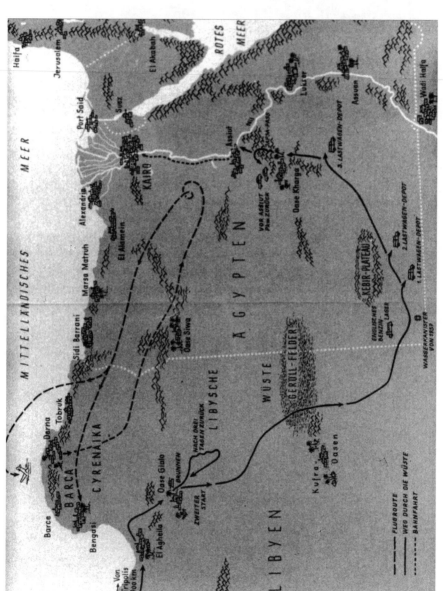

The big desert operation by the Brandenburgers.

Further Abwehr Operations in Russia

FORAYS TO BATAISK AND MAYKOP

The German 1942 summer offensive, whose objectives were the capture of the Caucasus and an advance as far as Stalingrad, also brought new missions for the Brandenburgers. In preparation for Operation Caucasus, at the beginning of July 1942 the II Battalion, less its 6th Company, boarded trains in Vienna and traveled via Odessa to Nikolayev on the River Bug. The individual companies arrived in the period from 10th to 12th July.

One week after the battalion's arrival in the area of operations, III Battalion also moved from Germany to Russia, traveling from Duren to the Stalino area. From there it marched to Rovenki, south of Voronezh. At first, however, only the 10th and 12th Companies went to Rovenki. The 11th Company followed at the beginning of August. The regimental commander Oberst Haehling and his staff first moved to Rovenki and later to Stalino.

1 Battalion had been in action in the east since the start of the campaign against Russia. The 1st Company under Oblt. Babuke had been assigned to the 14th Panzer Division and the 3rd Company under ObLt. John to the 13th Panzer Division, while the 2nd Company under Oblt. Pinkert was subordinated to the 4th Panzer Army. The missions assigned these companies were bridge actions and similar missions that did not require lengthy preparations.

On 13 July 1942 the 3rd Company under Oblt. John carried out a deep reconnaissance mission into the Don Bend ahead of the spearheads of the 3rd Panzer Division. Driving two captured American vehicles, the patrol drove 80 kilometers into enemy territory and came to a village filled with Russian troops. There, the Germans were halted by a Russian sentry. After being questioned by the local commissar they were allowed to drive on. After darkness fell the patrol returned to the German lines, returning with useful reconnaissance information.

On 23 July the 3rd Panzer Division established a bridgehead across the Don east of Konstantinovskaya. From there the Brandenburger companies swarmed into the open and into the enemy hinterland. When Russian resistance weakened east of Rostov it was time for the 8th Company under Hauptmann Siegfried Grabert to go into action. The 8th Company received its orders following the entry into the city of German forces on 24 July. It drove through the city and headed for the road and rail bridges over the Don in the Bataisk area. Its objective was to seize the bridges and hold them until the arrival of army units.

Hptm. Grabert and the leading group reached the first arm of the river in the Don delta while fighting in Rostov was still going on. The first half company crossed in inflatable boats under the command of Lt. Hillier. On the far side the company assembled at the command post of the 43rd Motorcycle Battalion under Obstlt. Stolz. From there five bridges spanned the entire Don delta north of Bataisk. A single raised road led through the wild marshy terrain between Rostov and Bataisk to the bridges and the road lay under constant Russian artillery and rocket fire.

When dusk arrived the Grabert Company moved out onto the raised road. On the left the large railway bridge was burning. Parachute flares rose and illuminated the advancing men. Mortar fire caused the first casualties. German mortars returned the fire. The first German bridgehead was at the near end of the enemy-held second bridge; it lay in a deep ravine in front of the river. It was held by the motorcycle troops who were firing at the Russians close to the bridge, preventing them from blowing it up.

A Russian heavy machine-gun was firing at the Germans in front of the second bridge from a pier of the burning railway bridge to the left. An hour after midnight heavy mortar fire opened up from the far end of the bridge. Suddenly there was a flash of flame on the bridge. Russian tracers had set a truck on fire.

At 0230 Hptm. Grabert gave the signal to attack across the bridge. The leading squad crept forward. The enemy spotted the movement on the bridge and opened fire. Then signal flares rose from the far end of the bridge; it was a signal to the men who had stayed behind with the heavy machine-gun that Grabert had taken the bridge. Hptm. Grabert suffered a minor head wound during the attack.

With ammunition running low, Grabert had to send a runner to the rear to request support. He ordered the attack on the third bridge to go ahead. Grabert stormed forward at the head of his company. The Russians blazed away with everything they had, including machine-guns concealed on the marshy islands left and right of the bridge. Several men fell. Hptm. Grabert was hit in the stomach. He nevertheless crossed with the others and helped subdue the Russians on the other side before he collapsed.

When the cry, "A shot of morphine for the chief!", came back, medical officer Dr. Weber and medic Uffz. Fohrer swam across the river. Crossing the bridge was still impossible as it still lay under heavy fire. Dr. Weber gave Grabert the injection.

The Brandenburgers were pinned down and could go no further. They just managed to fight off Russian counterattacks. Not until dawn, when the first German tanks arrived, was the enemy driven back. Stukas attacked the Russian battle groups and contributed to their destruction. The tanks rolled across the bridges and drove south. The 8th Brandenburg Company had successfully completed its mission but the cost was high: 17 killed, 16 missing (most of whom had been killed) and 54 wounded. With total casualties of 87 the company was no longer fit for operations. It was pulled out of the front to regroup.

Hauptmann Siegfried Grabert died on 25 July 1942. He was awarded the Knight's Cross with Oak Leaves posthumously on 6 November 1943.

Having cleared the Don delta, the gateway to the Caucasus was now open and nothing stood in the way of the 13th Panzer Division. Two Brandenburger companies, the 5th commanded by ObLt. Zulch and the 7th under Oblt. Oesterwitz, were at the front, as was the reformed 8th under Lt. Prochaska.

The latter received orders to take the road bridge at Belaya on the road to Maykop. The operation began on 9 August 1942. Lt. Prochaska took up position in front of the 66th Panzer-Grenadier Regiment's I Battalion and set off at 1300. But it was not until 1700 that the four captured trucks separated from the spearhead group. They were able to infiltrate the retreating Russian columns and slowly but surely they worked their way toward the Bataisk bridge. When they reached the bridge, the leading vehicle was stopped by a Russian policeman directing traffic, in order to allow the crush of traffic to thin out. At last the signal was given to move on, but now the truck's starter had failed. The Russian policeman pitched in and helped start the engine using the hand crank.

The vehicle rolled across the bridge. Far below the Belaya rushed past. At the far end of the bridge Prochaska gave the order for everyone to get out. The crew of a nearby Russian tank truck was overwhelmed. The pioneers ran to the bridge piers and removed the explosive charges. The main detonation wire was cut. Prochaska fired two white flares, the agreed-upon signal to the following tanks that the bridge was in German hands. When the first German tank reached the bridge it had to shove aside a panje wagon blocking the way. It tried the same with a Russian automobile, but it refused to budge.

The Russians fired across the river and the Germans answered. Lt. Ernst Prochaska sprinted back across the bridge to speed things up. He had just about reached the leading tank when he was hit and knocked down. He died that same day. Another Panzer IV cleared the obstacle and rolled across the bridge. Infantry and anti-tank guns followed and secured the other end of the bridge.

In the words of division commander Herr of the 13th Panzer Division, Leutnant Prochaska had saved the division four days. Ernst Prochaska was posthumously awarded the Knight's Cross on 16 September 1942.

INTO THE CAUCASUS

At the end of July a group from the Brandenburger Caucasian Company had been sent into the Caucasus to begin encouraging the mountain tribes to revolt against the Red Army. Another 30 Brandenburgers were sent into the enemy rear. They got as far as the Mineralny Vody area, where they blew up a bridge vital to Russian supply traffic. Two Abwehr agents were sent to the Kirovograd area, where the 46th and 76th Rifle Divisions, both made up largely of conscripts from the Caucasus, were deployed. There they successfully encouraged members of the two divisions to desert.

A special Brandenburg unit under the command of Leutnant Fölkersam, a descendant of the Baltic Admiral Fökersam, who had died in the naval Battle of Tsushima while in Russian service, carried out a series of missions. Under his command were 62 Baltic Germans who spoke perfect Russian. Disguised as NKVD Major Truchin, Fölkersam and several of his men, also wearing NKVD uniforms, stole vehicles from a Russian-occupied village in the Caucasus. These were needed to carry out their mission of stopping the Soviet demolition squads from carrying out their work in the Maykop area. The Russians had been ordered to destroy all the oil-producing installations in the area as well as storage facilities in the event of a retreat.

Fölkersam's special unit was under orders to prevent the destruction of as many drilling sites in the area as possible and to secure the oil stored there.

When the group in their captured vehicles crossed the embankment of the Armavir-Tuapse line they were stopped by a real NKVD patrol. "Major Truchin" was able to convince the NKVD officer leading the patrol of his special mission and had him lead them to Maykop, straight to the NKVD headquarters. There Fölkersam reported to the commanding general.

Now Fölkersam had to reconnoiter the area. Caution was required. The German attack was supposed to start on the morning of 8 August. That was still a week away. By the 7th Fölkersam had collected all the necessary information. That afternoon the Russians opened fire from the city; it was aimed at the approaching panzer spearhead. Fölkersam had assembled his men. When night fell they drove to the front, making their way through the chaos, and finally arrived at the communications central of the commanding Russian army. This they attacked with explosives. All of the front-line command's telephone lines were severed and its radios destroyed. Afterward Fölkersam and his men drove back to the city's telephone exchange and occupied it. Now the Russian-speaking soldiers came into their own; they advised everyone that the city had to be evacuated and that the telegraph office itself would cease operating in a few minutes. The confusion grew into chaos.

At the same time the special detachments raced toward the selected oil production facilities, which had been prepared for destruction by the Russians. They prevented all but one from being wrecked and secured the important oil storage sites.

When, on the morning of 9 August, the spearheads of the German V Army Corps approached Maykop, resistance was light, for thanks to the order to retreat which Fölkersam and his men had issued over the Russian army lines, the Soviets were already in retreat. Adrian von Fölkersam had won a battle. In recognition of his efforts he was awarded the Knight's Cross on 14 September 1942.

ACTION AT LENINGRAD

In the autumn of 1942 an operation was initiated in the northern sector of the Eastern Front that is among the most fantastic ever begun in the Second World War.

Agent handler Starkmann, a German from the Baltic States who spoke perfect Russian, was spirited into Leningrad by sea. There he was met by a number of Ukrainian nationalists who had been working in the city since before the war. They got him a position in a factory in which several saboteurs were at work.

In the period that followed machines repeatedly broke down in the tank repair shops of Leningrad, optical devices were wrecked. More and more Leningraders were recruited by the underground movement. Radio signals were passed on to German attack units from Kronstadt. Sailing times of submarines, gunboats and motor torpedo boats were reported by radio. The Starkmann group came to have a portentous significance to the city, which had been in the grip of the German units surrounding it since autumn 1941.

The Russians homed in on transmissions from Starkmann's command post and prepared a night raid. But Starkmann also had operatives inside the political police and he was warned in advance. He evaded the trap and was led by a resourceful Leningrader, who had joined the resistance group, to the city's main cemetery.

The man took Starkmann to a huge mausoleum dating to the time of the czars. An underground passageway led to the mausoleum, its entrance concealed by a dense thicket. Its original purpose had been to plunder graves, but from now on the mausoleum served as Starkmann's new headquarters. He was completely safe there. The radio antenna lead was passed through the roof of the mausoleum to one of the nearby trees and the antenna itself led upwards along a branch, allowing radio traffic to be conducted without drawing attention.

Operating by night, Starkmann and his men carried out a series of sabotage operations. Once he and his party ran into an NKVD patrol that stopped them and wanted to take them to NKVD headquarters. They shot down the three men and fled to the cemetery, where they disappeared from sight. Each time they sneaked into their "wolfs lair," as they had dubbed their hiding place, two inconspicuous looking "old ladies" erased every trace. Finally the NKVD caught one of Starkmann's NCOs. Under torture the man revealed the location of Starkmann's hiding place.

The cemetery was surrounded. Then a small group of about 30 armed-men surrounded the mausoleum. The captured NCO was forced to give the agreed-upon signal, and when Starkmann opened the door he was looking into the muzzles of several submachine-guns. During its three months of activity, Starkmann and his "fascist band" had inflicted serious injury on the Russians. All of the captured men were repeatedly brought before special interrogators. All those whose names they gave were quickly rounded up. There followed a show trial in which all the accused received the same sentence and were then liquidated.

OPERATION ZEPPELIN—THE PREPARATION PHASE

One of the most spectacular operations carried out by the Abwehr in Russia was undoubtedly Operation Zeppelin.

The Ausland/Abwehr was just one of the units which conducted this type of underground warfare, although it was the official office. Nevertheless its power was neither absolute nor the highest. It was in direct competition with the Reichssicherheitshauptamt of the SS and the Sicherheitsdienst. The OKH's Foreign Armies East department also became involved now and then, although its missions were of a special nature.

The foreign department of the Sicherheitsdienst, Office VI, under the command of Brigadeführer Schellenberg, carried out the same type of missions as Abwehr II. Office IV was under the direction of Oberfiihrer

Heinrich Muller, while Standartenführer Ohlendorf was head of the SD's operational groups.

When the leadership of the Reich found out that Admiral Canaris had been exchanging secret information with the British and Swiss secret services and was conspiring with them, he was "put on ice." The OKW department Ausland/Abwehr was paralyzed by Himmler's RSHA and the head of its Department VII, Brigadeführer Schellenberg, took over more and more of the role of Reich security service.

Prior to his removal, Admiral Canaris had reached a conclusion that was haunting many minds, and which only appeared to be waiting for a solution. In early 1943 he disguised agents as prisoners of war and secreted them into POW camps to ascertain the attitude of the prisoners toward "Mother Russia".

From the reports that went directly to him, the admiral learned that there was a great potential in men in the prisoner of war camps that could be exploited. In order to test to what extent this could be done, in late May 1943 he sent a representative, Generalmajor von Lahousen-Vivremont, on a fact-finding mission. He was also ordered to find out whether the rumors about the terrible things going on in the camps were true, especially those concerning the marches through Poland into captivity. After his return von Lahousen-Vivremont said that conditions were even worse than had been feared and that the agents of the orders were sitting in the Reichssicherheitshauptamt.

"It could be very different," declared the head of Office II. "I have visited the camp and spoken with Russian officers and men. Many of them would be ready to fight for us to free Russia from the Bolsheviks. If we removed the commissars and agitators who really do exist in these camps, we could win over the Ukrainian prisoners in particular with decent treatment and loyalty and could organize an entire army of liberation. In the Abwehr alone we have enough officers who were trained in Russia in the twenties and speak perfect Russian. They could lead the battalions, regiments and even divisions in the fight for freedom."

When asked by his superior if he wasn't closing his eyes to the real situation, the Russophile Lahousen-Vivremont answered that efforts were in fact being made in many camps to save Mother Russia. He stressed that Germany was facing a unique opportunity not only to win the war in the east militarily, but the political struggle for the minds of the Russian people as well.

Canaris found the theory credible. He turned to a prepared dossier, from which he saw that the present number of Russian prisoners of war was 2,876,566. Even if only every hundredth Russian responded, this would produce an army of 30,000 men. Transported behind the Russian lines by air, these men represented a unique, tremendously powerful dynamite charge which could shake the enemy so badly that he might fall. Equipped with weapons, radios and money, these men would be the terrible seeds of destruction for the Bolsheviks.

Canaris could imagine these "avengers" of Holy Russia coming down in the villages behind the lines in their parachutes, sent from heaven to summon the people of Russia to revenge. They would carry out acts of sabotage, report Russian troop movements and paralyze Russian transport.

Admiral Canaris formulated a plan. "We must send them in two waves. Neither must know of the other. The first wave will be ordered to report the basic facts and act as pathfinders. This second, smaller group must be dropped into those areas previously identified by the pathfinders as sympathetic to us. Their mission there will be to train White Russian partisan groups to fight the Russian Army and send them into action. Then we too will have enough partisan groups to make things difficult for the Russians."

Operation Zeppelin was on. Generalmajor Lahousen-Vivremont worked out all the details and set up the required training courses. He suggested initiating the action simultaneously with the start of the Russian counteroffensive expected after the German opening of the Kursk offensive. Reports from agents inside Russia suggested that the Soviets were already massing troops for such an offensive.

Admiral Canaris now began trying to improve conditions in the POW camps. The die had been cast. But what was going on in the RSHA in this regard; did they not have similar plans? Had not discussions relating to these plans begun even before those of the Abwehr?

HITLER, THE PARTISAN WAR AND "ZEPPELIN"

In summer of 1942 Hitler became aware of the growing difficulties facing him in Russia, in particular the guerrilla war going on behind the German armies. He demanded of Himmler that the secret service and the counterintelligence organizations step up their efforts against the partisans in order to keep the number of army security units fighting partisans to a minimum.

"The military situation requires," said Hitler, "that the secret service has to be reactivated in Russia. We have to be better and more adequately informed about the enemy's situation and his plans."

Himmler promised an immediate improvement in the situation and passed Hitler's request on to Schellenberg. The latter informed his chief that a massed use of agents would be necessary to take on such a powerful opponent. True, their intelligence contacts and those of the Ausland/ Abwehr in Sweden, Finland, the Balkans and Turkey were very active. But they were inadequate because they only brought in second-hand reports on the enemy situation at the front, troop movements and attack preparations. What was needed was agents at the scene of the action and behind the Russian Front, and not just a handful but thousands.

When Himmler then asked Schellenberg exactly how many agents were needed, the latter replied that at least 2,000 would be required with good language skills and excellent radio equipment. As well they would have to be equipped with Russian made vehicles and weapons.

"The Russians are a terrible foe, Schellenberg," Himmler declared, "but we must smash them. Prepare me a complete report immediately outlining the situation of our secret service activities in Russia."

In 1942 the German counterintelligence effort against the Soviet Union consisted of three branches: the outlying stations in all the capitals of Europe and the Near and Middle East, the local stations and message centers, and the front-line reconnaissance detachments. Now an unprecedented large-scale operation had to be started to make the net denser: Operation "Zeppelin."

This operation, which out of necessity was developed by both counterintelligence agencies, the admiral's as well as Himmler's, was not based on the until then standard practice of dropping individual agents or small groups, but on the employment en masse of Russians from prisoner of war camps who had declared themselves ready to fight to free Russia from bolshevism. The action also involved special operations by the Brandenburgers and lone agents of the very first order, who were located in Russian communications centers and even in the staff of Soviet Marshall Rokossovsky. For example, there were two Russian general staff officers working for the German side. Also involved in Zeppelin were the OKH departments Foreign Armies East and Foreign Armies West.

There existed in Germany a communications center which, under the direction of a White Russian officer, obtained information from many nations. Its most valuable service, however, was obtaining fresh and reliable reports from the staffs of the STAVKA, the Russian army command. Often it provided reports concerning new Russian offensives or troops movements from large-scale down to the division level two to three weeks before they began. The center was subordinated to Foreign Armies East, and if Hitler had heard of this unit it would have been possible to draw decisive conclusions from its reports in formulating his orders. However Hitler had an extreme dislike for the head of the Foreign Armies East evaluation section.

THE SELECTION PHASE

Operation "Zeppelin" began with the sorting out of thousands of Russian POWs who had previously been identified as legitimate by cleverly infiltrated "prisoners" who were in fact German agents. They were trained and ultimately, when their training was over, dropped behind Russian lines. Their orders were: "Submit regular reports on the status of the Red Army, carry out acts intended to demoralize the enemy as well as acts of sabotage, combat partisan groups by infiltrating observers into same and in so doing arrange the laying of ambushes for these bands."

Finally the Germans even resorted to using recently-captured prisoners of war, provided intensive questioning had revealed that they would cooperate and they were believed to be genuinely opposed to the Soviet regime. These missions were organized and carried out by Working Groups North, Center and South, which were attached to the corresponding army groups.

Most of those who went into the POW camps as "prisoners" to seek out such resistance fighters were Baltic-Germans. The Russians so chosen were sent to special camps and provided with good rations. After demonstrating their suitability and undergoing examination, in accordance with an agreement that had meanwhile been reached with the General in Charge of Volunteer Units, they became soldiers of the German Armed Forces and were issued German uniforms.

A large number of the volunteers came from the Vlasov Army that had been captured at the Volkhov. Vlasov and his men subsequently joined the German side to fight for the liberation of their homeland. These men approached their new mission with idealism and were for the most part reliable.

Special emphasis was placed on training these men to operate radio equipment. The Luftwaffe Command made available Kampfgeschwader 200, a unit formed for specialized bomber and transport missions, to deliver the agents to their destinations. KG 200 was equipped with specially equipped aircraft as well as captured aircraft from a number of other nations. Not until after the war did it become obvious that a Russian spy must have been active somewhere in the Reichssicherheitshauptamt, for on 2 July 1943 a radio message from Berlin was received by the Supreme Command of the Red Army in the Kirovskaya underground station in Moscow:

> From Justus to Director:
> OKW Dept. Ausland/Abwehr and SD planning an operation to infiltrate 30,000 former soldiers of the Red Army, now in Germany as prisoners of war, into the Soviet Union. Admiral Canaris and

Brigadeführer Schellenberg are working together closely on the details of this plan.

Purpose of the operation is: formation of partisan units for conducting espionage and sabotage behind the Russian lines, reports on troop movements in the Red Army's rear area and actions aimed at distracting the population. Movement is to be carried out in two waves. First wave expected at the end of September, second wave to follow in October.

Codename for the operation is 'Zeppelin.'

End of message.

Generalmajor Reinhard Gehlen, head of Foreign Armies East from 1942 until the end of the war, had the following to say about this complex of betrayal, the effects of which were often felt by the Brandenburg units:

During a lengthy conversation with Admiral Canaris I reached the conclusion that the Soviets must have a very well informed source in the very top level of the German command. In every case the enemy was informed in detail in a very short time about what was taking place and what was being considered by the German side. After a long silence I will reveal a secret concerning the fateful role which Hitler's closest intimate, Martin Bormann, played in the last years of the war and afterward.

He was the Soviets' most prominent informer and advisor and had begun working for the enemy at the start of the campaign in Russia. Canaris and I established independently of one another that Bormann had the only unmonitored radio station. But we agreed that at that time keeping Bormann—the most powerful man next to Hitler—under surveillance was as good as impossible. Any slip-up would have meant the end of the investigation and the end of us as well.

For this reason, therefore, they allowed the Brandenburgers to continue carrying out operations that were already known to the enemy and thus left them to the revenge of the Soviets in order to save their own necks.

Canaris described to me his suspicious facts, speculations and determinations concerning Bormann's treasonous activities. He saw as the most likely motivations Bormann's limitless ambition and his complexes toward his environment. And finally there was the ultimately unsatisfied ambition of Reichsleiter Bormann to one day take over Hitler's position.

I was unable to draw my own conclusions until I had the opportunity after 1946 to investigate the mysterious circumstances surrounding Bormann's flight from the Führer bunker and his disappearance. The claims that often appear in the international press that Bormann is living in the jungle region between Paraguay and Uruguay, have no basis in fact.

In the 1950' s two reliable pieces of information made me certain that Martin Bormann was living perfectly protected in the USSR. During the occupation of Berlin, the former Reichsleiter was picked up by the Red Army and taken to safety. He has long since died in the USSR.

OPERATION "DRUCHINA"

Among the Russians brought together for Operation "Zeppelin" were an army corps general staff officer and an engineer from a Russian deep mining operation. It was they who organized "Druchina." Under the leadership of general staff officer Colonel Rodionov, code name "Gill," battle groups were formed whose initial role was to guard the German Army's rear area. Other battle groups were trained in partisan warfare, then delivered to their areas of operation by aircraft of KG 200.

The larger main force led by Colonel Rodionov was deposited behind the Soviet front. Its mission was to carry out a secret march into a Russian partisan village and burn it down. Rodionov's orders were to kill all the inhabitants.

Colonel Rodionov followed his general staff training in preparing the mission. The force followed winding paths through an area of dense forest as it approached the partisan sanctuary. Now and then a twig cracked. All went smoothly. The unit surrounded the village and then conducted a thorough search it was completely empty. The huts were set on fire.

Suspicion grew when Colonel Rodionov suggested that they continue the search; everyone else wanted to head back at once. On the way the colonel led the group through a marshy area that was traversed by several water-filled ravines. It was a shortcut, he said. Just as the unit's point squad was leaving one of the ravines, machine-gun fire suddenly flared up in its rear. Then rifle and pistol fire cracked in the groups of partisan fighters. The first of the German officers with the unit fell mortally wounded. Then followed the NCOs and in a few minutes quiet reigned. Colonel Rodionov and his troops had done a thorough job. None of the German soldiers escaped with his life.

Headquarters waited in vain for the battle group to return. Search parties sent out 24 hours later found the bodies of the German soldiers, stripped of all clothing. But there was no trace of the Russian partisan fighters. Colonel Rodionov had been in radio contact with the partisan organization's communications center in Moscow for some time and had set the trap. After the massacre of the Germans he was picked up on the other side of the village by an NKVD staff car and driven to the nearest Red Army headquarters. There he was put aboard an aircraft, which immediately took off and set course for Moscow.

Seventy-two hours after the ambush, Colonel Rodionov was standing in front of Stalin. He reported on the German plans in general and his coup in particular. He was promoted to Major-General and received the Order of Stalin. One of the former Russian officer POWs who had freed himself by taking part in the operation subsequently worked his way up to the staff of Marshall Rokossovsky. There he was active as a specialist on the German Armed Forces. But the officer in question was not a true returned defector. He had gone along with his boss Colonel Rodionov but remained loyal to the Germans.

While in Rokossovsky's staff, at lengthy intervals he sent radio messages to Germany on the assigned frequency. However, with the catastrophic outcome of Operation "Druchina" the man was no longer trusted. It seemed more likely that he was merely sending material fed him by the Russians.

The accuracy of his reports should have convinced the Germans that he was genuine. But Hitler's bias after the debacle with "Druchina" was insurmountable.

Nevertheless, Operation "Zeppelin" was not a total failure. The planning staff, which assembled all available information on the potential target areas and decided where the next operations would take place and which industrial installations, supply centers or transportation junctions would be targeted, carried out a series of successful operations. However, the large action, in which at least about 1,000 men would be deposited behind the Russian front, was unfeasible. A lack of suitable officers and the unavailability of aircraft prevented the plan from reaching fruition.

A plan was later worked out to employ a manned version of the V-I flying bomb against targets in the Soviet Union. The V-I would be carried to the vicinity of its target by a long-range bomber; there it would be released and guided to its target by the pilot in a similar fashion to the Japanese kamikaze fliers.

A large number of Luftwaffe pilots volunteered to fly the suicide machines. Among the intended targets were Kuibyshev, Chelyabinsk and Magnitogorsk as well as factories beyond the Urals. Captured Russian engineers and technicians had provided the exact location of the targets; Russian cartographers were used to determine the routes to the targets which best avoided Soviet anti-aircraft defenses. The plan came to nothing, however, as Hitler was against it.

An SD agent reached the port of Murmansk aboard a British transport ship from Reykjavik. There he separated from the crew, and with the help of a Finn who had lived in Murmansk since the 1920's set up a radio station which he used to transmit important information on the sailing times of the QP convoys to German observation posts along the Norwegian coast.

Ultimately, however, a plan aimed at Moscow was worked out and put into action.

"STALIN HAS TO BE ELIMINATED!"— "FROM JUSTUS TO DIRECTOR!"

On 2 October 1943 Otto Skorzeny, who had received the Knight's Cross after freeing the Duce from the Gran Sasso on 13 September, sent a radio message to the Schellenberg office. It said: "Operation 'Red King Checkmate' is ready to go."

The message went on to provide details of a plan that had been in the works for several months: it involved nothing less than the murder of Stalin in Moscow.

A radio report was received in Moscow on 3 October:

> From Justus to Director.
> A plan has been adopted to murder Stalin.
> The execution squad consists of two agents, F.M. Savrin and his wife Olga. Different weapons and methods could be used. No date has yet been fixed, but the operation is to take place as soon as possible. The agents will be delivered by air. Possible landing sites east of Smolensk or near Rzhev. Further details to follow.
> End of message.

It was snowing in Moscow on 4 October. Two men sat facing each other in an office in the Kremlin. Between them on the table covered with files and maps lay the transcripts of several radio messages. The one on top of the pile was from Justus to the Director. The man in uniform was Major-General I.K. Lebedin, head of the NKVD's central counterespionage organization. The civilian with the pince-nez on his nose sitting across from him was Lavrenti Beria, the head of the NVD.

"What do you think of this story, Comrade General?" Beria asked the head of NKVD counter-intelligence.

"If the assassin is determined enough he will succeed, but we will stay his hand and regain the full confidence of Stalin, who appears to favor the rose-pinks. We will stop this Savrin. Since he was a Russian officer, we have to discover his unit and his commanding officer, who can give us more detailed information about this man."

"And how are we to do that, Comrade General?"

"By searching the personnel roster for a Savrin and requesting a picture of the killer from Germany."

"That won't be easy," observed Beria.

"But our contact in the Wehrmacht High Command will do it. He has a number of good people who are working against Hitler to choose from."

THE ASSASSIN AND HIS PREPARATIONS

The Russian Lieutenant Savrin had been captured while on a night patrol operation in the Volkhov area on 31 May 1942. The patrol he was leading was wiped out.

The leader of the German patrol, from the 5th Company of the 122nd Infantry Regiment, delivered the Lieutenant to the regimental command post for interrogation. Fyedor Savrin gave the regiment's intelligence officer a complete picture of the Soviet forces on the other side of the front. From there he was taken to the command post of the XXXXII Army Corps, which was in command in the area. There he was brought before Sonderfiihrer Kurbjuhn; a Russian specialist, he not only spoke excellent Russian, but was a good psychologist as well. Kurbjuhn had grown up on a farm in Lithuania. His clever questions allowed him to form a good picture of the Lieutenant.

Further interrogations followed and it became apparent that Savrin was a good candidate for an operation in Russia. Subsequently his name was passed on to Department II, the foreign intelligence section of the German intelligence service under Admiral Canaris. Savrin underwent a year of training in which, in addition to German intelligence techniques and weapons, he was taught everything that an agent had to do and know.

Meanwhile in a Russian field hospital two of the soldiers who had survived the patrol, members of the 336th Rifle Regiment, had told of the battle with the Germans. As a result Lieutenant Savrin came under suspicion and soon afterward his name appeared in a special card file of the NKVD.

The lieutenant from the 168th Rifle Division was thus in the central card file, with the remark that should he turn up again somewhere, Fedor Mikhailovich Savrin was to be handed over to the NKVD, unharmed if possible.

The RSHA very soon became interested in Savrin. They promoted him to the rank of Major so that he would not be so easy to identify if he was later caught during an operation in Russia. A major had a better chance of escaping the Soviets, especially if he was highly decorated. Savrin was therefore given the gold star of a Hero of the Soviet Union, something guaranteed to impress Russian sentries.

On 10 December 1943 several members of the SS and the Security Service met in Berlin with the head of Office VI of the Foreign Intelligence Service, Brigadeführer Schellenberg. The object of the meeting was to try to determine where the leak might be at the highest level of the German command, through which important information was flowing out of the country.

There, in Schellenberg's office in the Prinz-Albrecht Strasse, it became apparent that the "Citadel" summer offensive and the earlier operations at Stalingrad must have been leaked to the enemy in advance.

The Army High Command had created two specialized intelligence services in the "Foreign Armies East" and "Foreign Armies West" departments. For the German Armed Forces as a whole, however there was no similar intelligence service, although there had to be a man there "working both sides of the street", a spy who was passing important information to Russia.

It was Walter Schellenberg who came up with the idea of using an agent to kill the head of the Soviet secret service, Beria. But to do he job they needed someone who was ready to sacrifice himself. Those present knew no one and so Schellenberg continued:

"General Vlasov, the commander in chief of the 2nd Soviet Shock Army, whom we captured at the Volkhov last summer, is certain that there are plenty of men in the Russian prisoner of war camps who would be eager to risk their lives if the objective was to kill the red butcher."

When the talk turned to theoretical means of transporting such an agent, the Luftwaffe liaison officer brought up the 200th Special Purpose Bomber Wing. He explained that the wing had already carried out Operation "Druchina", the detachment commanded by the Russian colonel named Rodionov, code-named Gill.

Finally one of the security service officers present reported that the 647th Secret Field Police Group, based near Kodyma in the Riga area, had such agents, fully trained and standing by. Soon afterward "Director"—the head of the military intelligence service of the USSR RASWEDUPR, Lieutenant-General Ivan Ivanovich Ilyachev—received a call from "Justus", who informed him that an assassination attempt was being planned against Beria. The code word to initiate the strike was "Red King Checkmate."

The search for a determined and reliable Russian officer began. After a lengthy search he was found. His name was Savrin, Fedor Mikhailovich, a lieutenant. It turned out that he had lost his family during the Soviet purges of the 1930's, operations run by Beria. Savrin met a Russian female auxiliary in the camp at Riga where he was trained and they fell in love. This provided the Germans with added leverage, for the Russian lieutenant was promised that he might be allowed to marry the girl if he agreed to undertake a special mission.

On 31 January 1944 Justus reported to Director that "Red King Checkmate" had reached the decision phase and that a certain Savrin, a lieutenant who had deserted from the Red Army, was to carry out the assassination. The text of the radio message was as follows:

Method of assassination:
1. Poison bullet.
2. Panzerfaust rocket launcher
3. Magnetic mine, which can be affixed to the outside of a vehicle
4. Exploding belt worn by the assassin (suicide mission)
Date: Not yet determined. Possibly early summer 1944.
Site: Kremlin in Moscow.
Target: Lavrenti Beria
End of message.

A final period of training began, in which Savrin's young wife also took part. She became Savrin's radio operator. The girl was slim and well built, her hair shone like ripe wheat, but she had sparkling brown eyes, like old amber. Savrin would do anything for her, and so he dedicated himself one hundred percent to the mission, after which he could disappear in Moscow and await the German victory, when he would assume a high-ranking position.

NOT BERIA BUT STALIN
Brigadeführer Schellenberg went to report to his chief Himmler, who was aboard a special train near Berchtesgaden in order to be near Hitler. As soon as he had completed his report Himmler told him: "An assassination attempt on Stalin is being planned."

"And what about Beria?" asked a surprised Schellenberg.

"The plans have changed. You will be given further details by von Ribbentrop in Fuschl."

Walter Schellenberg, in whose sphere—Department IV of the Reich Main Security Office—the assassination plan fell, drove to Fuschl. There he met von Ribbentrop. At the end of a conversation filled with trivialities the latter sprung a surprise: "And finally I would like to discuss one other hot item with you, Brigadeführer. No one is party to it except for the Fiihrer, Bormann and Herr Himmler, therefore this part of the discussion must remain secret. As the Reich's most dangerous enemy, Stalin must be eliminated. This could only be done by someone meeting Stalin at a conference. We must establish a new contact with the Kremlin via Stockholm, then we'll see."

The entire plan seemed completely absurd. Why should Stalin meet with Ribbentrop in Moscow? It was Heinrich Himmler who referred to Savrin, already selected for a special mission, and proposed sending him against Stalin.

"This would even convince the Fiihrer, who wants to keep politics out of such an assassination attempt. It must be carried out by a Russian."

The agent was to attach an especially powerful hollow charge to the car used to drive Stalin from his home to STAVKA headquarters. It was no larger than a human fist and was designed to look like a lump of clay. A large-capacity aircraft of the 200th Special Purpose Bomber Wing was made ready.

Savrin was provided with a Russian motorcycle outfitted with a number of secret compartments and he practiced until he could master it in his sleep.

In summer 1944 it was determined that elements of Otto Skorzeny's 502nd Commando Battalion would scout and prepare the two potential landing fields.

OTTO SKORZENY REPORTS

On the morning of I August 1944 Sturmbannführer Skorzeny left his office at Potsdamer Strasse 28 and made his way to an imposing building in the Baeckler Strasse in the southwest part of Berlin. It was home to Department of the Reich Main Security Office under Walter Schellenberg. He had been asked to report on the progress of Operation "Red King Checkmate." Skorzeny had several errands to run, and by the time he reached his superior's office it was already near noon. As both men knew each other Skorzeny came right to the point.

"Rumors have reached me that the secrecy of this operation is not being maintained and that several ministers have already learned of the action. These ministers have suggested that a victim other than Beria should be chosen and what is more have submitted a list of names headed by Marshall Zhukov. Others have secretly suggested Stalin, as we have already done."

"I am sure, Skorzeny, that none of those who suggested Stalin know even the slightest about our plan. Nevertheless, the fact that his name was mentioned is alarming."

"We have to strike as quickly as possible, otherwise Moscow will know about our plan before we can put it into action," interjected Skorzeny. "If they haven't long since been informed already."

"Can you act at once, Otto?" asked Schellenberg.

"Savrin is fully trained and ready to go, all the necessary weapons and equipment are also ready. Only the Red Army medical certificate for all officers has been changed. Savrin's papers must therefore also be changed. We have to issue a new medical certificate for Savrin stating that he is no longer fit for active service. As well he has to have a large scar suggesting serious internal injuries."

"Can that be done?"

"Of course. Professor Dr. Ehricht has said that he can give Savrin a hellish-looking scar. This would only take about three weeks. If he was operated on today he should be ready for action again on 22nd August."

"Very well. See to everything else, Otto!" agreed Schellenberg.

On 27th August Major Savrin and his wife Olga reported to Schellenberg at Potsdamer Strasse. There it was determined that transport would be by aircraft and it was mentioned that a special detachment would prepare both prospective landing fields the night before.

Savrin received papers identifying him as Major Korolyov. He was also given a courier's pass and sealed envelope with a report from the high command of the 1st Baltic Front addressed only to Marshall Stalin. The courier's pass had been signed by Stalin personally. His wife Olga received a military pass identifying her as a second lieutenant from the staff of the 1st Belorussian Front. She was also given her marriage papers and her justification for travel was the honeymoon trip and a visit to relatives in several villages in the Moscow area.

"Takeoff," explained Schellenberg, "will be from Riga during the night of 6th September. "

For Savrin and his wife the last days were filled with hectic activity. The secret compartments in the motorcycle-sidecar had to be filled and checked. The battery powered radio was placed under the seat of the sidecar. German, Russian and English bank notes were packed in a precisely fitting, almost invisible sliding compartment. The machine's fuel tank was filled to the brim with Russian gasoline from captured stocks.

On the morning of 28th August, only 24 hours following this last meeting with Brigadeführer Schellenberg, Justus went into action again and reported to Director:

> Assassination team Fedor and Sonya Savrin will leave Riga at 22:00 hours on 3rd September.
> Landing site 1: Starytsa
> Landing site 2: Bakmutovo
> Alternate site: Rzhev, Moscow highway.

This third landing site, which the German Air Force had used as an auxiliary landing field for a time in 1943, did not—it should be mentioned—come under the same close surveillance because its exact location had not been given.

The operation could begin.

OPERATION "ZEPPELIN"—THE LUFTWAFFE

Kampfgeschwader 200's liaison officer had received orders to go to Berlin for a secret meeting in the Reich Central Security Office; as soon as he arrived, the Oberstleutnant was taken directly to the head of the RSHA, Kaltenbrunner.

At this time Dr. Ernst Kaltenbrunner from Ried in the Inn District of Austria was forty years old. He had been a member of the SA and SS since 1932. He rapidly progressed through all the developmental stages of the SS hierarchy and on 31 December 1944 was promoted to the rank of General of the Waffen-SS and of the Police. Previously he had "only" been a General of the Police.

Dr. Kaltenbrunner informed the liaison officer that the matter that he was about to discuss with him was of the utmost secrecy. KG 200 was to provide an aircraft able to fly to just outside Moscow, land there and deposit a large cargo unnoticed. Two passengers would be going along. The planned operation was important to the war effort, perhaps even decisive.

The operation was to take place as soon as possible, but at least before the onset of autumn weather. The landing site could not be more than 100 kilometers from Moscow. Kaltenbrunner asked, "Is this possible?"

After the Oberstleutnant said that it was, Kaltenbrunner continued: "Your mission is to deliver a man who will operate from Moscow. He will get from the landing site to Moscow by means of a motorcycle or other vehicle which will be brought along in the aircraft."

The Luftwaffe officer confirmed that this was also possible. Then Kaltenbrunner began discussing the operation in detail, and the officer in charge of the mission, Oberstleutnant Werner Baumbach, the sixteenth recipient of the Knight's Cross with Oak Leaves and Swords, learned that the objective was to assassinate Josef Stalin. A Russian officer, a deserter, had been recruited for the mission. He had been trained in various camps and had been found to be very suitable.

For this special mission Oberstleutnant Baumbach suggested the use of an Ar 234A or Ar 234B military transport; the aircraft was equipped with an hydraulic loading ramp which would simplify the loading and unloading procedure. There were, however, a number of detail questions still to be cleared up. The most important was determining the landing site. After several months of hectic deliberations a site was chosen on the Moscow-Smolensk highway. The alternate site was in the Rzhev area. An advance detachment was to check out both locations.

Russian volunteers were selected to form the advance detachment and were transported to the site of the operation. A short time later the leader of the detachment radioed that they had accomplished their mission and named a secure landing site far to the east of Smolensk. From there it was possible to reach the highway to Moscow quickly and drive to the city.

An alternate landing site was likewise found, in the former German salient at Rzhev. It was suspiciously close to Moscow and was to be used only in case of emergency. Radio communications with the advance detachment were ended, after which only brief messages were exchanged at lengthy intervals.

Meanwhile KG 200 had completed all the necessary preparations. An Arado 232 B was standing ready. The crew of the aircraft, commanded by an Oberleutnant, was not let in on the planning for Operation "Zeppelin." The selected aircraft was first flown to Riga, from where it was to fly the actual mission. Two passengers—a Russian major and a woman—boarded the aircraft in Riga. It also carried a Type M 72 Russian heavy motorcycle with sidecar, taken from captured stocks. Finally, on the night of 6th September, the aircraft took off on Operation "Zeppelin."

In the early morning hours of 6th September the crew located the alternate landing site, an abandoned airfield, and headed toward it. The aircraft lost altitude rapidly. The pilot set the heavy aircraft down safely and rolled down the overgrown landing strip. But then disaster struck: the port undercarriage leg rolled into a depression, the aircraft swung to the left and its wing struck a tree. Irreparably damaged, the Arado sat at the side of the landing strip.

KG 200's radio central and the RSHA maintained a constant listening watch on the Arado's frequency. Twenty-four hours later the major made radio contact and reported the landing accident: "Aircraft damaged landing at alternate landing site. Returning in two groups on foot." Subsequently nothing more was heard. Only Major Savrin continued to report in until he arrived in Moscow and found a place to stay. There he made contact with the German agent in the Kremlin. The agent reported that everything was progressing smoothly—too smoothly for the RSHA. There was no sign of complications. It was later learned that the information from Major Savrin and his wife was false. It seemed almost certain that they had fallen into the hands of the Russians.

In December 1944 one of the V-men who had landed with the advance detachment reached the German lines. Part of the group that had landed east of Smolensk, he was able to confirm that the advance detachment had been found and caught by the enemy as soon as it landed. The agents were forced to carry on with their mission as if nothing had gone wrong. Russian troops waited for the arrival of the aircraft carrying the agents.

When the aircraft began its approach to land at the primary site on the early morning of 6th September, it was fired on by a waiting Russian anti-aircraft gun. On meeting this unexpected resistance the crew abandoned its approach and pulled up. One of the V-men managed to escape in the wild confusion; it was he who reached the German lines.

The Arado now flew to the alternate landing field. The pilot tried to land there and as previously related the aircraft was damaged and left unable to take off again.

Several days after the disappearance of the aircraft Oberstleutnant Baumbach sent a Ju 188 to investigate the alternate landing site. When it over flew the target area it was fired on by Russian flak, but the crew were able to identify the Ar 232B at the side of the airfield. Nothing was seen of the crew. To the surprise of the RSHA, the alternate field had not been under surveillance when the Arado landed; the Soviets had evidently failed to realize that after overshooting the primary site it had flown on to the northeast and set course for its alternate.

The site of the landing was an abandoned airfield near Karmanovo. As soon as the Russian security forces became aware that an enemy aircraft had come down there, they dispatched troops at once. Led by the glow of a fire, they very soon discovered the aircraft. The available stopping distance proved to be inadequate and in spite of the crew's efforts the aircraft's starboard wing struck a tree and broke off. The starboard outer engine was also torn out. It caught fire and showed the search teams the way to the aircraft.

Nothing was found of the crew or the two agents. The subsequent search turned up nothing.

MAJOR SAVRIN AND SECOND LIEUTENANT SONYA SAVRIN IN RUSSIA

After the crash landing at the secondary landing site at Karmanovo the aircraft was hastily unloaded. The two "Russians" urged the crew to hurry. They were certain that the fire from the burning engine would be seen from far away and that Russian troops were already on the way to determine whether this was one of their own or a hostile machine.

With practiced hands, Major Savrin hid the things that could not be allowed to fall into Russian hands in the secret compartments beneath and on the sides of the sidecar, where they could not be found by a casual search.

These included conventional submachine-guns and poison bullets, which could kill no matter where they hit. As well there were small but highly potent magnetic mines and radio fuses with which to set off the mines from a distance. Since Stalin's habits and his route to the STAVKA were known, and brightly lit, chances of success seemed good.

The pair had with them a sum of 428,000 rubles, part of which was to be used to pay the few Moscow agents and helpers. Hidden in a compartment under the engine cover were 116 authentic and copied Russian stamps, forms and other personal papers that could be filled out as required. What was missing, however, was that little bit of luck that could turn this dangerous mission into a success.

Savrin with his wife Sonya breathed a sigh of relief when they came to a narrow forest path. Savrin started the engine and they drove carefully down the path toward the highway. About 200 meters from the road they came to a resting place, which fortunately for them had been abandoned by the troops bivouacked there. Savrin parked the motorcycle and crawled through the underbrush toward the highway. Peering through his Russian binoculars, he watched as two Russian armored cars turned into the forest down another path barely one kilometer away. Savrin had seen this path but decided not to use it on account of its exposed position.

To the southeast, in the direction of Moscow, he saw no movement at all in the light from the rising sun. He hurried back to the motorcycle.

"We have to go at once. If we can make the four kilometers to the side road we have a chance," declared the major.

His wife nodded and climbed onto the passenger seat. In the sidecar were odds and ends; they were the typical items which front-line soldiers brought home to their families from the field. They drove to the branch in the road and Savrin looked around one last time. Nothing to be seen. He opened the throttle and the set off toward the southeast. The three kilometers passed agonizingly slowly. Savrin forced himself not to speed, which surely would have attracted attention.

The pair breathed easier when they reached the side road. About ten kilometers farther they stopped; Savrin got out the small radio and began to transmit. This was the report that was received in Germany.

The radio went back into its hiding place and they drove on. Then they met a long column of vehicles; Savrin pulled off to the side of the road and let them pass. Now and then he was saluted. The gold star of a Hero of the Soviet Union proved its worth when an officer stopped beside the motorcycle. He introduced himself and asked where the major had come from and where he was going. Savrin reeled off his prepared story; he also introduced his wife. The officer wished them a pleasant stay in the capital and drove off to the front of the column again.

An hour later another column appeared; this time Savrin pulled off the road into a narrow forest lane. From there the pair watched as traffic grew heavier and heavier.

"We should have stayed on the main road," said Sonya.

"It would be just as busy; the troops who launched the offensive to the west need supplies and replacements," replied Savrin. Sonya nodded. They knew what they had gotten themselves into and they hoped that everything would turn out all right. In any case, as a result of landing at the alternate site they were much closer to Moscow and could hope to reach it by the following evening.

"We'll stay here for now," decided Savrin. Then they rolled the motorcycle into a dense thicket and made themselves comfortable in a small clearing. Four times Savrin crawled to the road to see if the traffic had abated. Finally, in the evening, the traffic did die down, and they left their hiding place and continued on their way.

When it became completely dark Savrin switched on the motorcycle's headlight. Ten minutes later they saw the leading car of a vehicle column. Heavy artillery vehicles forced them to leave the road and wait until they had passed. Back on the road again, the pair came to a roadblock; they were still 45 kilometers from Moscow. As they neared the barrier lights came on and two red flags were waved. Savrin slowed down and drove straight toward the roadblock. To the right and left he saw two soldiers of the NKVD. A sentry came out from behind the barricade and approached the motorcycle, his submachine-gun pointed at the pair.

"Be careful that you don't shoot someone, comrade," warned Savrin good-naturedly. "Or are there no bullets in your gun?" he continued with a smile. He undid the buttons of his leather coat; the sentry saw the decorations, however he did not appear to be particularly impressed.

"Your papers!" he demanded gruffly. Then, turning to Savrin's wife, "Yours too, Comrade Lieutenant!"

Sonya pulled her prepared papers from her tunic and passed them to the sentry, who disappeared behind the barbed wire. Three minutes later he returned. At his side was an officer with the rank of colonel. The latter stepped up close to Savrin. Even before he opened his mouth, Savrin knew that the game was up, for before him stood his former regimental commander.

"It is Lieutenant Savrin," the colonel called out in amazement. "We reported you missing and feared that you were dead. And now here you stand before me, in the uniform of a Russian major that surely came from Germany."

Savrin was about to reply but the colonel waved him off. "No lies Savrin. We caught the crew of the Ar 232 and they 'sang.' That is why I am here and the roadblock too."

Savrin tried to reach into his breast pocket but the colonel lunged forward and seized his forearm.

"No need to take your own life, Savrin. We still need you; and your wife too. Nothing will happen to you if you confess everything and maintain radio contact with Berlin for us."

"I wanted to get to Moscow, Comrade Colonel. That was the only way to get out of Germany and report back to my unit."

"All right Savrin, all right! Now come with me." Then the colonel turned to Savrin's wife, still standing by the parked motorcycle, pale with fright: "You too Comrade Lieutenant."

On the way to the Kremlin the colonel told them that one group from the crew of the aircraft had been caught barely an hour after their landing as they tried to make their way west. The second group was picked up later.

"And they betrayed the mission to you, sir," asked Savrin.

"As much as they knew about it, and that was enough for the NKVD leader to advise me. They spoke my name to the radio operator and he remembered it very quickly. They were therefore able to advise me, especially since I have been stationed in Moscow for a year."

"A very simple story and we had to stumble over it," thought Savrin.

"So you will work for us?" asked the colonel cordially. Savrin nodded.

"Of course Comrade Colonel, since it was my intention all along to reveal everything and turn myself in when I got to Moscow."

"Very well then. You are fortunate that the matter ended up in my hands. Otherwise you would have ended up rotting away in an NKVD interrogation camp."

Savrin and his wife continued communicating with Germany by radio. He named his contacts accurately and requested new ones. Within three weeks every German agent in Moscow, including the V-man in the Kremlin, had been arrested.

Major Reorganization

OVERVIEW

The end of 1942 saw the Brandenburgers relieved of their special missions-eliminating nests of resistance in front of the regular forces, securing bridges and ferreting out enemy headquarters. In spite of a special event, a crisis developed over how the Brandenburgers should be employed in the future.

The process of expanding the 800th Special Purpose Training Regiment Brandenburg into a special unit of greater than division strength began on 1st November. That December the special unit was enlarged to become the 800th Special Purpose Division Brandenburg and was placed under the direct command of the Ausland/Abwehr. Due to existing shortages of personnel, equipment and weapons, the expansion proceeded slowly.

On 9 February 1943, after the death of Oberst von Haehling, command of the division passed to Alexander von Pfuhlstein. Pfuhlstein had previously led the 154th Infantry Regiment and had won the Knight's Cross on 17 August 1942 while serving as its commanding officer. With the full support of the Army Personnel Office and the OKW Operations Staff, he had been able to turn the division into a capable combat unit. But it was not until 1 April 1943 that the OKW succeeded in having the division placed under its direct command and not the SS's Reich Central Security Office. However, at the same time the Abwehr lost all direct influence on its "house unit." Assigned to the Abwehr was the "Kurfurst Training Regiment," which had been subordinate to it since formation of the unit began in 1940. All the other activities of the Abwehr had been combined in this regiment—the Abwehr school, the V-man battalion, the interpreter company, and several other units that resided at the previously-mentioned Quenz Estate.

By this time counterespionage had been placed under the wings of the Secret Field Police (GFP), as Canaris had not yet been removed, and thus was under the authority of the security service. All this happened at a time when the Brandenburgers were supposed to become a division, one whose title was preceded by the title "special unit."

At the same time, since Oberst von Pfuhlstein was present at Fuhrer Headquarters, Canaris conferred there with Generalfeldmarschall Wilhelm Keitel, head of the OKW. Together with Generaloberst Jodi, von Pfuhlstein walked into the briefing room and made his report. Then he listened as Jodi spoke: "The Wehrmacht Operations Staff lacks a unit of its own for the OKW war theaters. We have to go begging to the Army High Command for every division, a tiring and often annoying practice. This is an unworthy and at the same time unbearable situation! The newly-formed Brandenburg Division will therefore be placed under the direct command of the Wehrmacht Operations Staff as its sole house unit and will be deployed by it." The Brandenburgers had thus gone from being the private unit of the Abwehr to the house unit of the Wehrmacht High Command.

Oberst von Pfuhlstein was instructed to work out proposals for the future employment of the division. He submitted these proposals on 27th March. They were supported by the Wehrmacht Operations Staff and after receiving authorization from the OKW an order was issued to the appropriate offices which was based on the proposals by the division commander. This marked the completion of the process by which the Brandenburg Training Regiment became the Brandenburg Division.

THE DIVISION ORDER OF BATTLE

Division Commander:	Generalmajor von Pfuhlstein
First General Staff Officer	Major Frankfurth
Ia:	Hauptmann Wülberg (until 31/5/43)
IIa and Division Adjutant:	Hauptmann Pinkert

Base headquarters (which emerged from the headquarters of the Brandenburg Training Regiment) was Berlin.

DIVISIONAL UNITS

Signals Battalion

Brandenburg:	Hauptmann Eltester
Base Headquarters:	Berlin

Brandenburg Tropical Battalion

(the von Koehnen Battalion)	Hauptmann von Koehnen
1st–4th Companies	

Brandenburg Coastal Raider Battalion

1st–4th Companies:	Rittmeister C. von Leipzig
Home Base:	Langenargen, Lake Constance

Brandenburg Parachute Battalion

1st–4th Companies:	Hauptmann Weithoehner
Home Base:	Stendal

THE REGIMENTS

1st Brandenburg Regiment:	Major Walther
Regimental Units:	1st Co., Brandenburg Signals Battalion
I Battalion:	Rittmeister Plitt
	Hauptmann John
1st–3rd Companies and the Legionnaire Company	
II Battalion:	Hauptmann G. Pinkert
	Oberleutnant Rosenow
5th–7th Companies	
III Battalion:	Hauptmann Froboese
	Oberleutnant Wandrey
9th–12th Companies	

2nd Brandenburg Regiment:	Oberstleutnant von Kobelinsky
	Oberstleutnant Pfeiffer
Regimental Units:	1st Co., Brandenburg Signals Battalion
I Battalion:	Hauptmann Weithoener
1st–3rd Companies	
II Battalion:	Haputmann Oesterwitz
5th–7th Companies	
III Battalion:	Hauptmann Renner
9th–11th Companies	

3rd Brandenburg Regiment:	Oberstleutnant F. Jacobi
Regimental Units:	1st Co., Brandenburg Signals Battalion
I Battalion:	Oberleutnant Kriegsheim
1st–3rd Companies	
II Battalion:	Hauptmann Bansen
5th–8th Companies	
III Battalion:	Hauptmann Grawert
9th–12th Companies	

4th Brandenburg Regiment: Oberstleutnant Heinz
   I Battalion: Hauptmann Hollmann
                                      Hauptmann Gerlach

   1st–4th Companies
   II Battalion: Hauptmann Dr. Hartmann
                                        Oberleutnant Lau

   6th–8th Companies
   III Battalion: Hauptmann von Koehnen
   11th–13th Companies

Independent Companies
   14th (later 16th) Company: Oberleutnant Hettinger
   15th (Light) Company
      (parachute):   Oberleutnant Oschatz

Auxiliary Units of the Brandenburg Division
   Brandenburg Training Regiment: Major Martin
   I Battalion: Brandenburg, Havel
   II Mountain Infantry Battalion: Baden, near Vienna
                                   (later Veldes, Oberkrain)
   "Alexander" Legionnaire Battalion: Hauptmann Auch
   1st (White) and 2nd (Black)
     Companies

Operations in the
East and Southeast

EARLY ACTIONS ON THE EASTERN FRONT

Even while the Brandenburg Division was still being formed, its individual units were thrown into battle as soon as they were brought back up to strength. The first unit sent to the east was the Ist Regiment's I Battalion under Rittmeister Plitt. It was transported by rail from Berlin to Idriza in the northern sector of the Eastern Front via Frankfurt, Stettin and Konigsberg. The campaign waged there against Soviet partisans was fought in the notorious partisan area of Krestcy, east of Novgorod. The partisans lurking in the impenetrable marshy area were inflicting serious damage on German forces and the goal was the elimination of this threat.

The battalion under Rittmeister Plitt was one of nineteen large size battle groups that were employed on anti-partisan duties on the Eastern Front in 1943. Powerful partisan units were active in the battalion's new combat zone in the Vitebsk area, supporting the Red Army's attack that had begun in January 1943 to take those fortresses and fortified places still held by the Germans—such as Velikiye Luki.

The first major battles against the partisans occurred on 21 April 1943. The Brandenburgers succeeded in reopening the vital supply road from Liliupova to the Deminez position that had been cut in several places.

When fighting flared up in the north, the unit was sent into the Alolia area in Estonia. The platoon commanded by Leutnant Heinemann of the 4th (Legionnaire) Company arrived there on 13th May to carry out an undercover mission. Forty of his legionnaires followed him deep behind the Russian lines. On 15th May there was a mutiny over a trifling matter, which threatened the success and the life of the entire patrol. In accordance with military law, Lt. Heineman had nine of the mutineers shot. The other 24 soldiers who returned with him were handed back over to the prisoner of war camps because they were undependable.

On 15th May another combat group under the commander of the 3rd Company, Hauptmann Babuke, carried out a surprise raid. It overran a

Russian outpost. Hptm. Babuke was wounded in the close-quarters fighting and Oblt. Schulte took over the company in his place. Subsequently almost the entire battalion was committed on the threatened road from Pustoshka to Vitebsk. This resulted in dramatic battles with partisans in which no quarter was given or expected.

The battalion made repeated forays into the impenetrable swamps. The enemy's camouflaged camps were ferreted out and the fleeing partisans shot down. Ambushes by both sides led to further casualties. The main burden of these attacks was borne by the 3rd and 1st Companies. The 1st Company suffered casualties of two killed and five wounded when it was caught in an ambush 12 kilometers south of Alolia. Meanwhile, the 3rd Company prepared to attack a partisan base.

ATTACK BY THE SCHULTE COMPANY

During the night of 12th May the 3rd Company under Oberleutnant Schulte made preparations to advance behind the recognized partisan positions. Divided into three groups and led by Oblt. Schulte with the company headquarters squad and a machine-gun squad, the men worked their way through the swamps. The main group stayed on a reconnoitered path that led through a dense wilderness of birch trees. The ground was soft and yielded beneath the men's boots. In the deceptive light of the half moon, now and then they could see areas of open water to the left and right.

Oblt. Schulte held his submachine-gun at the ready in the crook of his arm. The man with the backpack radio, who was walking directly behind him, called his name softly. Schulte gave the hand signal to halt.

"What is it Beller?" asked Schulte.

"Right group has picked up a partisan sentry. He was taken without making a sound."

"That looks good," replied Schulte.

Moments later they came to the end of the swampy area and tried to find a way through the dense undergrowth. A spade rang off a gas mask container. Schulte raised his hand in warning. They stopped, listened in the darkness. Somewhere off to the front right an owl cried and then another to their left.

"Those are no owls, Oberleutnant," whispered the leader of the company headquarters squad softly. 'There are no owls here!"

"Schellermann squad to me!"

The squad under Uffz. Schellermann moved up. The Unteroffizier looked at his company commander expectantly.

"Looks like a partisan sentry at two o'clock," Schulte whispered to him. "Go and check it out."

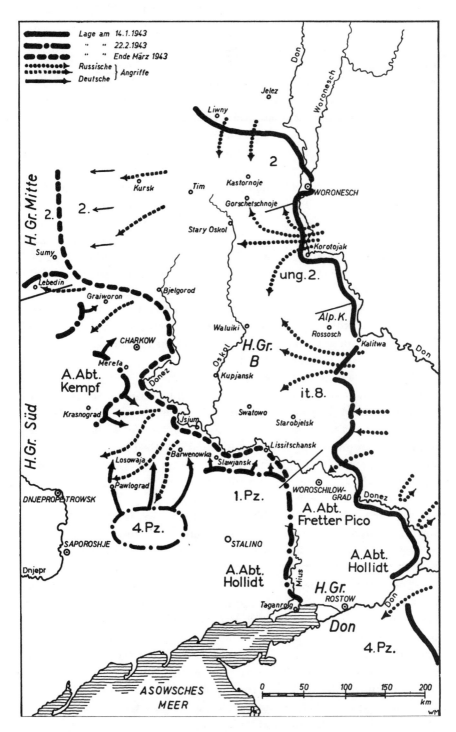

Russian attacks against Army Groups Center and South, January–March 1943.

Uffz. Schellermann and his squad moved out. The main body stayed where it was, waiting for his signal. Then they moved on. Weapons at the ready, after a half-hour march they reached the spot where scouts had been the night before. This was the jump-off point for the attack. From there they had to take a path that led over a corduroy road through the middle of the swamp to the partisan camp on an island in the swamp.

The troops advanced over the spongy ground. Suddenly shots from a number of submachine-guns and Russian automatic rifles rang out to the left and right. Both of the flanking groups had apparently made contact with the enemy. As well there was Russian gunfire in front of and behind them.

"Ambush, Herr Oberleutnant!" shouted Oblt. Schulte. They dove into the muddy soil, literally burrowed into the bushes and tried to make out the enemy. Schulte saw a muzzle flash. He squeezed the trigger of his sub-machine-gun and fired four bursts, emptying the magazine. He pressed the release button, the magazine dropped out and with a quick movement he rammed another clip into the weapon. His men fired in all directions. The machine-gun went into position in a dense thicket and opened fire on the partisans, who were now becoming visible.

"Withdraw slowly. Watch out for an ambush!"

As they crawled back, several of the men sank into and extricated them-selves from muddy holes. The partisans in their rear were still invisible. The only indication of their positions came from muzzle flashes when they fired at the men around Oblt. Schulte. Just when it looked as if none of them would get out alive, they heard the familiar sound of German submachine-guns and an MG-42 firing.

"That's Schellermann!" one of the men cried out enthusiastically.

"Up! Forward!" shouted Oblt. Schulte. He got to his feet and began to run along the corduroy road, firing as he went. Then, suddenly, he seemed to freeze in the hail of bullets from a Russian automatic rifle before he fell to the left and disappeared in the mud.

The company reformed and succeeded in escaping the ambush, tak-ing it's four wounded with it. The four members of the company who had been killed had to be left behind, however. The operation had failed. It had demonstrated to the Brandenburgers that the partisan units were employing the same tactics as they and that they held a distinct advantage as far as knowledge of the local terrain and concealment were concerned.

Leutnant Hebler took over the decimated 3rd Company, which had lost two commanders in a few days. The fighting in Army Group North's sector went on and the situation looked bad.

In the northern sector and in the area held by Army Group Center, the soldiers of the Brandenburg Division fought one of the most costly campaigns of the Second World War. A request to transfer the decimated units back to Germany to rest and refit was turned down by the OKW Operations Staff.

OPERATIONS IN THE BALKANS

More units were sent to the Eastern Front and the bloody summer of 1943 that demanded great sacrifices from the Brandenburgers. It took a great deal of effort on the part of Generalmajor von Pfuhlstein to gradually bring his unit back together. On 5th August the 1st Brandenburg Regiment's I Battalion under Rittmeister Plitt was withdrawn from its area of operations at Orodesh and transported by rail to Baden near Vienna. The unit began occupying quarters in Neuhaus on 10th August. Refitting and reorganization, as well as the disbandment of the 4th (Legionnaire) Company, proceeded very quickly and on 10th September Hptm. Plitt reported that his unit was once again fit for front-line service. The battalion's next area of operations was to be northern Greece.

The Ausland/Abwehr had become aware of Allied plans for an advance by British forces from Egypt and the Near East against the European mainland, specifically Greece and the Pelopponese. Following the receipt of this report by the OKW, more and more Brandenburg units were sent to southeast Europe. For example, the 4th Brandenburg Regiment under Oberstleutnant Heinz transferred from Brandenburg, Havel to Yugoslavia. Heinz and his staff preceded the unit to the Balkans. The first combat unit to follow was II Battalion under Hptm. Dr. Harmann. The unit detrained in Raska, near Nish Lud, on 28th April and from there was trucked to Sjenica. There it was placed under the command of the 1st Mountain Division. The last unit to arrive, 4th Regiment Headquarters, reached Yugoslavia on 16th May, and Oberstleutnant Heinz reported that he and his II Battalion were ready. However his I Battalion under Hptm. Hollmann had been diverted to southern Greece with the 104th Light Infantry Division.

The loss of one of its battalions seriously weakened the regiment. Oberstleutnant Heinz complained to the division and in response he was sent II Battalion, 1st Brandenburg Regiment under Hptm. Pinkert as a "replacement." The first action in Yugoslavia was launched from Ckovinnice through Gorazde and Gacko to Krivi Do.

During May 1943 Serbian General Dragoljub Mihailovic, who had been named Minister of War by the Yugoslavian exile government in Lon-

Feindlage nach einer deutschen Lagekarte vom 10. 1. 1943

The enemy situation in Yugoslavia 1943.

don in January 1942, approached Oberstleutnant Heinz and proposed that the Brandenburgers and his nationalist-Serbian Chetniks join forces in the struggle against Tito's communists. After getting the "green light" from the Abwehr, on 9th May Heinz concluded an agreement with General Mihailovic for combined operations against the Tito partisans. This secret agreement resulted in the formation of the Montenegrin Legion, which was supposed to be attached to the 4th Brandenburg Regiment. Unfortunately the agreement was ultimately rejected by the Wehrmacht Operations Staff and no joint operations took place.

Several days earlier, on 7th May, the division suffered its first casualties in Yugoslavia when elements of the 4th Brandenburg Regiment took part in fighting in Dormitor in the Sutjeska Gorge.

Major Walther, commander of the 1st Brandenburg Regiment, led his unit into the Balkans beginning on 11 July 1943. Like the commander of the 4th Regiment, he arrived with only his III Battalion. The regiment's I Battalion under Rittmeister Plitt was still fighting on the Eastern Front. Walther's zone of operations was the area between Thebes and Amphissia northwest of Athens. There he was to engage both nationalist and communist guerrillas as the situation required. As it turned out, the nationalist guerrillas took little action against German installations because the two guerrilla groups were locked in a bitter struggle.

The next unit to transfer to the Balkans was the 2nd Brandenburg Regiment. Commanded by Oberstleutnant von Kobelinsky, the regiment, whose last elements were not withdrawn from the Caucasus area until March-April 1943, was ready for action again in July. The unit had been reorganized as follows: I Battalion under Hptm. Weithoener; II Battalion under Hptm. Oesterwitz; and III Battalion under Oblt. Renner

Oberstleutnant Kobelinsky developed a serious illness and died at the end of June. Oberstleutnant Pfeiffer stepped in to the breach to lead the unit. On 9th July the regiment entrained for Greece. Following the completion of all the transfers, the units of the Brandenburg Division were deployed as follows:

1st Regiment: Major W. Walther
    I Battalion: Pustoshka area, USSR
    II Battalion: Sarajevo area, Yugoslavia
    III Battalion: Thebes area, central Greece
2nd Regiment: Oberstleutnant Pfeiffer
    I Battalion: Ptoleais area, northern Greece
    II Battalion: Ptoleais area, northern Greece
    III Battalion: Ptoleais area, northern Greece
3rd Regiment: Oberstleutnant Fritz Jacobi
    I Battalion: Pustoshka area, USSR
    II Battalion: Pyrenees, southern France
    III Battalion: Karachev area, USSR
4th Regiment: Oberstleutnant Heinz
    I Battalion: Pelopponese, southern Greece
    II Battalion: Sarajevo area, Yugoslavia
    II Battalion, 1st Rgt.:   Sarajevo area, Yugoslavia

"Operation White" at the beginning of 1943.

The war against the partisans was unbelievably harsh. Neither side gave any quarter. One of the most remarkable actions was carried out by Oberleutnant Konrad Steidl, whose description of the action is taken from his war diary:

"After days of scouting I was able to determine that strong bandit forces had moved into the area surrounding Klisoura. I advised Oberstleutnant Heinz and received orders to carry out a motorized advance into the gorges south of Klisoura.

Driving in a motorcycle-sidecar combination, I led the column with the machinegun squad. The regiment had placed at my disposal the heavy tractor with mounted quadruple flak. When we approached a village driving carefully, as the roads were mined in places, I was shot at from some bushes. I jumped from the motorcycle and opened fire at two fleeing partisans with my submachine-gun, knocking both to the ground.

The village was full of partisans. We left our vehicles and charged the village. The houses went up in flames. The partisans fled the village but continued to fire at anyone who showed himself from the slopes above. We could not get at them and I had to order my troops to fall back. Uffz. Grober had his head taken off by a stray antiaircraft shell.

The next action brought us up against strong partisan groups in the Vlasti area. Moving by night, we arrived at the jump-off point by way of Ptolemais. My company drove point. We moved up into the mountains. There was a full moon and it was almost as light as day. At midnight we stopped to rest in a sunken road that, lined with dense bushes, offered good cover. Vlasti lay before us. We crept up to the village, bypassed some stone barricades, and reached the entrance to the village. The fighting began and by morning the village was in our hands.

The next afternoon we reached Weithoener's command post. Several hours later General von Pfuhlstein arrived on an inspection tour.

After night fell we continued on. Meanwhile Renner and his company had stormed the Klisoura Pass, and we moved toward Eratira. The bulk of the enemy had withdrawn south over the Aliakmon. Several bandit-occupied villages south of the Aliakmon were taken in a night action. Once the Aliakrnon had been crossed, the attack on the city of Neapolis, which was full of communist guerrillas, turned out to be a dangerous undertaking. I crawled forward to Weithoener and received instructions to take the company left of the road and attack toward Neapolis. This in 40-degree heat. But we took one hill after another. Our attack was supported by the light guns of the parachute troops and by 75-mm anti-tank and anti-aircraft guns.

At the same time Oesterwirt attacked along the road. Heavy fire came from the houses and positions at the outskirts of the town. I broke in with a platoon from my company and drove out the enemy in heavy house-to-house fighting. I blew up a munitions dump in the center of the town with a hand grenade. Oberstleutnant Pfeiffer arrived and congratulated us on our success."

This ends the Steidl account. Let us now turn once again to the Russian theater, where the activities of the Brandenburgers had diminished but had not yet ended.

The 3rd Brandenburg Regiment's I Battalion arrived in the Pustoshka area on 6 July 1943 and the next morning relieved the war-weary I Battalion, 1st Regiment. Under the command of veteran Brandenburger Oblt. Kriegsheim, the battalion took over the sector between Idriza and Sokolniki.

During the night of July 19th the battalion was awakened by a call for help. Oblt. Kriegsheim learned by telephone that the regiment's 4th Legionnaire Company was under attack in the town of Sarethsje. Russian officers serving in the legionnaire company had arranged an ambush. At least 70 legionnaires were killed in the slaughter. When Oblt. Kriegsheim arrived he found the mutilated bodies of the legionnaires as well as those of 14 German members of the unit and its commander, Oberleutnant Kohlmeyer. Initial questioning of those still alive and the legionnaires who had hidden themselves revealed that the approximately 50 Russian legionnaires responsible for the massacre had taken off in two trucks. These reports soon proved to be true.

"We have to go after them and see to it that they are punished, otherwise none of our lives will be safe any more," declared Oblt. Kriegsheim.

While the main body secured the town, a reinforced platoon led by Oblt. Kriegsheim set off on the trail of the two trucks. Finally they were found on a side road in a forest, having run out of fuel. They had been rolled down an embankment and tipped over, rendering them useless.

Oblt. Kriegsheim and his men continued on. Toward midday they were fired upon from numerous hiding places in an area of difficult terrain. Oblt. Kriegsheim deployed his force and advanced on the partisans. Their positions and machine-gun nests, which were equipped with German weapons, were taken after a flurry of hand grenades. Not a single partisan escaped. The German uniforms and the personal items taken from the slain legionnaires and German soldiers were recovered.

The 4th Company of the 1st Brandenburg Regiment was subsequently disbanded and was not reformed. More than a year before the chances of a German victory over the Soviet colossus had appeared good; but now the tide had turned and Russian troops who had chosen to serve with the German forces attempted to escape retribution from the Red Army by carrying out massacres such as this one.

The war against the partisans in the area of the Dvina River and its tributaries exacted a heavy toll from the Brandenburgers. An advance on Rybaki by the 3rd Regiment's I Battalion and an attack on Kulino and a subsequent action at Lake Sarre by III Battalion were successful. The action in the area west of Vitebsk from 24th to 28th August was bloody and terrible. Code-named "Harvest Aid II", the operation was carried out by the Holtzendorf Regimental Group made up of the first three companies of the 1st Brandenburg Regiment. Soon afterward Oblt. Kriegsheim left the Brandenburgers and the former adjutant of the 3rd Regiment, Hptm. Wasserfall, took over command of the battalion.

During and after Operation "Zitadelle", the final German offensive in Russia, small Brandenburger battle groups fought many defensive actions. In each of these numerous missions, including one ordered directly by Generaloberst Model, the Brandenburgers were able to do what was requested of them. The 3rd Regiment's III Battalion in particular was called upon to carry out many difficult missions in the period from 11 September to 2 October 1943. It eliminated a Russian breach in the 110th Infantry Division's lines and took over the defense of Semeretschi for the 20th Panzer Division. At Iput it was once again committed to assist the 110th Infantry Division; a battalion counterattack sealed off and destroyed a penetration by enemy forces.

By the time the battalion was withdrawn from the front on 2 October 1943, it had sustained casualties of 17 killed and 74 wounded from an initial strength of 9 officers, 32 NCOs and 319 enlisted men. In a letter of gratitude to the regimental commander, the commanding officer of the 707th Infantry Division said: "Your Third Battalion distinguished itself magnificently in action against the enemy. It is truly a joy to fight shoulder to shoulder with this outstanding battalion."

From there the 3rd Brandenburg Regiment was transferred into the area south of Minsk. Elements of the Brandenburg Division also saw action in the Crimea, near Zhitomir and during the German retreat. When the battle for the Crimea began, the enemy broke through near Krivoy Rog. Soviet tanks drove out of the area northwest of Kiev and entered the city. The 3rd Brandenburg Regiment's I Battalion was once again thrown into the thick of the fighting, spearheading the battle group that was sent against the enemy in an attempt to thwart his breakthrough. In an effort to once again achieve the impossible the scratch force was sent Luftwaffe field units and alert units dispatched by the army high command.

In the midst of this polyglot force, which in spite of its lack of cohesion fought to the last drop of blood, the battalion under Hptm. Wasserfall was a tower of strength. Wherever the fighting was heaviest, wherever the Red Army had torn a gap in the German lines, the Brandenburgers stepped in and stemmed the raging flood. Night counterattacks pinched off penetrations, after which the enemy troops were attacked from behind and wiped out.

On 6th October the battalion—which was subordinated to the 246th Infantry Division—was sent to the 2nd Luftwaffe Field Division, part of Battle Group Schafer. The latter was holding against enemy attempts to break through and was under heavy pressure. Hptm. Wasserfall was wounded there. On 9th October he was relieved by Hptm. Gerhard Pinker, who had formerly commanded the 1st Regiment's II Battalion. The battalion remained in action near Zhukovo until late October. It fought off no less than seven heavy attacks, often with strong tank support. Seven times panzerfausts and anti-tank mines stopped the Soviet armor:

The enemy made repeated attempts to surprise the defenders in night raids. This was man against man, and although the Brandenburgers were practiced in this style of fighting the tenfold superiority of the enemy made it a costly affair. The battalion was reduced to about 70 fighting men before the regimental commander appealed to the headquarters of the 3rd Panzer Army in person. He was able to bring about the withdrawal of the battalion, which was transferred to the Luchesa area in the rear where it could rest and integrate replacements.

It was only five days before the situation at the front demanded the return of I Battalion. Those elements that had been brought up to strength and issued new weapons were directed into a blocking position southeast of Dretin. In this area, southeast of Polotsk, enemy forces which had advanced out of the Nevel area and reached the Polotsk rail line were supposed to be halted. But stopping such a powerful force was out of the question. The Brandenburgers and the other infantry units had to conduct a fighting withdrawal. By 13th November they reached Schily, where hastily prepared defensive positions were occupied.

The enemy ultimately reached the villages of Ostroff and Kuliki, in front of and to the side of the defense front, threatening the battalion's positions. A night counterattack was ordered. Hauptmann Pinkert led the counterattack. The Brandenburgers reached Ostroff and then struck out to the left and right. They outflanked the town, taking out two Soviet outposts in the process, and then entered Ostroff from behind. Almost noiselessly they disabled the Russian weapons then entered the houses and overwhelmed the sleeping Red Army troops. When the enemy realized they were under surprise attack and opened fire, the four MG 42s, which could fire 1,200 rounds per minute, opened fire and swept the streets clear.

Leaving behind one platoon, the battalion moved on to Kulki. There, too, surprise was achieved. The enemy were defeated. Everything the Brandenburgers could not take with them was blown up and then the remaining Soviet stores were set on fire.

Exactly 24 hours later the Brandenburgers were summoned to the area of the 211th Infantry Division, one of the divisions of the LV Army Corps. Sirotino, situated on the Polotsk- Vitebsk road, had to be cleared of the enemy to enable German forces to fall back to the west on the road unhindered. The attack was a success and the battalion played a significant role in the 211th Division's success.

On 19th November I Battalion, 3rd Brandenburg Regiment was placed under the command of Battle Group Wagner of the 211th Infantry Division. General Staff Oberst Wagner was Ia of the LV Army Corps and had already successfully completed many such assignments. He had worn the German Cross in Gold since 11 April 1942 and was considered a gifted but nevertheless aggressive officer. Under his command the Brandenburgers saw several days of extremely heavy fighting. Defensive battles were fought and counterattacks carried out, after which a staged withdrawal began into the next position, where the men dug in again.

When the 3rd Brandenburg Regiment's I Battalion was pulled out of the line on 9th December and transferred to Koslovo, everyone hoped for a lengthy rest. But the Red Army had already launched a new offensive. Throughout all of December the battalion was repeatedly sent back into action in bitter cold and fierce snowstorms. It was not until the turn of the year that the front quieted down and the Vitebsk area could be considered secure.

Another element of the 3rd Brandenburg Regiment, III Battalion under Hptm. Grawert, fought a weeks-long battle against partisan forces operating in the area southeast of Minsk. At the Beresina it had to battle both partisans and regular elements of the Red Army that had broken through. It was a struggle for survival, man versus man against the dangerous Russian opponent who possessed an advantage in knowledge of the local terrain and conditions. At the beginning of December Hptm. Grawert was ordered to lead a patrol across a river; intelligence needed prisoners. Every able member of the unit answered his call for volunteers. The patrol was led by Oblt. Ramstetter, commander of the 10th Company, who selected mostly members of his own company to accompany him. On the evening of 2nd December the company was moved forward into the sector held by an infantry regiment on the west bank of the Beresina east of Bobruisk.

Oblt. Ramstetter received the express order to bring back live prisoners. He was advised that the infantry group stationed there had been unable to take even a single prisoner. After a briefing by the commander of the infantry company holding the center of the line, Ramstetter first deployed a squad to scout ahead. This was followed by a conference with the unit commanders in whose area the night raid was to take place. The three squads of the 10th Company received the following orders: "The firs two squads will scout the terrain to the left and right of the third squad and will be assigned specific objectives. The company commander will remain with the third squad opposite the Russian main line of resistance on the east side of the Dniepr on the river ice. Third squad will cover departure and arrival and give supporting fire."

The following is Oblt. Ramsteter's personal account of the action:

After moving up through our positions across the ice we reached the designated departure point. From there the two reconnaissance squads headed off in the assigned directions. Both squads managed to slip through the Russian lines into the rear without difficulty. During the course of the operation both squads were able to take prisoners from Russian-occupied villages without being noticed. They captured horses and sleighs that they used to transport back the prisoners.

In the early morning hours both squads arrived in front of our starting point at almost the same time, unaware of the other's presence. Each thought the other to be a Russian patrol. Not until the last second did the two squads recognize each other, and quiet returned after a few shots had been fired, which unfortunately wounded one man. They came through to our covering squad and together we withdrew across the ice to our own lines. Prisoners, horses and sleighs were turned in; the prisoners were immediately transported to division.

We were subsequently withdrawn from this sector.

Not until the beginning of January 1944 were the headquarters of the 3rd Regiment under Oberstleutnant Fritz Jacobi and the 3rd Brandenburg Regiment's III Battalion under Hptm. Grawert pulled out of the area southeast of Minsk. They were transported by train to Stolyn, east of Pinsk, where positions were occupied. Their orders: "Guard the seam between Army Group Center and Army Group South."

THE "ALEXANDER" LEGIONNAIRE BATTALION

Commanded by Hptm. Alexander Auch, the battalion was organized as follows. The 1st (White) Company, comprised of White Russians and Ukrainians, and the 2nd (Black) Company, comprised predominantly of Caucasians.

Born in Petersburg as the son of a salesman, Hauptmann Auch spoke perfect Russian. The battalion was formed under his command in Freiburg, Breisgau in January 1943. Some of the cadre and command personnel came from the old 2nd Company, 800th Special Purpose Regiment; the rest were convalescents from various companies returning to active service after recovering from wounds or illnesses.

Hptm. Auch thus had a core of capable, veteran Brandenburgers. From Freiburg the unit went for training to Kranepuhl near Brandenburg. There the unit was billeted in a barracks camp belonging to the flak artillery. At Kranepuhl the unit was joined by its Russian volunteers, men recruited from the prisoner of war and labor camps and who were ready to "join the fight against bolshevism."

The unit was sent to the Eastern Front at the start of Operation "Zitadelle." It occupied quarters in the Teterev area, from where it was to carry out its first anti-partisan operations. The "Alexander" Battalion was forced to withdraw after the Russian counteroffensive that followed "Zitadelle" began to gain ground against the 4th Panzer Army. It was deployed in the Zhitomir area, where it performed very well in the bitter fighting there.

The battalion held out against the Red Army in Zhitomir until 13th November. It took part in a counterattack on Pavoloch and Paripzy; both towns, defended only by regional defense and alert units, had fallen, and Red forces poured through the resulting gap.

The 4th Panzer Army readied seven divisions to close this gap in the German defensive front and placed them under the command of the XXXXVIII Panzer Corps. The counterattack's objective was to reach the Kiev-Zhitomir rail line and from there advance to the major Kiev-Zhitomir road. This supply line, which had become vital to the enemy, was to be cut.

The attack began late on the evening of 19 November 1943. Driving with the lead tanks, in some cases riding on them, the men of the "Alexander" Battalion stormed back into the city of Zhitomir. While the tanks rolled through quickly, the Brandenburgers had to clear the city house by house. The result was dramatic man-versus-man combat. The fleeing enemy was chased from floor to floor up to the rooftops as one house after another was cleared. Zhitomir was retaken by the German forces. The night attack on the city was described in a report by the panzer division: "Zhitomir was taken in the early morning hours of 19th November in a night attack by tanks and panzer-grenadiers of the 7th Panzer Division led by the division commander (Generalleutnant Hasso von Manteuffel). Oberstleutnant Schulz, commanding officer of the 25th Panzer-Grenadier

Regiment 'Rothenburg', also took part. Cooperation between all arms was outstanding."

Approximately 100 men of the "Alexander" Battalion stormed into the city with the tanks. They overran the drunken crew of a Russian anti-tank gun and reported this to Oberstleutnant Schulz, who immediately followed up with six tanks. In the midst of the mass of armor was the armored troop carrier of the division commander (7th Panzer). Hasso von Manteuffel wrote:

> The large fires at the eastern outskirts of the city helped us find our way among the blocks of houses. But even more helpful was the splendid cooperation with a battalion of panzer-grenadiers. It was several days later before I learned that they were members of the Brandenburgers' 'Alexander' Battalion.
>
> The last organized resistance in the city was eliminated by 3 A.M. on 19th November. The task of clearing Soviet troops still holding out in the houses fell to the Brandenburgers. For me, seeing this cooperation, this readiness for action and this terrific offensive spirit, was one of the strongest impressions of the war.

On 20 November 1943 the Armed Forces High Command announced: "Occupied by enemy forces several days ago, yesterday the city of Zhitomir was surrounded by our troops and taken by storm."

For his role as leader of the operation, on 23 November 1943 Hasso von Manteuffel became the 332nd German soldier to be awarded the Knight's Cross with Oak Leaves. After the war he told the author: "I owe this high decoration to the fabulous performance of all the soldiers of my battle group, which of course includes the Brandenburgers. who threw themselves into the wildest fray."

The subsequent defensive battles saw the Brandenburgers once again fully committed. Some days later Generalmajor von Pfuhlstein lauded their efforts: "The reliability and competence displayed by the legionnaires in battle is first and foremost thanks to the German officers, NCOs and men of the division who fought at their side in this battalion."

In his "Christmas order," von Pfuhlstein also praised the unit's efforts in its most recent battle, when he said: "Our veteran Russian legionnaires under Hptm. Auch covered and made possible the called-for withdrawal of German troops from the Zhitomir area. Our legionnaires were the last to leave Zhitomir, and they were the first to reenter the city during the counterattack."

These legionnaires of the Alexander Battalion were to fight several more hard battles before fate caught up with them too.

Now back to operations in Greece and Yugoslavia.

IN THE BALKANS

After a quiet summer in the Balkans—apart from some ambushes—the bulk of the Brandenburg Division was stationed there against Greek and Yugoslavian partisans. The latter blew up important bridges and rail lines and carried out night ambushes, for which the preferred weapons were daggers and knives. The partisans received deliveries of supplies of all kinds by night, especially from British sources.

July 1943 saw the 1st Brandenburg Regiment's III Battalion in action against communist partisans in the Thebes-Amphissa area of Greece. I Battalion, 2nd Regiment fought a terrible battle against these night ambushes, which claimed a steady toll of German troops, near Olympus.

At this time there also occurred an incident in which Admiral Canaris allowed himself to be led astray by the head of Italy's military secret service, General Arne. It had filtered through from various sources that the Italian command was about to abandon the Axis. A general conference between the German and Italian secret services became necessary after the arrest of Mussolini on 25 July 1943. This took place in Venice on 30th July. General Arne assured Canaris that the Italian government was determined "to continue the war with all means." Separate peace negotiations with the enemy by Italy were out of the question.

Admiral Canaris advised the Wehrmacht operations staff of what he had been told. In spite of their assurances, however, the Italians left the Axis several weeks later, a development which apparently escaped the Abwehr, if such a thing was still possible, for it was said at the time that "the sparrows were already singing from the rooftops" about the Italian move.

In the autumn the 2nd Brandenburg Regiment's II Battalion under Hptm. Oesterwitz was transferred to Albania to take possession of that country's ports, another land was added to the list of those where partisan activities were noticeable, although they lacked the intensity of the Greek or even the Yugoslavian efforts.

In September 1943 III Battalion, 1st Regiment was transferred to Larissa as partisan bands had become a problem there. By the end of the year the 1st Mountain Infantry Division had assumed most of the responsibility for anti-partisan activities in Greece, allowing the elements of the Brandenburg Division released from there to be moved to Yugoslavia.

Among the provisions of a Führer Order issued on 4 October 1943, which included directives for the Commander-in-Chief Southeast, was a decree that the 1st Brandenburg Regiment should remain under the command of Army Group E in the Pelopponese, while the main body of the Brandenburg Division "was to be employed to guard lines of communication in the rear and participate in the war against the partisans." Generalmajor von Pfuhlstein received this order as an extract from the Führer Order on 6th October.

As per instructions contained in the Führer order, on 8th November the 2nd Brandenburg Regiment under Oberstleutnant Pfeiffer was transferred to Raska, Montenegro. Following this the division commander initiated a number of exchange measures: the 1st Regiment was to remain in the Thebes-Levadia area and the battle group made up of I Battalion, 4th Brandenburg Regiment under Hptm. Hollmann, was to be exchanged for II Battalion, 1st Regiment, which was attached to the 4th Regiment. The division commander was at least able to avoid total confusion, but the return of II Battalion, 1st Regiment to its parent regiment was not authorized. Now under the command of Oblt. Rosenow, the battalion continued to be attached to the 4th Brandenburg Regiment. The reason: "It is expected that the bulk of the 1st Regiment will also be moved to Yugoslavia in the near future." In any case I Battalion, 4th Regiment did rejoin its parent regiment in Sarajevo. At this point the 4th Regiment was organized as follows:

Regimental Commander:	Oberstleutnant von Hugo
Commander I/4:	Major Hollmann
Commander II/4:	Hauptmann Lau
Commander III/4:	Hauptmann von Koehnen
Commander I/I:	Hauptmann Rosenow (subordinated)

OPERATION "ZIETHEN"

The operation began on 6 December 1943. The attack units advanced over the rugged mountains and finally came to a long, narrow lake where the mountains divided. Quarters were occupied in Livno. The headquarters of the 4th Regiment transferred from the Banja Luka area to Sinj, leaving behind Oberstleutnant von Hugo, who had sustained a leg injury. It would remain in Sinj until mid-January 1944.

The move was linked with forays into the Lim Valley and the high mountain passes between Sjenica and the area east of Prijepolje. This operation, code-named "Kugelblitz", saw the 2nd Brandenburg Regiment in action beside the 1st Mountain Division, then under the command of Generalleutnant von Stettner.

On 23 November 1943 preparations began for the destruction of all Tito units in the large rectangle between Sjenica-Prijpolje in the north, Plevla in the west, and Brodarewo in the south. Because of the difficult road and weather conditions, it was 1st December before the units were ready to attack.

One of the most difficult tasks was given to the 2nd Brandenburg Regiment's I Battalion: occupy the city of Prijpolje in the valley of the Lim River. Once again we are able to turn to the war diary of then Oblt. Konrad Steidl, who recorded the details of this operation:

> Summoned by the regimental commander, I received orders to seize the bridge near Prijepolje, which was vital to the crossing of the Lim River, and hold it until the arrival of the main force. Obstl. Pfeiffer said that the outcome of the entire operation depended on the outcome of this mission.
>
> I will thus have to shoulder the blame if anything goes wrong. I am therefore working out my battle plan especially carefully, even though I lack information on the enemy, the most important factor in precise planning.
>
> Elements of the 1st Mountain Division and the Renner Battalion have already moved out to seize the mountain passes between Sjenica and the area east of Prijepolje. After bitter resistance from the partisans our attack spearheads are west of Gvod.
>
> Until then I must move the battalion forward in order to conduct reconnaissance and to make an assessment of the terrain. There is still some snow on the slopes, but the roads are muddy. We took refuge in some poor farmer's huts. A Moslem from Prijepolje came and told us what was happening in Prijepolje. We learn that the city is held by Tito partisans and Italians whose armory includes heavy weapons, tanks and artillery.

Oberleutnant Steidl included all this in his plan, including the fact that the bridge was mined and prepared for demolition. Several bunkers guarded against removal of the mines and severing of the wires to the explosives.

Reconnaissance during the two nights preceding the attack revealed that the Tito partisans had extended their positions from the Milesevo monastery across the Kosevina ridge to the Lim Valley and that tanks were guarding the road. Manned by troops of the 1st Mountain Division under Generalleutnant Stettner/Ritter von Grabenhofen (Generalleutnant von Grabenhofen had received the Knight's Cross on 23 April 1943. He was shot by partisans near Belgrade on 18 October 1944), the most forward German positions were on Kocevo Mountain.

The attack began early on the morning of 3rd December. The men of the Steidl Battalion had procured pack animals so that they would not have to carry all their equipment. The final rest stop was made when they reached the forward German outposts near Kocevo. At 2 A.M. the next morning began Operation "Lim Bridge." The point platoon was led by Lt. Mark. After advancing several hundred meters he veered left while the main body of the company continued straight ahead.

This latter route led directly to the river. Movement to the left or right was impossible on account of the marshy terrain. The main body turned around and marched to a group of houses north of the bridge. When they approached the buildings they heard voices. They were Italians who were speaking to one another.

At this point we return to Oblt. Steidl's account:

> I instructed my interpreter Vladimir to speak to them. Vladimir called to them softly, 'Sono italiani camerati'. The Italians took cover and opened fire on us. Since we absolutely had to have Prijepolje in our hands by dawn I ordered my men to rush the position.
>
> We stormed into the Italian dugouts and took them. A number of my men were wounded. We took them with us and moved as quickly as possible down into the Lim Valley, hoping that the enemy in the city would not be alerted. We still had four kilometers to go and it was already 4 A.M.; the first pale light of morning was already moving up the mountain peaks. Moving quickly, we took out the last bunker sentry positions before the city.
>
> A few hundred meters before us lay the city. The large bridge was clearly visible. We had the objective in sight and now it was up to us. I could see busy traffic on the far side of the Lim. The embrasures of bunkers peered across at us. They were only 60 meters away. There were guns there as well. The enemy had seen us, but they mistook us for their own because we were shrouded in fog.
>
> We marched single file down a path. To our right was the enemy-held mountain slope, to our left the rushing Lim. I ordered my men to attack—maximum tempo.

Attacking from on the move, we stormed the first bunker at the town limits and then charged toward the center of the town. We came under furious return fire from there, from across the road that ranched off to the bridge. We reached the bunker at the bridge. A flurry of hand grenades and we moved on. We found and cut the wires leading to the explosives. Vladimir had already crossed the bridge, I ran after him at a crouch. Sparks flew as bullets smacked into the bridge's iron superstructure. But we made it across and established a small bridgehead on the other side. I had lost many of my brave men. Only the 2nd Company was with me; the 1st Company was still on the other side engaged in bitter, house-to-house fighting.

By now the enemy had recovered from their shock and launched the first counterattack. As soon as they were within range we tossed our hand grenades. But they kept coming, even though their numbers were reduced. Max Kohlhuber, one of my veterans, was killed beside me. The number of wounded climbed, even Vladimir was slightly wounded in the shoulder. A quick survey revealed that I had only about 30 men left from the entire company. Vladimir was shot in the head and killed at my side. By now we had about 80 prisoners and only about 18 fit men remaining.

One of my handful of surviving soldiers shouted, 'The tanks are coming!' And there they were. The first one rolled across the bridge, and with it our regimental commander and a relief platoon commanded by Oberleutnant Haut.

Now the advance continued. Oblt. Steidl and the reinforcements moved on the nearby barracks, from which we were under an almost uninterrupted stream of fire, but they were unable to get through.

The tanks moved into position and were joined by several anti-tank and light infantry guns; together they placed the barracks, which were defended by about 300 battle-tested partisans, under direct fire. Nevertheless this attack also failed.

"We have to have possession of the barracks before night falls," ordered Oberstleutnant Pfeiffer. "We will attack after dark with all the men and drive the enemy out."

Bolstered by the arrival of reinforcements from III Battalion under Hptm. Reuner, the attack began in total darkness. Escorted by two tanks, an assault team led by Oblt. Steidl made it to the barrack gate. Smoke candles and gasoline blew in the gate and the last resistance was broken. 180

enemy dead were left behind in the barracks. It was exactly 10 P.M. when Prijepolje and the west bank of the Lim were in our hands. But reconnaissance patrols revealed that victory had not yet been won.

More Tito partisans were approaching from the area south of Sjenica-Prijepolje-Plevlja and soon they were in the rear of the German forces which were attacking west and northwest. In order to meet this danger, on 7 December 1943, Oberstleutnant Pfeiffer sent his regiment's I Battalion south. Trucks carried the soldiers as far as Brodarewo. From there the battalion fought its way on foot through densely wooded terrain through Bukovic into the Grab area. There it linked up with the Jaksch Company and several Moslem units. From there Oblt. Steidl stormed toward Draskow-ina and reached the outskirts of the town. Patrols discovered enemy forces west and south of the town, all moving toward Draskowina. The battalion held its position until 12th December, when, running low on ammunition and with no supplies getting through, it was forced to withdraw.

Taking all its wounded with it, the unit pulled back to the hills on both sides of the Grab. There, acting as a forward screen, at dawn it repulsed numerous enemy advances made in heavy snow showers and dense fog.

Another attack was repulsed on 11th December, then the next morning the following order arrived by radio from regiment: "Fight your way through to the hills near Petulja, where you will be relieved by the Vinzenz Company. Once again establish a covering position."

The retreat was conducted during the night and on 18th December the surviving members of the battalion were relieved. The unit moved to Prijepolje, where it was placed in reserve and had some time to take on replacements in weapons and personnel and to some degree restore its fighting strength.

At the beginning of January 1944 Hptm. Weithoener—having recovered from his wounds—once again took over command of the battalion. Oblt. Steidl was promoted to Hauptmann for bravery in the face of the enemy and sent on a battalion commanders course. There, on 26 January 1944, he received word from division commander Generalmajor von Pfuhlstein, congratulating him on the award of the Knight's Cross that day.

At this time the 2nd Brandenburg Regiment's II Battalion under Hptm. Oesterwitz rejoined the regiment from Tirana. This left two army units in Albania, albeit with no supporting forces from the Brandenburg Division: the 100th Light Infantry Division and the 297th Infantry Division, both of which were part of XXI Mountain Corps.

Following the unit's anti-partisan activities in Yugoslavia, Greece and Albania in 1943, the division commander issued the following Christmas and New Year's order:

Brandenburg Division   Headquarters, 24/12/1943
The Commanding Officer
No. 747/43 secret
SOLDIERS OF THE BRANDENBURG DIVISION!

To all officers, NCOs and men, the first-aid officers and officials of the division at the front, in the hospitals and at home I send comradely greetings and best wishes for Christmas and the New Year.

As the old year gives way to the new, I wish to give you all a summary of what the past year had brought the Brandenburg Division.

In January 1943 almost all the elements of the then Brandenburg Special Unit were on the Eastern Front, especially in the south of the same. In ice and snow, engaged in heavy fighting, the weak companies of the Brandenburgers formed the rear guard for numerous divisions and panzer corps. Their sacrifices made it possible for these units to withdraw.

Not until the end of January, but in most cases not until February and March, was it possible for the Brandenburgers to be pulled out of the line and sent home temporarily. They took only themselves and their weapons with them. But one other thing came with them from the Russian expanses: the absolute feeling of the superiority of the German soldiers and especially the Brandenburgers over the Russian foe.

What happened then?

After a few weeks of outstanding work all the companies of the Brandenburg Special Unit were combined to form the Brandenburg Division. The battle-tested companies formed the backbone of new battalions, command over which was assumed by the veteran company commanders. They were joined by new men, and older and younger officers and non-commissioned officers. In this way companies became battalions and battalions regiments.

At this point I would like to gratefully acknowledge the outstanding work of the division's First General Staff Officer, Hauptmann Wülbers, who has since been seriously wounded on the Eastern Front. The first battalions returned to the front in April. The last elements of the division followed in May. I admit everything happened too quickly. It would have been better if a few more weeks or even days had been available. But they were not! Command and front demanded the rapid deployment of every available Brandenburger.

What was accomplished in 1943?

The 1st Regiment, the 4th Regiment's parachute company under the command of Oberleutnant Oschatz and Leutnant Horl, the 1st Coastal Raider Company with its now severely-wounded Hauptmann Kuhlmann, played a major role in the capture and clearing of the islands of Cos, Levita, Stampalia, Kalimnos, Leros and Samos. Several of these important islands were taken exclusively by Brandenburgers in surprise raids. When a crisis arose on Leros after four days of heavy fighting and a serious setback appeared possible, the 1st Brandenburg Regiment's III Battalion under the command of Hauptmann Froboese, who was wounded in the process, brought the operation to a victorious conclusion. Oberleutnant Wandrey and twenty men broke through the heavily fortified English line, took out a series of especially stout bunkers in the deepest part of the English front, and finally personally took prisoner the commander of the island, General Tilney. Our division's III Battalion, 1st Regiment and the daring action by Oberleutnant Wandrey and his men had a decisive influence on the surrender of the numerically superior and far better armed enemy on the heavily fortified and defended island.

Under the energetic and at the same time caring command of its commanding officer, Oberstleutnant Pfeiffer, the 2nd Regiment daily inflicted heavy losses on the enemy in men and materiel in numerous battles and engagements in Northern Greece, Albania and especially in Serbia. Compared to the enemy's extraordinary losses, our casualties were minimal. This is due to the 2nd Regiment's especially successful use of our proven special operations style of fighting. I give special credit to the three battalion commanders, Hptm. Weithoener, Hptm. Oesterwitz and Hptm. Renner and to Oberleutnant Steidl. All four are veterans of special operations.

For months I and III Battalions of the 3rd Regiment have been at one of the hot spots in the fighting in the east. It is a position that is mentioned almost daily in the Wehrmacht communique. These two battalions have come to know the fury and determination of the Russian attacks. The battalions have fought magnificently in heavy engagements against numerous heavy tanks, marauding cavalry units and numerically superior infantry forces, against artillery and mortar units and rocket launchers, often with no friendly units left or right. Hptm. Pinkert (Gerhard), Hptm. Grawert and Hptm. Mertens played a large role in these successes.

By comparison Hptm. Bansen's battalion in Italy had it somewhat easier, but it has carried out its orders to the complete satisfaction of the division.

Also brought together in a battalion under Hptm. Auch, our old Russian legionnaires formed the rear guard which made possible the withdrawal by German army units in the Zhitomir area. They were the last to leave Zhitomir and, fighting as part of the 7th Panzer Division, were the first to reenter Zhitomir. The reliability and skill of the legionnaires in battle is due in large part to the German officers, NCOs and men of my division serving in this unit.

The division has also not forgotten the difficult and costly battles in Africa, especially in Tunisia, by the von Koehnen Battalion and the coastal raider company under Hauptmann Kuhlmann. But on Cos and Leros the coastal raider company showed that its spirit and verve were the same as in Africa. III Battalion under Hauptmann von Koehnen has also long since returned to action against the enemy.

At present the units of the 4th Regiment have been deployed separately. Several elements of the regiment recently joined combat. Operations by the 4th Regiment will not get fully under way until 1944.

The operation on Leros by the 1st Company under Oberleutnant Solder, who was wounded there, the numerous actions by the parachute company and, not least, the daring surprise raid by the Hettinger Company which led the to capture the island fortress of Maddalena (where it was thought that the Duce, Benito Mussolini, was being held prisoner), are a prelude to further successes by the division.

Our radio operators have again proved that they are masters of their trade. They established all the desired communication links, often over many hundreds of kilometers.

The medical officers have distinguished themselves, and not just as doctors. When the situation required, such as in the east or on Leros, they proved equally capable leaders of units and fighters. Our special thanks is also due to the division's officials, who worked conscientiously and carefully to ensure that the field forces received the necessary supply.

On the eve of the New Year, however, we especially remember our fallen comrades with reverence and gratitude. They await the victory that we must now win for them.

We want to keep in touch with our comrades in the hospitals. No one must be forgotten! 'We want to have them all back with us soon by way of the convalescent companies.

What will 1944 bring us?

Our ranks have been thinned by the battles at the end of this year. This will change at the start of the new year. Beginning in January we will be joined by picked volunteers from every branch of the armed forces, who will be assigned to the front-line regiments. As well we will be receiving the first young soldiers who were carefully trained in the new training regiment under the command of Major Martin. I have seen these recruit companies, they are trained in all styles of fighting and have exercised in the field. The regiments will be keen to get these excellent young soldiers.

Our weaponry will be improved to the maximum degree possible. NCO courses, combat school courses and other opportunities for the best possible training will be exploited to the utmost.

In the preceding summary I have named several officers by name. But our success would not have been possible if these officers had not had hundreds of brave NCOs and men standing at their side as part of a true fighting team. To all of them goes an equal measure of my thanks and recognition.

The Brandenburg Division enters the New Year self-confident, its head held high. No one in the German Armed Forces, and certainly no one on the enemy side, can impress or outdo us Brandenburgers!

Our motto for the year 1944 is the same as in the old year. It is:

BRANDENBURGERS FORWARD EVERYWHERE!

VON PFÜHLSTEIN.

This order of the day provides a brief outline of the actions in which the Brandenburgers took part. But it is also in recognition of the efforts of the division's troops and therefore deserves to be included in this work.

FURTHER FIGHTING IN YUGOSLAVIA— NEGOTIATIONS WITH TITO

Before proceeding with the account of the Brandenburg Division's subsequent operations in Yugoslavia I wish to bring to the reader's attention an explosive political interlude in Yugoslavia which, if it had been handled properly by the German supreme command, could have prevented many bloody sacrifices on both sides.

It is a well-known fact that there were two competing political groups in Yugoslavia, each trying to outdo the other. What is not so well known, however is the fact that both the loyalist General Dragomir Mihailowitsch and the communist leader Josef Broz Tito were ready to reach an understanding with Germany to possibly work together and informed her of this in conversations.

The Chetniks—loyalist troops under general Mihailowitsch—had begun the fight against the German Armed Forces long before Tito. When the communists formed their partisan units, hostilities soon broke out which escalated into pitched battles. This strategy first led to negotiations between Mihailowitsch and the Wehrmacht in Yugoslavia, which were terminated by Hitler.

But in February 1943 it was representatives of General Tito who met with Professor Buerger, director of the Klagenfurt Abwehr office, behind the German lines to hold initial talks about a common effort against the then mutual enemy England.

Tito, who felt he had been left in the lurch by the Russians, and who no longer expected the English to live up to their promises, was furious and ready to call a halt to the war against Germany if he was given authority in Yugoslavia and Croatia—under overall German control. However, this condition doomed the enticing offer to failure. Giving up Croatia to the communists and thus losing a loyal ally, which was kept at Germany's side by its leader Pavelich, was out of the question.

However, General Mihailowitsch, who was supported by England, on behalf of whom he concluded the secret agreement with Italy in spring 1943 that paved the way for the Italian departure from the Axis after the fall of Mussolini, was at first on the German "peace list." But then it filtered through that the Italian forces were supplying the Chetniks with weapons and ammunition and wanted to give them a free hand, and that General Mihailowitsch was parleying with the Italian commander in Podgoritza over a joint strategy with the Italians against the Germans—after the Italians changed sides. The German side now went all out.

The commander of the 4th Brandenburg Regiment received orders to break into the headquarters of General Mihailowitsch, capture him and place him in German custody. Spies reported that he was staying in the town of Kolaschin in Montenegro.

The regimental commander, Oberstleutnant Heinz, and two of his best men, who spoke the local language, set off through the enemy lines.

They reached the bridge across the Lim near Prijepolje which was to be the scene of such bloody fighting in December (see previous chapter) and found Mihailowitsch, who was residing in Kolaschin with his two chiefs of staff, Generals Dyuresetsch and Pugowitsch.

In conversation with the general the latter declared that he had more than 200,000 of his own troops and that his main foe was not Germany but Tito's partisans, and therefore he had called a halt to the war against Germany. Mihailowitsch stated that he would make available a fully trained and equipped division for the war on the Eastern Front if his demands were met. These were: "Restoration of the Serbian state with me as minister of war. Recognition of my Chetnik troops as the German Armed Forces' shield against the Tito partisans."

Led by Oberstleutnant Heinz, the three Germans returned safely to their own lines. Heinz telegraphed a detailed report to the Abwehr office in Klagenfurt, which immediately passed this "hot iron" on to Fuhrer Headquarters. From there orders were issued, not just to arrest Mihailowitsch, but also his two chiefs of staff, who as per agreement were waiting for the result of the report at the command post of the 4th Brandenburg Regiment. This against Oberstleutnant Heinz's promise that they had the status of emissaries.

Immediately afterward an SD detachment appeared at the regiment's headquarters and relieved Oberstleutnant Heinz of command. The two Serbian negotiators were taken away by the SD.

After ratification of the agreement reached between Oberstleutnant Heinz and General Mihailowitsch on 9 May 1943, the formation of a "Montenegrin Legion" was to have begun at once. Oberstleutnant Heinz was to have appeared before a court-martial, however Admiral Canaris was able to have the proceedings quashed. Once again a great opportunity had been squandered.

THE HUNT FOR TITO

On the night of 1 January 1944 the Croatian defenders of Banya Luka, reinforced by units of the Brandenburg Division, repulsed an attack by ten (!) partisan brigades, which according to legend were commanded by Tito himself. It was the opening act of a cat-and-mouse game that was to last for a month. The Chetniks employed a whole network of patrols that, accompanied by radio teams provided by the Brandenburgers, searched for traces of the partisans in enemy territory. While taking part in these missions the Brandenburgers wore Croatian uniforms.

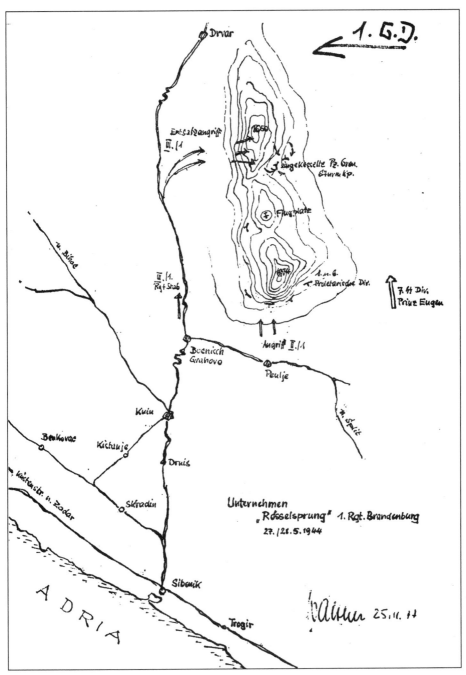

The Special Purpose Training Regiment 800 Brandenburg during "Operation Rosselsprung" (Knight's Move), May 1944.

Under the command of the Brandenburgers, a militia was formed in Kotor Varos by the mayor. The village was often fired on by the partisans and thanks to this organization it fought off a number of night attacks.

Stationed at the base of the Brandenburgers, in Kraljewo, was the Wild-schütz Unit, which consisted of soldiers of the 4th Regiment. They carried out reconnaissance of the enemy and, with permanently or temporarily attached V-men, kept an eye on enemy troop concentrations. As well there were a number of Brandenburger combat teams.

By 2 January 1944 the defenders of Banya Luka had been squeezed into a small area in the center of the city and the order was given for all-round defense. They clung grimly to the airfield as well as the Loga barracks and the citadel.

The remaining Brandenburg units were now ordered to intervene in the battle and go to the aid of Major Benesch and his "Wildschütz" unit. They worked their way up to the Vrabas Bridge in the west of the city and reinforced the police company there. On the way there the Brandenburgers came under heavy fire and suffered one killed and 13 wounded. Nevertheless, they reached the bridgehead and held it against several enemy attacks. When all the men had moved up the bridgehead was expanded. During the fighting an agricultural building on the far bank of the river belonging to the Trappist monastery was set afire.

On the third day of the fighting the exhausted Brandenburgers were relieved by men of the 92nd Motorized Brigade. This unit's self-propelled guns drove through all the streets and alleys of the city and systematically eliminated all remaining nests of resistance. The partisans fled Banya Luka and disappeared into the surrounding forests. Together with the main body of the 92nd Motorized Brigade, the Brandenburgers reached the village of Jaice. Until very recently this had been home to the headquarters of the partisan army and General Tito. His quarters, which were located in a chemical plant, were still "warm" so to speak.

Soon afterward information came from the village of Drvar that Tito was nearby. In an effort to catch him and eliminate the expected partisan threat, the 2nd Panzer Army moved in an SS parachute battalion and assembled the 4th Brandenburg Regiment, bolstered by units of the 1st Regiment (II and III Battalions), elements of the 92nd Motorized Brigade still in Jaice, and a special battle group of the 7th SS Mountain Division "Prinz Eugen."

HQ 2nd Panzer Army sent its forces concentrically from various directions toward the location where Tito's headquarters and Tito himself were suspected to be. But the supreme commander of the partisans escaped at the last second. Not until it was all over did the detachment of SS paratroopers, moving on foot, arrive on the scene. The attempted coup failed, but interrogation of locals revealed that Tito had in fact been living in the house.

Tito and his headquarters, which at that time included a British military delegation, had relocated to Dvrar, a mountain retreat about 100 kilometers west of Jaice, at the beginning of January. First it was housed in several abandoned homes, but for security reasons—in particular as a precaution against German bombing raids—it was moved to several nearby caves. Finally, fearing that German spies had found his domicile (which they had) Tito and his closest staff moved to the Bastasi area, six kilometers outside Drvar. There there was an especially roomy cave that was quickly outfitted to serve as his headquarters. Officer trainees of the Tito Escort Battalion and a unit of an engineer brigade assumed responsibility for protecting the commander in chief.

After another V-man was discovered in Tito's closest circle on 27 March 1944, it became clear to Tito and his staff that the Germans must also know about his new hiding place. Incidentally the German agent escaped before an execution squad came for him. The mood turned to one of panic when another captured agent, who had also been searching the area, revealed to the partisans that he had betrayed the hiding place to the Germans.

The decision came on 4th May. During an ambush on a platoon of Chetniks on security duty, a map was captured showing a series of military strong points and bases: all were located in the area around Dvrar and Bastasi. In order to deploy the SS paratroopers exactly and at the right time, Hauptsturmfiihrer Skorzeny, from whose special unit the paratroopers came, was asked to come to Yugoslavia to prepare and coordinate the action.

The Benesch Special Unit, now organized into two battle groups under the command of Lt. Kirchner and Lt. Böckl, were placed under the command of the airborne unit and moved into the assembly area. The following is from a report by the commander of the regiment:

> III Army Corps in Knin and the nearest division headquarters in Drnis were too far from the scene of the action. Nevertheless, the 1st Brandenburg Regiment received its orders direct from the corps instead of from the division in Drnis, which was at least closer to the action. We received as reinforcements the 2nd Panzer Army's panzer-grenadier assault battalion, which at this time was comprised mostly of officer cadets who had been sent to Belgrade for operational training. A Croatian volunteer company was also sent and finally a reconnaissance battalion.

The 1st Regiment with its two battalions and the reinforcements were supposed to attack through Bosnian Grahovo on the left wing of the 7th SS Mountain Division "Prinz Eugen" and seize Tito's headquarters which had been located near Dvrar.

The operation began early on the morning of 25 May 1944. A half hour earlier German bombers had begun pounding the area. They succeeded in knocking out the partisan headquarters' radio center. For communications Tito was left with just one telephone line. At first the partisans in Dvrar and in the headquarters in the cave near Bastasi were shocked and paralyzed.

It was precisely 7 A.M. when the first wave of paratroopers under Hauptsturmführer Rybka came down in the Dvrar Valley and the cargo gliders were let go over Dvrar to begin their spiral descent prior to a pinpoint landing. There were scarcely any partisans left in the city itself. Most had fled to the mountains when the bombing began. However at the mountain cave the 100 officer cadets of Tito's guard were ready to fight. They were the first to engage the German paratroopers.

An hour after the landing most of the city was in German hands. Hand grenades and explosives were used to clear the last of the houses. However the officer school, Well protected by the rocks and well armed with machine-guns, withstood every attack. The second wave of paratroopers landed at about 11:50 A.M. and attacked the partisan positions with great élan, but the officer cadets fought just as bravely.

An hour later, summoned by means of the sole remaining telephone line, the leading units of the 3rd Lika Brigade arrived on the battlefield. German losses now began to mount as well.

During this time the Brandenburgers were still on the march from Knin in the direction of Bosnian Grahovo. Several times they came under attack by enemy fighter-bombers. These aircraft operated from a forward airfield situated on the rocky plateau atop the twin-mountains of Sator and Jadovnik. A strike on the airfield to eliminate the attacks by the enemy fighter-bombers was not possible, for several agents had reported that the partisans' 1st and 6th Proletarian Divisions were holding impregnable positions around the airfield.

The Brandenburgers nevertheless attacked the airfield as their first objective. While II Battalion, 1st Regiment was deployed frontally from Peulje, III Battalion stormed out of Bosnian Grahovo and attacked with artillery support.

All attacks by the Brandenburgers failed in the face of massed defensive fire. Here the partisans were able to fall back on several medium and one heavy battery of Italian artillery. When II Battalion succeeded in fighting its way to near the outskirts of the airfield and drove enemy troops from their trenches and dugouts there, it was immediately counterattacked. The partisans charged the German positions, resulting in a wild melee. Thanks to their superior numbers the partisans were able to throw the Brandenburgers out again. The German wounded had to be left behind. An immediate counterattack by the regiment's reserve retook the positions. The German wounded were found there, horribly mutilated.

The regimental commander wrote of this decisive situation:

I sent reinforcements to the battalion in order to take the hill in front of us and the airfield on it the next morning.

My staff moved there in order to be present for the decisive attack. But the partisans had evacuated their positions during the night, and the airfield, which we reached shortly afterward, was empty. The last aircraft had flown out with the English military commission in the late afternoon of the previous day when my men reached the first positions.

In this situation the report reached me that a company of the 2nd Panzer Army's PGR-SR had been surrounded by partisans on Jodavnik Mountain and was almost out of ammunition. We had to get the company out as quickly as possible. I therefore moved my command post back to Bosnian Grahovo, where my III Battalion was standing ready. I led it down the road to Dvrar in order to storm the hill near Jadovnik from the flank. The attack was a success because the partisans were occupied with the surrounded company and were seemed determined to destroy it, causing them to disregard even the most minimal security measures. We stormed up the hill and in a single rush, firing from the hip and lobbing hand grenades, we crushed the enemy.

The entire regiment joined the company and pursued the enemy as he fled to the north. The latter offered no resistance, because their objective of enabling Tito to escape had been achieved. Tito got away, though not dressed as he might have—he had to leave his brand new Marshall's uniform behind, along with some papers which proved very informative.

Pursued by the Prinz Eugen Division, the partisans and the fighters around the headquarters withdrew to Potocki, which lay west of Jaice. From there Tito's staff and closest advisors drove to an airfield near

Kupreskopolje. From there they flew to the island of Vis (Lissa), where
Tito and his staff arrived on 4 June 1944.

The attempt to capture Tito and eliminate his entire staff had failed.
Nevertheless, the operation, which was code-named "Rösselsprung," did
give the German side a considerable breathing space, during which the
Tito units had to undergo reorganization.

The Dvina bridge near Dvinsk.

Brandenburgers in Soviet uniforms.

General Dietl bids farewell to his infantry as they set out to seize Murmansk.

The CIC of the Lapland Army, Eduard Dietl, with his commanders: Gen. Böhme, commanding general VIII Mountain Corps, and battalion commanders.

Night battle for a Russian village.

Forward observer in the southern sector of the Eastern Front.

A Soviet rocket
launcher captured
in the southern
sector.

In the central sector
of the Eastern
Front, 1943.

A wounded soldier
is evacuated to the
rear. No one was
left behind.

Marshall of the Soviet Union Ivan Stepanovich Konev. As commander of the 1st and 2nd Ukrainian Fronts he received reports on the activities of the Brandenburgers. In autumn 1961 he said in Berlin: ''The Brandenburgers fought like the devil!''

When asked about the Brandenburgers by the author, Generalfeldmarschall von Manstein said: "The Brandenburgers I met on the battlefields of Russia were not just soldiers, but patriots who answered the call to arms from all over the world."

GenOberst Walter Wiess also employed the Brandenburgers in the northern sector of the Eastern Front. "When I am asked to name a unit that surpasses all the others I immediately think of the Brandenburgers."

GenOberst Gotthard Heinrici, CIC of the 1st Panzer Army, had much to be grateful to the Brandenburgers for at the start of the Russian campaign when he was commanding general of XXXXIII Army Corps.

General of Mountain Troops Hans Schlemmer had Brandenburgers under his command near Orel and south of Parichi.

Oberst Albert Brux saw the Brandenburgers in action several times, including near Maykop as they cleared the way for his tanks.

Generalmajor Erich Bärenfanger, from March 1945 commander of Sector A in the Reich capital. He fell on 28 April 1945.

GenLt. Dr. Karl Maus first saw action with the Brandenburgers in 1941 in the central sector of the Eastern Front as commander of the 69th and 33rd Rifle Regiments.

The grave of Oblt. Wolfram Knaak and his men, near Dvinsk.

German sniper with telescope-equipped rifle, part of the unseen war between opposing snipers.

Counterattack near Zhitomir.

Shot-up Russian Stalin II tanks in the southern sector.

Prior to the recapture of Kiev by the Red Army.

Issuing Panzerfaust anti-tank weapons.

Panzer General Kempf also relied on the assistance of the Brandenburgers as commanding general of XXXXVII Panzer Corps.

Field Marshall Carl-Gustav von Mannerheim, CIC of the Finnish Army, received the Knight's Cross on 18 August 1941. On 5 August 1944, shortly before Finland left the war, he became the seventh foreigner to receive the Oak Leaves.

Generalluetnant Paul Klatt fought with the Brandenburgers in the far north.

4 June 1942: Hitler congratulates Field Marshall Mannerheim on his 75th birthday. In the center is Gen. Keitel.

GFM Günther von Kluge found the Brandenburgers' help invaluable, first in Poland as commander of the 4th Army and later in Russia as commander of Army Group Center.

Soviet T34/85 tanks break through at Neisse. Among the defending forces were Brandenburgers.

Russian soldiers raise the Soviet banner on the Crimean Peninsula.

Street fighting in Berlin.

April 1945: Russian tanks, in this instance US built M4A3E8 Shermans, roll through Yienna toward Linz.

Troops of the Red Army in the capital.

Soviet SU 100 tank destroyers in Berlin.

The German command is placed under arrest: from left, Minister Speer, GA Donitz, and GenOberst Jodl.

General de Artillerie von Küchler during the surrender negotiations.

The New Brandenburg
Training Regiment

Aware that replacements were not arriving fast enough to keep pace with the heavy casualties being suffered by his units, GMJ von Pfühlstein proposed to the head of the Abwehr, General Canaris, that he form a replacement and training regiment. The idea fell on fertile ground, and in May 1943 the Brandenburg Replacement Battalion was formed from the personnel that had been left behind by the division in Brandenburg. Under the command of Maj. Martin, the battalion consisted of the detachment's personnel, who had been acting as instructors, and new recruits.

Mid-August saw the formation of II Battalion in Baden bei Vienna and the process that would lead to the Brandenburg Training Regiment had begun. The new battalion was transferred to Brandenburg, Havel, where both battalions subsequently carried out their training. Then, under the command of Hauptmann von Einem-Josten, a mountain infantry replacement battalion was formed, which was based in the Neuhaus-Tristingthal area. It was to ensure an adequate supply of replacements to the 2nd Brandenburg Regiment. The home headquarters of the 2nd Regiment were incorporated in the same way. In order to provide the optimum in high-mountain training, several months later the battalion moved to Admont in Styrian Salzkammergut.

On 5 March 1944 a request was sent from the Wehrmacht Operations Staff Army to all existing elements of the training regiment to provide soldiers for an alert regiment that was to see action in the area southeast of Krakow in connection with Operation "Trojan Horse." The units were instructed to have the men ready to transport by 10th March.

The planned action never took place, however, and the two battalions that had been formed for it returned to the bases at Admont and Brandenburg, Havel.

OFFENSE AND DEFENSE IN ITALY

The Allies broke out of their constantly expanding bridgehead at Anzio-Nettuno on 12 May 1944, as a result of which the alert regiment was once

again placed on alert. Its two fully equipped battalions were rushed to
Istria, where they occupied quarters in the Trieste-Fiume area. The regiment's chief purpose there was to guard the coast against possible enemy
landings. Oberstleutnant Martin was in command, operational conditions
were simple, and there was not the slightest sign of an enemy landing. In
fact by this time no landings were expected. On 17th June, therefore, the
two alert battalions were disbanded. III Battalion under Hauptmann
Grawet moved to Stein and IV Battalion under OberZeutnant Bostrick to
Domzale, in the then "Reichsgau Oberkrain" northwest of Laibach.

The Brandenburg Alert Unit was now officially made part of the Brandenburg Training Regiment; the unit's ultimate organization was as follows:

Following this first movement, on 9 June 1944 the Wehrmacht Operations Staff issued an order, part of OKW /WFSt./Op (H), Südost. No. 00
6053/44 Secret Command Matter, according to which the entire Brandenburg Training Regiment under Oberstleutnant Martin was to transfer into
this "Reichsgau." The specified quartering area encompassed the towns of
Domzale, Stein, Krainburg, Radmannsdorf and Veldes. There the regiment was subordinated to Headquarters, XVIII Army Corps. However the
latter was only permitted to employ the alert unit to secure the quartering
area and—when training activities permitted—engage in anti-partisan
activities.

The Brandenburg Alert Unit was now officially made part of the Brandenburg Training Regiment; the unit's ultimate organization was as follows:

Regimental Headquarters:	in Veldes (Bled am see)
18th Heavy Training Company:	in Veldes
I Battalion:	basic training battalion in Veldes and Lees areas (formerly Freiburg)
II Battalion:	mountain infantry basic training battalion in the area of St. Veit an der Save (formerly Admont)
III Battalion:	field training battalion in the Stein area (formerly III Battalion of the Alert Regiment)
IV Battalion:	field training battalion in the Domzale-Hannsburg area (formerly IV Battalion of the Alert Regiment)

Under Hauptmann Auch, ethnic Germans recruited in Hungary were
formed into Training Battalion "U" and placed under the command of the
training regiment.

The 1st and 2nd Convalescent Companies remained behind in
Freiburg as did the 3rd and 4th Convalescent Companies in Brandenburg.

The 17th Training Course Company was also quartered in Brandenburg, Havel.

The Legion Training Company, on the other hand, was transferred from Kranepuhl near Brandenburg to Freiburg on orders from the division command. There it was subordinated to the leader of the combat school course.

At the end of April 1944 the training regiment was re-designated the 5th Führer Panzer-Grenadier Regiment and was pulled out of the area around Laibach, from where it had been employed in the anti-partisan role, and under the command of Oberstleutnant Schwarzrock was transferred into the Stockerau area. Nominally, at least, the unit had left the Brandenburg Division; however, several months later it was incorporated into the Brandenburg Panzer-Grenadier Division. For the time being, however, it was stationed in the Stockerau area under the command of the Führer Grenadier Division.

There now follows a summary of the final actions by the division in Yugoslavia.

BITTER RETREAT

Its headquarters in Saloniki, at the start of 1944 the units of Army Group E included the Ist and 2nd Brandenburg Regiments. The 2nd Regiment was withdrawn from the Ionian front, where the threat of a landing by the enemy was minimal. The 1st Regiment, however, remained in the Piraeus-Athens-south Attica area, engaged in anti-partisan operations under LXVIII Army Corps. The latter was supported by the 1st Regiment, which had been released from its coastal defense role and was now deployed in the Levadia-Lamia area. In addition to operations against the growing partisan threat in Greece, the regiment was also expected to guard the through roads through Thermopolae to southern Greece and the coastal area opposite the long island of Euboia. Patrols had alerted the commander of the 1st Regiment, Maj. Walther, to a massing of communist EAM units in the Sperchia Valley. Additional well-armed patrols were sent against these partisan nests from Lamia as well as from the Kamena Wurla area. The men of III Battalion were specialists in such operations, but they suffered the first casualties in this area. While leading a patrol by the 10th Company, on 3 January 1944 Oberst Minzenmay, III Battalion adjutant, was killed along with two of his companions. The patrol had arrived just as an infantry company was being pinned down by enemy fire at a bridge that the partisans had blown. The patrol succeeded in freeing the bridge.

On 14th January, Oberst Spath, commander of the 2nd Company, assumed temporary command of I Battalion in Atalanti. He instructed

Leutnant Stahl to take a well-armed patrol and scout the EAM partisans near Sklitron. The company patrol set off from the village of Evangelistria. It was accompanied by Feldwebel Koch with a number of heavy weapons. A halt was made near Sklitron to take on water. The point moved out again and reached the entrance to the village, then the unit was showered with rifle and machine-gun fire from behind left and right. Luckily Fw. Koch and his men were following 200 meters behind as the rear guard. They opened fire and then took cover at the exit from the valley beyond the village. There they formed a defensive hedgehog; several members of the leading elements of the battalion arrived there after nightfall.

Lt. Stahl, Uffz. Schmiedel and a female Gefreiter were caught in an ambush and shot. An immediate counterattack created a breathing space, but the advance was called off for the time being, to be repeated three days hence. During the night of 18th January the battalion fought its way back through the valley into Sklitron. Accompanied by a 20-mm Vierlings-flak and other "heavy" weapons, it recaptured the village.

The partisans subsequently withdrew into the mountains and the battalion's activities were limited to patrols until 20 February 1944. On that day the entire regiment was ordered to depart, and the move subsequently began at 5 A.M. on 21st February. The unit's destination was Prilep, which it reached by way of the Servia Pass, Kozani, Ptolemais and Bitolj. From there on 25 February the regiment moved on to Diakowa, Albania by way of Prizren.

The regiment was subordinated to the 2nd Army and was ordered to stand by as operational reserve in the event of an enemy landing on the Dalmatian coast between Zadar and Split.

Commanded by Oberst Seuberlich, who had taken over from Haupt-mann Wandrey after he was sent on a training course, the 1st Branden-burg Regiment's III Battalion undertook a transfer march to Skradin north of Sebenik. The regiment's I Battalion transferred from Skutari to Tirana, where several patrols were carried out in order to show the partisans "that they were there."

During the period from 18 March until the end of May 1944, III Battalion was involved in close-quarters fighting on a total of ten days, several of which resulted in heavy casualties. Operation "Bora" in particular was very costly, as was the assault on Hill 214 near Ceranje and another line of hills to its west.

On 14 April 1944 it was announced that the Brandenburg Division was going to receive a new commanding officer. The officer was Generalleut-nant Fritz Kühlwein. Born in 1892, and thus already 52 years old, Kühlwein had led the 45th Infantry Division until 28 April 1944 and had been decorated with the Knight's Cross. On 19 January 1942, while an Oberst and commander of the 133rd Infantry Regiment, he had become one of the first commanders at the front to receive the German Cross in Gold. Fritz Kühlwein led the division until it became part of the Großdeutschland Panzer Corps. He was thus the last officer to command the division as originally created.

From the Benkovac area the 1st Brandenburg Regiment's I Battalion carried out a number of difficult anti-partisan operations, frequently cooperating with the regiment's III Battalion. This battalion recorded no less than 22 close combat days. On 20th May Hauptmann John took over I Battalion. He had recovered from his wound and was eager to be among his comrades again after this difficult time. He led the battalion in the bitter June battles near Benkovac, where the battalion was repeatedly attacked by fighter-bombers. Walther, now an Oberstleutnant, and his headquarters were in Skradin. Hauptmann Wandrey, who had come back from a battalion commander course, once again assumed command of III Battalion, 1st Brandenburg Regiment. Not until mid-May, when II Battalion was released from its subordination to the 4th Regiment, was the 1st Regiment complete again.

The final actions until that fateful 24th September, when the Brandenburg Division ceased to exist, were connected with anti-partisan operations and were among the worst experienced by the Brandenburg during the Second World War.

Increasingly the fighting in Yugoslavia concentrated itself around Belgrade in September. One of the most turbulent scenes of the war took place there when, on 29 September 1944, the Red Army launched an attack with fresh divisions from its bridgehead on the west bank of the Danube on both sides of the mouth of the Timok River in the direction of Negotin. More large Soviet units approached Zajedar from the south and southeast, threatening the Petrovac-Bor supply line, the only avenue of retreat for the German units (which, incidentally, also included the 2nd Brandenburg Regiment, which was subordinated to the 1st Mountain Infantry Division) fighting in the bend of the Danube south of Turnu Severin.

South of Belgrade near Topola, III Battalion, 1st Regiment was locked in combat with partisan units, while I Battalion was in action against partisans in the area of Sabac on the Save River. Elements of I Battalion, 4th Brandenburg Regiment were still in Belgrade, where III Battalion arrived on 27th September after its retreat from Topola in order to join the withdrawal to Smederewo.

I Battalion, 1st Regiment under Oberst Hebeler was still fighting at the bridgehead near Sabac. A mixed force of Red Army troops and partisan units attacked the German bridgehead in extremely heavy rainstorms. The companies of the battalion were encircled. They held out until 10th October when, in a desperate charge, they broke through the encircling ring and subsequently fell back to Sabac and from there to Ruma, in the course of which they had to break through a Russian blocking position in a night attack.

Those October days saw Oberstleutnant Walther constantly en route to his battalions. During one such drive on 13th October he was wounded and had to be evacuated to a hospital in Germany. His successor, Oberst von Brückner, who came from the 23rd Panzer Division, arrived on 15th October. A veteran officer, on 11 March 1945 Erich von Bruckner won the Knight's Cross while leading his regiment—by then designated the 1st Brandenburg Light Infantry Regiment. During the night of 15th October Soviet tanks broke through the outer defensive ring around Belgrade in the south and reached the city suburbs. The entire defense in that sector collapsed. A few strong points held out until 20th October.

Battle Group Stettner, elements of the 1st Mountain Division, and Battle Group Wittmann linked up in the area near Pozarevac on the Morava. Battle Group Stettner was supposed to break through to Belgrade and force the crossings over the Danube.

The final battle in Belgrade began on 15th October. By then Battle Group Stettner had fought its way into the Mokri Lug area. Both Stettner's and Wittmann's groups included Brandenburgers: the 2nd Regiment with the 1st Mountain Division and I Battalion, 4th Regiment with Battle Group Wittmann (in command of Battle Group Wittmann was Generalleutnant August Wittmann, commanding officer of the 117th Light Infantry Division).

An attempt on 17th October to reach the still open Save bridges failed. The Red Army had positioned strong forces at the south end of the city. As the unit that had been ordered to attack the enemy from the city did not arrive, during the night of 18th October Generalleutnant von Stettner was forced to decide to break out to the west in the direction of the crossing over the Save near Sabac.

Under attack from the rear and both flanks, only company-size groups were able to reach the north bank of the Save. The Red Army reported a large number of prisoners taken. During the night of 20th October the Germans recaptured their bridgehead at Belgrade and moved it to the north bank of the Save. Tito's army, led by several partisan formations, stormed into Belgrade, the city they had been forced to leave three and a half years before.

The 20th of October was named a national holiday in Yugoslavia.

That day Oberst Schulte-Neuhaus took over command of the surviving Brandenburg battle groups in Novi Sad (formerly Austrian Neusatz). At the same time he assumed responsibility for the defense of the Theiss River line from the mouth of the river to Szeged. Titel formed the focal point of this sector.

There was further heavy fighting and losses were heavy. The 1st Regiment's II Battalion under Hauptmann Wandrey, in particular, was heavily engaged. Wandrey was wounded on 16th October and had to leave the field to Hauptmann John, who was still walking with a cane. On the 18th John suffered a serious abdominal wound and Oberleutnant Friedrichsmeyer took over the battalion.

The Red Army, which was attacking virtually without pause in an effort to expand its bridgeheads at Apatin and Barina to prepare for its next offensive, did not advance one step farther. But German counterattacks also failed to throw the enemy back across the Danube. Not until early on 21st October did the Red Army succeed in rolling up the German main line of resistance north of its bridgehead at Apatin. The 1st Regiment's II Battalion under Hauptmann Heine was almost wiped out in the fighting there. The Soviet troops attacked from all sides. So fierce was the close combat that even the severely wounded Brandenburgers kept firing at the numerically-superior enemy until they lost consciousness or died.

During a final breakout, 22 of the 24 surviving men were killed. Only Hauptmann Heine and his runner survived this disastrous defeat.

During the German withdrawal it was always the 1st Regiment that established new blocking positions and allowed the retreating soldiers to establish themselves there. Fünfkirchen was reached on 27th November. The enemy attacked at once and the retreat had to be resumed during the night. The troops withdrew to the northwest, over hills and through ravines and forests, hard-pressed by enemy tanks. A blocking position was established at Kaposvar on 3rd December. T 34s attacked in large numbers. The Brandenburgers allowed themselves to be overrun and only when the tanks had passed did they emerge from their holes to attack with anti-tank mines, demolition charges and hand grenades. Fifteen T 34s were destroyed with "bare hands" in a terrific battle.

On 8th December, with the Puszta under deep snow, the regiment was assigned its first rest areas near and in Szenyer. Just like the 1st Regiment, the 4th Regiment had undergone a severe test. Major Pinkert, the regiment's CO, reported that Major Hollmann, who had commanded IV Battalion until then, succeeded him during this critical period. The regiment had to endure difficult weeks and months following the return of the Tito partisans to Serbia on 21 March 1944. As described elsewhere, elements of the regiment took part in Operation "Knight's Move," the attempt to capture Tito, and after the escape of the communist commander they took up the pursuit of the partisans. On 11th June the 4th Regiment's III Battalion under Major Koehnen engaged strong partisan units near Kupres and drove them back. On 2nd July the battalion again engaged Tito units and casualties were heavy.

On 22 August 1944 Major von Koehnen was killed near Visegrad. The initial report stated that he had been shot in his car during an ambush. It was later discovered that the actual circumstances were somewhat different:

"During the drive to his new quarters, Major von Koehnen sat next to the driver in the first car. The battalion adjutant was behind him in the back seat. Suddenly there was an outbreak of heavy rifle fire from partisans. The convoy halted. The car took a direct hit. Major von Koehnen was killed instantly. The adjutant was wounded but played dead when the partisans approached. Three or four men jumped out from behind cover, ran over to the car and ripped Major von Koehnen's Knight's Cross from his throat. The adjutant's wedding ring was taken from his finger. The briefcase von Koehnen had been carrying, which contained secret papers, was simply thrown away by the attackers. They did not need it, for they were not partisans but simple robbers, otherwise they would have taken the important papers with them."

In Bugojno Hauptmann von Kriegsheim temporarily assumed command of the regiment.

On 23 August 1944 there was a revolt in Romania and General Antonescu was arrested. The CIC Southeast received orders from FHQ to assemble a group of forces in the Nish-Belgrade area to put down the revolt. Elements of the 201st Assault Gun Brigade were brought in, as was the entire 4th Brandenburg Regiment and the Brandenburg Parachute Battalion from Montenegro.

The two battalions of the 4th Regiment that first landed in the Klausenberg area of northern Romania became involved in bitter fighting with the arriving elements of the Red Army. What was left of the two units fought its way back into Hungary.

I Battalion, 4th Brandenburg Regiment under Oberleutnant Schonherr, which faced the attacking Russian armored units on the west bank of the Morava, was ordered back after the Russian breakthrough. Like I Battalion, 1st Regiment, it also fought in Belgrade. Hauptmann Gerlach was killed and Oberleutnant Schonherr assumed command. Oberleutnant Schonherr, Leutnant Seeger and Leutnant Mundlos had to attempt a breakout with about 30 men. Ten soldiers were fatally hit. The remaining soldiers and the three officers were caught by the Russians seven kilometers south of the Save. Lt. Seeger was felled by a partisan bullet. The rest managed to escape and rejoined the regiment, now under the command of Major Pinkert, in the Esseg area.

The fighting in Yugoslavia and Romania was approaching its end. The Brandenburg Division's days were also numbered.

Already on 27 May 1944 Generalleutnant Kühlwein had collected in a memo to the OKW/WFSt the ideas for the subsequent conduct of the war that had long been under discussion in division headquarters. The following are the main points contained in the memo.

New Missions—New Formations
New Attack Units
Headquarters, 27/5/1944
The commanding officer:

The Brandenburg Division was created as a special unit for offensive operations. Since the German Armed Forces have been fighting on the defensive, it has adapted to this changed situation and has become the 'OKW's standing anti-partisan unit.'

The division's experiences during the fighting withdrawals in the east, anti-partisan warfare in the Balkans, France and Italy, show that the division can only carry out its assigned tasks when it has the support of a sufficient cadre of fighting interpreters and recruited natives. It is proposed that such native units be formed to enable the division to keep up with the constantly growing demands.

Proposal: Division of the Brandenburg Division into:

(a) a patrol corps,

(b) light infantry regiments and special units.

(Re. a) The patrol corps to be established in all existing and possible theaters of war as native units with division fighting interpreters from recruited locals. Its role is to carry out small-scale operations in cooperation with the division.

(Re. b) The division's light infantry regiments, the coastal raider battalion and the parachute battalion are fast, mobile units with concentrated firepower which can be used anywhere regardless of the theater of war.

Roles: Establish contact with the patrol corps in the various areas of operations. Running battles with the support of the patrol corps. During offensive operations they make possible the deployment of undercover patrols, provide backup and relief, or make possible their recovery.

Elements of the former Canaris intelligence organization were about to be incorporated into the SS security service, and this memo was an attempt by Generalleutnant Kühlwein to prevent elements of the Brandenburg Division from being included in such a transfer.

The Wehrmacht Operations Staff quickly approved the formation of the patrol corps. It requested that it be operational by 1 August 1944.

THE ONLY PATROL CORPS

The 8th Company of the 3rd Brandenburg Regiment, which had been pulled out of Italy at the end of July, was built into the "Patrol Corps Southern France."

A platoon from the 8th Company was taken from its parent unit to form Operations Group Pyrenees together with Spanish legionnaires. This in turn was a sub-unit of the Patrol Corps Biscay.

Formation of Operations Groups Brittany and Flanders of the Patrol Corps Northern France took somewhat longer. Both patrol corps were supposed to be employed in France.

Operations Group Slovakia, on the other hand, was part of the planned Patrol Corps Carpathians. Also part of this patrol corps was the hastily formed Operations Group Romania-Transylvania.

When all the Brandenburg units were then combined to form a new division, the patrol corps took on lives of their own. They subsequently saw action until the end of the war.

Following the assassination attempt on Hitler on 20th July and the related departure of the Abwehr under Admiral Canaris along with Hitler's turn toward the RSHA and the security service, fears arose that the Brandenburg might be absorbed by the military office of the security service under Otto Skorzeny. Under these auspices it was the division's 1st General Staff Officer, General Staff Major Erasmus, who together with the headquarters came up with new ideas. These put Generalleutnant Kühlwein's patrol corps in the corner and called for the reorganization of the Division as a fighting division of the Army. It was to become either a light infantry or panzer-grenadier division. This proposal was made in a report to the Wehrmacht High Command on 30 August 1944. Titled Abt. Ia No. 362/44 Secret Command Matter, it stated:

The units now belonging to the Division have been employed on anti-partisan duties behind our front for years. With the exception of minor elements they carry out their combat duties as normal panzer-grenadier or light infantry regiments. The weak forces still carrying out special combat duties are the commando platoons with the battalions and regiments of the patrol corps. From a total strength of 14,056 German soldiers they comprise only 900 officers, NCOs and enlisted men. They contain the bulk of the available language experts. These consist of 210 Russian-speaking, 181 English-speaking, 185 Serbo-Croatian-speaking and 310 Italian-speaking soldiers and 610 who speak other languages.

The bulk of the division today consists of light infantry units (motorized) which in terms of firepower, training and fighting spirit are at the top of their form but which share the fate of all the shattered units. The planned transfer by the WFSt. of 140 of our soldiers into units of the RF SS would mean the end of the efforts to keep together the personnel suited to special operations.

The following solution is proposed in the event that the release of these 140 soldiers proves unavoidable: Remove all units of the division suited to special operations and transfer them to the RF for the large-scale formation of such an organization for these roles.

There followed a list of special operations units which the RF SS would then have to raise; the list was so long and diverse that Himmler dropped his plan.

Based on this report the WFSt decided to relieve the Division of all its roles as a commando unit and place it at the disposal of the Army General Staff for reorganization as a regular army division. On 8 September 1944 the Wehrmacht High Command issued the necessary order, number 0010994/44 g.K. WFSt/Op. The dissolution of the division had become a fact and it was confirmed in an order of the day issued by Generaloberst Jodl:

Chief of the Wehrmacht
Operations Staff   FHQ, 11/9/1944
Soldiers of the Brandenburg Division!

The division is being relieved of its duties as a special operations unit and reorganized as a motorized light infantry division. You are therefore leaving the area of my direct command.

I thank you for the readiness for action and willingness to sacrifice that you have shown. The division has fulfilled all my expectations in the infantry role and in the area of special operations.

That orders for your reorganization as a light infantry division have nevertheless been given, is so that all forces that have proved themselves in the area of special operations might be employed en masse under a unified command and thus achieve new successes.

The name Brandenburg is an obligation! I am certain that in its new form the division will do its duty and continue its glorious tradition.

Heil to the Führer!

Jodi, Generaloberst.

The Division existed no more, but that did not mean that its old units would not continue to make a name for themselves until the very last day.

The Brandenburg Coastal Raider Battalion: The Abwehr's Navy

FORMATION AND INITIAL EMPLOYMENT

By spring 1942 it had become obvious that the 800th Special Duties Regiment could not do without water craft if it wished to successfully take part in difficult river missions or carry them out independently. In the past difficulties had always arisen when rivers had to be crossed and the regiment's forces were assigned assault boat detachments from the infantry, which were often situated far behind the scene of operations.

The formation of the Light Pioneer Company was begun aboard the training vessel Gorch Fock in Swinemünde. The company was formed from a cadre of personnel from the 800th Regiment, and from landing and assault pioneers, small vessel pilots from the navy and Caucasian and Baltic legionnaires. At the start the company was equipped with sailboats, inflatable boats and Type 39 light assault boats. These were used to carry out the first landing exercises in the Bansis-Heringsdorf area. Training assistance was provided by the Kriegsmarine and in particular by the 2nd Pioneer Replacement Training Battalion from Stettin-Podejuch with its Training Platoon "L" based at Dievenow.

At the end of the training period the company's 1st Platoon under the command of Oberleutnant Kuhlmann was moved by train from Swinemünde to Brindisi. An independent operation in Egypt under the command of the German Africa Corps was planned.

The 2nd Platoon under Oberleutnant Kriegsheim, as well as the 3rd Platoon led by Oberleutnant Dr. Wagner, were moved to Nikolayev by train under the command of the company commander, Hauptmann Horlbeck. The company's officer complement was as follows:

Company Commmander: Hauptmann Horlbeck, 1942
Oberleutnant Kriegsheim, 1942–43
Rittmeister von Leipzig, 1943–45
Oberleutnant Bertrand, 1945

1st Platoon:	Oberleutnant Kuhlmann
2nd Platoon:	Oberleutnant Kriegsheim
3rd Platoon:	Oberleutnant Dr. Wagner

During the summer of 1942 the 2nd and 3rd Platoons moved from Nikolayev to Mama Tatarskaya near Kerch in the Crimea. The first mission was a reconnaissance in force by light assault boats against the island of Kossa Tusla in the Strait of Kerch. During the night of 2 September 1942, without its 1st Platoon, the company undertook three operations simultaneously. The objective was to eliminate the Russian positions on Cape Pekly on the Taman Peninsula. Further, the island of Kossa Tusla was to be occupied and a Russian shallow-water steamer—the Gornyak—stranded off the Bay of Taman was to be stormed. An enemy observation post had been identified on the steamer.

All three operations were necessary in the course of Army Group South's advance through Anapa to Novorossisk.

The assault group that landed at Cape Pelky arrived unnoticed. When they came to the first sentry position they were hailed. The Russian sentry raised his weapon but he was knocked to the ground by a burst of submachine-gun fire before he could press the trigger. The six members of the raiding party stormed the bunker and trench. They lobbed grenades into the observation trench, then ripped open the door of the bunker and tossed in a satchel charge. Taken completely by surprise, the enemy was overwhelmed.

The second assault boat silently came alongside the land side of the stranded steamer. The first two Brandenburgers to go aboard reached the deck of the ship without being heard. They secured both gangways. One of the men quietly eliminated the Russian sentry on the bridge and after all of A Squad were on board, the sleeping Russians, including their lieutenant and a political commissar, were rudely awakened.

The third and probably most difficult action was aimed at the island of Kossa Tusla. Three assault boats first sailed around the island in a wide arc. The last stretch of water was covered silently using paddles. The first boat landed by a dense tangle of bushes not far from the island's lookout post. The men moved silently through the bushes and approached to within about 50 meters of the enemy, who were in a blockhouse built low to the ground.

Then they waited for a signal flare that one of the other two boats was to fire from the flank of the island in order to startle the enemy. The third boat was to come ashore on the other flank at a distance of 600 meters. Before the agreed upon signal was fired, the slow rattle of a Russian Maxim machine-gun was heard. Then submachine-guns joined in. The enemy had spotted the first boat.

"The signal flare," Uffz. Gregor whispered to the squad leader. The latter ordered his men to prepare to fire.

A second later the first Russians ran out of the blockhouse into the open. When they were all in the open the squad leader opened fire. Several brief bursts mowed down the enemy, then hand grenades flew into the trenches and the men stormed the bunker. During this phase of the fighting one of the soldiers running behind the squad leader was hit in the back by a bullet fired from a Russian pistol. The force of the shot from the Russian commissar's Nagant pistol knocked the man to the ground. He was killed instantly.

Two more men from the assault squad in the first assault boat, which now headed for the shore at full speed, were wounded. But Kossa Tusla was in the hands of the Brandenburgers. The threat posed by Russian occupation of the Taman Peninsula had been eliminated.

When the 11th Army commanded by GFM Erich von Manstein (he had been promoted to this high rank after the fall of Sevastopol) crossed the Strait of Kerch in driving rain early on the morning of 2nd September and reached the Taman Peninsula, the two platoons of the Coastal Raider Battalion had already moved farther inland. Near Saporoshskaja, south of Cape Pekly, they attacked an enemy battery and silenced it after three attacks. While advancing toward the city of Taman they met the leading elements of the 11th Army.

The company had achieved all its assigned objectives. Three days later it was transported back to Kerch. After being moved from there to Anapa, on 9th September it received orders to proceed by assault and inflatable boat behind enemy lines and carry out demolitions on the Tuapse-Novorossisk road. For the troops of the Red Army this road along the coast was an indispensable supply route. If it were cut, it would be impossible for the defenders, who were dug-in in the rocks between the mountains and the sea, to go on fighting.

The troops of the German V Army Corps had meanwhile arrived at the gates of Novorossisk. Decimated by the battles of the past weeks and at the end of their endurance, a further advance seemed impossible. It was the divisions of this corps the 9th, 73rd and 198th Infantry Divisions—under General der Infanterie Wilhelm Wetzel that had reached Krasnodar on 11th August, crossed the Kuban and moved through the land of the Chechens. The German troops had been warmly welcomed by the Muslim Chechens, who rejoiced in the liberation of their people from communist and thus atheist control.

After this victory and the crossing of the Kuban, Army Group Ruoff under Generaloberst Richard Ruoff was ready to take Novorossisk, Tuapse, Sochim Suchumi and Batumi. If this last big attack succeeded, it would deprive the Soviet Black Sea Fleet of its last bases. As well, it would make it possible for the Germans to supply the Caucasus front by sea.

An even greater success would lay in store for Germany's eastern armies, however, for (as the most recent feelers put out by the Abwehr had revealed), after the last eastern and southern strips of coast had fallen, Turkey would be ready to join the war against Russia at Germany's side. All of this was the part of the "Global Mission" plan, which in Germany was promoted mainly by the Abwehr.

After such a military success and the associated development just described, the North Persian position of England and Russia would have collapsed. At the same time the southern route for delivery of US military aid to the Red Army from the Persian Gulf to the Caspian Sea would have been cut.

At the same time—this is mentioned here in connection with the war plans of Hitler and the Ausland/Abwehr—Rommel's plan, namely a drive by Panzer Army Africa through Egypt into the region between the Tigris and Euphrates Rivers and from there occupation of all the important oil fields of Iraq and a pincer movement with the Caucasus front to take the Russian fields near Baku, would have been a complete success.

All the necessary conditions existed in the summer of 1942. The army of the Caucasus was near its objective, while Rommel was advancing on El Alamein and Alexandria. In both lands German agents and sabotage teams were ready to prepare the way for the arriving troops.

This unique plan was to go unrealized in the Second World War. The forces available to Germany were too weak to span and hold this global net. Yet it must be realized that, even though they are often scorned, the German plans were anything but utopian. It is the aim of this work, Global Mission, to portray this, no more, no less.

When one considers that bridging columns were already standing by to bridge the Nile and that the general objective of "to Ibn Saud" had been given, it is most surprising that these global ambitions have not been described long before. Since the Ausland/Abwehr and its house unit—the Brandenburgers—were closely involved with these operations and were in action in every theater and other anticipated intervention points around the world, it is appropriate that these plans at least be outlined here.

On 10th September, the day when I Battalion of the 73rd Infantry Division's 186th Infantry Regiment under Obit. Werner Ziegler launched its assault on Novorossisk, a small flotilla of assault boats and inflatable boats carrying the Brandenburgers sailed through the darkness in a wide arc around Novorossisk to the south. The 122-kilometer-long supply road between Tuapse and Novorossisk was to be cut approximately 30 kilometers southeast of Novorossisk. Towed behind the assault boats, the inflatable boats carried weapons and explosives.

Oberleutnant Ziegler, who already wore the Knight's Cross with Oak Leaves, entered the city, fought his way house by house to the harbor, eliminated the flak batteries there, and finally seized the city. Now it was the Brandenburgers' moment, for the next objective was Tuapse, and this key point in the narrow coastal plain was decisive. For the German forces to reach and take it, it was imperative that that the road be blocked to the Soviet forces withdrawing from Novorossisk to prevent them from reinforcing the garrison in Tuapse.

The small waterborne force under the command of Hptm. Horlbeck reached the turning point to the coast an hour before midnight. There was still no sign of the enemy and on the coast ahead there was no sign of resistance. Suddenly the observer squatting in the leading assault boat called out: "Shadows to starboard!"

The detachment leader swore softly. He turned to the right, raised his night-vision binoculars to his eyes and saw a Russian motor torpedo boat emerging at high speed from the fog in the southeast. Then, farther back, he saw a low silhouette that could only be one of the Russian cutters which patrolled the coast. It would surely report the approach of the German assault boats.

"First squad: machine-guns open fire!" ordered the detachment leader. When the assault boat was close enough to the Russian vessel, which then began signaling with its Aldis lamp, both machine-guns opened fire. Bullets struck the bridge of the Russian vessel, then seconds later a there was a flash as the 40-mm Bofors gun on the bow of the boat opened fire. The tracer shells whizzed past the bow of the leading assault boat like fiery comets.

The detachment leader ordered the boats to turn west. The first squad turned. In following, the second squad swung too far to the west and ran straight into the hail of fire from the motor torpedo boat. One of the inflatable boats, whose line could not be jettisoned quickly enough, was struck by a salvo of shells. There was a terrific explosion and the inflatable boat was thrown into the air like a fiery kite. The assault boat that was towing it sheared off course, looked like it too would be tossed into the air, but then recovered and reversed course. A burst of machine-gun fire struck the rear of the boat. This one burst of fire, which hit the wildly zigzagging boat, killed one man and wounded four others.

After jettisoning the inflatable boats, which were shot up by the enemy and exploded, the assault boats succeeded in returning to their base northwest of Novorossisk. There the four injured Brandenburgers, whose wounds were fortunately minor, were cared for and the dead man delivered to the burial detachment.

The operation had failed and as if it was a sign, this area also became the fateful point for all of Army Group A under Generalfeldmarschall Wilhelm List, who had won the Knight's Cross for the capture of Novorossisk. Later, on 23 October 1944, Werner Ziegler, by then a Major and the commander of the 186th Grenadier Regiment, would become the 102nd German soldier to be awarded the Knight's Cross with Oak Leaves and Swords. He was one of the few Majors to receive this high decoration.

THE BRANDENBURG TROPICAL BATTALION

The story of the Brandenburg Tropical Battalion's 5th Company is closely related to the history of the Brandenburg Coastal Raider Battalion, since the company originated from the coastal raider battalion's 1st Platoon. When the British counteroffensive at EI Alamein started, it was sent by rail from Brindisi back to Freiburg in Breisgau, there to be expanded into the 5th Company of the Brandenburg Tropical Battalion.

The battalion commander was Hptm. Friedrich von Koehnen. Acting as company commander was the first platoon commander, Oblt. Kuhlmann. While still in Germany the company's boat complement was bolstered. Unfortunately the new types of boat (Schneider boats, which instead of screws were each equipped with one or two Voith-Schndeider propellers, which made it almost possible to turn the boat on the spot) were not yet available.

During the period 4 to 8 November 1942 the Brandenburg Tropical Battalion was flown to Tunis in Ju 52 transports. The unit was assembled there in preparation for a move to Hammamet on 10th November. In the meantime the 2nd and 3rd Platoons of the Coastal Raider Battalion had won great acclaim for a successful long-range patrol. In November they landed near Cape Penaj to scout the possibilities for a commando operation against the Russian port of Gelendshik.

The patrol advanced to the outskirts of Gelendshik and was able to locate a favorable break-in point. It lay low as a Russian patrol heading for the German lines passed by not ten meters away. The German defensive positions were warned by radio and when the Russian patrol arrived there it ran into a hail of fire from two of the new MG 42 machine-guns. It was wiped out to the last man.

The Brandenburgers returned with important information for the German attack. The changed situation put an end to the planned operation but it did nothing to change the run of success by the small force of Brandenburgers in this area. Other Brandenburger detachments operated in the Caucasus, which will be described elsewhere In spite of the limited number of operations carried out in a small area, it was obvious that a larger unit should be formed for larger and more ambitious special operations and amphibious missions in other waters (in particular the Mediterranean). This idea did not occur just to the Ausland/Abwehr.

The Brandenburg Light Pioneer Company and the 1st Coastal Raider Platoon under Oblt. Kuhlmann were allocated to form the basis of the Brandenburg Coastal Raider Battalion, formation of which began at the end of 1942. The expansion took place in Langenargen on Lake Constance. The battalion commander was Hptm. von Leipzig. The battalion, which was fully motorized, was organized as follows:

Battalion Headquarters:	1 heavy Type 42 assault boat
	1 Type 41 pioneer landing boat
	2 light machine guns
1st Company:	2 heavy Type 42 assault boats
(230 men)	2 Type 41 pioneer landing boats
	9 light machine guns
	2 FlaMW 151/20 light
	anti-aircraft guns
	2 medium mortars

2nd and 3rd Companies were similarly equipped (230 men each).

4th Heavy Company:	6 commando boats
(appx. 230 men)	30 demolition boats
	14 light machine guns
	6 FlaMW 151/20 light
	anti-aicraft guns

The battalion's specified role was: Anti-partisan operations from the sea and commando operations behind the enemy's front, as well as against enemy vessels at sea and in port. Personnel support would come from the companies of the Pioneer Training Battalion in Lindau and its facilities in the Kressbronn area near Hard, Bregenz.

Then in January and February 1943 personnel were detached for service with the 5th Company, Brandenburg Tropical Battalion, which was moved by rail to Italy and from there by ship and aircraft via Palermo-Trapani to Bizerte. The two heavy assault boats (command boats) and two demolitions boats (with Schneider propellers) that were shipped across, together with their crews and the servicing and maintenance group were placed under the tactical control of the 3rd Motor Torpedo Boat Flotilla under Korvettenkapitän Kemnade. Their mission was to carry out defensive patrols from Ferryville.

During one such mission the company came upon and captured a British commando team in inflatable boats. Documents found in the boats, especially the radio code books and the call signs of the other side, made it possible for the Brandenburgers to subsequently capture several more British commando teams (also see operations by the von Koehnen Tropical Company).

Commando operations were also executed on land, at the Kasserine Pass for example. They also included glider operations and the formation of the Arab Legion in Enfidaville as well as other special operations.

In May 1943 the end of Army Group Africa was in sight, and the two demolition boats had been damaged by heavy seas and had to be blown up. The two heavy assault boats left Northwest Africa from Cape Ras Zebib exactly one night before the surrender of Army Group Africa. With general staff officers and other staff officers on board, they reached Trapani, Sicily after a zigzag crossing during which they were fired on several times.

The assault boats were supposed to bring General der Panzertruppe Hans Cramer and General Gustav Vaerst out of Africa but both officers elected to go into captivity with their troops.

The elements of the 5th Company that returned from Africa and those who had come home earlier after being wounded assembled in Langenargen and were incorporated into the 1st Company of the Brandenburg Coastal Raider Battalion.

In summer 1943 the bulk of the now complete battalion was moved by rail into the area of the Adriatic. The 1st Company was quartered in Brindisi, other elements of the battalion went to the Cote d' Azur.

In mid-June 1943 a commando squad of seven coastal raiders under the command of Lt. Brüggmann went to one of the German submarine bases for transport to the Indian Ocean. There it was supposed to destroy a dry-dock in a South African port which was of great importance to the Allied supply lines to the Pacific Theater.

When the submarine surfaced in the Atlantic to take on fuel oil from a depot sub, both vessels were attacked and sunk by Allied aircraft. The Abwehr men manning the submarine's anti-aircraft guns shot down one of the attacking bombers and damaged another and forced it to turn away.

They went down fighting with the submarine. The two German vessels were U 194 under Kapitänleutnant Hess and U 200 under Kapitänleutnant Hein Schonder.

COASTAL RAIDERS IN ACTION

The code-word "Axis" also resulted in the Brandenburg Coastal Raider Battalion being placed on alert. "Axis" was the answer to the Italian withdrawal from the Axis pact, which was announced on 8th September. The first objective of the German forces was to disarm all Italian military units and occupy the most important Italian bases.

1st Company, Brandenburg Coastal Raider Battalion, whose boats and related personnel had left Langenargen for Brindisi on 15th July, while the remaining troops were flown to Piraeus near Athens, saw its first action. The boat section meanwhile set sail from Brindisi through the Adriatic in the direction of the island of Corfu. From there (the Italians had not yet pulled out of the Axis pact) it sailed via Ithaca and Patras to the port of Lutrakion, where it was united with the combat elements.

From its new base the 1st Company carried out various transport missions for the 1st Brandenburg Regiment. As well it patrolled the coast of the Gulf of Corinth.

On 8 September 1943 the battalion's individual companies were in the following ports and positions: 1st Company, Brandenburg Coastal Raider Battalion, in Athens-Larissa; and 4th Company, Brandenburg Coastal Raider Battalion, in Santa Lucia, Sardinia.

The battalion headquarters and 2nd and 3rd Companies had been subordinated to the Commander-in-Chief Southeast and deployed to the Adriatic on orders from the Wehrmacht Operations Staff. There the units were instructed to cooperate with the 771st Landing Pioneer Battalion. Elements of the 4th Coastal Raider Company were also moved there.

The Brandenburgers achieved their first success in the Athens-Larissa area on 9th September. Under the command of Korvettenkapitän Dr. Brand, chief of the 21st Anti-Submarine Flotilla, the boats of the 1st Company entered Piraeus harbor and seized an Italian torpedo boat there. The vessel was soon put to use by the Kriegsmarine and was a welcome addition to the German navy's limited resources in the Mediterranean.

From 23 to 28 September 1943 the company and its heavy assault boats were moved from Lutrakion to Igumenica. From there the assault boats transported the division headquarters of the 1st Mountain Division to Kajos. Operation Corfu thus moved from the planning stage to the decisive stage of the assault on the island.

Corfu, which was located off the northwest coast of Greece and was still held by Badoglio troops, was to be taken in a surprise attack.

While the Brandenburgers' assault boats carried the headquarters of the 1st Mountain Division to Kajos on the southern tip of the island, the alpine troops followed in the former Spanish freighter "Rigel." They saw no combat, for the Italian troops preferred surrender and disarmament. When the action was over, Hptm. Kuhlmann, the commander of 1st Company, Brandenburg Coastal Raider Battalion, received orders to proceed to Athens for a conference at the headquarters of the 22nd Infantry Division.

THE BRANDENBURGERS ARE READIED—THE CAPTURE OF COS

On Friday, 12 November 1943, all operations under way in Greece by the Brandenburgers were broken off. At 12 midnight on 13th November the 15th Company, which had captured Stampalia in a parachute operation on 22nd October and remained to occupy the island, was flown out in seaplanes. The company arrived at the seaplane base at Phaleron at 5 A.M. the same day.

Simultaneously III Battalion, 1st Brandenburg Regiment and the 1st Coastal Raider Battalion moved to Athens. From there a decisive action was to take place against British forces, which, beginning on 8 September 1943, were to realize their old plan of occupying the Greek and Italian islands. The British Special Boat Squadron landed near Castellrosso on Rhodes. The Italian garrison resisted until the morning of 10th September. When the following British 234th Brigade arrived on 18th September, Rhodes had already been taken by German troops. All 40,000 men of the Italian garrison were disarmed and the enemy was repulsed. British troops beat the Germans to the islands of Cos and Leros and on 18th September also occupied Symi, Stampalia and Ikaria. On Cos, Leros and Samos the British succeeded in reinforcing their forces to battalion strength and beyond.

After returning from the conference in Athens, Hptm. Kuhlmann issued the necessary orders by radio from Lutrakion to his companies still deployed in the Corfu area. The three raider platoons sailed their heavy assault boats direct to Naxos as ordered. The two landing boats with the company train arrived in Lutrakion 24 hours later.

On the evening of 2nd October the three heavy assault boats were at the rendezvous point of convoy "Olympus." This consisted of five transport steamers, six navy ferries and two militarized fishing cutters. The escort consisted of the minelayer Drache and six to eight submarine chasers of the 21st Anti-Submarine Flotilla under Korvettenkapitän Brand and four minesweepers of the 12th Minesweeper Flotilla under Korvettenkapitän Mallmann/Korvettenkapitän Brand was in tactical command of Operation "Polar Bear." The group sailed together to Amorgos. There it split up into three landing groups which sailed separately direct to Cos.

The Brandenburgers' three landing boats sailed with the escort UJ 2101 under Kapitänleutnant Vollheim in landing group three. The group reached Kamara Bay on the south coast of Cos at about 4 A.M. on 3rd October. The sea was calm and visibility good. Not until the landing began did the ships come under sporadic fire.

The coastal raiders stormed the Italian hill positions, firing their submachine-guns and MG 42s from the hip. When a coastal battery near Kephalos opened fire on boats lying off the port, Feldwebel Biallas attacked the position with ten men.

They rushed to within throwing range and lobbed their grenades, then sprayed the embrasures of the two flanking bunkers with their MG 42s and with a final rush seized the battery. Taken completely by surprise, the gun crews were unable to disable their weapons, which provided the Brandenburgers with a most welcome increase in firepower. They manned the guns and opened fire on the nearby airfield, which was still held by British troops.

The supporting fire from the captured British guns allowed the Brandenburgers to take possession of the airfield a short time later. A brief machine-gun duel broke out around the tower, but the terrific rate of fire of the MG 42 quickly decided the affair in favor of the German side. As soon as the airfield was taken, a radio message was sent and the 1st Company of the Coastal Raider Battalion was dropped over the airfield from Ju-52 transports. The remaining units were flown in.

At the same time as landing group 3, landing groups 1 and 2 also set out across Cos. Once, the landing groups were halted by enemy resistance and Stukas were called in. The dive-bombers appeared in two flights and bombed the enemy positions directly in front of the troops. As soon as the bombs had fallen, they stormed forward and took the English positions. Whenever the advance was stalled by resistance, this was overcome with the help of Bf 109s which swooped down and strafed the enemy.

In the early afternoon German troops reached the far side of the island, dividing it in two. The fighting lasted throughout 4th October. The Brandenburgers proved themselves capable and experienced bunker crackers and when evening came the 600 English troops still fighting and the 2,500 Italians who had joined them surrendered. The Brandenburgers had taken the island of Cos.

The capture of Cos eliminated the only two British airfields in the Aegean. The first German aircraft to use the fields were Bf 110 reconnaissance aircraft, which flew their first sorties from there on 5th October.

After the men were given a brief rest, the Brandenburgers' three heavy assault boats sailed to Kalymnos, which was also occupied by Badoglio troops. One of the boats, carrying Hptm. Kuhlmann, sailed into Kalymnos harbor under a white flag. Kuhlmann asked the Italian commander to surrender, but the latter refused to give up without a fight.

Kuhlmann now tried a bluff. He warned the commander of the island that he was in for a heavy attack by Stukas. As well he stated that an assault force of Brandenburgers wearing Italian uniforms had already placed an explosive charge with a time fuse in the commandant building.

The Italian commander finally decided to surrender. The two heavy assault boats loitering outside the harbor sailed in unmolested and disembarked their troops, who occupied all the important positions on the island. They found that the Italian garrison was already stacking its rifles.

That night there was an attack by British commandos who had hidden out on the island during the day. The commandos tried to overrun the Brandenburgers, who were bivouacked in the harbor area, but the enemy troops, their faces painted black, were spotted by a sentry. The man opened fire on the commandos with his submachine-gun. Within seconds all the Brandenburgers had their guns in their hands. They fought their way from building to building, from woodpile to woodpile. The Brandenburgers prevailed in the man-to-man fighting and forced the enemy out of the city. A well-armed patrol followed the British, who had fallen back into the hills. The result was a drawn-out battle in which the Brandenburgers also suffered casualties. The dramatic events on Cos ended when the last seven British commandos—all of whom were wounded—surrendered.

On 8th October the company was shipped to Kalymnos, from where it was to launch an assault on Leros. The bulk of the troops assembled for Operation "Leopard" were from the 22nd Infantry Division under Generalleutnant Friedrich-Wilhelm Müller.

Battle Group Müller embarked on several transports. The escort was provided by the 9th Torpedo Boat Flotilla under Korvettenkapitün Riede. It consisted of five torpedo boats, the motor-torpedo boat S 55, the 21st Anti-Submarine Flotilla under Korvettenkapitän Dr. Brand with five to six large and eight to ten small sub hunters and the 12th Mine Sweeper Flotilla under Kapitänleutnant Mallmann with ten to twelve minesweepers. The voyage to Cos was to be made in two stages, by night to Amorgos and from there by day direct to Cos, with arrival in Cos on 6 November 1943.

⌈The convoy assembled near Lavrion. There it was joined by reinforcements in the form of soldiers of the 9th Luftwaffe Field Division. The
order to sail arrived early on 4th November. Lavrion was reached at 8 A.M.;
however, the second leg of the voyage had to be postponed on account of
rough seas.

This delay gave the British a chance to strike. On the afternoon of 5th
November British torpedo bombers attacked the ships as they lay at
anchor. The massed antiaircraft fire from the ships shot down three of the
bombers before they could launch their torpedoes. All the aerial torpedoes that were dropped missed and exploded against the rocky shore. One
of the assault boats raised anchor and picked up six British aircrew who
had bailed out of their stricken bombers. They were then handed over to
the infantry unit stationed in Lavrion.

The second leg of the voyage was begun during the night of 6th
November and took the boats past Makronisi and Cos, south toward the
island of Paros. The ships dropped anchor in Naoussa Bay at 8 A.M.. There
they were attacked again, this time by six torpedo bombers. One of the
German minesweepers was struck by a torpedo. Once again three of the
attacking aircraft were shot down.

The ships raised anchor at 8 P.M. and then passed through the Paros-
Naxos narrows. They sailed north past Irakleia to the north coast of Amorgos. Several nautical miles later a sea battle was observed ahead, during
which one of the escorting sub chasers—GA 45, which was serving as a submarine lure—was sunk by the British destroyers "Penn" and "Pathfinder."

The loss of the sub chaser warned the entire convoy and allowed it to
avoid attack by sailing back to Paros. While approaching Naoussa Bay by
night, landing boats D and L of the 780th Pioneer Landing Company
under Oblt. Bunte sustained hull and screw damage.

The convoy set sail again at 3:20 A.M. on 8th November. Shortly before
arriving at Amorgos it was again attacked by British torpedo bombers. It
was 3 P.M., and force 5 to 6 seas made the job of the anti-aircraft guns more
difficult. Nevertheless, the curtain of flak that they put up caused the torpedoes launched by the 12 to 16 Beaufighters to miss their targets, as they
were dropped too soon. By 6 P.M. the ships were all hidden in different
bays on the north coast of Amorgos.

During the following night enemy destroyers appeared off the bay.
They shone searchlights into the German hiding place but failed to discover the small warships. The destroyers fired "blind" into one bay but it
was empty.⌋

After the enemy vessels had left, the convoy raised anchor and sailed
on, and on 10th November the ships rendezvoused off Cos with the group

of vessels approaching from farther north. Five of the coastal raider's boats were ordered into bays on Cos, five to Kalymnos. There the troops disembarked and took up position in concealed waiting areas.

At 8 P.M., enemy destroyers appeared and searched in vain for the German boats and troops. On 11th November 1943 the order was given to launch Operation "Typhoon-Leopard" as it was now called. Leros was once again in the crosshairs. The action on Leros will now be described in detail in the following section.

LEROS, THE VERDUN OF THE AEGEAN

On 28 September 1943 Hptm. Kuhlmann, the commander of the 1st Coastal Raider Battalion Brandenburg, was ordered to Athens, where he was to take part in a conference in the headquarters of Generalleutnant Müller, commander of the 22nd Infantry Division.

Generalleutnant Müller had received directions from the OKH to form a battle group to liberate the enemy-occupied islands in the Dodecanese. The first stage of the operation was the capture of Cos by the Brandenburgers. They stormed the Italian hill position and took the coastal battery near Kephalos by storm. With this battery they shot up nests of resistance on the outskirts of the British airfield at Antimacchia six kilometers away and then stormed it. A half hour later the 1st Company of the 4th Brandenburg Light Infantry Regiment (trained paratroopers) arrived by Ju 52 and occupied the airfield.

During the night of 4th October the Brandenburgers rolled up the last defense line in the west part of the island. They had thus achieved one of the most important requirements for the capture of Leros: the elimination of both British airfields in the Aegean. Brandenburgers sailing in assault boats secured Kalymnos. The rest of the company was sent across to Kalymnos, from where the assault on Leros was to be launched, on 8th October.

The three heavy assault boats of the Brandenburg Coastal Raider Battalion's 1st Company reached their departure point three nautical miles northeast of Alinda Bay at about 5:15 A.M. on 12th November. They formed the first of four attack groups.

Lt. Schädlich, the company commander, peered over the heads of his men into the bay. He saw the two navy ferries that were serving as escorts. Then he spotted the minesweeper that was acting as command vessel. Seconds later the radio operator on the command vessel received the following message: "Coastal raider vessels cleared for independent landing in Pandeli Bay. Good luck!"

The three heavy pioneer boats, which were 14.5 meters long with room for 40 men, were loaded to capacity. Each boat carried a platoon of light infantry with its weapons. The two diesel engines howled as the boats raced faster and faster toward the coast. Suddenly, from one of the hills on the island of Leros, two searchlights flashed on and swept the bay with their beams.

"That's coming from Monte Appetici, Herr Leutnant," said Obfw. Kuntze, leader of the 1st Platoon.

Seconds later there was a roar as 150-mm shells struck the water in front of them, causing geysers of spray to shoot upwards. The rumble of more gunfire rolled down from Monte Appetici. One of the raiders cursed as the second salvo fell closer to the boats. The boats increased speed in an attempt to drive under the fire. The 250 H.P. engines roared, driving the three heavy assault boats across the bay at 42 kilometers per hour. The first two boats cleared the enemy fire but the third suddenly lost speed, came to a stop and lay in the midst of a hail of shellfire.

The boat's radio operator signaled that they had engine damage. Looking back, Lt. Schädlich saw the shells falling ever closer to the assault boat, which had meanwhile been illuminated by the searchlights. Then mortars and heavy machine-guns joined in. Kuntze ordered his men to get ready. The raiders reached for their weapons. The coast rushed nearer. The motors died for a second and then roared again, turning the propellers in reverse. Nevertheless the bow of the first boat struck hard against the rocky shore. The raiders leaped from the boats and clambered up the rocks. The enemy fire could not reach them there for the position was in a blind spot. They heard the second assault boat hit the rocks behind them, then the voice of Fw. Burzius as he urged on his men. Then the first assault boat cast-off, followed by the second.

There was no turning back now; now they had to climb up, take the slope and eliminate the 150-mm battery so that the main body could land. The platoon leader, who was close behind Lt. Schädlich, slipped on a steep section and collided hard with Uffz. Finkler. The latter yelled at him angrily to watch out but nevertheless helped him up the steep section. The din around them was somehow eerie. Nothing happened to them but somewhere below in the bay the third motorboat with nearly 40 comrades aboard was drifting and under fire from all sides.

Then finally, gasping and fighting for breath, they reached the top of the steep slope. Just as they began to breathe easier and set out across the now flatter, brush-covered slope, the English troops covering the battery opened fire with machine-guns. The bursts of fire whipped over the flat. Hannes Baecker, who had jumped up to be near the Leutnant with the radio, saw flashes as the machine-guns fired. He dropped to the ground but too late. Baecker was hit by several bullets and the impact rolled him over. He lay still behind a bush.

He was shocked to see blood spurting from his left thigh and called out for a medic. Taking cover behind the boulders that covered the gentle slope, first-aid NCO Mandalka hurried over to Baecker. One look told him that the wound had to be bandaged at once. He grabbed an old pair of suspenders he had in his medic's bag and went to work. He heard the Leutnant's voice as he ordered the men to get up and advance and then saw them rush forward a short distance before taking cover again among the rocks.

The sun had come up and it was becoming increasingly warm. "Help me Fred," gasped Baecker when he came to again. He saw that the medic had already taken care of two other wounded who had made their way back to a small hollow. "Of course we'll help you," replied the medic.

Below in the bay the third, disabled assault boat lay under a hail of enemy fire. The boat's machinist worked feverishly. One of the machinist mates helped him. A look of hope appeared in the eyes of the men when one of the motors started.

"Go! Zigzag course to the shore!" shouted Feldwebel Meeser, the platoon commander. The boat began to move. Water sprayed high and when it was about 40 meters away from its former position four heavy shells fell into the sea in the exact spot where they had been only seconds before. It would have been their death sentence. The assault boat reached the bay safely; it had high, rocky sides and had been chosen because no enemy positions had been sighted there.

"Go! Up the hill!" shouted Meeser. Then he grabbed the MG 42 and jumped ashore.

Medical officer Dr. Droste, who had established a provisional aid station in a ravine, called to Meeser to leave the boat where it was and not have it cast off. "The boat can take off the wounded," he explained.

"First we have to repair the coolant line," replied boat's machinist Ewerth.

"Let me know when you're ready," shouted the medical officer through the din. The machinist nodded.

The 3rd Platoon now set out to climb the steep slope. Within half an hour it had joined the other two platoons and, like them, was pinned down by fire from enemy troops defending the battery.

"Good, there you are Meeser!" Leutnant Schadlich greeted the platoon commander. "Give us covering fire with your two machine-guns while

1st Platoon attacks. The 2nd Platoon will see to it that the flanking machine-gun over there is taken out."

When the machine-guns opened fire the Brandenburgers rushed forward. They ran for their lives, for they were still under machine-gun fire even though the flanking gun had been taken out. A man next to Obfw. Kuntze cried out and fell to the ground. Then salvoes of mortar shells struck the ground in front of them. Fragments sheared branches of the bushes at shoulder height. Someone yelled: "take cover!" but there was no need. Exhausted, parched by the sun, they lay where they were.

Unteroffizier Finkler, squad leader in the 1st Platoon, reached for his canteen. He felt his tongue sticking to the roof of his mouth and badly needed a sip of tea. As he unhooked the canteen it felt as if it were empty. He shook it—nothing! Then he saw the hole and examined it more closely. A bullet had made it; a few more centimeters and it would have entered his back.

"Do you have a sip of tea for me?" he asked Schneetz, who had crawled forward to him. He unhooked his canteen and passed it to the squad leader.

Finkler took a long drink and passed it back. Then Schneetz took a drink too before screwing the cap back on and hooking the canteen back onto his belt Moments later Gefreiter Kosters of the platoon headquarters squad reported that the medic needed assistance. "I need two men to help him bring back the seriously wounded. Dr. Troste wants to operate."

They handed over their submachine-guns and crawled back down the steep slope while left and right mortar detonating rounds spread deadly shrapnel. They slid down the slope to where Mandalka had indicated and breathed a little easier. No bullet could find them here. They picked up the wounded. Dr. Droste operated on the first man, for whom immediate intervention was the only hope. Then they carried the surgical cases to the assault boat, where they were carefully bedded down. More and more wounded arrived and when machinist Ewerth reported that they were ready to go and the one intact motor began to rumble, the last of them were put on board. The heavy assault boat cast off.

The men on the land looked back and saw the boat clear the cover of the rocky bay. But then all hell was let loose. As if every gun, every mortar and every machine-gun had been waiting just for this moment, hot steel suddenly began showering the boat. Zigzagging violently, the machinist tried to steer the boat out of the danger zone. But mortar rounds began falling into the sea all around the boat and then it took a direct hit amidships.

"My God!" screamed Dr. Droste in dismay as he watched the boat sink, "the wounded!"

The survivors tried to swim through the shell-torn water; most of the seriously wounded soon disappeared beneath the surface. To those watching the terrible spectacle from the land, the surface of the bay was so stirred up by exploding shells that it looked like one huge whirlwind. They made their way down to the narrow strip of beach to help the survivors ashore.

Finkler saw one man in difficulty about 30 meters from shore, He tossed his tunic to Schneetz and jumped into the water. After a few strokes he reached the man and swam back with him to shore. Of the 30 wounded headed for Kalymnos in the assault boat, 14 were missing.

THE ATTACK

Up above, on the second, less steep section of the slope, the Brandenburgers worked their way forward in stages. Then they came to a completely open plateau, which had neither rocks nor bushes for cover.

Dismayed, Gefreiter Kosters shouted, "Nobody can make it across there lieutenant!"

Platoon leader Kuntze looked at his watch: "Where are our Stukas? They should have been here long ago."

Leutnant Schadlich shook his head. "Remember we were late starting. If headquarters took this into account they will be here in five minutes."

No one could raise his head without being fired on. It looked as if at this spot the attack on the enemy battery had been stopped cold. During a pause in the firing the sound of battle rumbled over from the north side of the island. There the landing pioneers had ferried over the men of the 22nd Infantry Division.

Time passed. It was too long for one man; pressed close to the earth, he tried to crawl into better cover in a shallow crevice in the rock. He had gone barely 15 meters when a twin-barreled machine-gun opened fire and riddled his body with bullets. For a moment Leutnant Schadlich laid his head on the rocky ground. This was his company. He knew every single man. And in a daydream only a few seconds long he saw little but skeletons left of his company after this operation. But then he was jolted back to reality by a dull droning in the air.

"The Stukas are coming!" someone shouted. This was followed by a half hysterical, half relieved cry of: "Our Stukas!"

"Prepare to attack!" shouted the Leutnant. The order was passed on from man to man. Already the men on the ground could recognize the gull wings of the dive-bombers. They approached the island in a formation of twelve. Then with an ear-shattering din they peeled off and dove on the gun and field positions on the island, under wing sirens howling.

"Up!—Forward!"

The men got to their feet and raced across the plateau at a crouch. The Stukas had forced the crews of the machine-guns and the 20-mm anti-aircraft guns to take cover, helping the raiders cross the plateau. They staggered the last few meters, but they had done it. Amid the din of the dive-bombers and exploding bombs they had made it across the barren rock plateau.

The Stukas pulled up again into the sun, which reflected off the wings of the machines. Their engines howled at full power. Then, abruptly, the defenders opened fire again; but a number of the enemy positions were now silent. The bombs from the Stukas had turned Foxholes and bunkers into graves.

The raiders now advanced in stages across a shallow slope dotted with rock oaks. Low bushes gave them cover. The November sun blazed down as if it were summer. Finally out of breath, they lay where they had dropped. A second wave of Stukas attacked and created another breathing space.

"Damn it!" cursed Oberfeldwebel Kuntze, "are they just shooting at us? Are we the only ones attacking on this whole island?"

"The others are fighting over there," replied the Leutnant., pointing to the north side of the island. And so they were. The attack had begun at the same time on the north side of the island and in the northeast.

Leutnant Glaser, commander of the first of three platoons of the 780th Landing Pioneer Company, led the second of four assault columns in the eastern group. It was made up of Landing Boats C—under the command of Unteroffizier Michael Lehner, acting as command ship E, M and O. The eastern group landed in Alinda Bay at 5:15 A.M.; each of the four squads of troops had a special assignment. To port the soldiers in the slower landing boats saw the preceding heavy assault boats of the Brandenburgers sail into the midst of the beginning barrage of defensive fire. They also attracted the attention of the searchlights.

"Full throttle, Lehner!" Leutnant Glaser yelled to the boat commander. He turned half around, saw the snouts of the two boats, O and M, which were close behind, while boat O ran somewhat farther to starboard.

Within a few minutes they had run beneath the fire intended for them. Already the rocky shore was threateningly close. The men of the 65th Infantry Regiment's II Battalion were making ready when light machine-guns began firing from the dark bay. The platoon commander gave the order to fire. The landing boat's weapons, which included a 20-mm anti-aircraft gun roared to life. Their tracers flitted across to the enemy vessel lying in the bay.

Boat C traded fire with the enemy vessel as it closed. The men behind the machine-gun could already see the forms behind the weapons on the enemy boat, saw them fall, and then the landing boat came alongside the British MLK 456. A boarding party took the survivors prisoner and left two men behind to stand guard. Then they jumped ashore. The remaining boats carrying the first groups of the von Saldern Battalion landed. The platoons formed up and headed in the direction of the hill. Their objective was to capture the ridge northwest of Alinda Bay. If they succeeded, the parachute landing planned for noon could go ahead.

Here the advance progressed rapidly. The infantry of this famous division worked their way forward in steps. As he so often did, Major von Saldern was leading the way for his battalion. Wherever he went, his men followed. So they advanced, meter by meter, until they had reached the ridge and taken possession of it. Then Major von Saldern assembled his men.

The third group, which was designated to land farther north in Palma Bay, and which was supposed to fan out to the north as far as Cape Panozimi, was led by the second platoon commander, Stfw. Baumgart, in landing boat G. Boats H, J and N also carried men of the 65th Infantry Regiment's II Battalion.

By the time the boats arrived off Cape Panozimi it was already daylight. The coastal artillery of the defenders had the range. Nevertheless, landing boats G, J, N and A sailed beneath the enemy fire and landed at the specified location. But the navy ferry and landing boat H commanded by Unteroffizier Neitzcl were caught by mortar fire. The navy ferry took the first direct hit. A few soldiers jumped over the side and swam toward land. Then two near misses rocked the ferry. The vessel was holed beneath the water line and suddenly took on a severe list. The survivors jumped into the sea and tried to get away from the sinking ferry as quickly as possible Then the sea closed over the ship. Landing craft "H", which had also taken a direct hit, drifted off to the north listing heavily. The craft, which could no longer be steered, was carried toward the island of Strongilo.

With the landing craft less than 100 meters from the island and about to sink Unteroffizier Neitzel ordered everyone out. They jumped out and swam for the safety of the beach. Neitzel went back for a man in trouble and helped him ashore. At least some of those on the landing raft made it to shore. The other boats could not pick up survivors as they were under orders to return to Kalymnos as quickly as possible to pick up and deliver the heavy infantry weapons. And so boats "J" and "N" which had landed near Cape Panozimi sailed directly south after unloading their soldiers. When the enemy's guns were turned on them they made smoke and escaped with negligible damage.

Boat "A", however, which had the company medical officer on board, sailed to where the marine ferry had gone down and then toward the island of Strongilo. It rescued several survivors still in the water. At 10 A.M. it received orders to sail back to Kalymnos together with boat "G", which was sitting on the beach with about 30 wounded. The two boats arrived at noon.

The soldiers who had gone ashore fought their way up the hills step by step against English resistance.

The group designated to land on the north tip of Leros was commanded by Platoon Commander III, Stabsfeldwebel Wiegand. His force consisted of a navy ferry and landing raft "K". On board the two vessels was a company of II Battalion, 65th Infantry Regiment. With the ferry in the lead, the small group sailed roughly to the north tip of the Bay of Palma. There the fire from enemy batteries on both sides of the bay was so heavy that the commander of the ferry could not decide to land. He also ordered boat "K" with its load of infantry, including company commander Dorr, to return to Kalymnos at once. Dorr and the platoon commander, Stabsfeldwebel Wiegand, had no choice but to follow the order. Both ships sailed back to Kalymnos.

The boats that had landed in Griffo Bay were also supposed to return to Kalymnos immediately, but when they left the safety of the rocky slopes they came under such heavy mortar and machine-gun fire that they were forced to turn back. They had to wait there until the hoped for expansion of the beachhead caused the enemy fire on the bay to be weakened or eliminated.

By midday it appeared that the attack on the well-defended island of Leros had failed. It was 1:00 P.M. when the drone of aircraft engines was heard again. The Brandenburgers and the soldiers of the Saldern Battalion lying in sparse cover under the hot sun looked into the sky.

One of the soldiers identified the aircraft as Ju 52s. It was the promised paratroopers—the parachute company of the 4th Brandenburg Regiment under Oberleutnant Oschatz, with Leutnant Horl as his deputy and I Battalion of the 2nd Parachute Regiment under the command of Hauptmann Kuhne.

The spirits of the men on the ground were lifted when they saw figures spring from the doors of the transports. In seconds the parachutes had opened and the paratroopers drifted down toward the island of Leros.

THE PARACHUTE OPERATION

The parachute battalion was in central Italy when the order for this mission reached it. The 470 paratroopers were flown from the Ferrara airfield to Athens-Tattoi. There Hauptmann Kuhne and his company commanders used aerial photos to plan the mission; they also learned that a Brandenburger parachute company would be jumping with them. As planned, the Ju 52s carrying the paratroopers arrived over Leros at dawn on 12 November 1943. Shortly before the jump zone they were recalled by radio. The Brandenburgers and the assault groups of the 16th and 65th Infantry Regiments had not got ashore yet.

In particular the attempt by the marine ferries and I-boats of the western group to land in broad Gurna Bay had been repulsed three times. III Battalion, 16th Infantry Regiment under the command of Hauptmann Aschoff was unable to go ashore. Finally the attempt was abandoned and the troop carriers sailed back to Kalymnos.

Now the parachute troops would have to be committed if the operation was not to be a complete failure. The second takeoff from Tattoi took place at about 10 A.M. The 40 aircraft with the paratroopers and their weapons and explosives arrived over Leros at about 1 P.M. As they neared the island, Italian and British anti-aircraft guns opened fire. They fired salvoes at the approaching aircraft, which were at about the same height as the defenders in their mountain positions. The paratroopers were dropped over the designated point between Gurna Bay and Alinda Bay at the narrow waist of the island.

Hauptmann Kuhne succeeded in assembling his companies under heavy enemy fire. Oberleutnant Haase, commander of the 1st Company, received orders to seal off the north part of the island and prevent the enemy from breaking through to the south. The 2nd Company, led by Oberleutnant Fellner, and the 4th under Oberleutnant Moller-Astheimer assaulted Monte Rachi, Hill 105, about 600 meters inland. Oberleutnant Raabe received orders to seal off Alinda Bay and the island capital of Leros with his 5th Company.

Hauptmann Kuhne warned Fellner, the commander of 2nd Company, to watch out for the Brandenburgers who had come down on the other side of the mountain. The paratroopers worked their way forward. Oberleutnant Moller-Astheimer led the Fourth up the hill through an overgrown ravine. When they came under fire they took cover and fired back.

Oberjäger Franzrahe waved his two companions from the company headquarters squad to him. Together they crawled on all fours along the ravine, clambered uphill around a rocky crag and five minutes later found themselves level with the enemy machine-gun. They crawled on and reached an outcropping, where they were fired on from behind by another machine-gun. While Stabsgefreiter Zylinski used his submachine-gun to force the crew of the machine-gun to take cover, Franzrahe opened fire on the machine-gun nest below him just as one of the English soldiers was about to lob a hand grenade. The man was knocked down by a burst from the squad leader's submachine-gun.

Seeing this, the company commander ordered his men forward. Under covering fire from Franzrahe and Zylinski and machine-gunner Otte, they reached the top of the hill. Farther left the 2nd Company had also reached the hilltop. They stormed several field works, giving each other mutual support. Franzrahe and his two companions used hand grenades to take out a troublesome machine-gun position. Monte Rachi was in their hands. With the battalion staff, the runners and the reserve squad, Hauptmann Kuhne set up his battalion command post on Monte Rachi. A short while later the most forward of the paratroopers made contact with the Brandenburgers.

The klaxon sounded, the signal for the paratroopers to jump. Oberleutnant Oschatz nodded to his deputy, who was to jump first. Leutnant Horl leapt through the open door and sailed through the air. The shock when his parachute deployed was great, but that was a good sign, and he drifted beneath his open parachute toward the rocky island. Tracer flitted past him. To his right he saw several men leave a Ju 52 and watched as, hit by the tracers, they fell to earth like lifeless puppets.

The rocky ground came up quickly. Horl pulled up his legs, rolled over his left shoulder and felt a stabbing pain in his head. For a few seconds he lost consciousness but was wakened by the blows against his body as it was dragged over the rocks by his parachute. He grasped the quick-release handle and was free.

Horl collected himself, folded up his parachute, and then called to his men. He saw one hobbling toward him; with a sprained ankle this man was out of action. Paratroopers were landing all around. One came down on a rocky ridge and was injured. His cries reached the ears of his comrades, causing them to tense up with fear. After it had assembled, it was found that one third of the company was out of action due to injuries or enemy fire. By now the enemy mortars had turned the full weight of their fire on to the paratroopers. The machine-guns that had been firing at Leutnant Schädlich and his men now turned and poured rapid fire into the onrushing Brandenburger paratroopers. Then the enemy committed his artillery as well. Shells blasted the rocky ground, spraying splinters of stone in all directions.

The paratroopers scratched into the stony ground. It was just a matter of time before they were hit. If no one came to relieve the pressure they would be wiped out.

Leutnant Schädlich, who with his men had seen the paratroopers drifting down, saw that the fire previously been meant for them had been redirected at their comrades of the parachute company.

Realizing that the paratroopers needed help, Schädlich pumped his right arm three times and got to his feet. Crouched low, his submachine-gun at the ready, he ran forward over the rocky ground. Moved by the élan shown by their company commander, the men to his left and right got up and began to advance. Obergefreiter Roder of the Finkler squad took out an enemy machine-gun.

The English anti-aircraft guns, which had been firing at the cornered paratroopers, now turned their fire on to the troops led by Leutnant Schädlich. Then the machine-guns and mortars returned to their old target and forced the decimated light infantry platoons of the 1st Company of the Coastal Raider Battalion Brandenburg to again take cover in the rocks and crevices. A short while later the English launched a counterattack From their heavy battery position, taking the Germans completely by surprise. When they appeared before the raiders they were only 50 meters from their makeshift cover.

Roder loosed off a long burst that halted the English attack. Finkler and Kuntze lobbed hand grenades. The enemy assault faltered about 20 meters in front of the Brandenburgers. Three or four wounded English soldiers cried out for help. Their shouts rang out through the afternoon of that day, so costly to the Brandenburgers. When one of the raiders attempted to reach the wounded men, he was hit in the shoulder by a sniper. The sniper would have to be eliminated before a second attempt could be made. Finkler gave his friends a sign. Schneetz stuck his steel helmet met on the short entrenching tool and raised it above cover. When nothing happened, he moved the helmet slowly to the right. Meanwhile Finkler had taken aim at the sniper's suspected position, resting his carbine in a crevice in the rock.

Suddenly he spotted a glint from a rifle as the sniper moved his weapon from cover. Finkler aimed carefully and squeezed the trigger. While the sound of the shot echoed off a rock wall, the English rifleman fell back and disappeared. Schneetz and his friend crawled forward. They brought back three wounded Englishmen, who were tended to by the medical officer Dr. Droste.

The enemy still held the surrounding hills, from where he was able to observe the entire landing zone. This was kept under constant fire so that any movement was extremely dangerous. The temperature fell when night came and by midnight on 13th November it was ice cold. But what had happened at sea? What was the navy doing to bring relief to the Brandenburgers, the combat engineers and the parachute troops?

During the night of 11th November the captured Italian torpedo boats TA 14, TA 15, TA 17 and TA 19 of the recently formed 9th Torpedo Boat Flotilla set off on their first operation. They were to provide cover for the landing operations against the island of Leros.

The four boats assembled before the anti-submarine nets of Piraeus harbor near Athens and then set off at medium speed toward Leros. When they arrived off Leros with the other vessels of the convoy early on the morning of 12th November, they were met by heavy fire from the heavy battery on top of Monte Appetici. All around the torpedo boats huge fountains of spray spurted up from the sea. The boats made smoke to hide the small landing raft from the enemy gunners and tried to pinpoint the enemy positions.

But the enemy batteries had a good fix on their targets and fired without letup. The torpedo boats zigzagged in front of the landing raft, laying smoke, while shells continue to fall all around. Since they were under orders not to engage shore batteries, the torpedo boats withdrew as soon as the smaller vessels had landed.

Not until early afternoon during the course of their second sortie to Leros, bringing weapons and equipment from Kalymnos, did TA 14 and 15 open fire on targets on the island. Shells smashed into the rocks. The barrage lasted ten minutes, until the boats were recalled to Kalymnos. In the days to come they would get the opportunity to do more for Leros.

When darkness fell on the first day of the attack, the British destroyers Faulknor, Beaufort and Pindos of the 8th Destroyer Flotilla under Captain Thomas on the Faulknor together with motor boats DSC 266 and DSC 263 and the motor torpedo boat MTB 315 were waiting in the Leros-Kalymnos-Levitha area to prevent the Germans from delivering reinforcements and supplies to Leros. The remaining vessels of the flotilla, the Dulverton, Echo and Belvoir were located somewhat farther away and were bombed. The Dulverton took a direct hit from a glider bomb and broke in two. Men jumped over the side to escape the flames. At 1:45 A.M. on 13th November the Dulverton went down. When the attack was over the Echo and the Belvoir proceeded to the spot where she had gone down to pick up survivors.

But no German transports sailed that night, even though it was planned to try and land the men of II Battalion, 16th Infantry Regiment, part of the western group that had failed to get ashore, two hours after sundown. Their arrival could have tipped the scales in favor of the invaders, but force 6 to 7 winds and heavy seas prevented the operation from being carried out.

During the night of 13th November the marine ferries and the navy's I-boats sailed for Leros with III Battalion, 16th Infantry Regiment under Hauptmann Aschoff. They had been forced to abandon their attempt to land the previous morning and they were eager to try again. Through the heavy seas the ships reached the new landing sector on the northeast side of the island in Palma Bay and BIefuti Bay to the north. The battalion went ashore and worked its way some distance inland while it was still dark.

The heavy weapons were supposed to arrive by marine ferry, but these vessels remained tied up at Cos and Kalymnos throughout the 13th waiting for the storm to subside. Orders were issued in the late afternoon of 12th November by the battle group headquarters under Generalleutnant Müller for the Dorr group, which that morning had been forced to return to Kalymnos by heavy fire, to proceed by assault boat to the Brandenburger coastal raiders' beachhead near Pandeli.

It was 11 P.M. on 12th November when the loading of the infantry began. A half hour later the small flotilla set sail. In the lead was a navy minesweeper whose captain was in charge of the sea operation. Behind it followed landing raft "A", "B" and "C". By this time the sea state had already risen to force 6 to 7. When the boats sailed into Alinda Bay the destroyers of the British night patrol showed up. The minesweeper left the landing craft, which had much lower silhouettes, and sailed off to the northeast.

A short while later, with the landing craft struggling toward the coastal raiders' beach, the searchlights on top of Monte Appetici were switched on again and began sweeping the sea. Barely 30 seconds later the two beams caught and held the first landing craft. The boat commander was blinded. The group leader ordered the vessels to zigzag. The boat was bathed in brilliant light by the searchlight beam and shells began falling into the sea. A wall of fire and smoke rose up in front of the boat. It was impossible to pass through this barrage fire without being destroyed. Having decided that a landing was impossible, the boat commander applied full port rudder and turned around to the south.

Landing craft "B", which was somewhat off to starboard and lagging behind on account of the heavy seas, sailed unnoticed into the bay and then turned onto the designated course. On the shore flashlights were switched on, showing the helmsman the exact course. The landing raft headed for the makeshift landing site. Willing hands reached for the infantrymen of the Dorr company and helped them ashore.

Meanwhile boat "C" was now under fire. It was even farther back and after boat "A" had veered off to the south the enemy searchlights sought a new victim and found it in the form of boat "C". The first shells fell into the sea in front of the boat. The helmsman turned to starboard. He steered a wide arc and headed north, the only way to escape the enemy fire. The boat then landed on the beach outside Griffo Bay and in minutes the men of the Dorr company was ashore.

When the boat tried to sail away at dawn on 13th November it came under heavy fire. After taking a direct hit, which tore a large hole, the helmsman steered the landing craft back to the safety of the rocky shore. The other two heavy assault boats were battered by the heavy seas, now at force 8. "B" took on water and its electrical system failed. Unable to sail, the boat drifted on the sea and was not made serviceable again until the night of 14th November. It returned to Kalymnos on the morning of the 14th. Boat "A", which still had its weak platoon of infantry on board, just managed to remain afloat. Only an intensive bailing effort by everyone allowed the boat to return to Cos. From there it sailed on to Kalymnos after the storm had abated.

Without sleep since 11th November, the men of the engineer landing company's repair group went to work on the heavy assault boats, some of which had been badly damaged, in an effort to make them seaworthy again. Could Leros still be taken? Or would the few hundred German soldiers have to yield before the eight fold superiority of the defenders with their heavy weapons in prepared positions?

At dawn on 13th November Leutnant Schädlich was awakened from a brief, unsettled sleep by a runner. He brought the news that a platoon of the Dorr company had landed and was on its way up to them. Relieved that the enemy had not counterattacked during the night, Schädlich was determined to make use of the welcome reinforcements. He ordered his platoon commanders to report to him at 5:30 A.M.

Soon afterward the infantry came up the hill. Some were still green in the Face from their rough sea voyage and the strain of the climb was obvious. Platoon commander Schaller reported his arrival with 42 men. Sch dlich ordered him to rest his men and informed him that they were to provide covering fire when he and his men attacked in half an hour. The soldiers dropped to the ground and tried to regain their strength; meanwhile, the coastal raiders prepared for their second attack.

Schädlich deployed his 1st and 3rd Platoons on the left, the 2nd Platoon and the infantry on the right. He stressed to the platoon commanders that the left was to spearhead the attack, while the right provided harassing fire and a diversionary attack. It was still dark but the soldiers' eyes were accustomed to it and they could see the enemy positions. The men stared at the lieutenant, who was in the middle of the two attack forces with the company headquarters squad and two other runners. When the time for the attack came, the lieutenant raised his arm.

The entire company rose up and charged. They had advanced several meters before the surprised enemy opened fire. Lt. Schädlich ordered the right group to open fire so that it would seem that the main attack was coming from there. The enemy directed the bulk of their fire in that direction. Enemy machine-gun fire forced Oberfeldwebel Kuntze to take cover. He was joined by a machine-gun team and Kuntze pointed out the position of the enemy machine-gun. Spotting a muzzle flash, the gunner put a burst squarely on target. The enemy weapon fell silent.

Kuntze and his men advanced four or five paces before forced to take cover again. Like his men he was out of breath, but he knew that the sooner they crossed this open area the better. But for now it seemed that the attack was falling apart under the fire from an enemy machine-gun. Then gunner Roder got up and ran toward the enemy position, firing as he went. The enemy gunner turned to meet this new threat and Roder was hit. But as he fell his last burst silenced the enemy machine-gun. Unteroffizier Finkler crawled over to Roder but he was beyond help.

Another man took over Roder's weapon, inserted a fresh belt of ammunition, and then raked the upper edge of the concrete gun position with fire. With the two flanking machine-guns pinned down, Oberfeldwebel Kuntze and Gefreiter Kosters moved toward the enemy position. Each carried eight hand grenades. The two men dashed to the cover of a crevice in the rock, where they rested for a moment. After peering through chinks in the rock to get his bearings, Kuntze assigned Kosters to the left while he took the right. They laid out the hand grenades, unscrewed the caps, then stood up behind the cover of the rocks and lobbed them in the direction of the enemy machine-gun nests.

As the last of the grenades exploded Leutnant Schädlich came running with the two attack platoons. Kuntze and Kosters ran to the edge of the concrete position, jumped in and turned their weapons on the English, who surrendered immediately. The two platoons led by Lt. Schädlich arrived seconds later. There was sporadic gunfire and then silence. The position was in their hands. Medic Unteroffizier Mandalka and his two aids tended to the wounded of both sides.

Leutnant Schädlich positioned a machine-gun squad facing the next enemy gun position, from where a counterattack might come. Although a breach had been forced in the enemy defense, it was localized. The other groups were still pinned down. Stuka support had been requested to soften up the enemy. Then the dive-bombers appeared overhead and before there was time to layout the air identification panels they began their dives. Schädlich ordered his men to take cover. One of the Stukas selected the gun site they had just captured as its target. Its bombs fell close, wounding three men. But bombs also fell on the second, third and fourth guns.

Leutnant Schadlich led the men of the Meeser platoon forward. Together they dashed through the communications trench into the second gun position. They met a group of English troops. There was an exchange of fire and the lieutenant was wounded. Feldwebel Meeser led his platoon past the wounded lieutenant into the enemy position and overwhelmed the defenders. The second gun site was now in the hands of the Brandenburgers. Unteroffizier Mandalka and two aides came and carried the company commander into the concrete gun position and laid him near the gun carriage. He was bleeding heavily from a wound in his thigh.

Medical officer Dr. Droste was summoned and he hurried forward through enemy fire to save the life of the lieutenant. He stopped the bleeding and then turned his attentions to the other wounded.

Leutnant Schädlich regained consciousness and ordered his men to set up an all-round defense. The enemy would surely try to retake the position, he warned his men. No counterattack came, however, and early on 13th November the men of II Battalion, 16th Infantry Regiment linked up with the Brandenburgers; together they fought on against the well-entrenched enemy.

The anticipated counterattack came later in the day. While two British destroyers pounded the German positions, a fresh company of the King's Own Regiment attacked from the fourth gun position on Monte Appetici. The defense organized by Lt. Schädlich, held, however, and a critical factor was the high rate of fire of the German MG 42 machine-guns. Fighting continued throughout the 14th. The navy once again tried to bring ÜI16's heavy weapons to Leros but the ships were forced back by heavy seas.

Aware of this, the British intensified their attacks, but they were beaten back. Hauptmann Kuntze now decided to launch a counterattack of his own against Monte Meraviglia. The two companies made good initial progress, but then heavy machine-gun fire forced them to retire to their starting point.

Not until the evening of 14th November did the storm subside enough to allow the navy's I-boats and several assault boats to try to reach Leros again. A small convoy was formed, with the rest of the Dorr company in three I-boats. Oberleutnant Bunte, commander of the 780th Pioneer Landing Company, headed for Pandeli Bay. From there he wanted to look for and hopefully recover the remaining landing raft, which he suspected were still in Griffo Bay. On reaching Leros he was disappointed to find that only one of the boats was seaworthy. The others were pulled up on shore so that the holes in their hulls could be repaired during the night. The first boats slipped past the English guns to Kalymnos, but those that followed had to run the gauntlet of gunfire.

The numerically weak German units continued to attack and gradually gained the upper hand. Finally on 16 November 1943 it was over. 200 English officers and 2,000 men surrendered to a German force consisting of four battalions of infantry, a handful of engineers and the Brandenburg Coastal Raider Company. 359 Italian officers and 5,000 men also went into captivity. The conquerors of the island also captured 120 guns (76-150 mm), 16 heavy anti-aircraft guns and 20 light anti-aircraft weapons.

At 10 P.M. on 17 November 1943 the German radio network played the fanfares that presaged a special announcement. It was the last time during the course of the Second World War. The announcer declared that German troops under Generalleutnant Müller had taken the strongly defended bastion of Leros.

When the fighting on Leros was over, the Brandenburg Coastal Raider Company could muster just 37 effectives from a strength of about 120 men. Three quarters of the company's personnel were wounded, missing or dead. The victory had been won, but it brought no joy to the men. Too much blood had been shed in the battle for an island that, in their eyes, was no longer important.

BRANDENBURGER COASTAL RAIDERS IN THE AEGAEAN: PARTISANS AND THE ENGLISH

Bled white after Operation "Typhoon-Leopard," the 1st Coastal Raider Company under the new command of Leutnant Voight and soon afterward Leutnant Bertermann, was divided into two groups. The 1st Company remained under the command of Leutnant Bertermann in the area of the Dodecanese and was ultimately stationed on Rhodes, where soon afterward it was named Coastal Raider Company Rhodes. The remaining companies of the battalion were spread along the coast of Yugoslavia.

The new 1st Company was designated "Special Purpose Construction Training Headquarters" and was stationed in Bar. It served in the uniform of the Todt Organization. Its role: commando missions against partisans and against the British ships that supplied them.

The company under Leutnant Bertermann left in the Adriatic was given a special role, namely countering Allied commando raids. In addition to its two large assault boats it had received a Greek sailing ship, the Kajikis; these vessels were used for patrol missions and short-range commando operations. The unit's landing craft and I-boats of the 15th Landing Flotilla were available for longer-range missions. The 780th Pioneer Landing Battalion also made its boats available to the Brandenburgers or included them in its attack plans and actions.

On the morning of 9 April 1944 an armed sailing ship carrying a British commando team was boarded and the crew taken prisoner. A complete set of operational orders and radio codebooks were captured on the sailing ship. These were to be used often in the future to deceive the enemy. The captured ship was renamed the *Erika*. Since the vessel was known to the partisans and thus did not have to fear being fired on, it was used in successful undercover operations against the islands of Saria and Skarpanto in the period 3rd to 18th May.

On 20th June Leutnant Bertermann, who until then was still officially the battalion adjutant, was placed in command of the coastal raiders based at Castello; it was only then that they became the Coastal Raider Company Rhodes.

All German troops on Rhodes, including the Brandenburgers, were under the command of Generalleutnant Ulrich Kleemann, who had joined all those troops under the designation "Assault Division Rhodes." Kleemann led the 90th Light Infantry Division in Africa and had received the Knight's Cross with Oak Leaves on 16 September 1943.

Also under his command were the "Harbor Protection Flotilla Dodecanese" under Kapitanleutnant Brachvogel and the 6th I-Boat Group under Leutnant zur See Berger, as well as the 780th Pioneer Landing Company under Oberleutnant Bunte. Naval commander was Kapitan zur See Brennecke. While the bulk of the Brandenburg Coastal Raider Battalion was engaged in anti-partisan operations and actions against British supply vessels in the Adriatic region, under the command of the Naval Commander Dodecanese Leutnant Bertermann had to conduct operations against the three enemy groups active in this area, namely: elements of the Long-Range Desert Group, the Greek Holy Brigade, and the Special Boat Squadron.

Though far inferior to his opponents in ships and equipment, Leutnant Bertermann nevertheless achieved a number of notable successes, the most dramatic of which was probably an operation that took place in August 1944.

A DIFFICULT RECONNAISSANCE MISSION

On 19 August 1944 Oberleutnant Bertermann received orders from the Naval Commander East Aegean to form a well-armed platoon with which to reconnoiter the islands of Saria, Skarpanto, Stakida, Unia-Nisia, Kamiloni, Zaphrani, Syrina, Kandelousia and Perigousa for signs of enemy occupation.

With one I-boat as command vessel and two others for individual actions, the small force assembled on Alinna. At 9:00 P.M. on 23rd August it sailed with a total of 30 coastal raiders and landed early the next morning on Saria. One of the boats sailed on to Skarpanto. Both islands were unoccupied. Another battle group of similar strength scouted the islands of Unia-Nisia and Kamiloni and also found them to be unoccupied.

When the leaders of the two groups met on Zaphrani on 25th August they decided to sail on to Syrina at once. On arriving there they discovered an unidentified vessel in a neighboring bay concealed beneath bushes and camouflage netting. Two assault boats, commanded by Oberleutnant Bertermann and Oberfahnrich Brandt, and each carrying a raider with a machine-gun, made straight for the vessel at top speed.

Realizing their critical situation, the crew tried to remove the camouflage and open fire on the approaching Brandenburgers, but their attempt failed. To make matters worse, when they cast off the camouflage netting fouled the boat's propeller. The two assault boats came alongside the enemy vessel left and right and the Brandenburgers leapt aboard with submachine-guns and machine-guns at the ready. The 14 British commandos on board surrendered.

The enemy vessel was HDML 1381, a combat ship armed with a 40-mm Bofors gun in the bow, two 20-mm Oerlikon fast-firing cannon and two twin-barreled machine-guns. This small "floating fortress" was powered by two marine diesel engines, which gave the 54-ton vessel a speed of 12 knots. One of the first raiders to board the ship immediately went below and prevented the ship from being scuttled. The following I-boats took the captured vessel under tow. The camouflage netting was removed from the screws, after which the prize, now manned by coastal raiders, was able to sail on its own to Portolago on Leros. The ship was renamed KJ 25 and was put to use by the Brandenburgers, becoming the best-armed unit they had.

The next operation, a patrol in KJ 25 under the command of Leutnant zur See Brandt against the island of Calchi, was a success. The coastal raiders made a surprise landing and engaged a detachment of the Holy Greek Brigade. Following a brief but bitter firefight in which the tremendous rate of fire of the MG 42 was a deciding factor, the surviving Greeks surrendered. Among the dead was the commander of the unit. He was buried by the captured Greek troops with an honor guard provided by the coastal raiders.

On 28th October boats of the 3rd Company, 86th Pioneer Landing Battalion put two groups of raiders and a company of infantry from the Assault Division Rhodes ashore in the rear of a British commando unit that had landed on Piscopi. Heavy fighting broke out. After day and night fighting in which the upper hand was gained and lost several times, the commandos were completely wiped out. The British troops fought with equal determination, but in the Brandenburgers they had met an opponent whose will to win more than made up for their numerical inferiority.

On the night of 14 November 1944 a platoon of Brandenburg coastal raiders arrived on the island of Alinna, where they set up an observation post. When British commandos landed there three nights later, they succeeded in overrunning the post.

After the company lost radio contact with the observation post on Alinna, during the night of 18th November Oberleutnant Bertermann dispatched a search party to the island. The team landed safely and made its way toward the observation post; however, it had walked into a British trap and was captured. The captured Brandenburgers were taken to a British destroyer lying in Turkish waters.

Another reconnaissance operation in KJ 25 to the island of Calchi on 23 March 1945 was crowned with success. The raiders succeeded in overrunning a company of the Holy Greek Brigade that had landed in motorboats. The boats also fell into the hands of the Brandenburgers. Questioning of the prisoners revealed that they had seen the KJ 25 but took it to be a British vessel that they knew.

On the evening of 13th April, while carrying out an undercover mission disguised as an English vessel, west of Castellrosso the KJ 25 encountered a British armed sailing ship. The enemy ship was armed with three heavy machine-guns and had a party of armed commandos on board. The sailing ship was boarded and the nine British prisoners were taken to Rhodes. KJ 25 carried out its final undercover operation on 7 May 1945. Once again the area of operations was in the waters surrounding Castellrosso. The mission was subsequently aborted when a radio message was received from the OKW ordering hostilities to cease.

The next morning the German commander in the eastern Aegean, Generalmajor Droeger, sailed in KJ 25 to the British destroyer Active lying off Symi to sign the surrender document. When the general was piped aboard the ship, which was considered "soil of the British Empire."

The next day, 9 May 1945, the KJ 25 took the British advance party to Rhodes. On arriving in harbor KJ 25 once again became HDML 1381 and returned to the Special Boat Squadron. For this part of the Brandenburg Coastal Raider Battalion the Second World War was over.

The Final Stage: Panzer-Grenadier Division Brandenburg

THE TRANSFORMATION

On 13 September 1944, as the result of an order from the Führer, the Brandenburg Division was transformed into a panzer-grenadier division and was integrated into the newly formed Panzer Corps Großdeutschland. With this order, issued by the OKW/WFSt., the Brandenburg Division ceased to exist. It was no longer a special unit engaged in tactical missions for the Abwehr. Only the Kurfurst Regiment was spared by this tragic development. The division commander had obtained one concession, however; every Brandenburger could decide for himself whether he wanted to remain with the new division or transfer to another unit.

The most popular new units for the former Brandenburgers were the commando units of the Waffen-SS commanded by Obersturmbannführer Skorzeny. From this point on these units carried out the type of missions previously the preserve of the Brandenburg Division. Otto Skorzeny had a great deal of faith in the Brandenburgers. For this reason about 800 Brandenburgers transferred to his command. However the vast majority did not want to leave their old home and remained with the division when it became a unit of the army.

The Panzer Corps Großdeutschland under the command of General der Panzertruppe Dietrich von Saucken, was organized as follows:

Panzer-Grenadier Division Großdeutschland	Generalmajor Lorenz
Führer Escort Division	Generalmajor Remer
Panzer-Grenadier Division Brandenburg	Generalmajor Schulte-Heuthaus
Führer Grenadier Division	Generalmajor Mäder

General der Panzertruppe von Saucken told the author that, "the Panzer-Grenadier Division Brandenburg was a gain for our corps. Its' units

were motivated by an extraordinary fighting spirit. They were outstand-
ingly familiar with methods of combat as well as the Red Army and the partisan forces in the Soviet Union, in Yugoslavia and in Greece. All that it
lacked was experience in division-strength operations as part of an army
corps. But I was certain that it would clear this hurdle with bravado."

For the Brandenburg Division it was the end of a developmental
process that had begun in September 1939. After the last of its units
returned at the beginning of December, the division was badly weakened
and materially decimated. The two replacement and training units were
still in existence, however, and were quickly able to provide the necessary
replacement personnel. This was made easier by the fact that the number
of regiments had been reduced from four to two, each with just two battalions.

For the first time it became apparent that more than the initial esti-
mate of 800 Brandenburgers had gone to Skorzeny's commando units. At
this time the division command was as follows:

Division Commander	Generalmajor Schulte-Heuthaus
Ia	General Staff Major Erasmus
Ib	General Staff Major Uhl
	(later General Staff Major Spaeter)

General Staff Major Helmuth Spaeter was a highly experienced officer
when he joined the division staff. He had won the Knight's Cross when serving as commander of the 2nd Company of the Großdeutschland reconnaissance battalion. A short while later Hptm. Witauschek and Hptm. Volkmar
joined the division as Ib, and Hauptmann Werner Lau as division adjutant.
The following is the division order of battle:

Division Escort Company:	Oberleutnant Mischkeres
Anti-Tank Battalion:	Hauptmann Königstein
	Leutnant Kass
Armored Reconnaissance Battalion:	Major Bansen
	Oberleutnant Mücke
	Rittmeister Frey
Military Police Company:	Leutnant Feldmüller
Panzer Regiment:	
I Battalion:	Hauptmann Graf Rothkirch
II Battalion:	Major Waldeck
III Battalion:	Hauptmann Spielvogel
(Armored artillery battalion)	

Armored Assault Pioneer Battalion:	Hauptmann Müller-Rochholz
1st Company:	Oberleutnant Bank
	Leutnant Hertkorn
2nd Company:	Oberleutnant Schlosser
	Leutnant Clemeur
3rd Company:	Oberleutnant Laurenz
	Leutnant Prieß
Supply Company:	Hauptmann Michaelis
Armored Bridging Column:	Oberleutnant Hasper
Signals Officer:	Leutnant Küper
Army Flak Battalion:	Major Voßhage
	Oberarzt Dr. Braun
RUB Company:	Hauptmann Schmidt
	Leutnant Baumgarten
Armored Operations Battalion:	Hauptmann Bauer
	Hauptmann Franke
Bicycle Battalion:	Sturmbannführer
	Graf Egloffstein
II Battalion, Training Regiment:	Hauptmann von Einem-Josten
Adjutant:	Leutnant Ullmann
	Leutnant Mohrmann
Battalion Medical Officer:	Oberarzt Dr. Fischer
III Battalion, Panzer-Grenadier	
Replacement and Training Regiment	Hauptmann Schewe
Adjutant:	Leutnant Gerving
Battalion Medical Officer:	Oberarzt Dr. Hofmann
Battalion IVa:	Oberzahlmeister Kohl
Battalion V K:	Technical Engineer Ramboldt
	Technical Sergeant Prien
Ia Clerk:	Obeifeldwebel Korthaud
IIa Clerk:	Feldwebel Trebschek
Ib Clerk:	Unteroffizier Knieper
9th Training Company:	Leutnant von Bülow
10th Training Company:	Leutnant Feindauer
11 th Training Company:	Leutnant Becker
12th MG Training Company:	Leutnant Steinmann
Special Purpose Training Company:	Leutnant Braun
1st Conversion Training Company:	Oberleutnant Kappel
2nd Conversion Training Company:	Oberleutnant Horsthemke
Trained Replacement Company:	Oberleutnant Halbig
1st (Light Infantry) Regiment:	Oberst Brückner

	Major Wandrey
	Major Bansen
I Battalion:	Oberleutnant Hebler
	Hauptmann Froboese
	Hauptmann Schuster
II Battalion:	Hauptmann Hunold
	Rittmeister Sandmeyer
5th Company:	Oberleutnant Zülch
	Oberleutnant Steidl
6th Company:	Oberleutnant Röseke
7th Company:	Oberleutnant Geisenberger
8th Company:	Oberleutnant (Hauptmann) Grabert
	Leutnant Prohaska
1st Half-Company of the 8th:	Leutnant Haut
	Leutnant Gruber
2nd Half-Company of the 8th:	Leutnant Hiller
	Leutnant Prohaska
III Battalion:	Hauptmann Wandrey
Company Commanders:	Leutnant Klaus
	Leutnant Krosch
	Leutnant Bürck
2nd (Light Infantry) Regiment:	Oberstleutnant Oesterwitz
Regiment Adjutant:	Hauptmann Vincenz
Regiment Medical Officer:	Stabsarzt Dr. Backhausen
Signals Battalion:	Oberleutnant Schmalbruch
	Oberleutnant Brauschmidt
I Battalion:	Hauptmann Steidl
1st Company:	Oberleutnant Wirth
2nd Company:	Oberleutnant Kieffer
	Oberleutnant Gutweniger
3rd Company:	Leutnant (Oberleutnant) Haut
	Leutnant Mark
4th Company:	Leutnant Esser
	Leutnant Langer
5th Company:	Oberleutnant Gabel
II Battalion:	Major Renner
	Hauptmann Heine
	Oberleutnant Afheldt
	Hauptmann Zinkel

6th Company:	Oberleutnant Sautner
	Leutnant Maier
7th Company:	Leutnant Stalf
III Battalion:	Hauptmann Zinkel
	Oberleutnant Auer
9th Company:	Oberleutnant Planer

COMBAT IS JOINED—JANUARY 1945

On 13 January 1945 the Red Army launched its assault on Germany proper, with the 1st White Russian Front under Marshall Zhukov attacking from the Magnuszew and Pulawy bridgeheads and the 1st Ukrainian Front under Marshall Konev from the Sandomierz-Baranow bridgehead. The Soviet blow struck the south wing of the 9th

Army and the entire front of the 4th Panzer Army—which formed Army Group A under Generaloberst Harpe—after a tremendous barrage by 10,000 guns.

On 14th January Hitler ordered two divisions of the new Panzer Corps Großdeutschland to entrain for the front, namely the Panzer-Grenadier Division Brandenburg and the 1st Parachute Panzer Division Hermann Goring.

The cadre unit of this newly formed corps, the Panzer Division Großdeutschland, was still locked in bitter fighting in the area of Praschnitz. General Wenck tried to order this division into the threatened area too, but the situation in the Rozan-Pultusk bridgehead did not allow it. The two divisions rolled out of northern East Prussia into the area of Kutno-Litzmannstadt-Petrikau, almost parallel to the westward-advancing armored spearheads of the Red Army. The first elements arrived on the evening of 16th January.

The first transports carrying the 2nd Light Infantry Regiment Brandenburg under Oberstleutnant Oesterwitz arrived in the area south of Petrikau late on the evening of 16th January. The troops detrained using the temporarily loading ramps and took over the defense near Longinowka.

The regiment's II Battalion detrained in Petrikau. Oberleutnant Afheldt immediately moved into a billet southeast of the city. That same night Soviet tanks rolled into Petrikau. There was some vicious hand-to-hand combat during which the battalion was split up and scattered by direct tank and machine-gun fire. It lost the bulk of its vehicles and all its heavy weapons. Some soldiers made it to safety in the woods in small groups. Oberstleutnant Oesterwitz had lost almost his entire battalion at the very beginning.

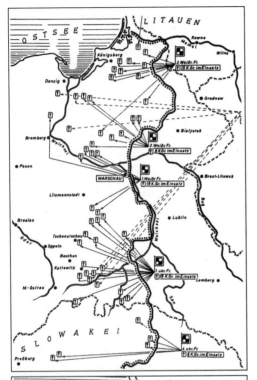

Soviet scouts search
for a weak spot.

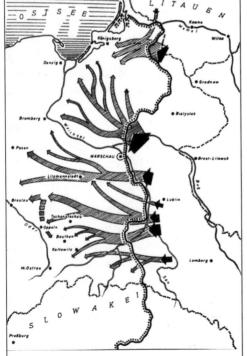

Soviet forces were
then committed.

The following companies detrained in the surrounding area on 17th January, the Assault Pioneer Battalion under Hauptmann Müller, for example, north of Petrikau. All the while it was detraining, Soviet aircraft bombed and strafed the vehicles. Luckily for the isolated units General Staff Oberstleutnant Erasmus was on one of the trains and he assumed temporary command. The 01, Oberleutnant Broker, gave him an order from Headquarters, 9th Army: "Panzer-Grenadier Division Brandenburg is to assemble in the forest east of Petrikau."

The order was crazy, as the Red Army had already advanced through that area. After a night of holding the entire division marched back into the Litzmannstadt area. There was no contact with division headquarters.

On 17th January the assault gun brigade Großdeutschland detrained in Litzmannstadt. Hauptmann Metzger reported to the Brandenburg Division, advising that the brigade had been subordinated to it. It was salvation at the last minute, for masses of Soviet tanks were already rolling toward Litzmannstadt and firing their cannon into the eastern suburbs. Hptm. Metzger led the 18 assault guns out of the southern suburbs to Pabianica. They were also attacked by enemy aircraft, but fortunately there were no losses. The assault guns engaged and temporarily halted the Soviet tanks.

Further elements of the Brandenburg Division continued arriving in Litzmannstadt and its environs until 18th January. Early that morning the first trains carrying the 1st Light Infantry Regiment under Oberst von Brückner arrived in Kutno. They detrained there as the Red Army was reported approaching Warsaw. Coming from the east and southeast, endless columns of refugees walked and drove to Litzmannstadt and entered the deceptive safety of the city.

The defensive struggle began at 8 P.M. on the 18th, when the first enemy tanks felt their way toward Litzmannstadt. Two veteran Brandenburgers. Obergefreiter Troger and Oberjäger Hahmann knocked out the first enemy tanks from close range, however three T 34s broke through. When the second tank assault reached the city, Gefreiter Kofler destroyed one tank with a Panzerfaust and two more with charges consisting of hand grenades bundled together. The 1st Regiment's 7th Company under Oberleutnant Geisenberger was attacked all night long and lost one third of its men.

On 18th January General von Saucken arrived in Litzmannstadt and moved with his staff into a cloth mill at the edge of the city. The first troops of Panzer Group Nehring arrived there on 19th January; the group was trying to escape Soviet encirclement by adopting the strategy of the "moving pocket." Litzmannstadt, too, was encircled and General von Saucken assembled the Brandenburg Division and the 1st Parachute Panzer Division Hermann Göring for a breakout to the west. During one Soviet attack on the 19th Brandenburgers destroyed 4 of 50 tanks using close combat methods.

Under unrelenting heavy pressure from the Red Army the Panzer-Grenadier Division Brandenburg left its positions and broke through to the west toward Grabica. With its infantry riding on the armored vehicles, the division broke through to Karezmy on the Gabria and linked up there with the division's armored assault pioneer battalion. The bridge was mined, but then General von Saucken ordered the mines removed as Panzer Group Nehring also had to drive over the bridge. Then a powerful force of Soviet tanks carrying infantry approached the concrete bridge. Two were knocked out by anti-tank guns positioned in front of the bridge, and the burning tanks blocked the way for the others. Only then did the division order the bridge blown.

Lt. Batzig was wounded by direct tank fire. The pioneer commander and 12 men drove to the bridge in three VW Schwimmwagen vehicles and positioned the mines, however they were unable to attach the detonators. The bridge remained standing. The two wooden bridges farther northwest were destroyed.

The retreat continued past Lask to the south to Shieratz. On 22 January 1945 Hauptmann Müller Rochholz and his pioneers reached Marcenin, where the first soldiers of Panzer Group Nehring were taken in. Leading them was an older colonel with a wooden leg who, deeply moved, hugged the captain.

The battle for the Warthe bridges on 20th January was also a dramatic one. The 3rd Company of the Armored Assault Pioneer Battalion was virtually wiped out there. Its commander, Oblt. Laurentz, was twice shot through the lungs and was rescued under heavy fire by his technical sergeant. Lt. Hertkorn was killed. Heavy bombing left the big Warthe Bridge impassable, but pioneers from another division repaired it sufficiently to allow vehicles to use it. Last to cross the bridge were the survivors from the 3rd Assault Pioneer Company. The Russians entered the city.

The retreat led the Brandenburg Division between Oppeln and Ohlau on the Oder, hotly pursued by large groups of Soviet tanks with mounted infantry. The two groups commanded by von Saucken and Nehring, which had linked up with the Brandenburg Division near Shieratz, fought their way back toward Kalisch-Ostrowo supported by the Großdeutschland's assault gun brigade. Repeated enemy assaults had to be fought off from the left and right. Ostrowo was already in Russian hands. Between Kalisch and Ostrowo the units fought their way through the Russian troops and by 24th January Korotschin was reached. But the division did not make it to

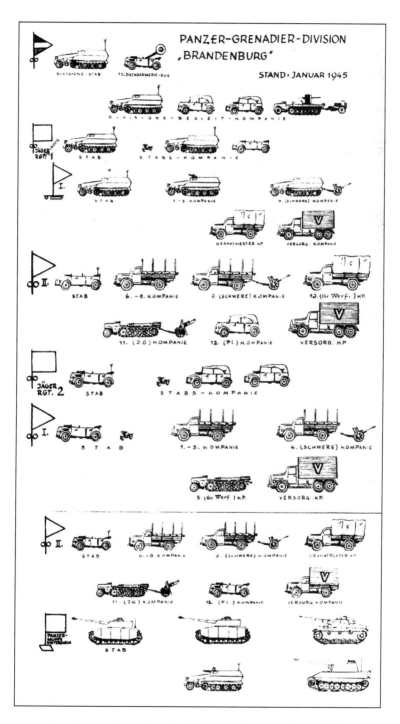

The Panzer-Grenadier Division Brandenburg (Jan. 1945)

the Oder, for on 27 January 1945 it was ordered to carry out an attack with the Hermann Göring Division which was supposed to destroy the entire enemy grouping in the Steinau bend.

It consisted of various corps of Marshall Konev's 1st Ukrainian Front. On 27 January 1945 it had reached the Oder on both sides of Steinau in spite of a desperate defense by students of an NCO school and even established a bridgehead across the river near Koben. They thus became the first Soviet troops to cross the Oder.

While striving toward the bridge at Glogau the von Saucken group came under enemy fire near Waffendorf and on 29th January it was ordered to halt, turn south while still east of the Oder, and immediately attack the forces of the 1st Ukrainian Front in the bend of the river.

Here once again there was a true Brandenburger-style surprise raid— by the Division Escort Company Brandenburg under Oblt. Mischkeres. Wearing Russian uniforms, Mischkeres and 12 men tried to seize the bridge over the Bartsch near Rützen. However, the company ran into an ambush and just managed to extricate itself.

In this situation the armored troop carrier battalion of the 2nd Light Infantry Regiment Brandenburg, led by several assault guns, rolled straight across the snow-covered fields in the moonlight toward Rützen. The assault guns opened fire from 1,000 meters. Enemy artillery firing from Rützen

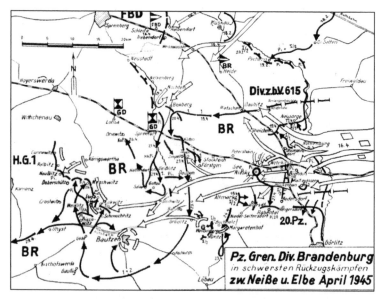

Map of the Brandenburg Division between the Neisse and the Elbe.

Castle, where the Red command staff had set up shop, met the attackers. The town was taken by storm but the Russians in the castle held on. There was a bitter struggle in which Hptm. Schafer, commander of the troop carrier battalion, was badly wounded. Finally the castle was taken.

During the advance on Wiersewitz II Battalion under Oberleutnant Afheldt fought its way through the enemy with the assault guns. The assault guns knocked out seven enemy tanks. A dug-in SU 100 was also destroyed. A Russian battle group supported by about 10 T 34s continued to hold and ultimately forced the attackers to withdraw. The attack cost the lives of 5 officers and 60 men.

The attack by the von Saucken group in the Raudten-Pilgramsdorf area began early on 1 February 1945. The armored patrols of the Armored Reconnaissance Battalion Brandenburg met the enemy before Pilgramsdorf. The Soviets were driven out of the town. The attack on 2nd February led by the Großdeutschland assault gun brigade, with I Battalion of the light infantry regiment under Hauptmann Froboese and elements of the Brandenburg anti-tank battalion under Hauptmann Konigstein, was met by heavy fire from the Red Army forces on the hills to the right and left.

Oblt. Planer, commander of the 7th Company, was killed. The 7th Company lost one third of its personnel. Toward noon the German forces reached the crossroads north of Mlitsh. Then approximately 20 T 34s suddenly emerged from hiding and overran the anti-tank guns under Lt. Kass guarding the crossroads. Seven enemy tanks were destroyed but the rest rolled west.

The fighting saw Generalmajor Schulte-Heuthaus in the front lines with his infantry. Near Toshwitz he and his men were almost cut off but at the last minute managed to break out.

The rest of the division held on at Polach. The village changed hands three times. Lt. Stalf and Lt. Kass fought with the courage of desperation. On 8th February the enemy broke into their positions and the fighting troops were forced to fall back toward Polach. II Battalion, 2nd Light Infantry Regiment set up its command post in the estate there. The Red Army continued to press and a further retreat began. During the course of 10th February the division's units were encircled south of Heerwegen. Gen-Maj. Schulte-Heuthaus and his light infantry were also in this trap. When night came General von Saucken courageously drove through the Russian lines into the pocket, where only the Brandenburgers were holding in good order. General von Saucken designated them to lead the breakout to the west. This great general—a wearer of the Knight's Cross with Oak Leaves, Swords and Diamonds—calmly organized the breakout.

Ultimately it was the Panther tanks of the Hermann Göring Panzer Regiment, which were in the rear guard under Major Dr. Roßmann, which swept aside the enemy and opened the way. By the early morning of 12th February the battle had been won. The three divisions of the von Saucken group had fought their way out, although casualties had been heavy.

THE BITTER END OF THE BRANDENBURGERS

A new defense front was established along the Lausitzer Neiße between Weißwasser and Gorlitz by the Panzer-Grenadier Division Brandenburg. From Forst to Muskau and Priebus to the Sänitz area the division went over to the defensive. Its sector of front was 32 kilometers long. The division command post was in Heide, on the Muskau-Rietschen road. The Muskau Forest extended to the Neiße River. For the veteran Brandenburgers this was a priceless advantage, because there they could erect their well-camou-flaged, almost invisible positions. On the other hand in several places it made it easier for the Red Army to cross the river almost undetected.

In no time at all there were bunkers and dugouts, communication trenches and ambush positions at the critical points. The first patrols went across the Neiße in the dark of night. The other side also conducted pre-liminary feeling-out operations. The division's pioneers were kept busy building bunkers. They also built a kilometer-long log road from Weiß-kessel to Weißwasser to allow supply vehicles to pass safely even through the worst mud. Valuable assistance was provided by the Volkssturm and a Cossack convalescent battalion. The first horse-drawn transport troop under Leutnant Grüber and Hauptfeldwebel Bohnke, consisting of two sections each with ten horse-drawn vehicles for a total of 120 horses and 80 soldiers, was the foundation of the Brandenburg Supply Train Battalion. The second horse-drawn troop was formed at the end of February under Lt. Gopfert. Senior Veterinarian Dr. Hein cared for the draft horses. When a third troop was formed in early March it raised the number of horses in the Brandenburg Supply Train Battalion to 352 and its total carrying capacity to 90 tons. It was a masterly feat by the division in the field of logistics. This was followed by the formation of a cavalry battalion, also of three troops. Its role was offensive and reconnaissance patrols and meeting enemy patrols. The cavalry were also employed against the "Committee for a Free Germany," which was actively engaged in propaganda and subver-sive activities at the Neiße.

The city of Weißwasser on the Berlin-Gorlitz rail line, which was of spe-cial importance as a front-line supply base, was turned into a fortress. In the city were large glassworks, such as the Osram works, coalfields, brick-works, a porcelain manufacturer and other factories.

Left table

Heeres-Gr.	Armeen	Korps	Div.
		XXIX.	8. Jg. / 19. Pz.+Sp.Vbd. / Olmütz / 271.
	1. Pz. / 304.	LXXII.	K.Gr. 76. / K.Gr. 15. / Sp.Vbd. 601 / K.Gr. 153.
		XXXXIX. Geb.	320. V.Gr. / 253.+16.ung. / Gr.Gen.Klatt / 3. Geb.+97. Jg.
		LIX.	/15. / 544. V.Gr. / 371. / 75. / 78. V.St. / 154.*
		XI.	4. Geb. / 10. Pz.Gr. / 16. Pz. / 254. / 17. Pz.
Mitte / 600. russ. / 2. SS-Pz. / »R«	17. / 18. SS-Pz. / Gr. / »H.W.«	XXXX. Pz.	68. / 1. Ski-Jg. / K.Gr. 168. / K.Gr. 45.
		XVII.	K.Gr. 31. / SS-Frw.Gr. / 359. / 208.
		Fest. Breslau	___
		VIII.	100. Jg. / K.Gr. 20. / Wff.Gr.SS / (estn. Nr. 1)
		LVII. Pz.	6. V.Gr. / 72. / 17.
		Gr. Kohlsdorfen	Div.Stb. z.b.V. 615 / Div.Nr. 464 / K.Gr. 545
		Pz.Kps. »G.D.«	1. Fsch.Pz. / »H.G.« / Pz.Gr.»Branden-burg«
	4. Pz. / K.Gr. 269	Kps.Gr. Gen.d.Art. Moser	20. Pz. / Div.Nr. 193 / Div.Nr. 404
		Fsch.Pz.Kps. »H.G.«	2. Fsch.Pz.Gr. »H.G.« / K.Gr. »Frunds-berg« / (Rst. 10. SS-Pz., »Frundsberg« / Fhr.Begl. 344)
		LXXXX.	464. / 469. / 404. / Kpf.Kdt.Chemnitz
		st. IV.	Kpf.Kdt.Dresden
	24.	Div. Nr. 405	
OB West / G	19. / Verbl. / z.Zt. / unbe-kannt	XVIII. SS	352. V.Gr. / 106. / 719. / 89.
		LXXX.	559. V.Gr. / 47. V.Gr. / 246. V.Gr. / 716.
		LXIV.	16. V.Gr. / 189.

Zahlenmäßige Übersicht der Divis.

Pz.Div.	11
Pz.Gr.	
Div.	4
I.D.	39
Jg.Div.	4
Geb. Div.	2
	60
Verb. Div.	1

Right table

Heeres-Gr.	Armeen	Korps	Div.
		XIII.	198. / 19. V.Gr. / 553. V.Gr.
	1. / Verbl. / z.Zt. / unbe-kannt	XIII. SS	38. SS-Gr. »Nibe-lungen« (Jun-kerschule Tölz) / 212. V.Gr. / 2. Geb. / 17. SS-Pz.Gr. »G.v.B.« / Div. Gr. v. Hohe / Div. z.b.V. 350
G		LXXXII.	361. / 416.
		Befh. Nordwest	K.Gr. MOk-West / RAD-Bef. / Verbd. IV / Höh.Pi.Kdr. XV
	Befh. Nordost		Vert. Ber. B'gaden-Salzburg
OB West		XII.	347. V.Gr. / 413. / Div.Gr. Bennicke
	7. / 2. Pz. / (in Zuführ.)	st. XIII.	11. Pz. / Pi.Brig. 655
		LXXXV. K.Gr.Bork	Kpf.Kdt.Passau / E. u. A.-Einh.
		IV. Flak-Kps.	Flak-Br. 508
	Armee Ligurien (LXXXXVII.) / 4.ital.Geb. »Monte Rosa« (o. 1. Rgt.)	LXXV.	5. Geb. / 2. ital. »Littorio« / 34.
		Kps.Lombardia	3. ital. Mar. »San. Marco« / F.Brig. 134. / 4. ital. Geb. »Monte Rosa«
C	14.	LI. Geb.	148. / 1. ital. »Italia« / 232. / 114. Jg. / 334. V.Gr.
OB Südwest		XIV. Pz.	94. / 8. Geb. / 65.
	10.	I. Fsch.	305. / 1. Fsch.Jg. / 278. V.Gr. / 4. Fsch.Jg. / 26. Pz.
		LXXVI. Pz.	98. V.Gr. / 362. / 42. Jg. / 162. (turk.)
		LXXIII.z.b.V.	Alarm-Einheiten

Zahlenmäßige Übersicht OB West

Pz.Div.	2
Pz.Gr.	1
Div.	
I.D.	21
Jg.Div.	—
Geb. Div.	1
	25 1/2

Zahlenmäßige Übersicht OB Südwest

Pz.Div.	2
Pz.Gr.	
Div.	2
I.D.	14
Jg.Div.	2
Geb. Div.	2
	21 1/2
Verb. Div.	4

Erläuterungen:
1/2 = Brig.
+ = E. u. A.-Divisionen

Zahlenmäßige Zusammenstellung wegen verschiedener Grundgliederungen und wechselnder Kampfkraft nur Anhalt!

Sa. 145 + 3/2 +

Order of Battle of the German forces 30 April 1945.

The military commandant of the city, Obersturmbannführer Graf von Egloffstein, received orders from panzer corps headquarters to prepare the city for all-round defense. There was a battalion of Volkssturm in the city under the command of Oblt. Jilski; it was to distinguish itself in the coming fighting. Elements of the Brandenburg Division's combat engineers oversaw the work on the defensive fortifications. Hauptmann Berghoff was appointed deputy commandant. The majority of the city's 15,000 inhabitants had already been evacuated. All the factories continued to operate at full capacity, however. Mayor Wenderoth had remained in the city to see to the needs of the civilians.

Late on 10th March the Red Army began pounding the bridgehead at Muskau with heavy artillery fire. The first attack struck the 1st Parachute-Panzer Division Hermann Göring. A Soviet rifle division attacked with powerful tank support, including several of the Josef Stalin type. After seven tanks had been knocked out the attack faded away.

In mid-March, under the command of Hauptmann Steidl, the 2nd Light Infantry Regiment Brandenburg undertook a large-scale raiding operation. The target was the "red house," which was occupied by Soviet troops. They had turned it into a small fortress which was joined to their lines by communications and combat trenches. Since minefields were expected, two squads of engineers were added to the assault group. Heavy 350-mm rocket launchers were to open fire on the "red house" to support the surprise attack.

During the night of 20th March Feldwebel Resch and his men, part of the first group, crossed the Neiße in inflatable boats into the small German-held bridgehead on the other side of the river. At 5 A.M. the Nebelweifer opened fire, filling the night with the shrieks and howls from their rockets. The first projectiles fell around the red house, while the artillery opened up on identified positions and bunkers. In the midst of this inferno Resch and his men ran toward the red house. They placed their explosive charges and took cover.

The red house exploded with a thunderous roar. Eleven Russians were pulled out of the trenches around the house and brought back as prisoners. While retiring to the river the assault team ran into a Russian minefield. Three men were badly wounded by the exploding mines. The rest of the assault team—without the prisoners, who had been left behind—reached the west bank of the Neiße. A total of five of the assault team's soldiers were killed during the course of the operation.

The next day large gaggles of Il-2 close-support aircraft flew over the Brandenburgers' front. The entire Brandenburg Division now lay before the Red Army's attack force. Both light infantry regiments were in the front line.

The Russian attack began on the afternoon of 15th April with the first artillery barrage. The next morning the Red Army attacked at first light; that Monday it took the offensive on the entire front. The enemy attempted to throw footbridges across the Neiße, which was only 15 meters wide at that point. The Russians were forced back by return fire and those that made it across were wiped out by a counterattack led by Leutnant Korte.

The Red Army resumed its attack in the late afternoon. Another crossing attempt was supported by heavy rocket fire. This time they succeeded in throwing a bridge across the Neiße. Under cover of heavy artillery, rocket and machine-gun fire, Russian units ran across the bridge onto the west bank of the river. The 2nd Light Infantry Regiment's 1st Company was forced to take cover. As soon as the enemy fire subsided, it attacked and drove the enemy back into the river. The next attempt by the Soviets to cross the river was also successful. Enemy troops broke into the German positions and decimated the 1st Regiment's III Battalion.

Major Steidl and his adjutant Leutnant Esser hurried forward and reached the First's command post. Lt. Huesker was ordered to lead an attack against the crossing point. While carrying out this order Huesker was killed by Russian barrage fire. There was fierce fighting with the Soviet forces and while the Germans were able to contain the bridgehead they could not eliminate it. The 1st Company's 1st Platoon under Ofw. Ascher held on. The reserve company under Major Renner, commander of the 2nd Light Infantry Regiment's II Battalion, was moved up and helped contain the bridgehead.

After this prelude the Red Army opened up its main offensive at the Neiße with a barrage that surpassed anything the Brandenburg Division had ever experienced. A hail of iron rained down on the bunkers. The artillery barrage, which included fire from the notorious Katyusha rocket launchers, lasted about three hours. When the barrage ended the Red Army attacked. They approached through the forest south of Kahlen Meile in dense masses, but also in smaller, fast-moving groups. Waiting for them there was I Battalion, 2nd Light Infantry Regiment under Major Steidl. The first T 34s had forded the Neiße. They drove west, planning to turn north in several kilometers and then encircle and destroy the Brandenburg Division.

The forest was the scene of horrible hand-to-hand combat. There "Pioneer Müller" and his assault pioneers destroyed the T 34s with Panzerfausts and explosive charges.

Standing ready at the von Arnim estate and castle was the Army Flak Battalion Brandenburg under Major Voshage. Voshage had already won the German Cross in Gold and he would receive the Knight's Cross for his actions here. He and his three flak eighty-eights withstood the Soviet assault. His other batteries had been assigned to the infantry regiments in the defense line. The Russian artillery concentrated on the castle and its large park in the center of the town of Wehrkirch. Voshage arranged with Major Müller that his engineers would fall back to the castle if they were dislodged from their positions.

Toward noon Major Steidl met Generalleutnant Schulte-Heuthaus, who had driven through heavy enemy fire to encourage his men at the front. The division commander ordered Major Steidl to fight his way through to Kaltwasser and once there to dig in and hold. Already there was Oberstleutnant Oesterwitz and II Battalion. The train and alert units had also fallen back toward Kaltwasser.

Soon after the Steidl unit arrived, a group of T 34s emerged from a wood to the right of the town and made straight for Kaltwasscr. The tanks were accompanied by infantry, some of who rode on the armored vehicles. The handful of German antitank guns opened fire. Smoke and flames showed that several tanks had been hit. Machine-gun fire chased the infantry off the tanks. Nevertheless it was not enough to stop the assault. The infantry were forced to pull back to the forest behind them, but they were surprised to find enemy tanks and infantry there too. The Renner Battalion was in a desperate situation; it fought desperately in an effort to stop the attack. "Vineyard hill" was defended by Oberleutnant Schlosser and his 2nd Assault Pioneer Company. Schlösser was shot and killed from point-blank range. A number of his men were also fatally hit. The wounded, some only able to crawl, tried to get to safety. They were picked up by the rest of the unit when it fell back. When evening fell the Russians were on the hill to stay and had surrounded the remaining pioneers.

The battle for Wehrkirch castle went on. "Pioneer Müller" and his men fought their way through to Lower-Wehrkirch; they retook the houses that had fallen to the Russians and chased them back to the station. The first Russian tanks had rammed a breach in the castle wall and drove inside. They were immediately attacked and destroyed by soldiers armed with demolition charges. Panzeifaust anti-tank weapons cracked and from ranges of 40 meters and less every shot was a direct hit. Major Voshage proved that he was also a master of the Panzerfaust by destroying two enemy tanks in rapid succession.

Soviet artillery continued to pound the park even though its own troops were there. The Russians pulled back toward the houses outside the castle park.

Forty assault pioneers under Hauptmann Müller reached the park and joined the defenders. The 3rd Flak Battery also arrived and was assigned a place in the all-round defense.

On the evening of that 16th April the Red Army also broke through the Neiße River line on a width of eight kilometers and advanced as far as 15 kilometers. The 1st Light Infantry Regiment was cut off; due west of the regiment's command post the Russians marched past about 1000 meters away and reached the village of Spree in the regiment's rear. Contact between regiment and division was severed. Major Bansen, the commanding officer, assembled the unit around the command post for a last stand. After giving the matter much consideration he issued the following order: "We are going to turn south and thus establish a new line. We are of no use to anyone here any more. The regimental command post will be the last to leave and will cover the withdrawal."

The enemy attacked with the same fury on 17th April. A fresh tank attack struck the castle at 3 A.M. The battle lasted several hours. Forty of the estimated 100 Soviet tanks were knocked out and the attack was beaten off before it reached the wall of the estate. The light and heavy anti-aircraft guns played a pivotal role in this defensive success, also a contribution was made by the pioneers with their close-attack weapons and the infantry with their Panzerfausts.

A fresh artillery barrage struck the castle at 9 A.M. The first preparations to retreat were made. Under the care of Medical Officer Dr. Braune, the wounded were first transferred to the wood west of the castle. At 1 P.M. an order came from division to evacuate the village and castle of Wehrkirch. Covered by the ever-watchful flak crews, the move was made to the next prepared position in the wood. The new halt line extended from Niesky to Neuhoff and along the road to Rietschen.

Niesky was found already swarming with plundering Russians; they were blasted out of the town. The retreat from Weißwasser also took place on 17th April. Early the next day every defensive position reported enemy tanks approaching. The Führer order to "hold at any price" could not be ignored. And so soldiers from the Brandenburg regiment had to go down fighting in the towns of Niesky, Kodersdorf, Ullersdorf and Spreefurt to allow the others to establish new positions. The corps command post in Spreefurth castle was prepared for all-round defense. The IIa and adjutant of the corps, Major Bethke, scraped together several alert units and, armed with only a pistol, attacked. Hit by several bullets, he fell to the ground but then got up and shouted for his men to follow him. But in the face of the murderous fire they all stayed in cover. After advancing a few more meters Major Bethke fell in the heavy defensive fire from the enemy.

Major Bethke was brought back after darkness fell. Still alive, he was operated on immediately by the 2nd Corps Medical Company Groß-deutschland, but in vain. This courageous officer died under the hands of the doctors fighting to save his life.

The division commander said,

Theo Bethke is an example to us all of the kind of soldier one rarely meets. He was a person with an unsurpassed strength of character. He first fought in the Panzer-Grenadier Division Großdeutschland. Then he came to us and became not just a member of our staff personnel but also a friend to us all, including me. Everyone who knew Theo Bethke, especially me, mourns his death.

HOERNLEIN, General der Infanterie.

Early on 19 April 1945 the 20th Panzer Division drove up in the rear of the Brandenburg Division. After giving up Kodersdorf and Ullersdorf the 2nd Brandenburg Light Infantry Regiment assembled in the Altmark area next to the 20th Panzer Division and linked up with Panzer Group von Wietersheim.

The 1st Light Infantry Regiment, in the north with the group of forces around the 615th Special Purpose Division, left that unit, withdrew from the Daubitz and Rietschen areas, and occupied a new defense line near Spreefurth. An attack was scheduled with the 20th Panzer Division for 20th April, to cut off the enemy forces that had broken through to the west. However, elements of the 2nd Light Infantry Regiment took part in an attack by Panzer Group von Wietersheim against Ullersdorf and Jank-endorf. Both villages were retaken despite fierce resistance from a Polish division and units of the Committee for a Free Germany. The villages had been burnt to the ground.

In Niesky the pioneers and other partial units under Hauptmann Müller-Rochholz were still fighting. After the Russians moved in reinforce-ments in German trucks, the three still-serviceable assault guns were deployed at the critical points. After moving ahead 250 meters, one of these was able to fire high-explosive shells directely into the Soviet infantry as the trucks were unloaded.

A short while later an attack by a unit of Cossacks was smashed before it could begin. The afternoon attack continued with hourly intervals. Under the command of an unidentified Oberleutnant, the three assault guns waited until the enemy came into view. With their guns fully depressed, they opened fire with HE rounds from just 140 meters away. This attack was literally blown to pieces.

This day had seen both the Soviets and the Germans take heavy casualties. That evening Hptm. Müller-Rochholz and his engineers broke out. The three assault guns towed trucks whose tires had been shot up. The 80 wounded were placed in the trucks.

The breakout began at 2 A.M. on 21st April. After the last bursts of fire in the direction of the Russian positions they set off. Federal Road 115 was reached. The engineers retreated through the Russians who were settling in. At the intersection of Federal Road 115 and the road to Kodersdorfer See there was a Russian machine-gun. It opened fire but was immediately silenced by a Panzerfaust round. Then, suddenly, a long Russian convoy came toward them from the opposite direction.

Müller-Rochholz ordered his men off the road. Miraculously the Russians in their vehicles drove past the soldiers and assault guns and disappeared in the direction of the front. Oedernitz was reached at dawn. A Russian battery still barred the way to the German lines. Müller-Rochholz gave the decisive order for the armored troop carriers and assault guns to break through, towing the trucks.

The assault guns blasted the enemy battery as they passed. They reached the positions of the 20th Panzer Division's 20th Pioneer Battalion and temporary safety. While the rest of the men dropped from exhaustion, Müller-Rochholz hurried to the division command post in Bischdorf and reported his return.

The two other attacks, whose preparations were already mentioned, were a success. More than 50 enemy tanks were knocked out, over 100 vehicles destroyed and much material captured, including food and gasoline. The units supplemented their vehicle pools with captured American-made trucks. Weißenberg was stormed by the 1st Light Infantry Regiment. The Russians fled the town in panic. Hundreds of panye wagons rolled across the plain, where they were caught and destroyed by the German guns. Approximately 1,500 enemy vehicles were counted destroyed.

But this last success did not alter the fact that the area around Bautzen could no longer be held. The corps was now to turn south around Bautzen and go into attack positions west of the city. When several other divisions attacked toward Bautzen, it was to carry out its own attack to the north on the left wing.

The assault pioneers under Hptm. Müller-Rochholz were there once again, having gone into position north of the Bautzen-Dresden highway. They were to attack with Panzer Group von Wietersheim and reach Storcha with its famous white church.

The 20th and 21st Panzer Divisions attacked at 1am on 26 April 1945. Their objective was Bautzen. The Panzer-Grenadier Division Brandenburg drove north on the left wing of the attack and cut off the Soviet spearhead driving toward Dresden.

These battles spared Dresden from the avalanche of Soviet tanks. During the night the Brandenburg Division was relieved by elements of the 269th Infantry Division. It subsequently drove to rest quarters near Ottendorf, Leppersdorf and Lomnitz.

On 1st May the division left the Panzer Corps Großdeutschland and a short while later drove back toward the Erz Mountains to occupy defensive positions there. The roads were clogged with countless vehicles. New positions were first occupied in front of the Elbsandstein Mountains and shortly thereafter on the mountain crests. The Panzer-Grenadier Division Brandenburg moved into positions in the Olmütz area. There, on 8th May, the men of the division heard on the radio that Germany's armed forces had surrendered unconditionally. The commander of the Panzer Corps Großdeutschland now gave the order for his units to withdraw to the Oder ahead of the Soviets, cross over and surrender to the Americans.

THE END OF THE PANZER-GRENADIER DIVISION BRANDENBURG
From the unloading station in Dresden, which was still in German hands, on 1 May 1945 the division rolled through the protectorate of Bohemia and Moravia past Glatz and Prague roward Olmütz. The division was preceded by the Ib, General Staff Major Spaeter. He had with him a few vehicles and specialists to make the necessary arrangements for a smooth arrival of the division at Olmütz.

Generalmajor Schulte-Heuthaus' order read: "In addition to the tasks associated with detraining, you are to find out as much as possible about the division's next mission."

After dropping off the specialists in Olmütz, therefore, he drove directly to the command post of IL Mountain Corps that was in the area of Mahrisch-Ostrau.

The division arrived in Olmütz on 2nd and 3rd May. At that time the troops of the Red Army were attempting to break through the front of IL Mountain Corps, seal off the last avenue of retreat to the west and bag the troops still on their way to Olmütz.

From the northeast Soviet artillery had been firing into the city, through which an endless stream of refugees was passing, since 2nd May. The mostly horse-drawn vehicles made slow progress. In order to hold this last bastion against the Russians, Army Group Schörner and its chief-of-staff, Generalleutnant von Natzmer, sent the Brandenburg Division there to cover the retreat of the entire corps.

Why did the Brandenburgers go into this final battle, which must end badly, without complaint? Hptm. Müller-Rochholz gave the answer:

The war would not last much longer, then there would be chaos. In these days we wanted to remain true to ourselves until the last second and see our fate through to the end. The spirit of our battalion, our comrades and our dead obligated us. Our shield of honor was to remain pure to the end. No one ran away! All our battles had proved that we did not go under if we stood together as one man.

So it was with us. To the last order.

The bulk of the division reached Olmütz. Its objective was to allow German infantry units to pass through the city by fending off all enemy attacks. Since the highest-ranking officer in Olmütz was General Staff Major Spaeter, he assumed command to cover the retreat of the 1st panzer Army. When Oberstleutnant Oesterwitz then arrived with his infantry and the Steidl battalion worked its way as far as Tscheitzitsch, the old confidence returned. And finally on 5th May the Brandenburg Army Flak Battalion under Major Voshage arrived and the 1st Light Infantry Regiment detrained at Stefanau.

The last battle began, and even Generalfeldmarschall Schörner's order of the day of 5 May 1945 could not alter the fact that signs of disintegration were growing. The oath "our discipline and the weapons in our hands serve as our pledge to go out of this war with bravery," was not of much use. Nevertheless, on 6th May the 1st Light Infantry Regiment battled Soviet heavy tanks as they neared Stefanau. The final battle for Olmütz, the "fortress without a garrison," began early on 7th May. According to the rumors, the Brandenburg Division was to cover a 100-kilometer retreat the next day. As well, on the afternoon of 7th May all unnecessary baggage was destroyed, secret papers were burned, and on the early morning of 8th May the Brandenburg Division moved out. It drove all day and reached Bistrau. Czech partisans were already active there. That evening both signals officers of the 2nd Light Infantry Regiment, Oberleutnants Schmalbruch and Brauschmidt, intercepted radio reports which repeatedly used the word surrender. Oberstleutnant Oesterholt reported this to Generalleutnant Schulte-Heuthaus, who issued the following order:

"To the corps: Jodi and Keitel have betrayed us. All vehicles, weapons, ammunition, tanks and assault guns are to be destroyed immediately. The Panzer-Grenadier Division Brandenburg is to retain only the vehicles necessary for the transport of personnel and small arms. The division is to assemble at Bistrau and break through the Bavarian forest."

This order was sent by radio on 8 May 1945 at 6:05 P.M. A half hour later the explosions rang out. Major Spaeter issued fuel to the trucks and troop carriers for the long journey west. Then they set off. The road leading to the west was clogged with traffic. The Brandenburgers passed wrecked, burning vehicles that had been pushed off to the side of the road. The going was faster on a side road. Then they reached a broad asphalt road. Not until outside Freudenthal was the road blocked again. Armored troop carriers of I (APC) Battalion, 1st Light Infantry Regiment pushed the obstacle aside and the drive continued.

Deutschbrod proved to be held by the enemy. Acting on radioed orders from the division commander, the division detoured north. Several units did not receive the message, as a result of which (he division became split up. It was at this moment that Soviet close-support aircraft struck, sewing death and chaos. A number of officers and men went ahead by motorcycle-sidecar, north in the direction of Casslau. The road to Casslau was clogged by columns of vehicles. Heavy enemy fire from Casslau forced another detour.

On 9th May several units continued to search the area for a way to freedom. On 10th May the division finally broke through the Soviet front south of Taschaslau into the Tabor area. The general led the way in an armored troop carrier. The troops arrived in Beneschau, where, already marching in long columns, they were flanked by Soviet guards troops and barricaded in a courtyard. All the officers had already been arrested and were on their way to captivity in the east. The last survivors would not see home again for eleven years.

The Brandenburg Division, which had finally been reunited and then suffered through the final months of a pitiless struggle, was gone forever. Its story had become part of the history of the Second World War. The division, which for a long time consisted only of a few companies, lost approximately 30,000 men in this struggle. It had fought, had won and lost, on every front—indeed all over the world. It was misused like the other divisions, but it never lost its honor and never surrendered, not even during the final, difficult weeks of the war against an opponent with a huge superiority in weapons, men and material.

The Brandenburger fighting units, especially the Panzer-Grenadier Regiment Brandenburg, fought heroically in the final weeks of the war in order that hundreds of thousands of refugees might escape from German's eastern territories to the west—and ultimately also to save their own lives. In the end many had to endure years of captivity as prisoners of the Russians and only a few returned alive. Such was not the case for the senior officers of the Abwehr, however.

Like Generalmajor Reinhard Gehlen, the head of the Foreign Armies East department, who packed his files into 50 crates in order to hand them over to the western Allies and continue working in his chosen field, all of the remaining leaders of the Abwehr (with the exception of Admiral Canaris and some of his associates) escaped imprisonment and instead joined the intelligence services to which they had fled.

It is no wonder then that high-grade master spies found shelter and new work and bread in both the German Democratic and Federal German Republics (East and West Germany, in the USSR and in USA. They simply picked up where they had left off and now did most of their spying against Germany.

All of those who had secretly conducted espionage against Germany during the Second World War now surfaced on the Soviet side. Among them was their chief spy Martin Bormann. In the western part of the divided Germany all of those who had been taken in by the western Allies went back to work, now operating against East Germany and the USSR in order to learn their secrets.

The names were known to both sides. But neither side ever made an attempt to expose the other in this regard, because then the entire apparatus of the intelligence services in east and west would collapse like a house of cards and it would have become obvious that all of those services were nothing more than freeloaders. The results of this mutual spying were zero. Now and then a counter-spy was found in "one's own camp" and was exchanged for another in the enemy camp.

Those who were left by the wayside and had to pay the bill were the Brandenburgers in their many services. They pulled the chestnuts from the fire, they risked their lives in feats which went down in the history of the Second World War.

Their reward was imprisonment and death, jails and years of interrogations. They did not change sides and for that they simply had to pay—many of them with their health, but even more with their own lives.

Whoever reads this history of the Brandenburgers should not forget that these events, which took place in a global arena, occurred at a time when every German—in or outside Germany—was proud to serve in the German armed forces. And so they came: from Africa and Asia, from South America and other continents, often in a sensational odyssey to Germany, out of the conviction that that land, their homeland, needed them and that they had the damned duty and obligation, to heed the call.

They had no way of knowing that they—like all other members of the German armed forces—would ultimately be misused and sent to the slaughter by their leaders.

They fought, they triumphed—and lost!

The fact that all the files of the OKW department Ausland/Abwehr II "went missing" during the Nuremberg Trials is based in the nature of the matter. They had, as several members of the Abwehr sarcastically put it, "become lost".

Further proof that all the remaining files of this type remain under lock and key is provided by the "memoirs" of the former head of the German Intelligence Service, General Gehlen, from which a curious reader can gather little more than hot air.

And in this attitude East and West are in complete accord.

APPENDIX I

Oberkommando
der Kriegsmarine

MPA I Nr. 1454

(Bitte in der Antwort vorstehendes Geschäftszeichen
des Datum und kurzen Inhalt angeben)

An
Marineoberkommando Ostsee,

K i e l

Berlin W, den 21. März 19

Marineoberkommando Ostsee
- Offizierpersonalabteilung -

P. Eing. 27. März 194

12782

Der Oberbefehlshaber der Kriegsmarine hat dem Admiral
C a n a r i s am 10. März 1944 mitgeteilt, daß er seine Ent-
lassung aus dem aktiven Wehrdienst mit dem 30. Juni 1944 her-
beiführen wird.
Das Fürsorge- und Versorgungsverfahren ist einzuleiten.
Admiral Canaris wird zur Verfügung der Kriegsmarine ge-
stellt werden. Eine Wiederverwendung ist nicht vorgesehen.

Im Auftrage

The CIC of the Kriegsmarine dismissed Admiral Canaris on 30 June 1944.

APPENDIX II

Kp.Chef: Oblt. Zülch
Kp.Arzt: Ob.Arzt Dr. Schmid
Kp.Trupp: Feldw. Ladendorff

1. Halbkompanie

Führer: Lt. Lau
I. Einsatz: Lt. Seuberlich
1. Schützengruppe
2. Schützengruppe
Pioniergruppe
Panzerbüchsentrupp
Flammenwerfertrupp
le. Granatwerfertrupp

II. Einsatz: Obfw. Schmalbruch
Gliederung wie I. Einsatz
Halbkompanietroß:
Feldw. Wolfsberger

2. Halbkompanie

Führer: Lt. Steidl
I. Einsatz: Lt. Pils
1. Schützengruppe
2. Schützengruppe
Pioniergruppe
Panzerbüchsentrupp
Flammenwerfertrupp
le. Granatwerfertrupp

II. Einsatz: Lt. Lorencuk
Gliederung wie I. Einsatz
Halbkompanietroß:
Obfeldw. Goller

schwerer Zug:
Führer: Obfeldw. Martl
s.MG-Zug: Feldw. Ortner
s.GrW.-Zug: Objg. Majoni
Pz-Büchse 41: Feldw. Stemmberger

Kompanietroß: Hptfeldw. Röttges
Zahlmeister: Obzahlmstr. Stein

Legionärszüge

Kommandeure:
Hauptmann G. Pinkert
Oberleutnant Rosenow
III. Bataillon (Abk. III./1. Rgt. Brandenburg)
(mit 9.—12. Kompanie)
Kommandeure:
Hauptmann Froboese
Oberleutnant Wandrey

2. Regiment Brandenburg
(hervorgegangen aus dem II. Btl. des Lehr-Rgt. „Brandenburg" zbV 800)
Heimatstab: Baden bei Wien, später Admont
Regimentskommandeure: Oberstleutnant von Kobelinsky
Oberstleutnant Pfeiffer
Regimentseinheiten: 1 Kompanie der Nachr.Abt. Brandenburg
(zugeteilt)
1 Batterie (1944)
I. Bataillon (Abk. I./2. Rgt. Brandenburg)
(mit 1.—3. Kompanie u. 4. (Leg)Kp. — später abgegeben)
Kommandeur: Hauptmann Weithoener
II. Bataillon (Abk. II./2. Rgt. Brandenburg)
(mit 5.—7. Kompanie u. 8. (Leg)Kp. — später abgegeben)
Kommandeur: Hauptmann Oesterwitz
III. Bataillon (Abk. III./2. Rgt. Brandenburg)
(mit 9.—11. Kompanie, 12. Kp. nicht aufgestellt)
Kommandeur: Hauptmann Renner

3. Regiment Brandenburg
(hervorgegangen aus dem III. Btl. des Lehr-Rgt. „Brandenburg" zbV 800)
Heimatstab: Düren/Rhld.
Regimentskommandeur: Oberstleutnant F. Jacobi
Regimentseinheit: 1 Kompanie der Nachr.Abt. Brandenburg
(zugeteilt)
I. Bataillon (Abk. I./3. Rgt. Brandenburg)
(mit 1.—3. Kompanie u. 4. (Leg)Kp. — aufgelöst Juli 1943)
Btl.-Führer: Oberleutnant Kriegsheim
II. Bataillon (Abk. II./3. Rgt. Brandenburg)
(mit 5.—8. Kompanie und Ital.Kp. „M")
Kommandeur: Hauptmann Bansen
III. Bataillon (Abk. III./3. Rgt. Brandenburg)
(mit 9.—12. Kompanie)
Kommandeur: Hauptmann Grawert

The company commanded by Oblt. Zülch with the 5/BR near Nikolayev.

APPENDIX III

RECIPIENTS OF THE KNIGHT'S CROSS

(includes soldiers who won the decoration before or after joining the Brandenburgers)

Obit. Eckhard Afueldt
Knight's Cross on 8/5/1945

CO II/2nd Light Infantry Regiment

Uffz. Albrecht Bauer
Cross on 27/4/1945

Front-line Reconnaissance Knight's Detachment 202

Maj. Wilhelm Brockerhoff
Knight's Cross on 8/5/1945

CO Armored Artillery Rgt

Oberst Erich von Bruckner
Knight's Cross on 11/3/1945

CO 1st Light Infantry Regiment

Lt. Adrian Baron von Foelkersam

I/800th Special Purpose Construction Training Regiment

Lt.z.S. Heinrich Garbers
Knight's Cross on 1/11/1944

Leader of a special sea operation

Obit. Siegfried Grabert
Knight's Cross on 10/6/1941

Leader of a special unit of the 800th Special Purpose Construction Training Battalion

Hptm. Karl-Edmund Gartenfeld
Knight's Cross on 3/2/1943

Staffelfuhrer in the Reconnaissance Group of the Commander-in-Chief of the Luftwaffe

Hptm. Erich Haut
Knight's Cross on 10/5/43

CO I/PGR 86, KIA on 2/9/44 near Raska, Serbia

Obit. Hans-Wolfram Knaak
Knight's Cross on 3/1 1/1943

CO 8/800th Special Purpose Construction Training Regiment

Hptm. Friedrich von Koehnen
Knight's Cross on 16/9/1943

CO III/4th Regiment, KIA on 20/8/44 near Visegrad, Croatia

Obit. Erhard Lange
Knight's Cross on 15/1/1943

Company commander of a special unit of the 800th Special Purpose Construction Training Regiment

355

Lt. Werner Lau	Platoon commander in 5/800th Special Purpose Construction Training Regiment
Lt. Hellmut von Leipzig Cross on 28/4/1945	Platoon commander in the Knight's "BB" Armored Reconnaissance Battalion
Hptm. Friedrich MUller-Rochholz Knight's Cross on 8/5/1945	CO Armored Assault Pioneer Battalion
Obit. Karl-Heinz Oesterwitz Knight's Cross on 30/4/1943 Oak Leaves on 10/2/1945	CO 7/800th Special Purpose Construction Training Regiment while CO of 2nd Light Infantry Regiment
Lt. Ernst Prochaska Knight's Cross on 16/9/1942	CO 8/800th 800th Special Purpose Construction Training Regiment. KIA 9/8/42 near Maykop.
Genmaj. Heinz Piekenbrock Knight's Cross on 4/5/1944	CO of the 208th Inf.Div. (After leaving the Abwehr)'
Oberst Alexander von Pfuhlstein Knight's Cross on 17/8/1942	CO 154th Inf. Rgt.
ObIt. Erich Roseke Knight's Cross on 14/4/1945	CO 9/1st Light Infantry Regiment
Hptm. Hans-Siegfried Graf von Rothkirch und Trach Knight's Cross on 4/20/1944	2./31st Panzer Regiment as commander of I Battalion 26th Panzer Regiment
Obstlt. Theodor Rowehl Knight's Cross on 27/9/1940	CO Reconnaissance Group of the Commander-in-Chief of the Luftwaffe (operations for the Abwehr)
Rittm. Helmuth Spaeter Knight's Cross on 28/7/1943	CO 2/Großdeutschland Armored Reconnaissance Battalion
Obit. Franz-Karl Spielvogel Knight's Cross on 4/9/1942	2./Artillery Regiment GD
Hptm. Konrad Steidl Knight's Cross on 26/1/44	CO I/2nd Light Infantry Regiment
Obstlt. Hermann Schulte-Heuthaus Knight's Cross on 23/1/1942	CO 25th Motorcycle Battalion
Major Werner Voshage Knight's Cross on 8/5/1945	CO Brandenburg Army Flak Battalion
Obit. Wilhelm Walther Knight's Cross on 24/6/1940	Patrol leader in 4/800th Special Purpose Construction Training Battalion

Obit. Max Wandrey   CO 11/1st Light Infantry Regiment
  Knight's Cross on 9/1/1944
Oak Leaves on 16/3/1945   while CO II/1st Light Infantry Regi-
                                     ment (died from wounds in hospital
                                     in Krusinwitz, Saxony on
                                     21/2/1945)

RECIPIENTS OF THE GERMAN CROSS IN GOLD

Oblt. Hans-Gerhard Bansen	9/7/1942
Oberarzt Theodor Becker	31/1/1945
ObJag. Robert Breitkreuz	2/5/1944
Hptm. Wilhelm Brockerhoff	9/10/1942
Oberstlt. Erich von Bruckner	25/3/1942
Obit. Josef Burggraf	16/10/1944
Oblt. Ernst-Eberhard Frey	9/10/1944
Hptm. Gustav Froboese	???
Fw. Erich Glaser	22/3/1945
Maj. Dr. Kurt Gloger	21/3/1943
Lt. Karl-Heinz Gohlke	30/3/1945
Oblt. Erich Haut	14/3/1942
Hptm. Max Horlbeck	19/12/1943
Ofw. Erich Horsthemke	23/9/1944
Hptm. Werner John	2/4/1943
Oblt. Ernst Kiefer	13/12/1944
Oblt. Wolfram Kirchner	8/7/1944
Lt. Karl Klein	5/6/1942
Oberst Erwin Lahousen Edler von Vivremont	July 1944
Rittm. Konrad von Leipzig	20/5/1944
Lt. Alois Meixner	10/10/1944
Oblt. Karl-Heinz Oesterwitz	13/12/1942
Hptm. Gerhard Pinckert	???
Obstlt. Alexander von Pfuhlstein	4/2/1942
Oblt. Erwin Rocseke	22/3/1945
Lt. Hans-Erich Seuberlich	24/4/1943
Lt. Dr. Walter Slama	10/1/1943
FhjObfw. Willi Streich	9/3/1945
Rittm. Erwin Thun-Hohenstein	15/9/1943
Ofw. Heinz-Willi Toppner	15/12/1944
Hptm. Werner Voshage	29/3/1945
Lt. Dietrich Walter	12/3/1942
Lt. Max Wandrey	13/5/1942

Oblt. Walther Wilhelm,
patrol leader, 4th Company,
Construction Training Battalion
Brandenburg. RK on 24 June 1940.

Oblt. Siegfried Grabert,
leader special detachment of the
Special Purpose Training Regiment
Brandenburg. RK on 10 June 1940, EL
on 6 November 1943.

Oblt. Helmut Beck-Broichsitter,
commander 14th Company,
Infantry Regiment GD. RK
on 4 September 1940.

GenMaj. Dietrich von Saucken, commander 4th Panzer Division. RK on 6 January 1942, EL on 22 August 1943, S on 31 January 1944, B on 8 May 1945.

Oberstleutnant Rainer Stahel, commander 99th Flak Regiment (mot.). RK on 18 January 1942, EL on 4 January 1943, S on18 July 1944.

Oberstleutnant Hermann Schulte-Heuthaus, commander 25th Motorcycle Battalion. RK on 23 January 1942.

Oberst Alexander von Pfuhlstein, commander 154th Infantry Regiment (first commander of the Brandenburg Division). RK on 17 August 1942.

Lt. Adrian von Fölkersam, adjutant on staff of 1 Battalion, Special Purpose Training Regiment Brandenburg. RK on14 September 1942.

Lt. Ernst Prochaska, 8th Company, Special Purpose Training Regiment 800 Brandenburg. RK on 16 September 1942. Killed on 9 August 1942 at the Maykop bridge.

Oblt. Hans-Wolfram Knaak, commander 8th Company, Special Purpose Training Regiment Brandenburg. RK on 3 November 1942. KIA 26 June 1941 near Dvinsk.

Lt. Werner Lau, 5th Company, Special Purpose Training Regiment Brandenburg. RK on 9 December 1942.

Oblt. Erhard Lange, commander of a battle group, Brandenburg Special Detachment. RK on 15 January 1943.

Obit. Karl-Heinz Osterwitz,
7th Company, Special Purpose
Training Regiment 800 Brandenburg.
RK on 30 April 1943, EL on 10
February 1945 (as Obersleutnant
commander Lt.Inf.Rgt, 2
Brandenburg).

Major Otto-Ernst Remer,
commander I Battalion, Grenadier
Regiment GD. RK on 18 May 1943, EL
on 12 November 1943 (as commander
of the Fhr.Begl.Div. GD).

Rittmeister Helmuth Spaeter,
commander of 2nd Company,
armored Recon. Battalion GD (later in
general staff of Brandenburg Division).
RK on 28 July 1943.

Oblt. Max Wandrey, commander 11th Company, 1st Light Infantry Regiment Brandenburg. RK on 9 January 1944, EL on 16 March 1945.

Hptm. Konrad Steidl, commander of I Battalion, 2nd Light Infantry Regiment Brandenburg. RK on 26 January 1944.

Major Hellmuth Maeder, commander III Battalion, 522nd Infantry Regiment (last commander Fhr.Gren.Div. GD). RK on 5 April 1942, EL on 27 August 1944.

Hptm. Hans-Siegfried von Rotkirch und Trach, commander I Battalion, 26th Pioneer Regiment. RK on 4 October 1944.

GenMaj. Kurt Hähling, commander 126th Infantry Regiment (former commander of Special Purpose Training Regiment 800 Brandenburg). RK on 2 March 1945.

Oberst Erich Brückner, commander Brandenburg Light Infantry Rgt. RK on 11 March 1945.

Oblt. Eckard Afheldt, commander II
Battalion, 2nd Light Infantry Regiment
Brandenburg. RK on 17 March 1945.

Oblt. Erich Röseke, commander
9th Company, 1st Light Infantry
Regiment Brandenburg. RK
on 14 January 1945.

Lt. Hellmut von Leipzig, platoon
commander in the Armored Recon.
Battalion Brandenburg. RK
on 28 April 1945.

Hptm. Friedrich Müller-Rochholz, commander Armored Assault Pioneer Battalion Brandenburg. RK on 8 May 1945.

BIBLIOGRAPHY

Abshagen, Karl-Heinz   Canaris—Patriot und Weltbüger, Stuttgart 1959

Ibid   Verrat im Zweiten Weltkrieg, Düsseldorf 1969

Alman, Karl und Frans Beekman   Kampf um die Festung Holland, Herford 1978

Bartz, Karl   Die Tragödie der deutschen Abwehr, Salzburg 1955

Baumann, Felix   Die Weltkriegsspionage, München 1931

Bertold, Will   Division Brandenburg, Bad Worishofen 1950

Borcher, Will   Krieg ohne Menschlichkeit, Wackersberg 1975

Bovery, Margret   Der Verrat im 20. Jahrhundert, Hamburg 1956

Brissaud, Andre   Canaris—Fürst der deutschen Abwehr oder Meister des Doppelspiels, Frankfurt 1978

Brown, Anthony Cave   Fie unsichtbare Front, München 1976

Buchheit, Gert   Die Anfange des Regiments Brandenburg, Z.S. 4/1969 und 1/1970

Ibid   Der deutsche Geheimdienst—Die Geschichte der militäfischen Abwehr, München 1966

Ibid   Die anonyme Macht—Aufgaben, Metoden, Erfahrungen der Geheimdienste, Frankfurt/Main 1969

Ibid   Soldatentum und Redellion, Rastatt 1961

Carell, Paul   Die Wüstenfüchse, Hamburg 1961
Charisius, Albrecht und Julius Mader   Nicht langer geheim—Aufbau, System und Arbeitweise des imperialistischen deutschen Geheimdienstes, Berlin-Ost 1969
Cookridge, E. H.   Karriere Dopplagent, Oldenburg-Hamburg 1968
Dallin, David J.   Die Sowjetspionage, Köln 1956
Deacon, Richard   A History of the British Secret Service, London 1969
Detwiler, Donald S.   Hitler, France und Gibraltar, Wiesbaden 1969
Dulles, Allen, Welsh   Verschwörung in Deutschland, Kassel 1948
Faber du Faur   Macht und Ohnmacht, Stuttgart 1953
Farago, Ladislaus   Das Spiel der FUsche, Berlin 1972
Flicke, W. F.   Die Tote Kapelle, Hilden 1949
Foote, Alexander   Handbuch für Spione, Darmstadt 1954
Garby-Czerniawski, Roman   The Big Network, London 1961
Eppler, John   Rommel ruft Kairo, Gütersloh 1959
Gehlen, Reinhard   Der Dienst, Mainz-Wiesbaden 1961
Gerken, Richard   Spione unter uns, Donauwüprth 1965
Giskes, H.J.   Spione Uverspielen Spione, Hamburg 1949
Gisevius, Hans Bernd   Bis zum bitteren Ende, Hamburg 1947
Gramont, Sancho de   Der geheime Krieg, Wien-Berlin-Stuttgart 1962
Grunfeld, Frederick V.   Die deutsch Tragödien, Hamburg 1975
Gunzenhauser, Max   Geschichte des Geheimen Machrichten dienstes, Stuttgart 1968
Hagen, Walter   Die geheime Front, Linz 1950
Höher, Wolfgang   Agent 2996 enthUllt, Berlin-Ost 1954

Hohne, Heinz	Kennwort Direktor—Die Geschichte der Roten Kapelle, Frankfurt/Main 1970
Ibid	Pullach intern, Hamburg 1971
Ibid	Canaris—patriot im Zwielicht, MUnchen 1976
Internationaler Militärgerischtshof	Der Prozeß gegen die Hauptkriegsverbrecher vor dem Internationalen Gerichtshof, Nürnberg 1946–47
Jaus, Otto	Die Brandenburger Freiwilligen in: Ostereichischer Soldatenkalender 1975
Jong, Louis de	Die deutsche 5. Kolonne in Zweiten Weltkrieg, Stuttgart 1959
Jordan, G. R.	Sowjets siegten durch Spione, Gottingen 1960
Kern, Erich	Verrat an Deutschland, Gottingen 1963
Kiel, Heinz	Canaris zwischen den Fronten, Bremerhaven 1950
Krigsheim, Herbert	Getarnt, getauscht und doch getreu—Die geheimnisvollen Brandenburger, Berlin 1958
Kugler, Raodolf	Die Küstenjagerabteilung Brandenburg, in MS an den Autor
Kurowski, Franz	Leros, das "Verdun" in der Ägäis, Rastatt 1978
Kurowski, Franz	Brückenkopf Tunesien, Leoni 1975
Kurowski Franz	Von der Poliseigruppe Wecke z.b.V zum Fallschirmpanzerkorps "Hermann Göring", Osnabruck 1994.
Ibid	Endkampf in Afrika, Berg 1983
Ibid	Mit Rommel in der Wüste, Stuttgart 1975
Ibid	So war der Zweite Weltkrieg, Lioni 1989-95; 7 Bände
Ibid	Endstation Kaukasus, Elberfeld 1962

Ibid	Gespräche mit Mitkämpern 1948-1993
Leverkuehn, Paul	Der geheime Nachrichtendienst der deutschen Wehrmacht im Kriege, Frankfurt/Main 1951
Liss, Ulrich	Westfront 1939-1940, Neckargemünd 1959
Lissner, Ivar	Mein gefabrlicher Weg, München 1975
Loeff, W.	Spionage—Aus den Papieren eines Abwehr-offiziers, Stuttgart 1950
Mader, Julius	Spionagegenerale sagen aus, Berlin-Ost 1970
Moravec, Frantisek	Master of Spies, London 1975
Müller, Josef	Bis zur letsten Konsequenz, München 1975
Mulinero, Arturo	Unternehmen Silberstaub, das Platinkommando in Kolumbien, Leoni 1984
Nemis, Fred	Brandenburger in Nordafrika, Rastatt 1965
Reile, Oskar	Geheime Westfront, Die Abwehr 1935–1945, München 1962
Ibid	Geheime Ostfront—Die deutsche Abwehr in Osten 1921–1945, München-Wels 1963
Ibid	Macht un Ohnmacht der Geheimdienste, München 1968
Riess, Kurt	Total Espionage, New York 1941
Ibid	Der deutsche Faschismus in Latein-amerika 1939–1945,
Ritter, Nikolaus	Deckname Dr. Rantzau, Hamburg 1972
Schellenberg, Walter	Aufzeichnungen, Wiesbaden 1956
Ibid	Memoiren, Wiesbaden 1980
Schramm, Wilhelm von	Geheimdienst im Zweiten Weltkrieg, München-Wien 1974
Schreider, Joseph	Das war das Englandspiel, Müchen 1950

Schröder, Bern Philipp	Deutschland und der Mittlere Osten im Zweiten Weltkrieg, Frankfurt-Zürich 1975
Schulze-Holthus, Julius	Frührot in Iran, Eßüngen 1950
Skorzeny, Otto	Deutsch Kommandos in Zweiten Weltkrieg, Kömigswinter 1973
Spaeter, Helmut	Die Brandenburger, Eine Kommandotruppe z.b.V., Müchen 1978
Ibid	Geschlichte des Panzerkorps "Großdeutschland", Duisburg 1960
Stehlin, Paul	Auftrag in Berlin, Berlin 1965
Steffens, Hans von	Salaam, Neckargemünd 1960
Stephan, Enno	Geheimauftrag Irland 1939–1945, Oldenburg 1961
Strong, Sir Kenneth	Geheimdienstchef in Krieg und Frieden, Wien- Hamburg 1966
Ibid	Die Geheimdienstträger, Wien-Hamburg 1971
Stahl, R.W.	Geheimgeschwader HK 200, Die Wahrheit nach über 30 Jahren, Stuttgart 1977
Thorwarld, Jiirgen	Der Fall Pastorius, Stuttgart 1953
Thieke, Wilhelm	Der Kaukasus und das Öl, Osnabrück 1970
Töpelmann, Heinz	Die deutsche Kompanie, Berlin 1963
Wedemeyer, Albert C.	Wedemeyer Reports, New York 1956
Wheatly, Ronald	Operation Sea Lion, Oxford 1958
Whitting, Charles	Canaris, New York 1973
Wighton, Charles und Günter Peis	Hitler's Spies and Saboteurs, Based on the German Secret Service War Diary of General Lahousen, New York 1958
Winterbotham, F. W.	Secret and Personal, London 1969
Zacharias, Ellis M.	Secret Mission, New York 1946
Zolling, Hermann und Heinz Höhne	Pullach intern, Hamburg 1971

Index

Page numbers in italics indicate illustrations.